A Prisoner's Duty

A Prisoner's Duty

Great Escapes in
U.S. Military History

Robert C. Doyle

Naval Institute Press
Annapolis, Maryland

Library of Congress Cataloging-in-Publication Data

Doyle, Robert C.
    A prisoner's duty : great escapes in U.S. military history /
  Robert C. Doyle.
        p.   cm.
    Includes bibliographical references (p. 327) and index.
    ISBN 1-55750-180-7 (alk. paper)
    1. United States—History, Military.   2. Escapes—United States—
History.   3. Prisoners of war—United States—History.   I. Title.
E181.D69   1997
909—dc21   97-16453

Printed in the United States of America on acid-free paper ⊗

04 03 02 01 00 99 98 97   9 8 7 6 5 4 3 2

First printing

"Fellow citizens, we cannot escape history."

Abraham Lincoln

To all the men and women whose courage and determination to be free took them from the jaws of captivity to the warmth of their homes.

Contents

Preface

Although the biblical Jonah and Moses could be viewed as the first escapers in Western tradition, the first committed escaper of any consequence in North America was Squanto (Tisquantum), the Indian who taught the starving English Pilgrims how to survive in the New World. Taken prisoner by English fishermen working along the New England coast, Squanto was transported to England, where he learned English. He was sold into slavery but escaped and made his way back to England. Eventually, he shipped aboard another fishing vessel bound for American waters. As the ship dropped anchor near Cape Cod, Squanto escaped again, this time to return to his home and family. Like many escapers who came after him, Squanto found that the world had changed in his absence; his entire tribe had been wiped out by disease. Undaunted, he adopted the English Pilgrims of the *Mayflower* in 1621, saved their lives in the first year of the Plymouth colony, and was rescued by Miles Standish after his abduction by another tribe who opposed the Pilgrims. Throughout his travails, Squanto exhibited ingenuity and determination, traits that are characteristic of escapers. Thus it is not surprising that his dedicated work and pleasing personality were instrumental in establishing a peace between the tribes and the Massachusetts English that lasted for nearly fifty years.[1]

What makes one individual willing to brave any obstacle to attain freedom while another will wait passively for rescue? Why does cruelty make one person fearful and another fearless? What generates the spark that causes natural leaders to emerge in crisis situations? What causes the ordinarily untrained citizen to perform extraordinary acts in a time of emergency? These questions are all relevant to a discussion of escapers, those individuals throughout history who have responded to oppression and intolerable cruelty by escaping or attempting to escape, often again and again. This book seeks to answer such questions by reviewing the exploits of real people, some famous, some unknown to any but their immediate peers, who were subjected to captivity and who refused to accept that condition. It discusses their motives for taking action, as well as the means they used to do it.

My interest in the subject springs from an intense curiosity about the mindset of these individuals, some of whom I discovered while researching and writing. . . . Others I came across through various other means. In nearly all cases, these were interesting individuals with interesting stories to tell.

In my previous work *Voices from Captivity: Interpreting the American POW Narrative* (1994), I identified escape as an act of self-liberation and placed it within the context of the resistance aspect of the captivity narrative. This book examines the escape act in more detail by expanding the earlier treatment into a broader exploration of the dynamics of the Golden Rule, that practice of equal treatment for both sides of a conflict, citing additional military examples, citizen escapes from marauding Indian braves, slave escapes prior to the Civil War, and hostage-taking during the post-Vietnam era.

British and Commonwealth scholars and popular historians, many of whom were themselves former prisoners of war (POWs), have done more extensive historical research and analysis on escapes and escapers in wartime than have Americans. Their interest was due in part to the traditional homage paid to the British escape ethos taught to members of the officer corps before and during their military education and the "ludic" or playful atmosphere that existed within the British public school system from which many of these officers were recruited. More to the point, and I suspect more likely the heart of the matter, it was also due to the characteristic British respect and admiration for the battler, the person who struggles against adversity in a lost cause. During the twentieth century, when the United Kingdom and the United States joined as allies in two world wars and Korea, POWs from both countries, while in joint confinement, grew to understand and accept each other's views on escape.

Some critics believe that American captives remained passively quarantined in their respective POW camps, feeling sorry for themselves, contemplating their release, and continually complaining about unlawful enemy treatment. This impression is erroneous. To be sure, many Americans chose to remain in captivity for various reasons. Most, however, endured their hardships stoically; a few collaborated and decided to join their captors; some refused to break out even when given an opportunity, and some defied tremendous odds and escaped.

American history is replete with stories of prisoners who took extraordinary measures to regain their freedom. American settlers ran away from tribal villages during the Indian wars, and maritime privateers escaped from prison hulks, as well as from Forton and Mill prisons in England, during the Revolution. Americans climbed walls and dug tunnels in Dartmoor in 1814 and fled Mexican captivity to avoid the immediate execution ordered by Gen. Antonio Lopez de Santa Anna. They traveled the Underground Railroad during the Civil War and the escape lines established by the partisan resistance in World War II. They even outwitted their captors in Beirut. Americans escaped both as individuals and in small groups: some planned and executed great escapes, while others just saw an opportunity and seized it.

In all human endeavors, hierarchies of importance and deference play major roles in establishing social order. The POW escape experience is no different. Escapers stand at the pinnacle of the prisoner hierarchy, respected by their fellow prisoners after wars and feared by their captors during them. Moreover, when the word "great" is associated with an organized escape, the extent of the adulation grows in direct proportion to the difficulty of the escape and the risks run by the escapers. Thus, in wartime, people view those who escape from POW camps as the ultimate heroes and role models.

Civilian criminals commonly exhibit the same mindset as POWs. After teaching in a medium security prison for many years, I learned that these prisoners suffer the same feelings of isolation from society as do POWs. The major difference between these two types of prisoners lies in the cause of their imprisonment. POWs, journalists, runaway slaves, and civilian hostages may have represented the enemy to their captors, but they were not criminals in any legal or moral sense within their own societies. They had broken no laws. The exceptions were the slave escapers—known as runaways and later "contrabands"—who knew they were breaking the law prior to the Civil War, but when they were accepted by Union authorities for combat duty as United States Colored Troops (USCTs), they were criminals no longer. Both civilian and military prisoners were assured protection from harm during captivity under a large body of international treaties and conventions.

Were the escapers heroes? Some were; some were not. This book does not need the label "hero." It is about ordinary people who rejected the status quo, seized the initiative to create an opportunity, and carried out a freely willed action to its end. In an age when young people find their heroes on the television or movie screen, the efforts of actual men and women to escape from deplorable and dangerous conditions reflect the essence of human courage.

To recognize those individuals whose exploits required daring, resistance, organization, planning, luck, and risk in one volume has proved to be an ambitious project. The amount of information on escapes dating from the colonial period to the end of the twentieth century is voluminous. Since my objective was to use representative samples to understand how the process of escape worked and what factors motivated escapers, decisions had to be made, and many escapes that were similar in nature had to be omitted. By linking history with experience through published and unpublished narratives, oral histories, personal interviews, diaries, letters, and government documents, this book attempts to make sense of the scores of nearly forgotten escape experiences, some of which happened long ago, some within our own lifetimes. It is an effort to complete the portrait of the escaper painted by past studies of the American experience of war.

That American soldiers, sailors, and airmen escaped captivity is a matter of record, but that record is incomplete, especially since thousands of names never reached the public, except in fleeting accounts in home town newspapers. As readers of this book will discover, although these individuals may have simply wanted to go home, they actually escaped into history.

Acknowledgments

Special thanks go to the following people living and working on three continents and seven countries who were so generous with their time, expertise, and friendship: at Penn State University, to Stanley Weintraub, Samuel P. Bayard, Daniel Walden, Henry Albinski, William Crocken, and my students and research assistants, Barbara Bambarger, Leslie Alter, Gwendolyn Smith, and Wendy Zug; to Henry Burman and Joseph Consolmagno of the Stalag Luft III Association, Robert Blakeney in Needham, Massachusetts, Douglas Cotton and Air Vice Marshal Thomas Howell, RAF (Ret.) in England, and to many other veterans who responded to my requests; to Fred D. Crawford in Michigan, who was so generous with his time and editorial skills; to Richard E. Winslow III in New Hampshire, for his research assistance in matters pertaining to the American Revolution and the War of 1812. In Australia, special thanks go to John Dalton at Monash University, Melbourne, and to Jeff Doyle, Jeffrey Grey, and Anthony Bergin at the Australian Defense Force Academy for their invitation to a POW Studies conference in Canberra, where I met Australian World War II POW veterans who stimulated and sharpened my thinking about escape along the Death Railway. In Hungary, special thanks go to my friend and colleague, Simon W. Duke, at Central European University, Budapest, for his valuable reflections about escape in general, Korea, and the hostage crises. In Germany, special thanks go to Barbara Ischinger and Reiner Rohr at the German Fulbright Commission in Bonn-Godesberg for extending every courtesy to me during my Fulbright grant in 1994–95; to Herman-Josef Real, Director of the Englisches Seminar at the Westfälische Wilhelms-Universität, Münster; to my colleagues Peter Bischoff and Carin Freywald for their friendship, help, and encouragement; to my students in a unique graduate seminar about war and peace in our own time; and to Geoff Megargie of Ohio

State University who spent a Fulbright year at the German Military Archive and the University of Freiburg. In Austria, I would like to thank Stefan Karner, Barbara Marx, and the staff at the Ludwig Boltzmann Institut für Kriegsfolgen-Forschung in Graz; and in France, thanks to James Walker, Robyn Hackett, and all my colleagues at the Université des Sciences Humaines de Strasbourg II, Département d'Etudes Anglaises et Nord-Américaines. To my wife Beate, whose patience and love have no boundaries, I give my enduring devotion.

Introduction

Throughout the eighteenth and nineteenth centuries, statesmen working with the European legal community attempted to create international laws that mitigated the horrors of war for individuals, both military and civilian, who were taken prisoner on or near the battlefield. Several conventions met in Brussels, Geneva, and the Hague in order to establish definitions and formulate rules relative to the treatment of prisoners of war (POWs), internees, and those who were sick or wounded in wartime. If their purpose was to ban war and human suffering from the field of human endeavor, these conventions failed. Despite such efforts, during World War I the number of civilian deaths alone each month averaged 137,000, and by November 11, 1918, the total for the period had reached 7 million. These figures tripled in World War II, when 338,000 civilians lost their lives each month from 1939 to 1945.[1]

Although the overall picture remained bleak, the situation involving POWs improved. One significant innovation in the condition of wartime captivity that grew out of these conventions was the notion of POW quarantine. First established by European legalists who were confronted with endless religious wars and wars of conquest, the concept of quarantine assumed that captured individuals were not the chattel property of the captor, to be murdered, tortured, traded, or sold into slavery at will; instead, they were soldiers who deserved respect and reasonable treatment by the state while in public captivity. This concept evolved into the powerful social dynamic of the Golden Rule: if one side treated its prisoners humanely in quarantine, the other side was expected to do likewise, at least insofar as its means allowed.

For an individual prisoner of war, quarantine meant that the war was over for the time being. A POW's duty was simply to sit it out and let other soldiers continue the fighting. Why, then, did rational soldiers reject the relative safety of a POW camp and reintroduce peril into their lives? With the odds stacked against them, why did so many servicemen attempt escapes that seemed highly improbable? Why did they risk reprisals— even death—in order to escape? Some answers to these questions are relatively simple; others, as readers will discover as they meet these escapers, are much more complex.

The first duty of anyone in captivity is to survive. Research has shown that individuals who became POWs, hostages, civilian prisoners, and slaves at all stages of history had to make certain basic decisions concerning life and death, escape or patience, acceptance or rejection, and, in the end, they had to determine for themselves the degree of suffering they could withstand at any one time in any one place.

For a soldier, the second duty is to escape. Survival is perhaps the most fundamental law of nature. Although it may appear to be a logical solution to the problem of being held captive, escape involves a conscious act of risky decision-making at a time when captors may have attempted to destroy the prisoner's will by force. Military and civilian prisons are not hotels, and inmates are not guests, even in the most progressive prison systems. There is nothing more reprehensible to a human being than being placed behind bars or barbed wire, and there is something very human about wanting to break out. Thus the essence of this book is not only a historical analysis of military and selected noncriminal civilian escapes, but also a search for some general insights about the circumstances that often spark this action.[2]

In general, escapers differ greatly from other kinds of prisoners. Reasons vary. Some prisoners have unknown strengths that lie dormant in the psyche but surface in the face of adversity; others can accept only so much abuse, cruelty, or boredom before they cast aside safety and security and at least attempt to escape. No one can determine beforehand who will or who will not become an escaper; thus it is essential for military personnel to have a distinct mandate to escape. However, not all soldiers, including officers, take the notion of duty seriously. Many need to be confronted by a captor's objections to their duty before its meaning becomes clear and the choice obvious. Others need only a code to keep, one that clarifies and broadens ethical expectations. The military's mandate fulfills that need.

Military escapers are often set apart from their peers by their individual survival skills. These include common sense, possibly a common cause, cunning, luck, personal determination, opportunistic pluck, and, for many, a strong sense of loyalty to an organization. Other types of prisoners—those in bondage because of acts of fate, religion, matters of state, hostage-taking, or such conditions as American chattel slavery before the Civil War—also rely heavily on such skills when making their decisions to escape.

My book *Voices from Captivity: Interpreting the American POW Narrative* (1994) demonstrated that most captivity literature follows a strict structural pattern that corresponds to an escaper's experience: pre-capture, capture, long marches, prison landscapes, resistance or assimilation, release, and the prisoner's lament. The variety of these experiences clearly shows, however, that no two captivities were exactly alike, even in the same prison camp at the same time. A similar rule-of-thumb applies to the escape experience itself. Nevertheless, there has always been something fascinating about the notion of escape from captivity. In the wide spectrum of prison literature, I found that escape is often portrayed as daring, romantic, and fundamentally heroic, and it certainly caught the imagination of postwar writers and narrators of many nations.

British writers publishing after both world wars brought the escape experience to the attention of a reading public not only in the United Kingdom, but worldwide. One survey shows that the number of British escape books that appeared after World Wars I and II compared favorably with other kinds of clandestine wartime adventures. That people identified with the stark life of a POW and developed noticeable attachments to such realistic portrayals is evident in the continued popularity of the POW book in general and the escape narrative in particular.[3]

Americans were also interested in escapes. Demand for captivity and escape stories first escalated with the expanded production and circulation of newspapers and magazines during the Civil War and continued thereafter. Scores of narratives were published and distributed by both large and small firms, and often by the authors themselves. The amount of public interest in such stories testifies to the appeal of these intense personal narratives and their thematic consistency. In 1863, John W. Ennis published the story of his 1861 escape from Richmond as *Adventures in Rebeldom: or Ten Months' Experience of Prison Life,* and *The New York Times, Harper's,* and other publications, large and small, national and local, carried a variety of prison camp stories and prints that portrayed life in Southern prisons. For example, James D. English's "Life in Rebel Prison: Narrative by an Ohio Boy Just Escaped from Andersonville, Georgia" appeared in the *Cincinnati Commercial* on July 10, 1864, and was quickly reprinted in the *New York Daily Tribune* on July 26, 1864. Although some Southern escapers published their narratives in book form, like Decimus et Ultimus Barziza, who published his story in Texas in 1865, before the war's end, the Southern side was chiefly represented by the *Richmond Dispatch,* the *Macon Telegraph,* and the *Atlanta Constitution,* which were among the newspapers actively involved in publishing wartime propaganda.

After the war Southerners were restrained, publishing their narratives largely for local or regional consumption in the *Southern Historical Society Papers* or, later, their short reminiscences in the *Confederate Veteran.* On the other hand, Union escape narratives began to appear shortly after the war's conclusion. In 1865, Junius Henri Browne, a journalist with the *New York Tribune,* published his *Four Years in Secessia;* Frederick F. Cavada, his story of the great escape in Richmond as *Libby Life: Experiences of a Prisoner of War in Richmond, Va., 1863–1864;* and Joseph Ferguson, his bitter account, *Life and Struggles in Rebel Prisons.* Henry L. Estabrook's, *Adrift in Dixie; or, A Yankee Officer among the Rebels* and Gilbert E. Sabre's *Nineteen Months a Prisoner of War* appeared in 1866. William Burson's story of his escape from the Confederate prison camp in Florence, South Carolina, appeared as *A Race for Liberty; or My Capture, Imprisonment, and Escape* in 1867. One year later, James Madison Drake published the first of two escape books, *Narratives of the Capture, Imprisonment, and Escape of J. Madison Drake, Captain Ninth New Jersey Veteran Volunteers.* In 1880, Drake came up with a better title and republished his story as *Fast and Loose in Dixie.* Willard W. Glazier published his exciting memoir about his escape from Columbia, South Carolina, recapture, subsequent escape, recapture, trial as spy, and final escape from Sylvania, Georgia, as *The Capture, the Prison Pen and the Escape,* and John Vestal Hadley, his *Seven Months a Prisoner* in 1868. In 1870, John Harrold published *Libby, Andersonville, Florence, the Capture, Imprisonment, Escape, and Rescue of John Harrold.*

Eleven years later, John L. Ransom's popular self-published and widely quoted *Andersonville Diary, Escape, and List of Dead* appeared in 1881. Thomas H. Howe's story of escape with slave help was published as *Adventures of an Escaped Union Prisoner from Andersonville* in 1886, Alonzo Cooper's *In and Out of Rebel Prisons* in 1888, Benjamin F. Hasson's *Escape from the Confederacy—Overpowering the Guards—Midnight Leap from a Moving Train—Through Swamps and Forest—Bloodhounds—Thrilling Events* in 1890, and Simon Dufur's *Over the Dead Line, or Tracked by Bloodhounds* in 1902. As the government and people of the United States attempted to remain aloof from European political and military entanglements in the early years of World

War I, one of the last first-person Civil War escape narratives surfaced, Daniel Avery Langworthy's *Reminiscences of a Prisoner of War and His Escape* in 1915.[4]

Although the Spanish-American War was won in 1898 and the American Army was launching expeditions into Mexico in search of Poncho Villa in 1915, Americans in general continued to read about the adventures of their soldiers in blue and gray as if these later events were inconsequential. By 1917, however, European hostilities had spread to America, and despite cries for neutrality, the United States entered the Great War in Europe. During the course of the war, more than four thousand American servicemen were taken prisoner by the Germans. Only a handful managed to escape, but following the armistice in 1918, some began to write about their experiences. There were very few book-length escape narratives, except Pat O'Brien's *Outwitting the Hun: My Escape from a German Prison Camp* (1918) and Edouard Victor Isaacs's *Prisoner of the U-90* (1919). Some of their stories were told in popular magazines. For example, *Atlantic Monthly* published George Puryear's exploits in escaping from the Villingen camp as "The Airman's Escape" in 1919, and *Harper's Monthly Magazine* featured James Norman Hall's "pseudo" escape as "Escape De Luxe" in 1920. Most of the World War I escapers were British and Commonwealth soldiers, however, who found ink in their own press.

After World War II ended, significant numbers of escape narratives appeared, as British and Commonwealth POWs reflected on their experiences in print. A. J. Evans's *Escape and Liberation, 1940–1945* (1945) started the flow; T. C. F. Prittie and W. Earle Edwards's *Escape to Freedom* (1946) set the pace; and Eric Williams's *Wooden Horse* (1949), first published as the novel *Goon on the Block* in 1943, and Anthony Richardson's story of Sir Basil Embry's escape from occupied France, *Wingless Victory* (1950), accelerated it. Nevertheless, three names have come to dominate the field: Paul Brickhill, Patrick Reid, and Airey Neave. Brickhill's literary career began with *Escape to Danger* (1946), and he later wrote a series of popular escape books, including *The Great Escape* (1950), *Escape or Die: Authentic Stories of the RAF Escape Society* (1952), and his biography of Douglas Bader's POW experience, *Reach for the Sky* (1954). Patrick S. Reid's *Colditz Story* (1952), *Men of Colditz* (1954), and *The Latter Days of Colditz* (1954) have become staples of British escape literature. Airey Neave, a popular Colditz escaper who ran the *Comet* escape line in London and later became a politician, published several books, including his own narrative, *They Have Their Exits* (1953), and the first account of the inner workings of the secretive MI-9, *The Escape Room* (1969). Richard Pape, a member of the RAF's Guinea Pig Club, published his escape thriller, *Boldness Be My Friend* (1953), and Aidan Crawley published the second British escape anthology, *Escape from Germany: A History of RAF Escapes during the War* (1956).

Even as the British POWs grew older, the demand for their memoirs and commentary persisted into the 1970s, 1980s, and 1990s. For example, T. D. Calnan's *Free as a Running Fox* (1970) depicted his experiences as a tunneler and escaper; George Mann told the story of his escape and partisan fighting in Italy in *Over the Wire* (1988); and Dr. Bram Vanderstock, one of the three RAF officers who scored a home run after the Stalag Luft III great escape, published *War Pilot Orange* (1987) after he emigrated from Holland to the United States. Although two important books, Michael R. Foot's and James M. Langley's *MI-9: Escape and Evasion, 1939–1945* (1979) and Alan Burgess's *Longest Tunnel: The True Story of World War II's Great Escape* (1990), demythologized the British and American escapes, neither achieved the lasting popularity of Paul Brickhill's *Great Escape* (1950) or Patrick Reid's *Colditz Story* (1952).[5]

American escape memoirs, autobiographies, and adventure stories pale in comparison to the popularity of British, Australian, and Canadian publications from World Wars I and II. Those that have appeared have enjoyed reasonable popularity, however, especially within the POW veteran community, which avidly reads bulletins and newsletters such as the Stalag Luft III Organization's *Kriegie Klarion* and the American Ex-Prisoner of War Association's *Bulletin*. Although George Harsh's Stalag Luft III memoir *Lonesome Road* (1971) was an exception, few came from commercial presses. Most were published privately by or for the authors, no matter how prominent they might have been while in captivity. R. W. Kimball's *Clipped Wings* (1948, reprint 1992), for example, has the look and feel of an American high school yearbook; Joseph P. O'Donnell's *Shoe Leather Express* and *Luftgangsters* (1982) reached only limited audiences. Delmar Spivey, one of the senior ranking officers in Stalag Luft III's American South Compound, published his own account of camp life and American participation in escapes as *POW Odyssey* (1984). Jerry Sage, the "Cooler King" and an OSS officer undercover in Stalag Luft III, published his rambling memoir *Sage* (1985), and Joseph S. Frelinghuysen published *Passages to Freedom: A Story of Capture and Escape* (1990), describing his escape in Italy.

Two significant works about the escape experience provided an American historical context to the library of largely British memoirs: Arthur A.

Durand's well-researched *Stalag Luft III: The Secret Story* (1988), a scholarly account of the American contribution to the Great Escape in March 1944, and Lloyd R. Shoemaker's personal memoir, *The Escape Factory: The Story of MIS-X* (1990). Shoemaker described the activities of the American supersecret MIS-X organization, which was devoted to facilitating escape missions in Europe, along with its British counterpart, MI-9. On the other hand, stories about escape lines and evaders, as adventuresome as they were, like Sam Derry's *Rome Escape Line: The Story of the British Organization in Rome for Assisting Escaped Prisoners of War, 1943–1944* (1960), Clayton David's *They Helped Me Escape: From Amsterdam to Gibraltar in 1944* (1988), George Watt's *Comet Connection: Escape from Hitler's Europe* (1990), and Harry A. Dolf's *Evader* (1992), have remained far from the mainstream.

Given the substantial number of American escapers and evaders in the European Theater during World War II, it is surprising that they have generated so few publications. Perhaps one reason for the lack of American production lies in the overwhelming saturation of the market by the British. Another reason might be that American escapers were satisfied to tell their stories to one another and saw little need to recount them to the general public. Nevertheless, both British and American escape experiences received more attention in the United States through adaptation in films such as Billy Wilder's *Stalag 17* (1953), John Sturges's *Great Escape* (1963), Mark Robinson's *Von Ryan's Express* (1964), and Bill McCutchan's *Scarlet and the Black* (1983), than they ever received as simple memoirs or adventure novels. In Britain, Eric Williams's *Wooden Horse* (1958) became a popular film. The BBC also got involved, producing an acclaimed television miniseries based on Patrick Reid's epic escape narratives. Indeed, Colditz became so well known in England that spin-offs of the series included a board game and a bizarre prison camp-like weekend resort for people who wanted to experience what it was really like to be behind the wire.

Individual escape stories were often combined into anthologies, thereby expanding their popularity following the Civil War. For example, *Century Magazine*'s collection, *Famous Adventures and Prison Escapes of the Civil War*, appeared in 1893, along with a large number of escape narratives written by the Union and Confederate escapers themselves. Following World War I, H. C. Armstrong's *Escape* (1935) was a strong seller in the United States as well as in Britain and Australia. In addition, Paul Brickhill's *Escape or Die: Authentic Stories of the RAF Escape Society* (1952), Basil Davenport's *Great Escapes* (1952), Eric Williams's

Book of Famous Escapes (1954), and Aidan Crawley's *Escape from Germany: A History of RAF Escapes during the War* (1956) all enjoyed considerable popularity in England. Edward G. Jerrome's *Tales of Escape* (1959) surfaced in the United States as a children's adventure book.

Narratives of escapes by Germans in American and Canadian captivity appeared as well. For example, Kendal Burt and James Leasor's tale of Franz von Werra's flight from Canada and the United States became *The One That Got Away* (1957); John Hammond Moore's *Faustball Tunnel: German POWs in America and Their Great Escape* (1978) revealed that German submariners broke out of captivity in the middle of the Arizona desert. Rheinhold Pabel's personal memoir, *Enemies Are Human* (1955), John Melady's *Escape from Canada: The Untold Story of German Prisoners of War in Canada, 1939–1945* (1981), and Arnold Krammer's *Nazi Prisoners of War in America* (1979), as well as his collaboration with George Gaertner, *Hitler's Last Soldier in America* (1985), completed the German escape picture on the American continent.

As Chapter 8 will show, American escapes from Japanese captivity were relatively few, but with government permission, the escapers began to tell their stories in print before the war ended. The first and most popular of these memoirs was William E. Dyess's *The Dyess Story* (1944), followed by Melvin H. McCoy's and Steven Mellnik's joint narrative *Ten Escape from Togo* (1944). Historian Quentin Reynolds edited C. D. Smith's narrative *He Came Back: The Story of Commander C. D. Smith* (1945) and republished it in 1971. After the war, Edgar D. Whitcomb related his unusual experiences in the book *Escape from Corregidor* (1958), and Jack Hawkins told of his escape in the memoir *Never Say Die* (1961). Steven M. Mellnick's exploits were described in *Philippine Diary* (1969). Samuel C. Grashio remembered his escape in *Return to Freedom* (1982); William A. Berry's resistance, escape, and survival story came out as *Prisoner of the Rising Sun* (1993); and James D. McBrayer, among many other POW veterans, commemorated the fiftieth anniversary of the war's end with *Escape! Memoir of a World War II Marine Who Broke Out of a Japanese POW Camp and Linked Up with Chinese Communist Guerrillas* (1995).

After the Korean War, Sir Anthony Farrar-Hockley's *Edge of the Sword* (1954) became popular, and following the Gulf War, British SAS soldier Andy McNab published *Bravo Two Zero* (1993) for British audiences still hungry for escape thrillers. Similarly, James N. Rowe's *Five Years to Freedom* (1971) and Dieter Dengler's *Escape from Laos* (1979) are the only published narratives of successful wartime escapes during the Vietnam War.

Popular collections took on a Cold War dimension as the number of wartime escapers decreased. Clay Blair's *Beyond Courage* (1955) was perhaps the only collection of escape stories to emerge from the Korean War, and no complete collection has yet been issued about escapes during the long Vietnam War. One possible reason for the absence of such a collection is the fact that only the government has been able to gather all the narrative debriefs recorded by the servicemen who escaped captivity in South Vietnam and Laos. Government policy states that official debriefs will not be available during the expected lifetime of the Vietnam generation.[6]

Concerning the civilian hostages in Beirut, only two men actually escaped their captors, Jerry Levin and Charles Glass. Charles Glass's *Tribes with Flags: A Dangerous Passage through the Chaos of the Middle East* (1990) and Sis Levin's *Beirut Diary: A Husband Held Hostage and a Wife Determined to Set Him Free* (1989) recorded those events. A few major international publishers have created anthologies by combining Cold War escape stories with those of earlier wartime escapes. Ian Fellowes-Gordon's *World's Greatest Escapes* (1967), the *Reader's Digest* anthology *True Stories of Great Escapes* (1977) edited by Charles S. Verral, and Elizabeth Bland's *Escape Stories* (1980) are all examples of such broad-brush escape anthologies in the popular press.

Few penologists deny that escape functions as the most total act of resistance that one can perform in response to the condition of captivity: nothing can stand in the way of the escapers and they would go over, under, or through the barbed wire surrounding and imprisoning them. When one reads British and Commonwealth authors, one has the impression that British POWs obeyed their customary mandate: escape, fail, and escape again. H. C. Bates's introductory essay "Escape" in Paul Brickhill's *Escape or Die: Authentic Stories of the RAF Escape Society* (1952) characterizes the British escape ethos as a "sort of illogical pig-headedness" in the face of overwhelming odds.[7] In *They Have Their Exits* (1953), Airey Neave recalled his own escape experiences from Spangenberg (Oflag XIX A, near Kassel), Stalag XX A (Thorn, Poland), and Colditz (Oflag IV C, Saxony), and defined the escaper as ". . . a man who must never admit defeat . . . always ready to attempt the unknown to achieve the impossible with the minimum of aid."[8] As A. J. Barker, a British historian of the POW experience, wrote in *Behind Barbed Wire*

(1974), "The true escaper tries to get away because he is rebellious by nature and objects to his liberties being restricted by a lot of bastards whom he despises. He also enjoys the adventure for its own sake, and the fact that considerable risks are attached puts escaping into the same class as big-game hunting under difficult conditions."[9] Richard Garrett, another British author who dealt with escape and escapers, commented in his book *Jailbreakers* (1983), that in a large war, all sorts of talent existed in a POW camp, especially among conscripted soldiers and reserve or temporary officers. Their ranks often included lock-pickers, forgers, and what in civilian life would be considered criminal craftsmen. If these imprisoned soldiers were willing to form a cooperative organization, then all these talents could be used to one end—escape.[10] Ian Fellowes-Gordon noted that British POWs escaped not only for the Elizabethan-style adventure of it all, but because, like British working people at home, they seemed more interested in their good names than in good wages.

To deny that British military custom and tradition created a distinct escape ethos is wrong. History shows that there were many determined British escapers, from Winston Churchill in the Boer War to the RAF "Great Escapers" in Stalag Luft III in 1944, and to Sir Anthony Farrar-Hockley in Korea. If one accepts Fellowes-Gordon's analysis, the Americans were not "illogically pigheaded" but were more interested in the odds than the payoff.[11] This is also a fallacy. However powerful British "illogical pigheadedness" may have been, to overlook what Americans achieved in this arena ignores the courage and determination exhibited by many American escapers.

As weaponry became more sophisticated later in the twentieth century, fewer soldiers physically confronted their foes. Logistic and support personnel greatly outnumbered front-line maneuvering forces, and of those who did face an enemy, relatively few found themselves in captivity. Even earlier in the country's history, only a small percentage of front-line soldiers became prisoners, compared to the number who stood ready to do battle. For example, in the American Revolution (1775–83), 290,000 men served in the Continental forces; of those, 4,000 died in action and 18,182 were taken captive, approximately 8,500 of whom died in captivity.[12] Yet handfuls of prisoners did manage to escape. When Privateer Capt. Gustavus Conyngham and thirty men tunneled out of Mill Prison in England, it marked the first closely coordinated great escape executed by Americans. With the cessation of hostilities in 1814, British guards in Dartmoor Prison looked the other way as incarcerated American POWs climbed its granite walls.

Daring escapers were found in the Texas War for Independence, the Mexican War, and on both sides during the Civil War. John Hunt Morgan's departure from the Ohio State Penitentiary displayed the kind of stealth and courage expected of a Civil War cavalry officer; Col. Thomas Rose's organized mass escape from Libby Prison released 100 Union officers from captivity and became America's second great escape. Other wars found escapers whose stories lie hidden in the ashes of time: Edouard Isaacs, Harold Willis, and others in World War I; Samuel Grashio, Mark Wohlfeld, and the rest who escaped from Davao Penal Colony in the Philippines during World War II; the Americans who participated in *Comet* and other escape and evasion lines in Europe; Ward Millar and Melvin Shadduck who escaped from the North Koreans; and Dieter Dengler, Charles Klusmann, James N. Rowe, and other captives who escaped from enemy prison camps in Laos and South Vietnam. There are too many such individuals to ignore.

This book examines escape experiences from the earliest Indian wars to the most recent events in Somalia. It begins with a topological discussion of the major kinds of escapes and depicts how and why individuals arrive at the decision to risk their lives in such a venture. Because the political and cultural circumstances of each war vary considerably, the book approaches each war as an individual epoch, with forward and backward connective tissues. World War II was really two different wars, one fought in Europe and the other in the Asian-Pacific region. So too was the Vietnam War, with airmen fighting one war in the North while air and ground forces fought another in the South. As a result, each segment of both wars receives separate attention.

In addition to military escapers, four groups of civilian escapers are covered in this book: captives in the colonial Indian wars; slaves who demanded freedom; civilian journalists, mostly war correspondents, who broke away from their tormentors; and the hostages who slipped away from their captors in Beirut. Another chapter explores the wider issues of escape: the nature of prison raids. The last chapter looks at the legacies of escape, not only in terms of American wartime escapers but also in terms of certain larger issues such as those POWs who escaped from American hands, particularly German POWs during and after World War II and Cold War escapes. Although this book is not intended to be an encyclopedia of escape, it does show how and why many people throughout history have responded to captivity by acting alone or in concert with others in order to achieve one goal—freedom.

1

The Dominance of Will
Rejecting the Condition of Captivity

Escape by God! Never mind hunger pains, discomfort or any other agony. Let escape become your passion, your one and only obsession until you finally reach home.

—Wing Comdr. Douglas Bader, RAF (1943)

For the most part, captives, hostages, and prisoners provide footnotes to the military experience rather than a central focus. Wars over religion, territory, mercantile interests, colonies, or even ideologies, were too serious to devote much time to worrying about prisoners of war (POWs). Captured soldiers were, after all, public enemies and burdens to their captors and living symbols of lost battles to those at home. Prisoners were never really considered heroes, except to themselves, because wars were won or lost in spite of them, not because of them.

In the gray dawn of antiquity, a time without compassion, most captives were expendable. Becoming a soldier-captive resulted, if not in immediate death on the battlefield, then possibly in a ritual execution during a spectacle intended to entertain the victors. Egyptian and Assyrian bas-reliefs depict the inhumane manner in which POWs were treated; not only were these art works created to magnify the glory of the victorious sovereign, but also to broaden the ruler's gospel of terror. They show the horrors perpetrated upon the prisoners exactly as they were enacted: the gouging of the eyes, tearing out of the tongue, and lopping off of the limbs. Historian J. Fitzgerald Lee commented, "Long files of captives are led to the feet of the conqueror, to be butchered by his executioners or to be slain by his own hand." [1] Lee also recalled that Cleomenes massacred all his Argive captives after their ransom, Sulla murdered eight thousand Samnites and Lucanians, and Caesar permitted his legions to massacre the

Nervians. Sulla displayed his kindness by permitting some captives to live, but only after their eyes had been gouged out. Caesar exercised similar clemency, but ordered the prisoners' right hands chopped off at the wrist.[2]

Whereas the Romans tortured their prisoners in order to teach insurgent peoples to never again bear arms against imperial Rome, soldiers in the Christian era developed precepts like Richard II's *Articles of War* (1385), a code that required any soldier who killed a prisoner to forfeit his horses and armor to the constable.[3] In the European wars against Islam, soldiers captured in battle often could save themselves only by religious conversion. The Arab historian Masoudi reminded his readers that the great Caliph, Haroun al Raschid (Aaron the Just), contracted with the Eastern Empire in A.D. 805 for the exchange and ransom of prisoners. Many lives were spared in the process; however, Masoudi noted that many Christian prisoners in the Caliph's hands became Muslim and refused ransom.[4]

Hugo Grotius argued in *De Jure Belli ac Pacis* (1625) that whatever was taken from the enemy under the rule of *jus gentium,* the law of nations, became the lawful property of the captors; thus free men could be reduced to slavery legally.[5] In ancient times, if prisoners were permitted to live after capture, they were immediately stripped of their citizenship and made slaves with no rights. The only privileges granted to them came directly from their owners. Consequently, they could be bought, sold, traded, used to settle debts between free citizens, or killed with legal and political impunity. Often reprieve resulted only because of the captor's desire to generate wealth: he could sell them to the highest bidder. By ransoming his captives, a clever political leader could thus make the loser of the war pay all or part of its cost.

In terms of the seventeenth-century understanding of international law, POWs became the chattel property of their captors and owed them the same lawful service that they owed their own princes or states. On the other hand, escape was both possible and justifiable if the captives suffered intolerable cruelty, such as witnessing the murder of other prisoners, undergoing torture and endless solitary confinement, or being sold into slavery.[6] For prisoners who were not committed escapers by nature, Grotius's rule of intolerable cruelty became the first, and possibly the most significant, reason for breaking out of quarantine captivity, especially when they discovered that their captors intended to inflict unwarranted harm upon them. If they escaped during the war under these circumstances, the captives attained freedom.[7] By the eighteenth century, however, laws and policies regulating POW treatment among European and American armies favored the Golden Rule, that is, the principle of providing humane treatment for the enemy's soldiers with the reasonable expectation that one's own soldiers would be treated similarly, tempered by what Karl von Clausewitz a century later would call military necessity.[8]

Escape represents a traditional act of defiance and resistance to the condition of captivity in general; legally, it defines the status of prisoners who have placed themselves beyond the immediate control of the public authorities of the detaining power. The status of escaper terminates with recapture, death, or reunion with one's own or an allied state or army. If prisoners sit tight and await liberation and repatriation at the end of the war, they consider themselves safely quarantined for its duration. Escape breaks the quarantine. As a gamble for self-liberation, not only is escape dependent on the direct and practical preventive measures taken by the captors, but it also depends heavily on certain psychological issues that come into play during wartime captivity.[9]

The most important psychological dimension of captivity is the actual commitment to escape. The American philosopher and World War II combat veteran J. Glen Gray commented, "The soldier who has taken, or himself been made, a prisoner of war will inevitably be a changed man and fighter."[10] For some civilian and military prisoners, this commitment surfaced immediately following capture. For others, it developed after experiencing unendurable camp conditions or because of the fear of certain death regardless of what one did to survive. The popular British historian J. R. Ackerley called it the prisoner's "deep human instinct—the need for self-expression of a free and natural growth of individual life" that rejects quarantine captivity and generates a struggle to rejoin the battle.[11] What Ackerley meant was that in British military circles, there existed a clearly defined, duty-bound, and traditional mandate to escape that signified individual and community identity, morale, and self-respect among POWs. This mandate offered the individual a personal release from the stresses of incarceration, albeit temporary in most cases, while at the same time fostering a team attitude. Such a mandate existed among the Americans as well. In his study of British and American actions in Stalag Luft III during the 1944 breakout, American military historian Arthur A. Durand observed that no other camp activity so exhibited the prisoners' ingenuity, dedication, sense of community spirit and purpose than escape.[12] By 1944, the Americans and the British who were held together in camps in Europe and Asia had begun to better understand one another.

What if someone refuses to escape, even when there is a reasonable chance of success? Michael Walzer points out that even in a prison camp, one can always refuse to cooperate in an escape if one is willing to accept quarantine and refuses to accept the risk that an escape entails, or in some instances demands.[13] While refusal is an option, a price must be paid for this choice, one that can become very dear indeed. Prisoners who do not want to participate in an escape and who accept the quarantine position *in toto,* risk ill treatment not so much by their captors as by their peers. According to Richard Pape, the outraged Wing Comdr. Douglas Bader, one of the most committed British escapers ever held in a POW camp, refused to accept such behavior from the men in his compound. "Blast you and your kind!" yelled Bader. "You're getting paid while you're in captivity. Earn that money!"[14] In Bader's mind, even if the enemy recaptured a soldier twenty times during or after an escape, he must still continue the battle by making the enemy spend time, money, and manpower in organizing manhunts. He urged the POWs in his compound to become fighters—*homo furens*—again, whether they wanted to or not, and his attitude infected most of the prisoners around him. In an escape-minded community of POWs, it was nearly impossible to be neutral.[15]

What fueled these competing ways of thinking was not just the traditional battlefield ethic, but also what Johan Huizinga called the ludic aspect of combatants at war: the game or duel between two equally powerful, war-making parties who believe that they have the right to battle each other less from necessity or material interests, or even a lust for power, than from a struggle for prestige, pride, glory, or the extreme satisfaction of being "one up" on the enemy.[16] Thus, what could be construed as simple schoolboy pranks, the many so-called "one ups" gained by British prisoners at their captors' expense, exemplified Bader's attitude and attested to Huizinga's concept of *homo ludens.* This sort of playful, childlike behavior explained why and how individuals, as well as small groups and larger, organized units of prisoners, formed and bolstered their determination to defy, harass, and defeat their captors.

For the British, the escape equation evolved from the neutral quarantine approach first envisioned by the eighteenth- and nineteenth-century framers of international law, to a more radical evaluation of war's ends and means themselves. Prison camps became the battlefield, where a commitment to action involved making the ethical choice between a safe quarantine and the more dangerous, but greater good of gaining one's freedom. Echoing by chance Rudyard Kipling's words, "But yet somehow it sickens me . . . the meaning of captivity," Wing Commander Bader embodied this philosophy and exhorted his fellow prisoners to action: "Escape by God! Never mind hunger pains, discomfort or any other agony. Let escape become your passion, your one and only obsession until you finally reach home." For Bader and thousands of other Allied prisoners, the prison camp became an extension of the front, not a refuge from it. The objective was to return to battle, and they rejected quarantine as anything other than a starting point for escape attempts.[17]

Military authorities on both sides of the wire have always expected some prisoners to escape. Such expectations led to protection of prisoners' escape attempts under international law. The right to escape was never challenged; instead, laws provided clear statutes that regulated what someone might or might not do during an escape. If escapes became too frequent, captors established special camps to isolate known committed escapers, much like Colditz Castle (Oflag IV C, Saxony) in Germany during World War II. As Patrick Reid stated in his books about the Colditz experience, he earned the right to be there. To him and the other prisoners, being a Colditz prisoner brought with it certain obligations, the principal one being to escape. As Colditz internee Giles Romilly wrote in *The Privileged Nightmare* (1954), "The cult of escape held moral sway and had its priesthood in the Escape Committees with their acolytes of selected assistants. The cult was genuine, since the idea of escape had power to excite all prisoners irrespective of individual aptitudes."[18] Romilly added that escape at Colditz "hypnotized the many who elsewhere might have stayed aloof."[19]

Even those in the POW community not planning to escape worked to facilitate the escape of others. After his captivity, Aidan Crawley, an RAF officer and POW, observed that the effort to escape improved the morale of all the prisoners in the camp. "The mere fact," wrote Crawley, "that in preparing for a mass escape hundreds of people were cooperating in an enterprise which held the prospect of an immediate result, was the best tonic a prison camp could have."[20] The captives provided this assistance even though escape attempts would bring vengeance upon innocent, nonescaping prisoners. At the same time, most prisoners had high regard for all those who participated.

Surviving in quarantine was simply not an option for those prisoners who arrived at the camp committed to escape or for those who developed that commitment while behind barbed wire. In essence, the British passion for escape resembled a gaming process designed to defy the enemy's rules and defeat a captor's attempts to humiliate prisoners. As H. E. Bates wrote in the Introduction to Paul Brickhill's *Escape or Die* (1952): "The captor has the guns, the bullets, the mines, the tear-gas, the searchlights, the spies, the traps, the barbed wire, the dogs and all the countless refinements of mental oppression that make life in prison compounds a special sort of hell. Against these things the captive has only his wit, his resource, his inventiveness, his brains, his endurance, his humor, his luck—if fate allows him any—and, perhaps most important of all, his mental attitude." [21] At its best, escape gives purpose to life in captivity; at its worst, escape becomes a form of self- or group sacrifice for a cause larger than any individual consideration. From a practical point of view, however, the end in this case may well justify the cost, the risk, and, from time to time, the means.

Americans held a different view about rejecting quarantine. Lacking the British tradition of escape as a duel between equal antagonists, the American POW had to survive first, resist second, then escape if possible, given a reasonable chance of success. Behind that three-part ethos of survive-resist-escape lies a distinct synthesis of frontier mythology and hard-nosed pragmatism embodied in what Rupert Wilkinson called the American tough-guy tradition. The traditional image of the tough guy is personified in American folklore, popular culture, and modern memory, and is reflected in what Wilkinson calls American "dynamic toughness." Prisoners of the Korean War era referred to the dynamically tough prisoners as "tigers."

Rather than follow the battling gamesmanship model of the British, Wilkinson's tough guys faced their challenges squarely. They took care of themselves and mastered their dual roles as individuals and as members of captive communities. They were dynamic and celebrated action, speed, and efficiency; they could "take it" because they stood up to adversity and never feared facing down their rivals.[22] Why they "took it" will become clearer in subsequent chapters. Facing down or baiting their rivals—brinkmanship—is one thing; leaving them behind is another. One can face someone down without a catastrophic confrontation. Taking the risk, in many cases a deadly risk, of breaking out of a prison camp thrusts a POW back into the world of catastrophic conflict in which peacetime compromising is replaced by the wartime "all-or-nothing" position required to succeed in one's mission.

One clue to better understanding the Americans is that in hostage and military captivity, Americans consistently viewed themselves as plain and practical people. They relied on the patriotic individualism of their eighteenth-century privateer forebears and the nineteenth-century courage and passions exhibited by their ancestors clad in blue and gray. However, while Americans maintained their concern for toughness, they never totally abandoned their connection with frontier mythology, especially that which concerned the essentially Puritan view of the clear dichotomy between savagery and civilization.[23]

From the time of the Forest Wars in Puritan New England to the end of the Hostage Crisis in Beirut in 1991, this duality played a significant role in American attitudes toward captivity in general, as if captive Americans retained their roots in radical Calvinism. Because Puritan Calvinism prescribed rigid spiritual duty and individuals were valued for striving to achieve material success, escape attempts could be considered as practical and quantifiable for the Americans as they were ludic for the British. It is little wonder, then, that the Americans in World War II called successful escapes "home runs." In the game of baseball, the home run represents success: the player steps up to home plate and faces the pitcher squarely; he then commits to a full-force swing and hits the ball into the grandstand. After running past three bases, he scores a home run. If other players are also on the bases, they score too, and in baseball, of course, whichever side scores more runs, wins the game.

The rule that the end never justifies the means becomes less dogmatic when referring to captivity. Modified by the American Code of Conduct, the Uniform Code of Military Justice, and the 1949 Geneva Convention (GPW), the rules governing prisoner of war status indicate that some ends do justify some means. As natural pragmatists, American POWs determined that what was good could be construed as that which was useful for the survival and best interests of the captive community first and the individual second. By using this criterion, Americans in some cases eliminated, and in others escalated, the problems, conflicts, and negative impact of the actions of committed natural escapers on a society of prisoners. Like the British, American escapers dared to challenge the individual and organizational dependency of prison life in order to liberate themselves.

Aside from any national or stereotypical characteristics that may have surfaced in a particular captivity environment, the literature of escape identifies three variables that recur as major motivational factors: (1) the development of an individual commitment to escape; (2) the existence of some sort of an institutional mandate, or at least permission to escape, in the form of custom, tradition, or written code; and (3) the desire to seize the moment if an opportunity to escape presents itself.

Given these major variables, four patterns of individual and group behavior predominate, which are exemplified in four types of escapers: (1) *natural escapers* who, for reasons best known to themselves, resisted captivity irrespective of any risks to themselves or to the community of their fellow prisoners; (2) *individual opportunity escapers* who seized an opportune moment to gamble on an all-or-nothing dash from captivity; (3) *small groups* of escapers who formed *ad hoc* partnerships of three or more prisoners to plan and execute an escape; and (4) organizational or *great escapers,* tunnelers for the most part, who formed extensive secret organizations, sometimes involving whole units of prisoners, to plan and execute the hard and dangerous work aboveground and under it. Mass escape required an organized matrix of selected participants and non-escaping accomplices with one goal in mind—freedom. The classic "X" escape organization reflected the values of a disciplined primary military unit in which everyone had rank, a specific job, and a designated place in the organization. Although small in comparison to a military fighting unit, it nevertheless had internally recognizable subordinate hierarchies, distinct enough to focus on one activity with one goal and homogeneous in its military content and interdependent self-sufficiency.[24] As the Colditz experience showed, the captives took such delight in their mission and comradeship that the escape community formed a unified group with a purpose, resulting in an almost instinctive recognition of the connection between unity and strength.[25]

During a long confinement in the Soviet Gulag system with inmates of diverse Russian backgrounds, Aleksandr I. Solzhenitsyn began to observe escaper behavior closely. He saw firsthand that in a large prison population there were always a few individuals who refused to remain in captivity for any reason. In *The Gulag Archipelago Three 1918–1956* (1976), Solzhenitsyn called them committed natural escapers, solo players who split from the community and struck out on their own. He wrote, "It is for the committed escaper's benefit that window bars are set in cement, that the camp area is encircled with dozens of strands of barbed wire, towers, fences, reinforced barriers, that ambushes and booby traps are set, that red meat is fed to gray dogs. A committed escaper is also one who refuses to be undermined by the reproaches of the average prisoner, and of all possible means of struggle, he has eyes only for one, believes only in one, devotes himself only to one—escape!"[26] One example of the Solzhenitsyn-style committed natural escaper was Capt. Lance Sijan, USAF. Sijan was shot down on November 9, 1967, and captured by North Vietnamese soldiers. Sijan died in captivity on January 22, 1968, after successive escape attempts and received the Medal of Honor posthumously.[27]

If some committed natural escapers recklessly imperiled their lives for the sake of an escape, the second, and far more common, category of escaper has been the prisoner who, without prior planning, suddenly saw an opportunity to flee. When a captor dropped his guard, looked the other way, or neglected security for a brief moment, the opportunist saw a chance, took it, and fled. Subsequent chapters discuss a number of such opportunities; however, the best example is James N. Rowe, who escaped captivity in South Vietnam.

Finally, there are the captives whose experiences have angered or humiliated them to such an extent that they have little hope of eventual release, no matter how accommodating their captors are. In addition to being motivated by humiliation, frustration, and anger, these individuals have often claimed that their commitment to escape was based on witnessing terrible atrocities while in captivity. The Indian captives Barbara Leininger and John Knight fall into this category. Escapers in all three major categories, however, were individuals who assessed their immediate situation, calculated the risk, combined luck and opportunity, and in the heat of a pivotal moment, abandoned their paralyzing fear to make an escape.

Some American POWs have been committed natural and opportunist escapers, but most seem to have decided to escape only after witnessing various instances of intolerable cruelty. All three categories of escapers could be found in tribal villages during the Indian wars; on prison ships during the Revolution and the War of 1812; in Elmira, Johnson's Island, or other prison camps in the North, or at Andersonville, Libby, or other prisons in the South during the Civil War. They were in the Stalags and Oflags in Germany in both world wars, as well as in Korea, Laos, Vietnam, and Lebanon. Some escapers, like Dieter Dengler, shot their way out of a prison camp; some dug tunnels; others walked out the front gate. Some risked immediate execution by posing as enemy guards; others jumped from trains in transit. After 1954, some responded to the Code of Conduct that outlined their duty in the unique circumstances of wartime captivity. Throughout the American POW experience, however, escapes occurred when opportunity, whether deliberately created or fortuitous, was afforded to those prisoners who viewed freedom as an absolute necessity.

When two committed escapers joined forces to form a partnership, they linked elements of creative entrepreneurial opportunism with the benefits of shared skills, including stealth and a sense of responsibility. Partnerships were at best timely relationships, born of necessity and matured in adversity. Thinking small required partners to reject the mass escape structure because it impeded their instant decision-making ability. Then too, the possibility always existed that their captors could have planted spies among them, snitches, who, for a small reward, would facilitate their recapture and possible death. A large number of committed escapers thus operated alone or entered into a partnership with one or, at most, a small group of like-minded prisoners. This entrepreneurial attitude—working on one's own outside an organizational structure—often proved very productive when the moment came to act.

Escapers who chose small groups of more than two escapers but fewer than ten also combined elements of innovative, practical entrepreneurship with opportunism, but they generally operated outside Solzhenitsyn's model of the solitary escaper.[28] More than mere alliances of convenience, partnership relationships formed hierarchical structures in which members were assigned individual responsibilities. By enlarging such small structures into larger, more organized frameworks, prisoners created the escape model commonly referred to as the mass or "great" escape. This model, used mainly by POW officers, shows how hierarchical military organizations functioned behind barbed wire. Mass escapes were managed in much the same way as a large civilian business enterprise or an active military fighting unit. The effort was based on two simple concepts: escape was a duty that served the greatest number of prisoners with the greatest possible good, and the greater the risk one took, the greater the reward or, in some cases, the punishment. Everyone had a place in the escape hierarchy, even nonescaping accomplices. Each member had assigned tasks, a distinct and valued place in the organization, and individual responsibilities. Mass escapes have been rare in American military history, not only because of the unique wartime circumstances imposed in prison camps, but also because many Americans, especially lower-ranking soldiers and noncommissioned officers, were more entrepreneurial than cooperative by nature. Nevertheless, mass escapes did occur.

Whether compelled by boredom, torture, personal humiliation, or simply by innate natural inclinations, as Solzhenitsyn suggests, some POWs began to consider the risks of escape irrelevant to any form of retaliation that the captors might inflict on them or on those left behind. In the Indian wars, for example, a terrible death awaited prisoners who attempted to escape and failed. The alternative of "sitting it out," that is, remaining with the captors and hoping for liberation, rescue, or release at some later time, was always a more comfortable option. Thus escapers are the few, not the many. Winston S. Churchill, a British journalist in his youth, became a prisoner of the Afrikaaners in the Boer War. In his later years, Churchill described his sense of melancholy and offered some clues to the psychology of escape. He wrote, "You are in the power of your enemy. You owe your life to his humanity, and your daily bread to his compassion. You must obey his orders, go where he tells you, stay where you are bid, await his pleasure, possess your soul in patience. . . . Hours crawl like paralytic centipedes. Nothing amuses you. Reading is difficult, writing impossible. Life is one long boredom from dawn till slumber." [29]

If Churchill was correct, boredom often played a significant role in a prisoner's decision to escape. During the Civil War, a Confederate POW officer on Johnson's Island observed that men became listless and no longer cared about the things that had hitherto been either their work or their recreation. [30] Boredom and the helplessness of prison life humiliated these men and dulled their sense of duty and personal well-being. Boredom, like physical pain, was a form of intolerable cruelty, and Churchill responded to it by becoming a successful escaper.

Some POWs decided to escape because they began to feel personal guilt for having fallen into the enemy's hands, and they searched for the fatal mistake that caused their capture. "Was my shootdown, surrender, or capture my fault?" "What did I do wrong to get into this mess?" If a prisoner believed that he was at fault, he might attempt to redeem himself through some kind of escape. With no counteracting influences, guilt turned into utter listlessness, an opium-like lethargy of dull resentment, gnawing heartache, and feelings of oppression. [31] Acting in consort, extreme guilt and ennui combined in some cases to produce the condition called "wire fever," or "barbed wire disease." Saying "I can't stand it any more," hopelessly embittered prisoners made direct and usually fatal charges against the wire in full view of armed guards. Not committed escapers at all, they knew full well that only oblivion awaited them. The ill-fated Japanese breakouts from camps in New Zealand and Australia during World War II were examples of this condition. These mass Japanese suicides only served to concede victory to the Australians and New Zealanders, devastated Japanese POW group morale, and destroyed any spirit of resistance among the remaining prisoners. [32]

In his massive treatise, *De Jure Belli ac Pacis* (1625), Hugo Grotius (1583–1645) termed these reasons for escape the principle or doctrine of intolerable cruelty. In Grotius's view, if a captor's actions became inhumane and outrageous enough to go well beyond the confines of law or custom regulating the moral boundaries that exist in captivity, a prisoner could flee freely and legally with a brave heart, completely without guilt and with no regrets.[33] Far from being just a theoretical principle of law, Grotius's position on escape from intolerable cruelty resulted from his personal experience as a political prisoner in the early part of the Thirty Years' War. In 1618, he was arrested, tried for treason by a special state court, and sentenced to life imprisonment in Holland's Loevestein Castle. In prison he discovered firsthand that it was one thing to witness catastrophic cruelty, quite another to suffer it. With nothing to lose but a wasted life behind heavily guarded granite walls, Grotius hid himself in a box of books and escaped. Lawyer that he was, Grotius used his experiences to form the basis for *De Jure Belli ac Pacis*. Others simply wrote about their experiences from memory and published them as memoirs.

The traditional escape narrative became a means of bearing witness to the captivity experience in general and to the escape in particular. In their memoirs escapers naturally tend to focus attention on the escape itself, or on attempted escapes. There is no formula for these books in the popular literary sense: no two escapes are exactly alike. As in the nonescape captivity narrative, however, the escape narrative compresses chronological time; structurally, it consists of a hierarchy of six escalating stages of contemplation, decision and action that these individuals commonly experienced during the course of an escape.[34]

The first stage focuses on the decision to escape and how each prisoner arrived at that decision: duty, military mandate, custom or tradition, or the experience of witnessing numerous instances of intolerable cruelty. Escape narrators have often described seeing recaptured escapers killed, tortured, or both. Rather than being discouraged by these sights, however, the captives become more determined risk-takers. The second, or planning, stage centers on individual, small group, or mass actions inside the camp once the decision to escape was made, including the rationale for forming partnerships and escape committees. Narrators have revealed how they shared their plans with other prisoners, arranged for outside help, and prepared for the flight toward friendly lines. The third stage constitutes the act of escape itself. Following the breakout from the camp, the escapers reach the fourth stage, the flight to freedom. Here the escapers experience the high adventure of evading their pursuers and traveling through enemy-held territory. Close calls, friendly or unfriendly brushes with civilians, supportive guerrilla or partisan bands, near recapture, or recapture itself color the narrative, and memoirists tend to describe these experiences in great detail. The drama of the first contact with friendly forces constitutes the fifth stage, which also includes some initial details of the repatriation. The sixth and final stage usually consists of a reflection, often in the form of a lament, on the entire captivity experience. (See Appendix 1, *Oral History Formats*.)

Among former POWs and other kinds of prisoners, feelings about escape have never been neutral. Many military escapers have received high praise and decorations from their institutional hierarchies, but their fellow prisoners may not have held them in such high regard since they often bore the brunt of their captors' retaliation.

Throughout history, escapers have been those prisoners who rejected the condition of captivity, some regardless of the treatment they received, others because of it. In either case, this rejection has resulted in a personal commitment to take whatever risks are necessary, even the possibility of death, to liberate oneself and others if possible. Why some prisoners sought to escape when simply sitting it out was a far safer option is the question asked by every prisoner who has ever contemplated this action. It is not an easy question to answer. In his book *Democracy in America* (1848), a seminal study of the United States, American institutions, and Americans in general, Alexis de Tocqueville provided a powerful clue to solving this problem. "It is not exercise of power or habits of obedience which deprave men," he wrote, "but the exercise of a power which they consider illegitimate and obedience to a power which they think usurped and oppressive." [35] Escapers from the colonial period to the modern era have a simpler way of expressing de Tocqueville's theory—"There was a war on." [36]

2

Pioneers, Volunteers, and Privateers
Escape in the Wars of Musket and Sail

We committed treason through his earth and made our escape.
—Gustavus Conyngham (1777)

Prisoners who rejected the condition of captivity during the colonial wars set the tone for those who would later become escapers during America's national wars. Beginning in Virginia in 1622, Indian wars soon raged throughout the North American colonies.[1] In all these wars one simple pattern emerged: first, the desire to take possession of the wilderness inhabited by the native tribes; then, the changing or taming of the wilderness so that the land could be developed into rural and urban communities; and finally, the parceling out of the land into bordered, well-defined property that had to be individually and collectively defended. While the tribes wanted only to be left alone, this would prove difficult in an age of European discovery and conquest. The westward movement of hordes of immigrants armed with ever more sophisticated weapons spelled the end of the Indians' way of life as they knew it.

Those newly arriving from Europe came not only with a passionate desire for religious freedom but also with the longing for a new land that they could make their own. Some settlers wished simply to exterminate the tribes in the process; others wanted the Indians to assimilate into the European culture. Although the Pilgrims in New England strove to get along with their tribal neighbors, virtually no one regarded their views as of any consequence. One by one, region by region, the tribes were forced to defend their lands against encroachment, themselves from eviction, and their culture from total destruction. As weaponry became more technologically advanced, first the army and then civilian settlers succeeded in taking the steps necessary to remove the tribes, dead or alive, from the land. That many tribes were annihilated bears witness to the intensity of these wars of attrition; that many people survived and later prospered in modern America is more than a cultural paradox, it is nothing short of a miracle.[2]

Among the early escape narratives were Juan Ortiz's *True Relation of the Gentleman of Elvas* (1557), which told of his adventures among and escape from the tribes of the American Southeast, and Hans Staden's *True History of His Captivity among the Tulpi Indians of Brazil* (1557), which described his shipwreck, life, and escape from a tribe in Brazil. Both these works were essentially travelogues and ethnological studies of aboriginal life written for a curious European audience intent on learning about the inhabitants of the New World. Later, the focus of this type of literature shifted from such relatively simple, ethnological descriptions of Indian lifestyles to more propaganda-like writings with more diverse purposes, including the waging of war. As a result, the captivity experience became an effective propaganda tool that assisted the initial European conquest of America.

Hostilities between the French and the English began in North America in 1613, seven years before the *Mayflower* landed at Plymouth in 1620, and ended 150 years later with the French cession of Canada to England in 1763. Although the issues of land and trade were major points of contention between these two superpowers in America, religion played an equal, if not more important, role not only in establishing the battle lines, but also in identifying Indian enemies and allies. The gauntlet was dropped in Acadia (Nova Scotia), when French Jesuits and courtiers planted the cross at Saint-Sauveur, and, in so doing, effectively declared war on the English. Caught in the middle of this conflict were the settlers and citizen-soldiers who suffered terribly from the horrors of the wars raging around them. As the New England antiquarian C. Alice Baker noted in 1897, "It was an age of intolerance when frontier settlements suffered for the sins of individuals."[3] In 1995, military historian John Keegan took a stronger position, noting that "the military ethic of the tribes struck the Europeans as nothing better than savagery," and the "encounter with native America had no precedent and was to have no later parallel."[4]

Indians and Europeans began taking one another captive immediately after Columbus's discovery of America in 1492. For the Europeans, capture and ransom had become a standard military practice during the

Middle Ages and Renaissance, with the bodies-for-cash arrangements often allowing the winners to return prisoners to the losers for money that paid for the wars. Columbus thus felt free to take captives in order to display them to his Spanish sponsors. For the native Americans unfamiliar with European ways, captivity became a standard tribal military practice for a different reason, namely, to replace combat losses. By the time the European superpowers flexed their muscles in America, captive-taking had developed into a multitiered, cross-cultural, and highly effective tactic with three major benefits. For the Indians, it provided a steady stream of hostages for ransom, as well as a number of assimilators into rapidly depleting tribes; for the Europeans, it escalated the religious nature of the British-French hostilities.

Both the British Puritans in New England and the Anglican planters farther south considered French and Spanish Catholics to be religious heretics who posed a powerful danger to their political and religious freedom. The French in Canada held similar views. Thus most of the communication between the colonials from France and those from England came at the point of a musket. Although both sides maintained relatively large armies, much of the warfare was conducted by, or in most cases with, their Indian allies, who thereby were quickly introduced to the European ransom system. The warfare between the two countries continued until General Montcalm's defeat in 1763 and France's subsequent forfeiture of Canada to England.

Because their Indian allies had taken their captives either in battle or in small raids, the French considered those they purchased from the Indians to be war prisoners and, by European custom, the chattel property of their owners for the duration of the war. Led by militant Jesuits, the Catholic French felt that if they reintroduced the deeply religious Protestant English to the Catholic faith, they would gain converts for the Church. Indians, Christians or those native in their faith, who were captured by the British colonists were executed, indentured, or sold into slavery as punishment for their crimes against the crown.[5] As a result, the colonial wars, although largely about the acquisition of land and power, also acted as an extension of Europe's religious wars, and the Indian nations, who were fighting for their existence, became battlefield allies and surrogate armies of the two superpowers. As Emma Lewis Coleman showed in *New England Captives Carried to Canada* (1925), New England's tribes acted as mercenary conduits in the captive-for-ransom business with their respective allies until 1763.[6]

During the colonial wars, French Catholics paid well for English Protestants. The Calvinist English hated the Roman Catholic Church more than they feared God. Indeed, the Puritans viewed being captured by Indians and transported to Canada as the lowest form of punishment a Puritan could suffer. In 1699 Cotton Mather charged, "No words can sufficiently describe the cruelty undergone by our captives in those habitations."[7] Armed with steadfast Calvinist religious convictions and a certainty that Catholicism represented both superstition and idolatry, the English Puritans sought innovative ways to retrieve their prisoners from French Canada.

Mather and his Puritans believed that the Catholic French and their Indian allies were satanic and that the warfare between settlers and Indians represented a struggle between God and Satan for the possession of a person's soul. The captured Puritans thus felt an unbridled mandate to escape by any means possible. Between 1675 and 1677, King Philip's War ravaged New England, and captivities, escapes, and rescues reinforced Mather's arguments. Jonathan Haines of Haverhill, Massachusetts, was taken from his home, along with his one son and three daughters. Indians attacked his farm while he was reaping his fields and took the group first to Concord, where they separated them by sex. The women were never heard from again, but the men were taken to Maine where they escaped.[8]

Another example of the Puritan mandate to escape can be found in the narrative of Hannah Dustan, which was recounted by Cotton Mather. In 1690, Hannah Dustan, together with her week-old child and nurse Mary Neff, was captured in a fierce raid on Haverhill. Her husband, who had escaped with their other seven children, alerted the neighbors. Since Dustan had so recently delivered the child, she could not move very quickly. Following the capture, the raiders murdered her newborn child, then took the two women to a village, where they forced them to run the gauntlet. Later, the two Puritan women were given to a large Indian family for safekeeping before being transported to Canada. One can only imagine the terror that these devout Puritans suffered at the thought of being held prisoner by Indians and French Catholics for an indefinite period of time. According to Mather, Dustan and Neff found tomahawks and killed their new guards one by one while they slept. He wrote, "She heartened the Nurse . . . to assist her in the Enterprise; and all furnishing themselves with Hatchets for the purpose, they struck such Home Blows, upon the Heads of their Sleeping Oppressors, that e'er they could any of them

Struggle into any Effectual Resistance, at the Feet of these poor Prisoners, there they fell down dead."[9] Dustan and Neff then stole a canoe and escaped. They took with them ten scalps, for which the Massachusetts General Assembly paid a bounty of fifty pounds in colonial money.

Religion played a vital role in the lives of many New England captives. Such was the case with Thomas Baker, Christine Otis, Esther Wheelright, Eunice Williams, and Molly Finney, all Protestant captives who encountered French Catholic piety in varying degrees during their Canadian incarceration. Facing the fires of execution, Thomas Baker broke free from his captors and sought refuge with a friendly Frenchman, who bought him from the Indians for five pounds. The French governor, hearing about his escape attempt, put him in irons and kept him in close confinement for four months before freeing him to mingle with the other prisoners once again. Taking advantage of this situation, Baker, along with Martin Kellogg, Joseph Petty, and John Nims, made a successful escape and arrived home in Deerfield in 1705.[10] After a treaty of peace ended the hostilities, the French Canadians were prepared to begin repatriation proceedings to rid themselves of their nonconverted Protestant captives, but they wanted to keep their newly naturalized citizens.

Baker returned to French Canada as Capt. Thomas Baker and rescued Christine Otis, who had accepted Catholicism while in captivity but renounced it upon her escape. On the other hand, Esther Wheelright became Mother Esther of the Infant Jesus in the Canadian Ursuline Order and died committed to the Catholic faith. Eunice Williams married a Catholic Indian and remained in Canada for eighty-five years, less in captivity than in exile. Molly Finney never converted; she was rescued and returned to New England. Anthony Brackett and his wife were taken prisoner at about the same time. Their Indian captors took them to Casco Bay (Portland, Maine), where they learned that another Indian band had taken an English storehouse on the Kennebec River. Upon hearing this news, the Indians wanted to join forces with this group and gave Brackett and his wife materials to carry. As the Indians hurried ahead, Mrs. Brackett by chance spied a canoe, stole it, and seized the opportunity to escape with her husband to Black Point.[11]

In Virginia, Capt. John Smith was taken prisoner by the Powhatan tribe, led by their chief Wahunsonacook, commonly called Powhatan by the British. According to Smith, "As many as could laid hands on him, dragged him to them, and thereon laid his head and being ready with their clubs to beat out his brains, Pocahontas, the king's dearest daughter, when no entreaty could prevail, got his head in her arms and laid her own upon his to save him from death."[12] Pocahontas's intercession with her father saved Smith's life, and the rescue that he chronicled in *General History of Virginia* (1624) became an American legend.

More than a century later, on orders from Governor Dinwiddie in 1753, George Washington of Virginia, another American legend, launched an expedition into western Pennsylvania and eastern Ohio to establish friendly relations with the Indians and drive out the French. Once in Pennsylvania he heard that the Delawares had taken two young boys captive. Washington tried to negotiate their release but failed, since the Delawares had already delivered the boys to the French who wanted to discover what the English were planning in Virginia.[13] Washington thus learned firsthand that the Indians along the Ohio River were far friendlier toward the French than they were toward the English. More important, he realized that a new war was looming, later termed the French and Indian War, one that would make Pennsylvania into another international battleground.

Between 1754 and 1763, the French attempted to contain British trading and expansion efforts across Pennsylvania's western frontier by building a chain of forts along the major rivers from Lake Erie to Ohio. Early in the conflict, much of the fighting took place west of the Allegheny Mountains and at Fort Duquesne, now Pittsburgh, Pennsylvania. Although the French eventually lost Canada to the British, between the opening shots of the war and the final surrender, French and Indian guerrilla raiding parties attacked deep into British Pennsylvania, which was populated in part by German and Swiss Protestant immigrants. Two of the Pennsylvania German girls, Barbara Leininger and Marie LeRoy, were captured in 1755 during one such raid deep into the Susquehanna Valley. Leininger and LeRoy then became escapers.

Early in her captivity, Barbara Leininger attempted to escape, but she failed. After her recapture, she was condemned to be burned alive, a punishment traditionally reserved for heretics and witches in Europe. Her captors "made a large pile of wood and set it on fire, intending to put her into the midst of it."[14] According to her narrative, in a gender reversal of the Pocahontas story, a young Indian begged so earnestly for Barbara's life that her captors pardoned her after she promised not to escape again. Another escaper less fortunate than Leininger suffered an agonizing death after her escape and recapture, something which Leininger dreaded. She wrote: "First, they scalped her; next, they laid burning splinters of wood, here and there, upon her body; and then they cut off her ears and fingers, forcing them into her mouth so that she had to swallow them. Amidst such torments, this woman lived from nine o'clock in the morning until toward sunset when a French officer took compassion on her and put her out of her misery." After observing this act of intolerable cruelty, Barbara Leininger realized that escape represented an all-or-nothing choice: she could either remain a prisoner forever or risk a cruel death if recaptured after another failed escape attempt. If prisoners were fully resolved to endure torture and death, they might "run away with a brave heart."

Despite the threat of punishment, Barbara Leininger and Marie LeRoy made up their minds to escape. This time they succeeded after they formed a partnership with two captive men. On the last day of February 1759, most of the Indian men left their village of Moschkingo and proceeded to Pittsburgh to sell pelts. Meanwhile, their women traveled ten miles upcountry to gather roots. Leininger and LeRoy accompanied them. Two braves went along as guards. According to Leininger, "It was our earnest hope that the opportunity for flight, so long desired, had now come."

To facilitate the escape, Leininger pretended to be sick so that she might be allowed to set up a hut by herself. On March 14, LeRoy was sent back to the village to fetch two dogs that had been left behind. On the same day, Leininger visited a German woman who lived ten miles from Moschkingo. This woman had planned to flee with them, but she had become lame and could not go. Nevertheless, the woman gave Leininger the provisions she had gathered and urged a young Englishman, Owen Gibson, to escape with the two young girls. In the evening of March 16, Gibson reached Leininger's hut, and the entire party, consisting of the two girls, Gibson, and another prisoner, David Breckenreach, quietly slipped out of Moschkingo. They had to skirt several huts and knew that dogs roamed nearby. Their luck persisted; not a single dog barked. At this point, the escapers became evaders.

The party then began their journey through the wilderness, traveling without a guide, unacquainted with the trails, and having to cross many rivers and streams, even though the season was rainy and cold. After three years of captivity, they were hungry, half naked, and desperate.

Their luck continued to hold. Using a raft left by the Indians, they floated along the Ohio River for almost a mile before reaching the other side. Once on shore, the four escapers ran the whole night and the next day until fatigue finally forced them to rest for several days. After finding food in the forest, the group began to think about the next stage of the trip. The two Englishmen built a raft, which they then boarded, and the group safely crossed the river. At this point, they were about 150 miles from Fort Duquesne in Pittsburgh, and they decided to travel east toward the sunrise. Although it took seven days, they finally reached Little Beaver Creek and knew they were only about fifty miles from Pittsburgh.

The last miles were the most difficult. Everyone was weak from the perilous trip and lack of food. Leininger fell into the water and nearly drowned. Their provisions were gone, and they had no weapons with which to kill game. Four nights were spent in rain and snow without a fire for fear of alerting the Indians. At last, on March 31, they came to a river about three miles below Pittsburgh. They built another raft; however, this one proved to be too light and threatened to sink. LeRoy fell off and, like Leininger a few days earlier, narrowly escaped drowning. The group returned to shore, and the men decided to take the women across one at a time. What kept them going was the knowledge that they were near the Monongahela River and Pittsburgh. Soon afterwards they met some British colonial soldiers and arrived in Pittsburgh that same evening. Their ordeal was over.

As in all wars, the escapers were the exceptions. On the Ohio frontier, other captives decided to wait for rescue. For example, Barbara Leininger's cousin and fellow captive, Regina Leininger, remained with the Indians in Ohio for nine years until 1764, when Col. Henry Bouquet's rescue mission freed 206 captured settlers, 81 men and 125 women and children.[15]

Yet the war was fought on several fronts. Thomas Brown was a young man who served as a volunteer with Roger's Rangers in 1756. Only sixteen years old when he enlisted, Brown was captured by the French and Indians, wounded several times, and taken to Montreal. In *A Plain Narrative of the Uncommon Sufferings and Remarkable Deliverance of Thomas Brown* (1760), Brown wrote that he managed to escape his captors for a brief time and fled to Crown Point, New York. His luck failed, however, and he was recaptured and returned to Montreal, only to be exchanged shortly thereafter. Still full of youthful exuberance, Brown reenlisted, fought and was captured, was again imprisoned in Montreal, and finally was exchanged after three years of captivity on the frontier.

After the French and Indian War ended in 1763, the great Ottawa chief Pontiac realized that the French defeat and expulsion from North America deprived many tribes of a powerful ally against the British and the encroaching Americans, who lusted after the Ottawas' lands. In response, Pontiac used his diplomatic powers to convince the Shawnees, Delawares, and Ojibways that they needed to create a powerful coalition to wage war, the only solution to their fears of invasion and conquest. Shortly after the alliance was in place, fighting broke out.

Pontiac's Rebellion, as it was known, was the last major Indian war before the American Revolution. Chief Pontiac attacked Detroit on May 7, 1763, and the Shawnees and Delawares set upon Fort Pitt later that month. The situation looked bleak for the Red Coats as the Indian coalition successfully attacked all the smaller forts, like Fort Makinac in northern Michigan, on the British western frontier. Over a two-month period, the British lost most of their interests. Except for Fort Pitt, Fort Niagara, and Detroit, their forts were destroyed, and the settlers, traders, and garrison troops were either killed or taken prisoner. In June 1763, the British counterattacked and began to defeat the victorious tribes, one by one. Gen. Thomas Gage decided that the time was right to launch an expedition to subdue Pontiac and extend English domain over formerly French regions in Illinois and Michigan. After several battles, the British were successful, and by September 1764, the land was at peace once again.[16]

Captured by the Chippewa near Detroit in 1763, John Rutherford managed to survive by deception: to ensure his survival he pretended to embrace his captors so that he could be adopted into the tribe. He noted in his narrative that captives who showed any disdain toward the Indians were either executed in a ritual or murdered simply for target practice. Like Leininger and other prisoners, Rutherford became a committed escaper after seeing other captives murdered capriciously. As would be true of escapers in future wars, Rutherford was fortunate to receive assistance from friendly inhabitants along the way. In his case, assistance came from sympathetic French civilians.[17]

Years later, during the Revolution, the frontier continued to play a significant role in the military operations of the volunteer Continental Army. By the end of March 1781, the Ohio tribes again began to make incursions along the frontiers of western Pennsylvania. In response, the principal officers of Pennsylvania's western counties, Colonels Williamson and Marshall, planned a punitive expedition against the Wyandot towns in eastern Ohio. The call went out for volunteers, especially for those Pennsylvanians who had lost relatives or goods in the attacks. "Every one who had been plundered by the Indians," wrote John Knight, a surgeon and volunteer, "should, if the plunder could be found at their towns, have it again, proving it to be his property, and all horses lost on the expedition by unavoidable accident were to be replaced by horses taken in the enemy's country."[18]

Knight joined the volunteers under Col. William Crawford at Fort Pitt (Pittsburgh). Acting as the guide was John Slover, a former captive. The volunteers crossed the Ohio River on May 24, 1781, with 465 men in eighteen companies. The next day the expedition began heading west toward Muskingum, about sixty miles from their crossing point. On June 4, 1781, the expedition made its first contact with the enemy. Knight recalled, "The firing continued very warm on both sides from four o'clock until the dusk of the evening, each party maintaining their ground." [19] The next morning, the Indians moved closer and fighting resumed. The battle continued all day, and the situation worsened for the volunteers. American casualties increased, while the number of Indian defenders grew steadily. As the hostile fire intensified, the battle deteriorated into a rout. Terrified, the members of the American expedition fled in all directions to avoid capture. Knight and his companions headed east to what they thought was safety, but after a few miles, the surgeon was captured, along with Colonel Crawford.

For Crawford, captivity degenerated into a fierce personal holocaust of torture and death. His execution was especially grizzly. Stripped naked and beaten with sticks, Crawford was attached to a rope tied to a post so that he could walk around a few times. His captors then took up their guns and shot powder into Crawford's body, from his feet to his neck. According to Knight:

> I think not less than seventy loads. . . . They then crowded about him, and to the best of my observation, cut off his ears; when the throng had dispersed a little I saw the blood running from both sides of his head in consequence thereof. The fire was about six or seven yards from the post to which the Colonel was tied; it was made of small hickory poles, burnt quite through in the middle, each end of the poles remaining about six feet in length. Three or four Indians by turns would take up, individually, one of these burning pieces of wood and apply it to his naked body, already burnt black with the powder. These tormenters presented themselves on every side of him with the burning faggots and poles. Some of the squaws took broad boards, upon which they would carry a quantity of burning coals and hot embers and throw on him, so that in a short time he had nothing but coals of fire and hot ashes to walk upon. Colonel Crawford at this period of his sufferings besought the Almighty to have mercy on his soul, spoke very low, and bore his torments with the most manly fortitude. He continued in all the extremities of pain for an hour and three-quarters or two hours longer, as near as I can judge, when at last, being almost exhausted, he lay down on his belly; they then scalped him and repeatedly threw the scalp in my face, telling me "that was my great captain." An old

squaw got a board, took a parcel of coals and ashes and laid them on his back and head. After he had been scalped, he raised himself upon his feet and began to walk round the post. They next put a burning stick to him as usual, but he seemed more insensible of pain than before.[20]

Knight was aghast at Crawford's immolation. His captors then informed him that the same thing was going to happen to him.

Bound, the doctor waited all night for his execution, which did not come. On June 12, the Delawares moved him, and he had an opportunity to see Crawford's charred body. He recalled, "I saw his bones lying amongst the remains of the fire, almost burnt to ashes; I suppose after he was dead they had laid his body on the fire."[21] After a twenty-five mile hike toward the intended site of his execution, the doctor seized the opportunity to escape. As he rested for the night, he attempted to untie himself, but his captor was vigilant and scarcely shut his eyes. Around daybreak his guard untied Knight and ordered him to prepare a fire. Instead, Knight found a solid stick and, using all the force he could muster, he struck the guard on the head. He then seized his captor's gun, but it failed to fire properly, so the Indian escaped Knight's wrath. Knight wrote:

I took his blanket, a pair of new moccasins, his powder horn, bullet bag (together with the gun) and marched off, directing my course toward the five o'clock mark. About half an hour before sunset I came to the plains which I think are about sixteen miles wide. I laid me down in a thicket till dark, and then by the assistance of the north star made my way through them and got into the woods before morning. I proceeded on the next day, and about noon crossed the paths by which our troops had gone out; these paths are nearly east and west, but I went due North all that afternoon with a view to avoid the enemy. . . . I crossed the river Muskingum about three or four miles below Fort Lawrence, and crossing all paths aimed for the Ohio River.[22]

Knight finally came upon the Ohio River about five miles below Fort McIntosh in the evening of the twenty-first day after he had made his escape. The next morning, on July 4, 1781, although greatly fatigued, he reached the safety of the fort.

John Slover, the expedition's guide captured along with Knight and Colonel Crawford, had also been condemned to death, but he escaped before his execution by fire. Slover slipped from his ropes, stole a horse, and rode away from his executioners. After a long evasion, he arrived at the fortified town of Wheeling along the Ohio River.[23]

During both the Revolution and the War of 1812, privateering became an internationally accepted way of waging war at sea. Using Letters of

Marque that authorized Americans to assault enemy merchant shipping first in the name of the Continental Congress and later, the United States government, the Yankee privateers waged war at sea against the British merchant fleet as private ventures. The privateer system allowed individual captains to hire out to wealthy entrepreneurs who provided ships, guns, and crews for the sole purpose of marauding an enemy's merchant fleet for profit. With an increasing number of ships, crews, and fire power, the American privateers engaged and captured unarmed or lightly armed British merchantmen. After placing prize crews aboard, they sailed them to the closest friendly port, often in France, where the captain or an agent sold the ship and its cargo to the highest bidder. The profits were then divided on a sliding scale among all the interested parties, from the ship's owner to the captain, officers, and crew. The damage the privateers inflicted on the British was significant, and the British greatly resented them.

From 1776 to 1782, vessels, guns, and crews in the privateer fleet far outnumbered the fledgling American Navy. Founded on October 13, 1775, the Continental Navy had only seven small warships in service. It grew steadily, however, and by 1776, it had thirty-one warships carrying 586 guns. At the same time, the Americans sailed 136 privateers with 1,360 guns against the British merchant fleet. The most famous fighting naval captain of them all, John Paul Jones (whom the British called a pirate), sailed in the *Bonhomme Richard,* a frigate named after Benjamin Franklin's former nom de plume, Richard Saunders, or "Poor Richard." Jones raided coastal towns in England, Scotland, and Ireland, and on September 22, 1779, he engaged and defeated the British frigate *Serapis* almost within sight of the English coast. Other famous privateer captains were Joshua Barney, Gustavus Conyngham, and Nathaniel Fanning. Except for Jones, all of these captains were captured during the Revolution.

By 1782, the Continental Navy had again been reduced to only seven ships carrying 198 guns, whereas the number of privateers increased to 323 ships with 4,845 guns. By the war's end, only one of the warships built or purchased by the American government remained in American hands. The rest were either captured by the British or burned to avoid capture. It was a thoroughly deplorable record (see Appendix 2A: *American Armed Vessels, 1776–1782).*[24] At the same time, however, the American war fleet sailed 330 ships with 5,043 guns, mostly privateers, leaving little doubt that rich profits motivated American seamen every bit as much, if not more, than did simple patriotism. In all, 1,151 American and allied privateers roamed the seas and captured about six hundred British vessels, sixteen of which were warships. With a Letter of Marque in hand, any freewheeling captain could harass, raid, take prizes, and become a nuisance to enemy merchantmen and a real danger to undefended enemy coastal towns.

That the system was generally accepted throughout the western European maritime world is indisputable. No privateer was ever considered a mercenary at home, and there was never a lack of enterprising sponsors, swashbuckling captains, or adventuresome crews ready to go to sea. It is a matter of history that the privateers served American interests at sea during these wars. Although international privateering was abolished by the Declaration of Paris in 1856, active American privateering continued until the American Civil War, and it was not formally abolished by Congress until March 3, 1899.

Still, the British Navy ruled the seas. In response to the successes of American privateering as well as to the Revolution itself, the British government passed Lord North's Act of 1777, which legalized the British view of the rebellious Americans as rebels on land and pirates at sea, thereby assuring their status as criminals. The North Act made certain that the British government exercised all of its sovereign judicial powers of punishment against the sailors charged with or suspected of the crime of High Treason committed in "any of His Majesty's colonies or on the high Seas or with the Crime of Piracy."[25] Andrew Sherburne recalled his personal encounter with an Admiralty court. After the American privateer *Greyhound* was engaged and captured, he and his shipmates were brought before twelve officers for trial. After some interrogation, the court pronounced sentence. Sherburne wrote, "We were severally and individually committed to Old Mill Prison, for rebellion, piracy, and high treason on His Britannic Majesty's high seas, there to lay during his Majesty's pleasure, until he saw fit to pardon or otherwise dispose of us."[26] Sherburne's experience, like that of many other captured American privateers, confirms that the British were more outraged with the Americans for fighting a war for money like mercenaries than for fighting a public war in open, uniformed naval combat for reasons of state. In effect, American officers and seamen of the privateer fleet could expect to be tried and treated as criminals, not POWs.[27]

In America itself, captured American soldiers were cast into criminal confinement in church cellars and local jails.[28] Ethan Allen's memoir, *A Narrative of Colonel Ethan Allen's Captivity Containing His Voyages and Travels* (1807), covered the period of his captivity from May 1775 until his release in May 1778, and was the first distinctly American POW narrative of the Revolution to become a best-seller. According to Allen and other prisoners of the period, military security was tight, and it was nearly impossible for American prisoners of the British Army to escape. They were too well guarded in small groups. Most stayed with the British until they were exchanged or taken to England. A young surgeon, Elias Cornelius of the Connecticut militia, was an exception. He made his escape during a snowstorm while his sentry was distracted. Cornelius perched on a tombstone in the yard, and after jumping over a fence, he misled other guards by posing as a drunken civilian. Eventually he reached a safe house near the edge of town.[29]

Captured sailors languished below decks in the dreaded poisonous British prison hulks at Wallabout Bay near Brooklyn, New York.[30] In a relatively short time, the American POWs held in the *John, Whitby, Good Intent, Frederick, Kitty, Hunter, Judith,* and *Falmouth* were too sick, too weak, or both, to escape. Miraculously, a number of prisoners remained healthy, and when conditions improved, some made successful escapes. Christopher Hawkins, for example, was taken on board the British prison ship *Jersey* in 1781 and quietly slithered down the side of the ship into the water without arousing the guards' suspicions. After he swam to shore, however, Hawkins was recaptured and temporarily housed in a private home. Luckily for him, his guards were romantically interested in a girl who was preparing food, and Hawkins seized the moment to slip away again.[31]

Samuel Nowell of Boston, Massachusetts, also became an escaper. Nowell first surfaced in 1773 as one of the night raiders who threw British tea into Boston Harbor. In 1775, the American Commissary of Supplies, then residing in Charlestown, had rendered himself the object of British suspicion and hatred. The British began a general search for him, but he was concealed by local patriots. In the middle of the night, Nowell, with one companion, took the Commissary aboard his boat and ran the gauntlet of the British naval blockade to safety. The British responded by declaring Nowell a criminal and pursued him. Using a disguise, Nowell slipped aboard a British ship in the harbor sailing for Nantasket. Two years later, in 1777, he sailed on the American ship *Independence,* which was captured by the British brig *Hope.* Along with the other prisoners, Nowell was transferred to the *Vulture,* carried to Halifax, and then imprisoned for sixteen months before his exchange. While in Halifax, Nowell had devised an escape plan for all the American captives. He

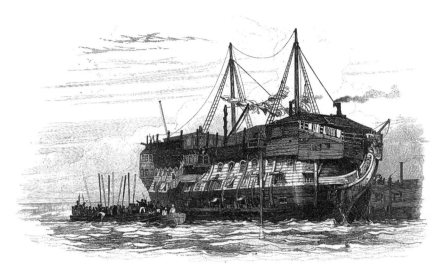

Unidentified prison ship of the nineteenth century. This is a clear illustration of what prison ships of the Revolution and War of 1812 looked like. French print

created an organization to tunnel out of the prison, but someone within the organization informed the British, and Nowell spent three months of close confinement in irons and manacles.[32]

Had Nowell escaped, he would have enjoyed several distinct advantages as a war prisoner on the loose in Canada. He could easily have disappeared into the native population because he looked and spoke like the residents of Halifax. Nor was he very far away from friendly territory by sea. It was a different situation for Americans in England, however. They faced a bounty paid for their return to prison authorities, the English Channel as a barrier to France, and the Atlantic Ocean as a barrier to America. Consequently, most Americans waited in close confinement for exchange; those who decided on escape from prisons in England needed outside help.

Despite the odds, captured American privateers in England began planning escapes soon after their incarceration in any one of several formidable British military prisons, including Millbay in Plymouth, Forton in Portsmouth, Deal near Dover, and Kinsale Prison in Ireland. Plymouth's Millbay naval prison was known simply as Mill Prison to the Americans; Fortune, or Forton, Prison began as a hospital and stood not far from the Portsmouth docks. Deal Prison was close to the coast, as was Kinsale Prison near Cork, Ireland. Using funds from the sale of prizes or donations provided by Britons friendly to the American cause, the captives made regular escapes from Mill and Forton, where prisoners reported that poverty made many of the guards susceptible to bribes. With planning and cooperative effort, individuals, partnerships, and small groups could burrow underneath the prisons or scale their lightly guarded walls. Because the British offered a reward of five pounds for the return of escaped Americans, a substantial sum at the time, those hunting the escapers became known as "five pounders." Although most men escaped in order to continue the lucrative business of privateering, it is conceivable that some enterprising prisoners feigned an escape simply to share the reward. Tunneling was by far the most common method for mass escape. In 1777, thirty-two American prisoners escaped from Mill Prison by digging an eighteen-foot tunnel to an outside field. Eleven were recaptured; the rest were free to fight again. American prisoners in Kinsale often seized small boats to make the passage to France.[33]

Many of the American captives proved to be very resourceful. For example, Eli Bickford of Durham, New Hampshire, was captured aboard an American privateer and imprisoned in the hulk *Jersey,* anchored with other prison hulks in Wallabout Bay, New York. After his transfer and removal to England, Bickford and a small group of other Americans dug a tunnel, keeping the dirt in their hammocks. When the moment came to break through the surface, the escapers discovered that a house blocked their exit. Instead of panicking or giving up, they dismantled a brick floor, climbed up into the house, unlocked the door, and walked out. After their recapture, the escapers were confined to the "Black Hole," where they lived on bread and water. Bickford then remained in prison for more than four years until his postwar exchange.[34]

Joshua Barney, a privateer officer of the Pennsylvania fleet, was captured in December 1780 by H.M.S. *Intrepid,* and he and seventy-four other American privateer officers were transported to England confined in chains deep within the warship *Yarmouth.* By the time they arrived in Plymouth fifty-three days later, eleven officers had died, and the survivors were in terrible physical condition. Barney and the remaining privateers were first sent to a hulk where they were charged as rebels and pirates. They were then removed to Mill Prison. Barney, believing that his life was worthless in British hands, lost little time in planning his escape.

In his first attempt, Barney dug his way through stone walls to a sewer, only to discover after a long walk through filth that the exit was blocked by an iron grating. He concluded that he needed a more inventive plan to break out of Mill Prison. He also needed some luck and a little help from

Joshua Barney, a privateer captain of the Pennsylvania fleet, was captured in December 1780 by H.M.S. *Intrepid* and later held in Mill Prison. After his final escape, Barney disguised himself and crossed the English Channel into France. Courtesy of the U.S. Naval Historical Center

the outside. After sounding out the sentries about their political views, he found a friendly guard who agreed to deliver a British officer's uniform that Barney could use as a disguise. On the appointed day, Barney covered the uniform with a large coat and had some of his friends distract the guards during roll call while others hoisted him over the prison wall. As a fugitive, Barney went quickly to a known "safe house" in Plymouth, owned most probably by Baptist minister Philip Gibb or Plymouth Tabernacle's Andrew Kinsman. Once there he explained his situation and received help for the next leg of his perilous journey. Barney knew that he had to leave England quickly, so he purchased a fishing boat for a trip across the

Channel to France. At sea, he managed to weave his way through numerous British warships at anchor. Finally, however, Barney met his match, a security-minded British privateer captain who refused to accept his cover story that he was on a secret mission to Admiral Digby himself. Realizing that the game was nearly up, Barney slipped down the side of the ship, stole its small dinghy, and made for land. After arriving in Plymouth again, a wiser Barney avoided public places on his way back to the "safe house" from which he had begun his journey. Since he knew that the British had placed the handsome price of five guineas on his head, Barney disguised himself for his final trip across the English Channel to France. Many years later, during the War of 1812, an aged Capt. Joshua Barney refused a commission in the United States Navy but sailed again as a privateer with considerable success.[35]

Barney was not the only privateer captain to make his escape from England. After his capture, Continental privateer Capt. Gustavus Conyngham, an Irish immigrant who arrived in America before the Revolution, was brought in irons to Pendennis Castle, where the British manacled his hands and held him in solitary confinement for sixteen days. Conyngham was then removed to Plymouth, where he was lodged in the Black Hole for eight days before being charged with committing high treason on "His Majesty's high seas." In Mill Prison, the British naval authorities convinced an angry and apprehensive Captain Conyngham that the gallows awaited him. As a result, he wasted no time devising a way to walk out of the prison gate dressed as a doctor. Recaptured and faced with what he believed was certain death for piracy, Conyngham began tunneling out as quickly as he could. The first two tunnels were discovered and destroyed, but Conyngham finally succeeded on his third attempt. On November 3, 1779, he and fifty-three other prisoners got away in one of the earliest highly organized mass escapes in American military history. Captain Conyngham later wrote about his cruises and subsequent captivity experiences. Concerning the escape from Mill, he wrote, "We committed treason through his [the king's] earth and made our escape."[36]

Forton Prison, a former naval hospital about one mile from Gosport and two miles from Portsmouth, operated from June 1777 to March 1783, although it was wholly unsuited for use as a military prison.[37] Eleven men escaped within days of its establishment in 1777. In 1778, the local militia found French and American prisoners climbing through a hole in the outer wall, and twenty-five prisoners escaped. Later that year, fifty-seven Americans dug a tunnel from the Black Hole, the area of the

Capt. Gustavus Conyngham of the Continental Navy. On November 3, 1779, Captain
Conyngham escaped from Mill Prison (England) with fifty-three other prisoners.
Upon reflection, Captain Conyngham later wrote, "We committed treason through
his [the king's] earth and made our escape." Artist: V. Zveg. Miniature published in
"Letters and Papers of Gustavus Conyngham" by the Naval History Society.
Courtesy of the U.S. Naval Historical Center

prison designated for punitive confinement, to a point beyond the prison
walls.[38] During the course of the war, there were rarely any more than
400 Americans in Forton at any one time. From 1777 to 1779, Forton's
American inmate population averaged about 200 to 250, but from 1779
onward, the average was closer to 350. After mid-1782, the number
declined steadily as a result of prisoner exchanges, yet even then little
could be done to stop the Americans from breaking out. Between June
1777 and April 1782, British records indicate that 536 Americans fled
from Forton. Of that number, only 112 avoided recapture.[39] In 1780,
more than a third of the American prisoners in Britain, 118 of 300 men,
escaped into the British population.[40] The English defeat at Yorktown
led to the end of the North ministry early in 1782. In April 1782, peace
was in the air, encouraged by the Shelburne government, and a general

prisoner release appeared imminent. Nevertheless, the Americans continued their efforts to escape from all the British prison facilities, especially from Forton.[41]

After their escape, whether in partnerships, small groups, or in mass escapes, the former captives found that stealth was not enough. They nearly always required some outside help in order to succeed during the most difficult phase of the escape—integrating into the indigenous population in order to reach the departure point for the journey home.

One influential American figure in Europe was Benjamin Franklin, who represented American interests in France from 1777 to 1785. Franklin's efforts on behalf of American prisoners lasted for the duration of the war, and his contacts in England were extensive. He made certain that incarcerated prisoners as well as those on the run received whatever help was possible, and he attempted to generate exchanges. Outside official channels, those Americans, both in prison and on the run, received the help they needed from several dissenting British clergymen, mostly radical Presbyterians, Unitarians, Quakers, and Methodists in England and Ireland, who supported the American cause. These men made a significant difference in the lives of several escapers.

William Hazlitt, a devout British Unitarian, tended to the needs of American prisoners held in Ireland's Kinsale Prison. Following the war, Hazlitt emigrated to America, but after finding the country more religiously conservative than he liked, he returned to England. Hazlitt's colleague, Reuben Harvey, a Quaker merchant from Cork, also helped to relieve the distress of American POWs in Ireland during the Revolution. In 1783, Harvey wrote to George Washington describing his activities and later received a commendation from Congress.[42] Robert Heath, who preached in Plymouth, became a regular visitor to the Americans in Mill Prison, where he dispensed his pastoral offices. Acting as conduits for aid given freely by sympathizers and expatriate Americans in Britain, Heath and his assistant, Miles Saurey, distributed funds, clothing, and food to the prisoners. In 1778, the British and the Americans began negotiating over prisoner exchanges, and Heath and Saurey found themselves caught in the middle, especially by providing comfort to the Americans whose releases were somehow delayed. Neither minister was active as a secret conduit for escapers, but the Reverend Thomas Wren was another story.

Wren ministered to the needs of the Americans in Forton. Like the others, his interest was spiritual at first, but gradually his efforts became more aggressively humanitarian when he began to solicit donations from friends and organizations for prisoner relief. Between June 1777 and

April 1782, 536 Americans escaped from Forton. Those who succeeded owed their success in no small degree to Wren and his confederates, who risked indictments for treason from the British government by offering escapers the safety of their homes, as well as intelligence concerning the safest routes through London. Whereas Heath's actions were oriented toward a spiritual ministry, Wren was a political activist who supported the Enlightenment ideas that he shared with the Americans fighting against the British crown.

After hostilities ceased in 1783, none of the American sympathizers in Britain, including Wren and Heath, ever asked the American government for any compensation for their acts of comfort. Their acts were grounded in the courage of their convictions, not in the expectation of any wealth that might accrue to them after the war. As a token of the nation's appreciation, the U.S. Congress passed a resolution in September 1783 acknowledging Wren's humane acts and thanked him officially for his benevolent attention toward the American prisoners incarcerated in England throughout the war. A few weeks later, the College of New Jersey, now Princeton University, granted Wren an honorary doctorate in recognition of his compassion and humanity. For Wren, a man of principle and courage, that was reward enough.

By 1783, America had grown tired of war and longed for peace. The country needed time to put its house in order before it could exert any influence abroad, but major issues remained unresolved concerning the British position in Canada and Michigan, as well as the continuing military relationship between the British and their allied native tribes. The American Articles of Confederation left room for the Canadian provinces to enter the Union if they freed themselves from England, and Americans worried about British control of the high seas and world trade. Each of these issues was resolved after the War of 1812, but unexpected events in the Mediterranean assumed greater importance.

In 1785, the Algerians began to take American captives, an activity that put the American government in the unenviable position of having to pay tribute and ransom to a Barbary power that it knew little about. There were also problems with France. Beginning in 1787 and continuing throughout the French Revolution, France grew increasingly hostile toward the United States. At sea, the two nations carried on an undeclared naval war until President Thomas Jefferson's Louisiana Purchase in 1803. Although the United States wanted to stay aloof from international entanglements in order to seek its own destiny at home and expand its trade abroad, the European powers continued to create policies that challenged American rights at sea and confronted U.S. interests on the North American continent. In 1796 at Jérémie in Santa Domingo, for example, the captain of a British warship in port needed men and boarded the American merchant schooner *Eliza* for the purpose of impressment. The American captain, David Porter, Sr., verbally resisted and took his ship to sea. Later his son, David Porter, Jr., was impressed during another such incident, but he slipped through a porthole and swam underwater to a Danish brig, which took him to Copenhagen where he transferred to a ship bound for the United States. As a result of such acts of British aggression, the second war against England, declared by Congress on June 18, 1812, came as little surprise to anyone.[43]

During much of the War of 1812, the American Army lost nearly every battle it fought. On July 13, 1812, after declaring that "no White man found fighting by the side of an Indian will be taken prisoner," Gen. William Hull surrendered Detroit and the Michigan Territory almost without a fight to British Maj. Gen. Isaac Brock and Tecumseh.[44] The Americans taken prisoner feared for their lives, but Tecumseh made certain that no massacres took place and won a reputation for fairness in his treatment of captives. This was not the case when a contingent of more than 850 Kentuckians lost the Battle of River Raisin in January 1814 to Col. Henry Proctor and a large Indian force. After the surrender, Proctor permitted the Indians to take bitter and bloody revenge against the Americans. Tecumseh was horrified to learn of this incident and knew that the Americans would retaliate similarly in the future.[45]

Subsequently, Fort Dearborn near Chicago was destroyed. Col. Winfield Scott was defeated at Queenstown in Canada, and the Americans lost large numbers of soldiers at the battle of Bladensburg in 1814. A British force of fourteen thousand soldiers, fresh from victories over Napoleon, was well trained and stirring for a fight in America. To make matters worse, the British burned Washington, the nation's capital, and the Royal Navy ruled the waves off the American coast with a two-hundred-ship blockade. In addition, strong resistance to the war was developing in America, especially in Massachusetts. Thus things looked bleak for the Americans, and the British were poised to make them accept nearly any terms of armistice or surrender—either would do—that Great Britain dictated. Not until the Gen. Andrew Jackson's engagements at Horseshoe Bend (1814) against the Northern Creeks or "Red Sticks" and at New Orleans (1815) against a veteran British force and Gen. William Henry

Harrison's victory over Tecumseh and the British near Thamesville in Canada did the Americans claim anything close to a victory.[46]

The war at sea, however, was another matter. Fighting was fierce, and the Americans made life miserable for the British naval and merchant fleets. The small American Navy made its power felt when the American frigate *Constitution* defeated the *Guerrière* on August 19, 1812, and the *Java* in December of that year. The American sloop *Wasp* destroyed the *Frolic* off the North Carolina coast; the frigate *United States* took the *Macedonian* captive; and the *Hornet* defeated the *Peacock*. The American deep-water navy lost only seven men-of-war but destroyed or captured twenty-six British warships and achieved success against the British on the Great Lakes.[47] The tide turned, however, and by 1814, most of the Navy's warships were blocked from departure and sat inert in port. On the other hand, the Americans issued 515 Letters of Marque, and the aggressive privateers resourcefully seized 1,345 British vessels. Consequently, treasures were won and lost at sea, and prices of imported goods soared in Britain. Feelings hardened, and captured American sailors remained in English prisons long after hostilities ended.

During the war, an extraordinary number of American naval personnel, privateers for the most part, were captured by British forces. About fourteen thousand men, out of a total seafaring manpower pool of approximately one hundred thousand, were held captive for some time.[48] The Revolution had taught the Americans bitter lessons about prison hulks, dungeons, and Black Holes in British jails, so they knew exactly what to expect. In England, American sailors were held in at least eighteen locations, ranging from prison hulks to the large prison at Dartmoor. However, the political situation in 1812 differed from that in 1776. The British now recognized the United States as a sovereign country, and as a result, no one was tried for piracy or branded a rebel, except for those sailors who had emigrated from England to the United States. The British considered these men to be British citizens and felt free to impress them, or worse, try them in Admiralty court as traitors. The others became prisoners of war with the rights traditionally accorded that status. In general, this meant that the officers were granted parole to house themselves in nearby towns, while the sailors remained in close confinement. From the autumn of 1812 to April 1813, nine hundred Americans were confined at Chatham, one hundred at Portsmouth, and seven hundred at Plymouth.

Early in the war most American sailors found themselves sent to the hulks *Hector* and *La Brave* under the supervision of the British Transport

Board. Both hulks were moored by chain to their respective piers about two miles from Plymouth. On April 2, 1813, approximately 250 American privateers and uniformed service personnel held in the prison hulks in Plymouth were moved to the newly constructed Dartmoor Prison in Devonshire.[49] Chosen both for its location near the moors and for Devonshire's dreary regional climate, Dartmoor was a thirty-six-acre complex enclosed by thick stone walls, about twelve to sixteen feet high. Originally designed in 1806–09 to hold 5,000 prisoners, it was always overcrowded, and, by the war's end, it contained 6,560 Americans.[50] In Dartmoor, disease was rampant, escape from the facility was difficult, and dungeon or "cachot" punishments upon recapture were severe. Although a few Americans escaped by climbing over the walls, local farmers and country folk turned them in for generous rewards.

From the beginning, the Americans proved difficult, sometimes even impossible, to guard. One daylight escape attempt took place in 1812 among the Americans imprisoned aboard the prison hulk *Canada*. As beef was being hauled aboard the hulk, six Americans cut the lines and managed to jump to the small boat swinging alongside. Dodging a hail of gunfire, they immediately sailed for open water. They may have been good sailors, but they had no knowledge of the navigational requirements of Commodore's Head, Gillingham, and the little boat ran aground. Although the escapers were recaptured and returned to their hulk, the British learned that the Americans never relaxed their efforts to devise escapes.[51]

The basic rule of pragmatic opportunism prevailed: given a reasonable chance to escape, any way was a good way if it worked. At sea, some American sailors decided that attempting to escape by rushing the guard and taking over the ship was better than endless POW incarceration. Benjamin Brown's journal, edited and published by Nathaniel Hawthorne as *Yarn of a Yankee Privateer* (1846), relates one such sad but pertinent experience. Brown, a pharmacist from Salem, Massachusetts, went to sea on the *Frolic* as the captain's clerk. Captured in the West Indies by the *Heron,* the *Frolic*'s crew was taken first to Bermuda for a brief stay and then to Medville Island near Halifax, Nova Scotia.[52] In the summer of 1814, 250 prisoners, including the crew from the *Frolic,* were removed from Halifax on board four transport vessels in a convoy bound for England. Leading the convoy was the *Goliath,* commanded by Capt. Frederick L. Maitland, RN, who later commanded the *Bellerophon,* and to whom Napoleon was to surrender after his abdication. Among the prisoners were the officers and crew of the American privateer *Diomede* out of Salem.

After being at sea for a few days, the British perceived little danger from the prisoners; in actuality, however, the men below decks were plotting to take possession of the ship. One group was to attack the quarterdeck to gain control of the helm; another planned to assault the fore hatchway to detain and secure the detachment of Royal Marines stationed there; and a third group was to take control of the forecastle to prevent the watch from taking its stations. The word "Keno" was to launch the assault. After the plan was prepared, however, one member of the group tipped off the British, who waited for the escapers to make their move. When the signal came, the Royal Marines on board shot the men as they rushed to their assigned objectives. The attempt to take over the ship had turned into a disaster. The *Goliath*'s surgeon, Barry O'Meara, treated the survivors with kindness, and after the ship docked in England, the Americans, including Brown, were deposited in Dartmoor.[53]

In addition to the thousands of white sailors held in Dartmoor, the British imprisoned approximately four hundred black American privateers from Baltimore and New England. Richard Crafus, taken prisoner aboard the Letter of Marque vessel *Requin* in 1814, was a professional boxer in civilian life. In prison, he established his reign over the black inmates and became known as "King Dick." He controlled the sales of spirits and beer, the prodigious amount of gambling going on to pass the time, entertainment, and religious services. Because of Crafus's extraordinary leadership, life in Barracks #4 inside Dartmoor Prison became bearable. One of Crafus's subjects was Charles Black, an impressed seaman who had refused to serve in the British Navy at the outbreak of the war. The British gave Black a choice, service at sea or imprisonment. With help from Crafus, Black became one of the few who managed to escape Dartmoor successfully before the war's end.[54]

When hostilities concluded with the Treaty of Ghent in 1814, the American prisoners believed that they had the right to leave Dartmoor and the other prisons in England. Instead, they received instructions to sit tight because a shipping shortage prohibited the American government from transporting them back to the United States immediately. In addition, Reuben Beasley, the American agent in London, discovered that the United States had insufficient credit to cover the cost of the return of its prisoners, and many men grew fearful and dangerously restless over their plight. Realizing that the war was over and there was no reason for these men to remain in prison, the British guards began looking the other way, making it easier for escapes to take place. Josiah

Cobb reported that in the space of four days and nights, "seventy-eight went out—eleven scaling the walls in open daylight, with their baggage, within full view of the sentinels, who looked on without seeing their movements." [55] Cobb explained how Dartmoor prisoners liberated themselves:

> The plan and price (from one to two pounds sterling) was agreed upon during the day, with the sentry posted in the yard, who likewise must purchase the confidence of two or three others, and wait till they were so placed on guard, in some dark night, as to hold the connection between them, when the prisoner was notified that all was in readiness. He that was to go out, gained the top of the prison through one of the cockloft skylights, none of which were grated, and with his rope already provided, descended to the yard. After the rope was detached from above, by a companion, it answered by throwing one end to the sentinel, to aid him in reaching the top of the wall, when he passed freely by as many of the guard as understood his purpose, and he was in safety outside the prison limits, beyond control of the soldiery. If then he had the requisite means and suitable clothing to travel genteelly, by stage or otherwise, he had no difficulty on reaching the coast, and securing a passage across the channel.[56]

So many men reached Reuben Beasley that he felt compelled to direct all would-be escapers to stay put until he could arrange cartel exchanges. Outraged at Beasley, the general attitude of the British government, and the still overcrowded conditions in Dartmoor, two Americans attempted to tunnel their way out of the prison. Digging was accomplished in three barracks simultaneously. Capt. Thomas Shortland, RN, the feared and hated interior commandant, discovered their efforts and shut them down. The Americans tried again, this time nearly completing their second tunnel, but liberation arrived at last, so the prisoners left the second tunnel unfinished. It was discovered in December 1911, nearly a century later, when Dartmoor's authorities excavated a foundation for a new prison hall.

It was logical for the American privateers to try to escape from prison hulks and major installations during the years of the Revolution and the War of 1812 because their living depended on the number of prizes they could take at sea. No one made any money while in jail. The prizes taken and the prisoners who could be exchanged for equal numbers of enemy combatants represented income and were far more important to these men than the numbers of soldiers slain on the battlefield or sailors lost at sea. For many of these prisoners, escape meant not only relief from incarceration but also the resumption of privateering and the possibility of continuing to earn huge profits. This is not to say that escapers fled their prisons solely to resume their profitable ventures, but they considered this combination of economic opportunism and simple but passionate patriotism to be their national duty. In language characteristic of nineteenth-century popular prose, Warren Wildwood described American prisoners of the British as a troublesome and restless lot, observing, "They will not settle down to inactivity under any wrong or oppression; they will not bear any burden meekly or tamely; nurtured in the lap of freedom, they chafe fearfully under any restraint; their liberty they will seek at any hazard—they pant for it as for the air they breathe; show them the remotest possibility of accomplishing their purpose, and no danger, no thousand dangers, will deter them from the attempt; destroyed they may be but not subdued."[57] But patriotism had its limits on both sides.

Although the British forces vastly outnumbered the Americans, the protracted raiding war at sea, the British defeats on the Great Lakes, and American victories on land altered the British negotiating strategy at Ghent during the autumn of 1814. Indeed, both nations had grown tired of war, but the British government had continued to covet American territories until the military reversals dampened its aspirations. The British offered terms for ending the conflict, but the Americans rejected them over and over again. Finally, after giving serious consideration to the costs of continuing to prosecute the war, it was decided that it would be cheaper to make peace. Both nations signed the Treaty of Ghent on December 24, 1814; the treaty was more an armistice than a clear-cut victory or defeat for either side.[58] Fortunately for the United States and the United Kingdom, it was the last incidence of declared, open hostilities between the two countries.

When one examines who escaped and why during this period, two types of individuals stand out: the roguish, committed natural escapers and the simple opportunists. Although most of the American prisoners were privateers, some were navymen like Capt. David Porter, who terrorized the British whaling fleet in the Pacific. In 1814, after his frigate *Essex* was destroyed in battle, he informed his captors, "I . . . consider myself . . . at liberty to effect my escape if I can."[59]

During the war, American prisoners escaped knowing full well that they were POWs; after the war, they sensed that they had become hostages not only of the British military establishment but also of their own government's inability to pay its bills. Whereas earlier the Americans tunneled out with only the clothes on their back, later they left bag-and-baggage, in many cases with sympathetic guards looking the other way as they climbed over the wall. On April 20, 1815, a total of 263 Americans left Dartmoor: a few days later another 5,193 freed prisoners followed, carrying a large white flag that depicted the goddess of Liberty sorrowing over the tomb of their dead compatriots with the legend, "Columbia weeps and will remember!"[60] What Columbia really wept for in the nineteenth century was the toll of American lives taken in Texas and Mexico and later during the Civil War.

3

Soldiers of Manifest Destiny
Escapes South of the Border

I have seen a letter from Santa Anna to General Waddy Thompson, saying that he was on the point of releasing the prisoners, when the news of the escape of sixteen reached him, which rendered us unworthy of his magnanimity. Devil take such magnanimous men; he has no such feelings.

—Joseph McCutchan (1844)

The issues that prompted men to fight during the American war with Mexico (1846–48) dated back to the Texas War for Independence in 1836 and well before. Old Mexico was a huge Spanish colony that extended north and west past present-day Mexico to Texas and into Arizona, New Mexico, Nevada, and California. After Mexico won its independence from Spain in 1821, part of the legacy of the colonial period included ongoing Spanish-American disputes over the national boundaries established by Thomas Jefferson's Louisiana Purchase in 1803. To keep the peace, the United States renounced its formal claims to Texas in the Adams-Onis Treaty of 1819. In turn, Mexico permitted *empresarios* like Moses Austin and three hundred American families to establish colonial residence in sparsely populated Texas. Upon Austin's unexpected death, his son Stephen carried out his plans and founded a permanent Anglo-American settlement at San Felipé de Austin in December of 1821. In 1826, the United States recognized Mexico as a sovereign nation.

In the space of fifteen years, more than thirty thousand Americans immigrated into the new land. Because of Austin's brilliant leadership, Mexican authorities gave the newcomers, mostly slaveholding Southerners and entrepreneurial Westerners, citizenship and free land taken from the Indians, but there were political and religious strings attached. The new Texans were forced to accept the Spanish custom of absolute rule by absolute rulers. More accustomed to laws fashioned from a combination of British and German political traditions, the Americans had already fought two wars against the English crown to establish and maintain representative democracy and to secure the specific personal and institutional freedoms included in the American Constitution. In that sense, patriotism and a spirit of political justice ran high among the Americans in Texas, and absolute rule by anyone was detested and scorned as tyranny, especially if Texans were the victims. The Mexicans also demanded that the American Protestant immigrants convert to Roman Catholicism, the state church of Mexico. This practice of forced conversion in the New World had begun in the sixteenth century with the Spanish issuance of the *Requerimiento,* a proclamation that called upon the Mexican Indians to acknowledge the supremacy of the Pope and the Spanish crown under pain of enslavement and confiscation of all personal goods.[1] At best, the new Texans gave this Spanish colonial relic only lip-service. Although many immigrants went through the motions of conversion to secure land grants, the Texan immigrants ignored the idea of a state religion and considered it an unjust infringement upon their personal rights.

The Mexicans saw the issues very differently. Texas was a part of Mexico, and in their view, traditional Spanish political and social customs were reasonable and enforceable. It became obvious that the American immigrants would not abide by the contract they had made with the Mexican government. Religion in Mexico was a state rather than a personal affair, and the American refusal to abide by Mexican civil and religious codes, authoritarian or not, was considered unlawful. These issues, coupled with the amount of land at stake, were enough to start a war in 1832. Beginning with a battle at Anáhuac between a small detachment of the Mexican Army led by Col. Domingo de Ugartechea and the Anglo-Texans led by John Austin (no relation to Stephen), the war eventually turned into a protracted struggle for political independence. The Mexicans, however, considered the struggle to be a manifestation of the Texans' inordinate greed for land, as well as a criminal insurrection against the state, punishable by death.

If ever a cultural clash erupted between authorities and immigrants, it was the Texas war. After an internal revolution, the dashing Gen. Antonio Lopez de Santa Anna became dictator of Mexico in 1834. Issues and passions came to a head in 1836, when the Texans under Sam Houston declared their independence from Santa Anna's Mexico and established a republic on paper. Bands of Texans then initiated attacks against Mexican Army outposts with some success. Built in 1744 as the Spanish mission San Antonio de Valero, the Alamo (Cottonwood) became the Mexican military headquarters in 1788. In January 1836, the Texans seized the small Alamo garrison from the Mexican Army, and from February 26 to March 6, 1836, the Mexicans retaliated vigorously. Led by Santa Anna, a Mexican force of about 4,000 soldiers marched into San Antonio to engage and destroy the 187-man Alamo garrison commanded by the Alabama firebrand, William Barrett Travis. The Alamo defenders saw the hated red flag that signaled "No Quarter" hoisted on a town church and responded with a blast from their cannon.[2]

When the smoke cleared at the Alamo, Travis, along with Davy Crockett from Tennessee, Jim Bowie from Georgia, and all other defenders, was dead. Those men who were not killed in action were immediately executed by a Mexican firing squad or were bayoneted where they had fallen wounded. The Mexicans lost about fifteen hundred soldiers at the Alamo, and Santa Anna was satisfied with the victory. In his view, the Texans were beginning to learn that armed insurgency in Mexico met with certain death. R. M. Potter memorialized the defeat in his "Hymn of the Alamo," published at Columbia, Texas, in the *Telegraph and Texas Register* on Wednesday, October 5, 1836:

> How Travis and his hundred fell
> Amid a thousand foemen slain!
> They died the Spartan's death
> But not in hopeless strife—
> Like brothers died and their expiring breath
> Was Freedom's breath of life![3]

Although the Texans gained a lasting battle cry, "Remember the Alamo," they learned that surrender was impossible and that Santa Anna's penalty for defeat was execution.

The Texans fighting the Mexicans at the town of Goliad, the second major battle of the war, were about to learn the Alamo lesson all too well. From survivors of smaller skirmishes, Col. James Fannin learned that one of Santa Anna's field commanders, Gen. Don José Urrea, patrolled the region. On February 16, 1836, Fannin received a message from Travis at the Alamo requesting reinforcement. Fannin stood his ground and refused to move his army of five hundred volunteers to San Antonio, but he eventually changed his mind and began the march. With the volunteer army only four miles from San Antonio and the Alamo under siege, Fannin called for a council of war among his officers, and together they decided to withdraw, leaving the Alamo defenders to their own fate. After he returned to the garrison at Goliad, Fannin received orders from Houston to evacuate his army and as many Anglo-Texan settlers as possible to friendlier territory to the northeast. Fannin detached a group of more than one hundred soldiers to evacuate the settlers from the town of Refugio, but General Urrea found and destroyed them quickly on March 16. Two days later, on March 18, 1836, Fannin engaged General Urrea several miles from Goliad to buy time for Sam Houston's forces training near the town of San Jacinto. In the battle, Fannin realized that his men were outnumbered, outgunned, and outmaneuvered by General Urrea. Instead of fighting to the end, Fannin arranged to surrender his command of about four hundred men under the assumption that they would be accorded the traditional treatment due POWs.[4] Fannin was wrong.

When Santa Anna, flushed with victory at the Alamo, received notice of Fannin's surrender, he ordered the immediate execution of every officer and soldier in the command. After a week in captivity, the Goliad soldiers, mostly volunteers from Tennessee, Alabama, Louisiana, and Kentucky, thought that they were being taken by ship to New Orleans. Instead, they were separated into three large groups, marched half a mile from the fort, and shot down in cold blood. Most of the officers, including Fannin himself, were shot later. Twenty-seven were hidden by friendly Mexicans and sympathetic foreign officers in the Mexican Army, but in all, 390 Americans were executed and, like the Alamo defenders, passed into martyrdom for Texas. J. M. Parmenter's "Texas Hymn" (1838) remembered the slaughters at Goliad and the Alamo:

We'll never trust his honor, assassin he is bred,
Brave Fannin and his warriors thus found a gory bed.
And Travis with his heroes on San Antonio height,
Before the foeman legions fell unequal fight.[5]

When reports of the Goliad massacre reached Sam Houston, a Tennessean who had been appointed commander in chief of the Texan army, his hatred for the Mexican Army in general and for Santa Anna in particular escalated considerably. The Texans wanted to exact retribution immediately, but Houston preferred to select the battlefield. After a series of retreats, Houston lost many of his volunteers, who left him to help their families flee to safety in the face of the Mexican advances. Houston's moment of decision arrived: with his back to a river, his 783 angry Texans engaged the Mexican Army on April 20–21, 1836, at San Jacinto. The battle cry was "Remember the Alamo."

During the battle and after it, Houston destroyed the Mexican force. Actual losses among the Texans were 2 killed in action and 23 wounded,

6 mortally. Mexican losses were significant: 630 men killed, including 1 general, 4 colonels, 2 lieutenant colonels, 7 captains, and 12 lieutenants. Mexican wounded amounted to 280 and included 3 colonels, 3 lieutenant colonels, 2 majors, 7 captains, and 1 cadet. The Texans also took 730 prisoners, including General Santa Anna himself, as well as 600 muskets, 300 sabers, 200 pistols, several hundred mules, and $12,000 in specie.[6] Even more significant than guns and money was the fact that human emotions came to a head when the enraged Texans shot many of their defeated enemies in cold blood as they tried to surrender. The Texans sought justice in its simplest form, *lex talionis,* an eye for an eye. In their view, what was just for one side was just for the other: the men whom they executed at San Jacinto had executed Texans either at the Alamo or at Goliad.

Although it outraged his officers and fighting men who demanded more blood and revenge, Houston permitted General Santa Anna to surrender and attempted to treat him with respect. Despite his own troops' raucous clamor for Santa Anna's execution, Houston wanted something more important for Texas than Santa Anna's life. He wanted his signature on a treaty recognizing the independence of Texas. After innumerable threats, Santa Anna signed Texas away and ordered his army to retreat south of the Rio Grande River. The Texans shipped the captured general to Vera Cruz, but immediately upon his return to Mexico, Santa Anna repudiated the treaty. For the time being, Texas and Mexico remained in an uneasy state of near-war despite Houston's desires for sovereignty and a lasting peace for Texas.

There was no doubt that the bloody Texas War for Independence had been won and that it created the Republic of Texas in 1836. Contrary to Houston's wishes, however, the fight evolved into a long war in the frontier tradition of Jacksonian Democracy, one that intensified as both sides sought to protect and expand their interests. On his last day in office, March 3, 1837, President Andrew Jackson granted the wish of his old friend Sam Houston by recognizing the Republic of Texas as a sovereign country, an act that added international dimensions to an already unsavory border conflict. In spite of Mexican protests, Britain, France, Belgium, and Holland followed the United States' lead and recognized the Texas Republic. What ensued were several years of political and military bungling, as well as personal tragedies for many Texan soldiers fighting to expand the Republic. Bolstered in spirit by international recognition but suffering from an empty treasury, the Texans became more aggressive in their pursuit of power and influence.

In 1841, a band of 321 armed Texans, under the leadership of Gen. Hugh McLeod, journeyed west to Santa Fé, New Mexico, where they hoped to offer the inhabitants the protection of the Republic of Texas and expanded trade with the new Republic. Harassed first by the Kiowas, then by the forces of nature, the citizens of Santa Fé rejected the Texans' offer. New Mexico Governor Manuel Armigo dispatched troops who disarmed and captured all the Texans and marched them to prison in Mexico City.[7] The Santa Fé prisoners were not executed outright, as had been the case at the Alamo and Goliad. However, on the thousand-mile march to Mexico City, their captors drove the Santa Fé prisoners without respite. At night they slept on frozen ground without blankets. Many died from exposure on the way, and some were shot for lagging behind. After the Mexicans crossed the Rio Grande, the overall treatment that the Americans received greatly improved until their release and repatriation in April 1842.[8] When word of the failed expedition and reports about the treatment of the prisoners reached home, the plague of war psychosis—escalating hatred for the enemy—took hold of both Texans and Mexicans once again. The Texans believed that they were invincible; the Mexicans wanted Texas back. Just as Spain had wrested its territory from the Moors in the fifteenth century, so General Santa Anna embarked on his own mission to reconquer the lost state of Texas and restore it to Mexico.

As retribution for the Santa Fé expedition and to reassert his position that Texas remained a part of Mexico in spite of the existence of the Republic's recognized sovereignty, Santa Anna ordered Gen. Mariana Arista to send a Mexican force to raid San Antonio and open limited hostilities on the Texas frontier. Under orders from Arista, Gen. Rafael Vasquez marched north and arrived in San Antonio on March 5, 1842. While the force stayed only two days, it was time enough to generate war fever among the Texans. Houston well knew that his Texans were bellicose and fully capable of fighting the Mexicans. He also knew that the Texan treasury was depleted and could ill afford an expensive war against Mexico or any other adversary. Mexico had a strong leader in Santa Anna, a skilled general capable of exercising his political and military will. Houston thus ordered Gen. Alexander Sommervell to San Antonio to command a group of about 750 Texan volunteers, with the objective of preventing them, if possible, from marching headlong into Mexico.[9] It was at this point that Sam Houston discovered that his own political will was not law in Texas in 1842.

The obedient and frustrated Sommervell tried to hold his men back by intentionally dragging his feet, but the Mexicans went on the offensive.

After Vasquez's force retreated south across the Rio Grande, news of his San Antonio raid was greeted with parades, cannon fire, and celebrations in Mexico City.[10] On September 11, 1842, another Mexican force entered San Antonio under the command of a French immigrant to Mexico, Gen. Adrian Woll. After a brief fight, the Texans found themselves surrounded and surrendered. Shortly afterwards, Woll was attacked by a small contingent of Texas Rangers, led by Maj. John C. Hayes, along with a group of volunteers under the command of Matthew Caldwell, a survivor of the Santa Fé expedition. Woll then hoped to lead the Texans into an ambush, but the astute Hayes halted and returned for reinforcements. Seeing a tactical opportunity, Woll decided to engage, but the long skirmish cost the lives of sixty of his men. The Texans, firing from protected positions, lost only one. Another group of fifty-two Texans, under Capt. Nicholas Mosby Dawson, attacked Woll and was soundly defeated. Only two Texans survived the battle, and a limited war, declared or not, was on.

Even the peaceful Sam Houston could not control the war fever that burned among the Texans. In San Antonio, more than three hundred armed men defied Houston's wishes and Sommervell's orders not to invade Mexico. In October 1842, they raided the Mexican village of Mier. After a futile fight, the surrounded and thoroughly defeated Texans wisely surrendered. The survivors became known as the "Mier Men." Because they had acted contrary to Sam Houston's wishes, the raiders, who were under the command of William Fisher, were scorned as independent operators, mercenaries warring outside the public interest and domain.[11] Unlike the outcome at the Alamo and the massacre at Goliad in 1836, those who survived remained in captivity for twenty months and twenty-one days. Scorned or not, the captured Texans began making war within a war, and escapes were imperative.

The first mass escape took place at the Salado prison compound, where Ewen Cameron and Samuel Walker led 170 resentful "Mier" Texans in a mass prison break. It began when Cameron signaled the others in the compound to create an armed skirmish between the prisoners and the guards. Chaos reigned over the compound as the Texans seized weapons and assaulted the surprised Mexican guards, who were in the middle of their breakfast. Startled and frightened, the guard force ran from the compound. In five minutes, the Salado prison break was over, but five prisoners and five guards lay dead. From the debris, the Texans armed and provisioned themselves with ninety mules and horses, 160 muskets, a cache of ammunition, money, swords, and pistols. Outside the hacienda, Cameron met Salado's commandant, Colonel Barragàn, who asked him to return to Salado with impunity. Cameron refused.[12]

The Texans' plan was simple and sensible: march west and turn north toward the Rio Grande River and Texas. With such a determined, well-armed force, it is likely that Cameron would have been successful had he not given in to the independent nature of his subordinates. One group under Capt. John G. W. Pierson decided that the road was too open and far too vulnerable to attack. Pierson's contention that the escape force was vulnerable may have been correct, and his desire not to be recaptured was understandable given the fresh memories that Santa Fé and Mier added to the past memories of the Alamo, Goliad, and San Jacinto. Cameron took stock of the situation and made a series of fatal decisions. Listening to Pierson, he split his force and made his way into the mountains, where travel became nearly impossible and where there was no food or water to support a large body of soldiers on the run.

Starving and dying of thirst, the escapers soon became lost and disoriented. In short order they were easy prey for recapture. All the Mexicans had to do was wait for the large, powerful force to dissolve into smaller, more vulnerable groups of desperate men. One *ad hoc* escape partnership consisted of Claudius Buster and John Toops. They left the mountains on their own and met some friendly inhabitants who gave them food and shelter. Arriving at a point near Laredo, they were discovered by the Mexican cavalry who recaptured them before they could cross the Rio Grande. John Alexander and Maj. George Oldham did manage to reach San Antonio; however, in all, only four Salado escapers arrived home. The rest were recaptured. Because they had the good will and support of most of the local people, the Mexican authorities were informed when evil, bellicose Texans were sighted wandering about the barren mountains in search of food or water. The Mexican cavalry started to round up the stragglers, group by group. Most were dying of thirst. Cameron, bound and walking in front of his men, saw many of them retaken when they were unable to walk any farther; the Mexican cavalrymen simply threw the prisoners across their saddles.[13]

General Santa Anna, hearing about the escapes and recaptures and outraged that several Mexican guards had been killed in the prison skirmish, wanted to execute the entire lot as he had done at Goliad, but the American and British envoys to Mexico, Waddy Thompson and Richard Pakenham, stepped into the conflict. Santa Anna faced a classic dilemma: these Texan escapers were protected by no law or tradition of public war, but he could not execute them without angering two major military powers, Britain and the United States, that recognized the Republic of Texas and whose representatives had interceded on the escapers' behalf. Yet Santa Anna had to do something, not only to save face among his own people but also to teach these prisoners another lesson about insurrection in Mexico. In place of mass executions, Santa Anna decided to use the old Roman method of decimation—executing every tenth man—to discipline the Texans.

The surviving Mier prisoners were forced to draw white and black beans from a jar. White beans meant reprieve and survival; black beans meant death by a firing squad. Seventeen men died against the wall on March 25, 1843. Ewen Cameron, the leader of the Salado escape, was executed a month later on April 25, 1843, at Huehuetoco by order of the Mexican government.[14] The survivors, one of whom was Texas Ranger Samuel Walker, were marched in chains to the Castle of Peroté.[15] For most of them, being spared outright execution was enough; they were content with quarantine. For that group, final liberation came in August 1844. A few others, like Walker, refused to accept quarantine. They had already seen what they considered to be arbitrary executions committed by the Mexican Army and opted to continue exploring escape opportunities.

On March 25, 1844, sixteen men formed a secret tunnel organization and escaped from the Peroté Castle. Nine reached Texas safely, and Santa Anna was furious. Before the escape, he had been ready to release all the Texans, but after it, Santa Anna changed his mind. The Texans were outraged. Joseph McCutchan's diary described the prisoners' indignation and their resolve to oppose the Mexicans: "I have seen a letter from Santa Anna to General Waddy Thompson, saying that he was on the point of releasing the prisoners, when the news of the escape of sixteen reached him, which rendered us unworthy of his magnanimity. Devil take such magnanimous men; he has no such feelings."[16] With more than a touch of irony, McCutchan added a defiant afterthought, "I am proud to think that some have made their escape . . . done on the 25th of March, the anniversary of the day on which the decimation took place."[17]

The anniversary date of the Mier executions meant something to Samuel Walker as well. Walker was certainly not the kind of man who was content to sit in quarantine and wait for statesmen to negotiate his liberation. He had participated in the Cameron escape fiasco at Salado in 1843 and nearly died on the trail in the mountains. Along with two friends, James C. Wilson and D. H. Gattis, Walker was part of the sixteen-man escape from the Peroté Castle on March 25, 1844. Their escape route took them first to Mexico City, where Walker was recaptured briefly. The wily and determined escaper broke out of an unguarded jail, and the team continued its flight. They trekked through the mountainous countryside trying to avoid hostile Mexican towns, but hunger demanded unusual action and they turned to deception. Posing as an Englishman, Walker convinced some suspicious civilians that he and the others were British immigrant workers. With that crisis behind them, they reached Tampico on August 12, 1844, and aided by the American consul, they signed on as deck hands aboard an American ship sailing for home. Six other Texans escaped later in 1844 as well.

On April 12, 1844, Texas nearly became a Territory of the United States; however, the agreement was rejected by the Senate in Washington, D.C. which was embroiled in arguments over expansion and slavery. A year later, the United States annexed Texas, and to Sam Houston's joy, Texas became a state on December 29, 1845, an event that changed the nature of Mexican-American relations permanently. Alarmed at this clear manifestation of American expansionism, the Mexicans broke diplomatic relations but stopped short of declaring war on the United States. Responding to the popular cry of Manifest Destiny, a term first coined by journalist and editor John L. O'Sullivan in 1845 in the *Democratic Review*,[18] and to what he perceived as a military threat to the newly acquired state, President James K. Polk of Tennessee sent U.S. Army troops, mostly Southerners sympathetic to Texas in the first place, to occupy the disputed territory along the Rio Grande River. American and Mexican patrols clashed on the morning of April 25, 1846, when a detachment of Mexican troops crossed the Rio Grande River and battled a U.S. Army scouting party. The Americans lost the skirmish and prisoners were taken. President Polk then declared that American blood spilled on U.S. territory demanded satisfaction, and the next war was under way.

As early as 1826, the Texas Rangers, initially a temporary militia of minutemen employed against the Indians of the region, served the Republic as peacekeepers; however, by 1840 they had become a corps organized by Jack Hayes and other captains. In the beginning these carefully selected men rode alone or at most in pairs, but by 1846 they fought in their own cavalry units. Individual rangers also joined the American Army as nonuniformed guides, interpreters, and scouts.[19] All Texans knew General Santa Anna's basic method of dealing with Texan prisoners in an armed insurrection: any Texas Ranger captured with the Rangers or serving in the American Army could expect nothing less than an immediate death sentence. The interpreter for the Louisville Cavalry,

Daniel Drake Henry, had fought the Mexicans in the Texas War of 1836 and so knew what to expect. Shortly after the Mexicans captured his unit, Henry seized a brief opportunity, mounted an officer's horse, and escaped. Five Mexican cavalrymen chased him for miles but returned empty-handed. Embarrassed, the pursuers reported to their commanding officer, Colonel Sambranino, that Henry was gone, and the colonel was furious. He drew his pistol and held it against the American commander's chest but hesitated to take his life. At that moment, another American officer ordered his men to the ground and told Sambranino that they had no intention of escaping. A third officer said, "Shoot and be damned." [20] The tense confrontation ended when the Mexicans tied the Americans together for the long march to Mexico City.

Capt. Samuel Walker of the Texas Rangers achieved even wider acclaim as a cavalry commander during the Mexican War than he did as an escaper from Peroté Castle in 1844. During the interim between 1844 and his return to a new field of battle in 1846, he helped design the Walker-Colt six-shooter, a weapon that became legendary in the history of the American Civil War and then on the frontier. Walker died fighting the Mexican Army with his Rangers at the town of Huamantla near the war's end when Santa Anna's army was all but destroyed. One chronicler described the battle and Walker's demise: "Suddenly a small body of horse broke from our ranks, headed by a tall cavalier, and dashed like a thunderbolt into the midst of the glittering Mexicans. They wavered a moment, then broke, and fled in confusion into the town, followed by all our cavalry. It was Walker and with his Rangers who performed this gallant feat, with 80 men dispersed 2,000 lancers." [21] Walker died in his saddle, re-forming his company after he had withstood two bullets. "He was, in the opinion of all who knew him," wrote the soldier, "the bravest and most dashing officer in our army, a man who seemed to be devoid of fear, and who could and would lead his company against any opposing force." [22] As a Texas Volunteer cavalry commander in the American Army, Walker set the tone for J.E.B. Stuart, George Armstrong Custer, Nathan Bedford Forest, and John Singleton Mosby, who led Union and Confederate cavalry units in the upcoming American Civil War.

Most of the non-Texan American soldiers held prisoner by the Mexican Army were kept in Mexico City, until it became obvious that the city itself was about to come under siege. Santa Anna then gave the order for their removal to areas more remote from the fighting. Those officers who gave their parole could not legally escape, but those who refused to give parole could. Midshipman Robert C. Rogers, USN, captured with a small naval party surveying the coast two miles from Vera Cruz, refused to give parole. To his surprise, the Mexicans still allowed him the run of the city. The prisoners knew that the American Army was in Puebla, and they also knew that in the confusion of having an enemy army at their doorstep, the Mexican guards had grown more careless. Taking advantage of the situation, Rogers and one other prisoner stole a hack and drove it to a nearby canal. Then they took a boat and rowed to Lake Chalco, where they found some horses. At last, both men reached safety and reported their adventures to their commanding officer, Gen. Winfield Scott, who had been a prisoner of war himself in Canada during the War of 1812. Scott must have been pleased to see his young escapers.

Transcendentalists and abolitionists in New England opposed Texan and American actions against Mexico because they saw both wars from a comfortable distance. To them, the Texans and their allies in Washington were merely adventurous and opportunistic Southerners who wished to spread their philosophy of economic dependence on the plantation system and social dependence on African chattel slavery. This was partly true, but Manifest Destiny, as it evolved, was one of the most powerful ideas to arise in America in the nineteenth century. Born after Thomas Jefferson's purchase of the vast lands of French Louisiana in 1803, the concept of Manifest Destiny—the expansion of the United States westward to the Pacific Ocean—captured the American imagination even more than the moral precepts concerning the evils of chattel slavery. Expansion meant progress and limitless opportunities for newcomers. Anything or anyone opposing this progression west and southwest became an enemy.

The native tribal assumption that land belonged to no one and everyone at the same time confounded both southern and northern Europeans. The Mexicans had derived their land from the Spanish discoverers, who seized it through the doctrines of discovery, conquest, and effective occupation. America's European settlers shared that view and set about vanquishing the native inhabitants. Although it took roughly three hundred years to defeat the tribes and conquer all the lands east of the Mississippi River, the same process required only thirty years in the West following the Civil War. The dramatic leap in military technology that wars inevitably produce partly accounted for this acceleration; in addition, however, in 1846 enthusiasm for Manifest Destiny went into overdrive, leading to calls for conquest by any means. The only road block was the Civil War.

Frontier settlement, the establishment of state sovereignty, defense of the state by its citizens, and, ultimately, the expression of political will made themselves felt as the United States consolidated its power and aimed at forging a new nation. The Texas War for Independence from 1836 to 1844 propelled this process to eventual fruition because the Texans were, for the most part, conventional Southerners and individualistic Westerners itching for new land. Both cultural communities shared roots in the American Revolution and the War of 1812 against England and believed passionately in the expression of individual, community, and national strength and determination through the use of arms.

At the dawn of the Revolution, the British temporarily replaced the Indians as America's mortal enemies. For the Texans, the Mexicans filled much the same role. The war in the 1830s and the subsequent expeditions in the 1840s, punitive or otherwise, were expressions of a policy aimed at defeating political and religious oppression, establishing a republic, and joining the United States. From the Mexican point of view, the Texan intruders practiced insurrection and partisan guerrilla warfare, both capital crimes against the state. As a result, the surviving defenders of the Alamo were slaughtered after the battle, and Fannin's men at Goliad were executed following their tragic surrender. Both these incidents served not only to heighten the hatred between opposing soldiers, but also encouraged the rising war psychosis between the two cultures. Common stereotypes like McCutchan's descriptions of the Mexicans as "devils" and "poor soldiers" are better understood in this context rather than simply passing them off as reflections of period racism. This is not to argue that racism played no role in the Texan-Mexican conflicts; rather, its role was less significant in the larger scheme of things. After all, a large number of Mexicans lived among the Texans in the border areas, and some fought hard for the Texas Republic against Mexico. Ethnicity counted a great deal in determining on whose side one fought, but the new opportunity-oriented political culture of an emerging nation-state counted for more.

Captivity and escape in the Texas wars represent two opposing paradigms of thinking. General Santa Anna viewed the Texans as insurrectionist criminals guilty of treason and deserving only of execution. In his view, any punishment short of death was a reflection of his personal magnanimity and benevolence. The Texans saw themselves as both Jacksonians and the embodiment of the rapidly expanding Manifest Destiny in America. When they fought as soldiers and lost, the Texans at first expected treatment as traditional POWs. The executions at the Alamo and Goliad shocked and angered them to the point where they were willing to undertake vengeful forms of retribution. Santa Anna believed that the decimation following Cameron's mass escape was just; the Texans saw it as cause for another war if the United States became a participant.

Sam Houston wanted nothing more than annexation and statehood for Texas. Like George Washington less than a century before him, Houston understood war and preferred negotiation and diplomacy to fighting. Although Houston sacrificed his soldiers at the Alamo and Goliad, he won the Battle of San Jacinto decisively and proved that he knew how to fight. He also proved that he felt no blood lust when he spared the hated Santa Anna. Although Houston was certainly no pacifist, he detested armed conflict but could do little to stop Santa Anna from exploiting the Mexican desire for the reconquest of Texas. He failed in his attempts to restrain Texans from the expedition to Santa Fé. He failed again when he tried to stop them from going to Mier on a punitive expedition as revenge for General Woll's raid against San Antonio. Good luck came Houston's way, however, because of the excellent relationship shared by Santa Anna and the American envoy, Gen. Waddy Thompson. Texans would have suffered a great deal more had it not been for Thompson's interest in the prisoners' welfare and his subsequent intervention. Analogous to Ben Franklin's intervention and intrigues with British diplomats and preachers friendly to the American Revolution, Thompson's work in Mexico City saved lives.

By the end of the Mexican War in 1848, fighting had cost the U.S. Army the lives of 1,721 soldiers killed in action or dead from wounds. Additionally, 11,155 died of disease and 4,102 were wounded but lived.[23] Santa Anna's officers understood the traditional rules of war that dictated reasonable treatment for POWs in their charge, and thus the non-Texan prisoners suffered little or no intolerable cruelty, and most remained in quarantine captivity until the war's end. On the other hand, the Texas Rangers were considered partisans by the Mexican military. These individuals were aware of Santa Anna's directive for their execution shortly after capture and escaped at all costs. Uniformed Americans from regular and volunteer units became conventional POWs and enjoyed what can only be termed the chivalrous quarantine captivity common in the period. They escaped because they followed the traditional mandate that quarantine was less than honorable and that it was their duty to harass the enemy even while in captivity. The Mexican War ended in 1848 with the Treaty of Guadalupe Hidalgo. Mexico ceded Texas, New Mexico, Arizona, California, Utah, and parts of Wyoming, Nevada, and Colorado to the United States. Mexicans living in those regions retained ownership of their properties, but relations with Mexico remained strained throughout the nineteenth and twentieth centuries.

Intrusions by Americans and Europeans in Mexico began with free-booting or plundering. Independent invaders known as Filibusters included the Irishman Philip Nolan in the eighteenth century; Aaron Burr, the former vice president who wanted to break off the newly purchased Louisiana from the Union and establish his own empire in Mexico in 1806;[24] and the shady privateer and opportunist Jean Lafitte, who helped Andrew Jackson defeat the British at the Battle of New Orleans on January 8, 1815.[25] Although each failed to seize power, they previewed the Texan experience of conquest and expansion not only in Mexico but in Cuba and Nicaragua as well. In 1851, well after Texas entered the Union, William J. Crittenden of Kentucky and Cuban radical expatriate revolutionary, Narciso Lopez, led an expedition of 420 exuberant paramilitary Southerners into Cuba in order to incite rebellion against Spain and generate a political passion to join the United States. Spanish forces defeated this new generation of Filibusters and publicly executed fifty of the interlopers in Havana, including Crittenden and Lopez. The 160 survivors were sent to Spain as prisoners. In 1860, Central Americans defeated similar efforts led by the exotic William Walker (no relation to Samuel), who had at one time taken over Nicaragua's government. Walker published *The War in Nicaragua* (1860), in which he preached his gospel of American expansion into Central America, but like many of his predecessors in the wars of Manifest Destiny, Walker was defeated and died in front of a firing squad.[26]

For America's soldiers in Mexico who later became generals and statesmen in the 1860s, like Robert E. Lee, Ulysses S. Grant, Jefferson Davis, and many others, the lessons of the Manifest Destiny campaigns in Texas and Mexico, as well as the adventures in Cuba and Central America, did not go unheeded. After eleven states seceded from the American Union and opened fire on federal forces in 1861, regular and volunteer soldiers in the next American war fought, captured, and imprisoned half a million other Americans. For Union and Confederate soldiers who rejected the condition of captivity and quarantine, the escape experience became another war within a war. While Confederate escapers on their way to Canada and Dixie matched and raised the stakes established in the wars south of the border, Union escapers often relied on bondsmen still in chattel slavery to lead them to the promised land in a makeshift version of the most elaborate and sophisticated escape line in the American experience of captivity and escape, the Underground Railroad.

Escape from *Durante Vita:*

Breaking the Chains the Masters Made

Let him be a fugitive slave in a strange land—a land given up to the
hunting-ground for slaveholders—whose inhabitants are legalized
kidnappers—where he is every moment subjected to the terrible liability
of being seized upon by his fellow men.
—Frederick Douglass (1845)

Bondage, as it was practiced in the seventeenth century,
consisted of several common conditions: military POWs taken in battle,
who were required legally to render service to their captors for the duration of the war; civilian criminals, who transgressed civil or religious law
and became the chattel property of the state; and two kinds of indentured
servants. One group entered freely into service contracts with their masters; the others were civilian criminals who were transported to a foreign
land and forced into indenture to work off their time. Each condition was
regulated, more or less, by codes of law that protected servants to varying degrees from abuse, ill-treatment, and wrongful death.

Of the three major conditions of servitude, noncriminal indenture was
the most benign; it carried no assumption that a person had committed
a crime or carried arms against the state. Nevertheless, the individual
became the chattel property of the master and labor could be bought,
sold, or rented. A common practice in Europe and America, indenture
was a system of bondage for a specified period of time as agreed between
the servant and the master in return for service and support. In Europe,
parents often made the contract for their children, with hopes that they
could learn a trade, and by the end of the indenture become self-sufficient
freeholders or at least skilled journeymen.

Criminal indenture was less benign. Begun as an alternative to the hangman, the practice lasted for about 150 years. After prosecution and guilty verdicts in court, often for minor crimes, thousands of condemned English men and women received orders for transportation and were brought from English prison hulks and jails to America as indentured servants. In 1788, five years after the peace treaty between the United States and Great Britain, the U.S. Congress finally decided that enough was enough and banned the practice. Beginning in 1787, the British government decided to transport their civilian prisoners to Australia. Transportation to New South Wales finally ceased in 1840, to Tasmania in 1852, and to West Australia as late as 1857.[1]

The situation of African immigrants was far more humiliating. Rather than coming to America as indentures, they came in chains. Slavers either bought unfortunate captives or assisted in their capture. Guilty only of being in the wrong place at the wrong time, they came to America against their will, neither as indentured servants nor as criminals bound for exile, but as human property bound *in durante vita,* captivity for life. During the forced migration from Africa to North, Central, and South America, somewhere between fifteen million and sixty million Africans landed alive.[2] The number who died before or during transportation remains a mystery.

The European slave trade began in 1442, when a Portuguese ship's captain, Antam Gonçalvez, captured several noble Arabs who offered ten blacks as ransom for their freedom. The offer was accepted, and the unfortunate individuals were brought to Lisbon and sold at the market. In 1443, slavers sent a shipment of 234 slaves to Portugal. By 1455, although the crown and the church opposed the practice, Portuguese slavers were kidnapping free Africans on the Gold Coast for sale in Europe and North Africa as slaves. By 1474, enslaved Africans abounded in Lisbon, and the taxes imposed upon their masters enriched the city's coffers considerably. In 1482, the Portuguese built the first slave-trading port, Sao Jorge de Mina, on the African Gold Coast.[3] Slavery became a business on the move. When Portugal and Spain divided up the New World in 1493, the African slave trade increased quickly, and owning slaves changed from something only the wealthy could afford to a necessity for developing sugar plantations and gold mines in the New World.

In 1511, the first Africans arrived as slaves in the Portuguese Antilles. In the years between 1511 and 1600, approximately nine hundred thousand Africans were brought to Latin America in slavery, and by the time England had established its colonies in North America, African slavery had been firmly entrenched in the Spanish and Portuguese colonies to the south.[4] Europeans, alone or in consort with African partners, made trips into the African interior to attack small villages and bring their quarry bound in chains back to the coastal areas, where they waited in stockades for transport to oblivion. Hundreds of ships, thousands of sailors, and hundreds, possibly thousands, of individuals, partnerships, and companies, were engaged in bringing to the New World—south of what became the United States—more Africans than Europeans for the entire colonial period.[5]

Africans in slavery rejected the condition of endless captivity when they could, and often revolted against their oppressors in desperation. The Jamaica revolt in 1522 marked the first such effort; it was not the last. African slaves in Panama revolted in 1531, in Cuba in 1533, and in Mexico in 1537. By 1542, Spanish law prohibited slaves from going out at night for fear of escape or revolt. The 1560s saw the English also entering the slave trade, when John Hawkins brought a shipload of slaves to Haiti (Hispaniola) and sold them to the planters at a huge profit. The French prohibited slavery at home and in 1607 declared, "All persons are free in this kingdom; as soon as a slave has reached these frontiers and becomes baptized, he is free." Labor needs in the New World caused the French to revise their thinking considerably. Between 1670 and 1672, French colonials imported more than three thousand slaves from Guinea to labor on the plantations of their island colonies in the West Indies. Slavery was legalized in French Canada in 1709, and in French Louisiana in 1716.

The Spanish and Portuguese understood from the revolts and streams of individuals fleeing bondage that their slaves desired freedom. As a result, they devised sets of laws that regulated retributions for escape. In 1571, for example, Spanish law listed several punishments for recaptured fugitive runaways: fifty lashes for an absence of four days; one hundred lashes plus a ball and chain for eight days' absence; two hundred lashes for being gone for four months; death for leading a mass escape; and large fines for any citizens helping slaves to escape.[6] By 1574, Spanish slave laws against escapers had become more sophisticated and created a bounty-hunter system that paid enterprising individuals, slave and free, to recapture escapers either for cash or, from time to time, for their own freedom. In effect, the Spanish and the Portuguese created a system that set slaves against slaves.

In the beginning of the forced African migration to North America, there were no codes or statutes that defined the nature of the relationship between master and slave. Africans arrived in the Virginia Colony in 1619 aboard a Dutch slave ship and were sold more as indentured servants than as slaves. After they completed their term of service, like other indentured servants, they were freed from bondage and were permitted to purchase land and lead lives similar to the other Virginia colonists. Although there was no legal slavery in North America, things changed in the 1640s, when slavery began to emerge as a matter of practice as the coastal plantations developed the tobacco trade.[7]

Slavery in the English colonies was widespread for several reasons outside the economic sphere. Whereas Spanish and Portuguese clerics believed that the life of the spirit transcended the miseries of life on earth and converted Indians and Africans to Catholicism, the rigidity of English Protestantism, and even Catholicism, seemed to exclude Africans from any saving grace. Slavery became a life sentence not only for those caught in its web at any one time, but also for those born into it or yet to be born, depending on the condition or status of the mother. A 1663 Maryland law, for example, stated the case: "All negroes or other slaves within the province, all negroes hereafter to be imported, shall serve *durante vita*."[8] As secular laws tightened the slaveholders' grip, opposition emanating from religious circles diminished, and Christian baptism played no role whatsoever, especially in the British colonies. Even if freed by a legal means such as manumission—the legal term for a master freeing his slaves— former bondsmen were often apprehended and reenslaved. A 1660 Virginia slave law stated that any English servant recaptured after running away with slaves, who were incapable of "making satisfaction by addition of time," shall serve not only his own sentence, but also the amount of time the slave was away from the plantation.[9] Simply stated, there was no way out.

In 1621, the Dutch West India Company was formed with the intention of creating a monopoly on the slave trade. Not only did the Dutch transport slaves from Africa, Dutch ships brought them north from Brazil to New York. By 1629, slavery came to the Puritan colonies, first to Connecticut, then to Massachusetts in 1630, Maryland in 1634, and Delaware in 1636. In 1638, the American colonials in New England took up the trade, sailing from Salem, Massachusetts, to the West Indies to exchange captured Pequot Indians for goods and slaves. The British recognized that the slave trade was lucrative as well. The Duke of York, along with King Charles II and several prominent English merchants, formed the Royal Adventures in 1663, renamed the Royal African Company in 1672, to compete with the Dutch and form a monopoly for the English colonies in America. The British trade was centered in Liverpool, and by the end of the eighteenth century, more than 130 English merchant ships sailed the Atlantic Ocean in the slave trade.

During the colonial period in North America, the first significant antislavery voices were raised by the German Mennonites in Philadelphia in 1688. Having suffered considerably from near slavery in Germany from the time of the Reformation to the end of the Thirty Years' War, the Mennonites, led to Pennsylvania by Francis Daniel Pastorius, urged the British Quakers to take a stand against what Pastorius called the traffic in menbody.[10] In 1700, however, Rhode Island recognized the legality of slavery. In Pennsylvania, the Quakers began to provide their slaves with religious instruction—something rarely done in the other colonies—but Pennsylvania legalized slavery anyway. In 1711, the Quakers in Pennsylvania reversed the decision. Between 1715 and 1750, more than twenty-five hundred Africans were imported per year and sold as property in all the North American colonies. By mid-century, feelings began to change, but not enough to make a difference. In 1769, Thomas Jefferson introduced a bill into the Virginia House of Burgesses that abolished slavery. It was defeated. Slaves and available free black men served in colonial militias from 1689 through the Revolution, not as first-call volunteers but as replacements for white soldiers killed, wounded, or captured by the enemy.[11]

By 1776, the slavery issue began to divide the country into political sections based on the inhabitants' collective feelings toward slavery as an institution. On the one hand, black men readily joined the Continental Army when they could; on the other, various colonies prohibited the arming of slaves for fear of revolts. Vermont forbade slavery in 1777 during hostilities, and more slaves joined state militias, especially if freedom was the reward for service. By 1778, slaves were joining both the British and the American colonial armies, and Jefferson believed that large numbers of slaves were on the run in Virginia alone. Slaves and free blacks also served in the Continental Navy, where they helped to man American privateers, or worked as coastal pilots in the Chesapeake Bay and the James River. At Savannah in 1779, between six hundred and eight hundred slave troops of the Black St. Domingo Legion from Haiti served with Comte D'Estaing and defended the American retreat. After these troops returned home, some participated in slave revolts. Henri Christophe, who served at Savannah as a boy of twelve, fought in Haiti with Toussaint L'Ouverture against French rule in 1791.[12]

Massachusetts had abolished slavery by the war's end in 1783. Virginia and New Jersey granted freedom to those slaves who had served as soldiers and sailors in the Revolution, and Maryland prohibited the slave trade. British ships carried thousands of escaped slaves, some of whom fought in the British Army, from America's shores, and in 1784, Rhode Island and Connecticut abolished slavery entirely. New York followed suit in 1785, and the political sentiment in the North began to favor dismantling the institution and establishing slave-free zones in the Northwest Territories. By 1802, the Northern states had adopted laws ending slavery, and the American military services, especially the North-dominated navy, received free blacks into the ranks.

The War of 1812 and the Battle of New Orleans on January 8, 1815, where more than six hundred black soldiers fought elite British troops, brought the era of hope to a close. In the same year, more than three hundred runaway slaves from Georgia joined about thirty Creek Indians and occupied Fort Blount, with the objective of creating a safe place for runaways and a protected base for raiding slave owners. On February 18, 1820, a general order from the Army's Adjutant and Inspector General's Office forbade any more black recruits. In the South, slavery took a different, more dangerous turn. Fearing a replay of the bloody Haitian slave revolt of 1791 and a series of revolts throughout the American South in the nineteenth century, Southern lawmakers tightened their grip on the slave communities. The use of the cotton gin had expanded the need for slave labor exponentially, while at the same time the legal codes extended their reach from the state to municipal levels, which had the effect of increasing and tightening the legal boundaries. The American Union divided in two over the politics and morality of the issue, a division so fundamental that the United States required a brutal civil war from 1861 to 1865 to settle it.

The prodigious amount of literature on American chattel slavery agrees, at least in part, that if there ever existed a classic application of Grotius's principle of intolerable cruelty, it made itself plain in American chattel slavery.[13] In England, the "Act to Regulate the Negroes on the British Plantations," passed into law in 1667, referred to the enslaved Africans in terms of their "wild, barbarous, and savage nature, to be controlled only with strict severity."[14] With little or no humanity built into the slave codes, treatment was based strictly on the whim of the master, and it is no wonder that by 1640, fugitive escapers became an enormous problem for slaveholders, even for those who thought they were benignly tolerant with their slaves. Chattel slavery in America was by its very nature intolerant. Between 1640 and 1699, fugitive laws were instituted throughout North America, and the intercolonial agreement of 1643 concerning fugitives in the New England Confederation served as the basis for all the subsequent fugitive laws written in the United States in 1787, 1793, and 1850.

Like settlers held by Indians, Indians held by the Army, and soldiers held by opposing armies, slaves during the nineteenth century had two fundamental choices to ensure survival: submit to the personal will of the slaveholders and endure the condition until death provided relief; or break the law and escape to the North, where the institution had been cast by the wayside. The paradox lay in the fact that the free states never guaranteed freedom to runaways, only to their own citizens. Slaves were considered by law and custom to be private property, and escapers were viewed as fugitives. Under the antebellum fugitive slave laws, including the American Constitution, slave owners were free to pursue runaways or hire others to apprehend and return them to their owners. Article IV, Section 2, stated, "No Person held to Service or Labour in one State, under the Laws thereof, escaping into another, shall, in Consequence of any Law or Regulation therein, be discharged from such Service or Labor, but shall be delivered up on Claim of the Party to whom such Service or Labour may be due." The famous Dred Scott Case, decided before the U.S. Supreme Court in 1857, assured slaveholders of their rights in this regard until 1865, when the Civil War and the Thirteenth Amendment abolished slavery completely with the words, "Neither slavery nor involuntary servitude, except as a punishment for crime whereof the party shall have been duly convicted, shall exist within the United States, or any place subject to their jurisdiction."

On the plantations, many slaves had established close familial relations with slaveholding families, and life in waiting was bearable. For those who worked in the tobacco, sugar, or cotton fields from dawn to dusk, however, waiting meant suffering unending physical abuse and personal humiliation. Before the federal government amended the Constitution in 1865, slaves used the biblical term for the traditional fiftieth year birthday celebration, or "Jubilee," to represent freedom. Africans in American chattel slavery coded its meaning differently, to what they understood as the only freedom available, death. Regardless of how a slave's life was lived, bearably in the plantation house or miserably in the fields, the condition of bondage was the same.

It infuriates most captors when their charges escape. In a miliary prison camp, for example, escape reflects a breakdown of security at best, poor or inadequate leadership on the part of the officers in charge, or, at worst, dereliction of duty. For a slave to escape, however, was an economic loss as well as a display of insolence toward the slave owner. Although punishments for military escapers were occasionally severe, for recaptured slaves, they were almost always extreme and often inhumane. Some runaways received lashings of up to five hundred strokes, cat claws drawn from the shoulders to the hips, whippings, or beatings with shovels; at times they were even buried up to the neck for days. Others were confined in stockades without food and suffered such cruel but common retributions as dismemberment of toes or half the foot. An observer recalled that one runaway's hands were tied, and he was hanged from a tree until his toes barely touched the ground. His captors tied his feet together and then thrust a rail between his legs with a weight on it to keep his body stretched out, thus preventing him from moving under descending blows.[15]

For upland slaves in Delaware, Maryland, Virginia, and North Carolina, intolerable cruelty most often took the form of fear of sale or transport to the Deep South's cotton or rice plantations in Mississippi, southern Alabama, or Louisiana.

Women who were recaptured were no less immune from torture, especially flogging or whipping, than were men. Not only were runaways almost certain to receive retributive punishment, but they were likely to be sold to anyone who needed another field hand. Yet they persisted in their attempts to escape. Their motivation came from within each individual, what W.E.B. Dubois called "a dogged strength" that went far beyond any fear of retribution.[16] Generations of bondage dictated the necessity of learning how to escape the lash, the whip, and a life in slavery far from family and friends.[17] Escape was indeed a risk, but it also was the one permanent action in a slave's life that denied the imposition of the master's will totally and irrefutably.

Runaways knew that their journeys were dark, dangerous routes with an uncertain outcome. One false move, one wrong turn on the road, or one wrong word to a friend might precipitate a disaster, even death. Thomas Likers, born a slave in Maryland, wrote, "I should be a fool if I didn't take my liberty if I got the chance. No matter what privileges I had, I felt that I had not my rights as long as I was deprived of liberty."[18] David Barrett, a slave in Kentucky in 1818, was tired of being whipped for no reason that he could understand, and took his leave. He said, "I loosed my horse from the plow, but instead of obeying orders, I mounted and rode in haste to the opposite side of the field, dismounted and skulked in the woods. This was the last my master ever saw of me."[19] Levi Douglass and James Wright feared that they would be "sold down the river" from the relative safety of the upland South down the enormous Mississippi River to places and conditions unknown. They resolved not to go; escape became their only alternative.[20]

As Frederick Douglass pointed out, there was no part of a slave's life that was not defined by captivity: food, clothing, shelter, work, family, attitudes, identity, and, finally, self-esteem. Unlike military captivity or civilian indenture, most slaves had no memory of a life once lived freely, no family ties that kept individuals close to home, and no hope for any kind of life other than the one they knew. Slavery was a cradle-to-grave arrangement. In his speech, "The Nature of Slavery," Frederick Douglass explained the predicament: "The law gives the master absolute power over the slave. He may work him, flog him, hire him out, sell him, and in certain instances, kill him, with perfect immunity. The slave is a human being divested of all rights—reduced to the level of a brute—a mere 'chattel' in the eye of the law—placed beyond the circle of human brotherhood—cut off from his kind—his name . . . inserted in a master's ledger, with horses, sheep and swine. In law, the slave has no wife, no children, no country, and no home. He can own nothing, possess nothing, acquire nothing."[21]

What Douglass told the world was that to be born into bondage was intolerably cruel; to die in it even crueler. Douglass thundered: "Let him be a fugitive slave in a strange land—a land given up to the hunting-ground for slaveholders—whose inhabitants are legalized kidnappers—where he is every moment subjected to the terrible liability of being seized upon by his fellow men. . . . I say let him be placed in this most trying situation in which I was placed—then, and not till then, will he finally appreciate the hardships of, and know how to sympathize with, the toil-worn and whip-scarred fugitive slave."[22] Each day in bondage meant that fewer persons were set free, yet, as their narratives record, successive generations of slaves managed not merely to survive, but were determined to escape.

Long before the Union Army liberated anyone during the Civil War, strong-willed individuals in hundreds of slave communities on small farms, in Southern cities, and on large plantations, defied the law, their masters, and sometimes one another to liberate themselves. In the Deep South, some escaped slaves found refuge with the Spanish in Florida or the Southern Creek tribes. By the 1840s, not only did slaves hear the booming voices of white abolitionists like William Lloyd Garrison, but also the voices of escapers like Frederick Douglass, William Wells Brown, and Henry Bibb. By and large, many antebellum slave narratives are actually escape narratives that express their authors' moral outrage at the treatment they received at the hands of masters and those who controlled their fates.[23]

Although the goodness of the individual and the evils of slavery, rather than escape per se, are the central themes of these narratives, antebellum narrators readily told their audiences about the kinds of intolerable cruelty they suffered before making the decision to escape. In that sense, slave escapers reached their decision to run away from bondage in much the same way as the military escapers did. This is not to argue that slave narratives and POW narratives mirror each other completely. National and international laws afforded POWs some protection from harsh treatment at the hands of their captors. Slaves, on the other hand, were victimized by the law, which, instead of protecting them, established slave codes that kept them in perpetual bondage.

There were other differences between these two types of escapers as well. Escape from a heavily guarded prison camp was difficult and required much preparation, stealth, wit, and, often, organization. Escape from an unguarded plantation, on the other hand, was relatively easy, especially when it was surrounded by woods or swamps. Some escapers remained in the South to find family members who had been sold to new masters or sent to a different part of the region. Others became fugitives or runaways but often kept in close contact with their friends and family who remained on the plantation. Many stayed in the woods for years. With provisions provided to him by his mother, one Louisiana escaper hid out in the forest so long that when he finally emerged, he was completely covered with hair.[24] Nat Turner, one of the most skillful organizers of his era, escaped to the South Carolina forest after his revolt collapsed.

Although it was not always difficult to escape the immediate confines of a plantation, reaching the North was another matter entirely. In general, the escapers had a long distance to travel, and they had little choice but to walk. Roads and trains were not viable options. Slaves needed travel passes for uninterrupted passage on public roads, and any white person could stop them and ask for written identification. Rewards for runaways were handsome, and many rural residents were not wealthy. Consequently, slave-escapers kept far from the roads, traveled mainly at night, and avoided civilians. Much like their military counterparts, they begged for food along the way; sometimes they stole it. In most cases, they developed clever ruses to fool would-be informers into believing they were either free or on a mission for their masters. James W. C. Pennington lamented his use of deception. He wrote: "If you now ask me whether I now really believe that I gained my liberty by those lies? I answer, No! I now believe that I should be free had I told the truth; but, at that moment, I could not see any other way to baffle my enemies and escape their clutches."[25] After several close calls, Pennington made his way to the home of a Pennsylvania Quaker, perhaps the strongest group of abolitionists living near the Mason-Dixon Line, and gained his freedom.

Coastal steamers and river boats were a useful means of transportation if a runaway could devise a clever scheme to stow away. William Wells Brown's *Narrative of William W. Brown, a Fugitive Slave* (1847) described his escape on a steamboat to Ohio in 1834. Trains required both travel passes and money for tickets, and thus were unlikely modes of transport north. For every rule, there are exceptions, however. Henry "Box" Brown's *The Narrative of Henry Box Brown: Written by a Statement of Facts Made by Himself* (1849) recorded his escape on two trains and a steamer, not as a paying passenger but as cargo in a box. With money he received from abolitionist contacts in Philadelphia, Henry Brown paid a carpenter to build a container that looked very much like a cross between a coffin and a wooden mail sack. Hoping to make the trip more comfortable for Brown, the carpenter marked the box, "This Side Up with Care." At the freight office, the workmen loaded the box on the baggage car upside down, but after seeing the instructions, they corrected their error. When the box was transferred from the train to a steamboat bound for Washington, it was again placed upside down. Brown's luck held, however, as the workmen righted the box once more. In Washington, Brown's box was first jostled and then loaded on a train to Philadelphia upside down yet again. With some humor, Brown wrote, "As I seem to be destined to escape on my head; a sign probably of the opinion of American people regarding such bold adventurers as myself; that our heads should be held downwards, whenever we attempt to benefit ourselves." Finally the box containing Brown arrived at his friend's home, and a voice said, "Is all right within?" "All right," replied Brown. His friend opened the box, and like a resurrected Lazarus, Henry Brown rose to begin life as a new man.[26]

There were many such narratives, some coarse, some eloquent, including the stories of fugitives collected by antislavery advocates and published in the abolitionist press, as well as those gathered for publication in nineteenth- and twentieth-century documentary accounts.[27] Prior to the Civil War, forty-eight full-length escape narratives appeared in the popular press, the most important of which was Frederick Douglass's *Narrative of the Life of Frederick Douglass, An American Slave, Written by Himself* (1845). Because he knew that those who remained in bondage needed all the escape routes they could devise, Douglass said little about his own escape on September 3, 1838. He only commented, "How I did so—what means I adopted—I must leave unexplained."[28] However, his advice, "Trust no man," became a byword for fugitives before the Civil War. Too many, including Douglass himself, were betrayed by other slaves and free blacks looking for rewards.

When slaves escaped, much like their military and colonial counterparts, they had to believe that they really had a destination. Masters excelled at discouraging their slaves from running away by filling their heads with visions of a life worse than the one on the plantation. Often they were told that free states were far away, or that Canada was little more than a frozen wilderness, where nothing grew. Some slaves were told that abolitionists were white cannibals who delighted in eating them, and if runaways avoided being on the menu, then they were likely to be sold back into slavery by profit-hungry Yankees. Yet slaves defied the negative folklore and developed a grapevine of their own. The slave grapevine, an expansive oral information network, played a large part in providing accurate information to potential escapers about their options. It carried stories of daring escape attempts and praised those who successfully disappeared. Eventually, it became the framework for a system of relatively sophisticated escape lines that began with maroon colonies, those small groups of plantation escapers who formed communities in the mountains, in the woods, or in nearby swamps. Between 1672 and 1864, approximately fifty major maroon communities, as well as untold numbers of smaller ones, thrived from eastern Appalachia to Louisiana. Some of these communities lived off the land; others lived off banditry against plantations and local towns. The residents of maroon communities near Florida fought with the Seminoles against the Americans, who were intent on annexing Florida into the Union in the 1840s.

Whether regarded as insurrectionists, partisan guerrillas, freedom fighters, or fugitives, those living in the maroon communities aided fellow escapers. Indeed, the conditions around the communities themselves were often enough to discourage even the most ardent slave hunters or "patrollers," from entering the dense, unknown forests in search of their quarry. Some escapers lived in maroon colonies for years, finding the peace, food, community, and security to their liking. One escaper, Octave Johnson, commented that after he discovered his overseer's intentions to have him whipped, he ran away to the woods, where he stayed for a year and a half, joining a community of more than thirty maroons. According to Johnson, "I had to steal my food, took turkeys, chickens and pigs . . . sometimes we would rope beef cattle and drag them out to our hiding place." Although they were free, they knew they were being hunted. Johnson remembered that they relied heavily on help from their friends who remained captive. He noted, "We obtained matches from our friends on the plantation, we slept on logs and burned cypress leaves to make smoke and keep away mosquitoes." [29] Others longed for life in the North. Johnson's maroon community and others like it were the first in a series of small steps that the artful escapers could use in freeing themselves from human bondage.

Eventually, some escapers secured funds from abolitionist allies and established connections between the maroon colonies to create an escape network. In 1838, the network, set up in Philadelphia with funds by Robert Purvis, became known as the Underground Railroad, the first truly organized escape line. There were difficulties. Directions north required escapers to possess the ability to read road signs, and if slaves encountered white passers-by, they could be required to produce travel passes. Since most slaves were illiterate by law, they could not fabricate or counterfeit their own travel passes. Deception and cunning often replaced the written passes, and slave escapers used other means to their advantage. They knew Polaris, the North Star, and the Big Dipper that in song they called the "Drinking Gourd." They also learned how to read trees and moss for weathering: the north side was more heavily weathered than the south side. To travel north, as the song text suggested, one had to "follow the drinkin' gourd."

As Southern slaveholders saw their chattels attempting to escape, they reacted. In 1850, Congress passed the last Fugitive Slave Law, which called for legal action against those people who assisted slaves in their escapes and required the return of runaways regardless of where they might live in the slaveless North. This action prompted slave escapers not only to continue their journey farther north into free Canada, where the wilderness and international border provided refuge, but also west into Indian lands where they were often welcomed into tribal communities. Henry Stewart, after his escape north, commented, "We rode to Canada and have been here ever since. I undertook to buy six acres of land in the country, and am now living on it." Stewart longed for home and friends, but he was adamant about remaining in Canada, declaring, "I have no idea of going back unless freedom is established." [30] George Johnson felt the same way. "My reason for leaving Pennsylvania," he said, "was that I always felt myself a freeman, and wanted to be a freeman, as the government didn't give me the liberty I wished, I concluded I would go where I could possess the same liberty as any other man." [31]

Abolitionists like William Lloyd Garrison wrote about freeing bondsmen, and men like the Reverend Henry Highland Garnet took action. For years Garnet preached to slaves about the process of resistance and sacrifice, saying that the "diabolical injustice by which your liberties are cloven down, neither God, nor angels, or just men, command you to suffer for a single moment." [32] It was one's duty, therefore, to use every means—moral, intellectual, and physical—that might promise freedom. Responding in force, slaves escaped alone, in small groups, and even with entire families. Josiah Henson led his family from Maryland to Canada. Later he commented, "They too must share with me the life of liberty." [33] Some slaves who escaped alone vowed to return for their families; some came back in uniform after the federal government established regiments of the United States Colored Troops (USCT) during the Civil War. One Union soldier escaped from both worlds. John Wesley Whitten first went north by way of the Underground Railroad into Pennsylvania, then joined the Union Army. Captured as a soldier near the end of the war, Whitten was sold into slavery in Cuba. Twenty-four years later, with the help of a sea captain, Whitten escaped his Cuban bondage and returned to his home in central Pennsylvania. [34]

To escape, slaves needed outside help. The Underground Railroad, or the "Freedom Train," provided that help. Nevertheless, secrets, especially those associated with the Underground Railroad, were hard to keep. Disclosures were dangerous, sometimes lethal, for people in the pipeline. Frederick Douglass strongly urged people to stop making reference to the existence of such organized undertakings, declaring, "We owe something to the slaves south of Mason and Dixon's line as well as to those north of it; and in discharging the duty of aiding the latter on their way to freedom, we should be careful to do nothing which would be likely to hinder the former in making their escape." [35]

By 1850, the Underground Railroad had developed a system of agents like Harriet Tubman, who traveled among the slaves and encouraged them to escape. Tubman became a hunted criminal in 1849, when she escaped from a Maryland farm, where her overseer had beaten her repeatedly. Migrating to Philadelphia, she washed dishes in order to save enough money to return to Maryland to lead her sister and two children out of bondage. A few months later she led her brother and two other slaves north. On her third trip she searched for her husband, but finding him remarried, she left him in Maryland. From 1849 to 1859, Tubman led more than three hundred slaves north, and rewards as high as $12,000, an enormous sum for the time, were posted for her capture.[36] At its peak, more than thirty-two hundred volunteers staffed the Underground Railroad. Heading the organization was Levi Cofin, a Quaker merchant in Cincinnati, Ohio, and Newport, Indiana, who personally arranged safe passage for more than three thousand escapers.[37]

The knowledge that secret travel lines with stops at "stations" existed all the way to Canada prompted many of the more timid to escape. They rested in barns and old houses by day and traveled at night. They marched through woods and along deserted roads, hid in wagons and carts, and took rowboats and cargo barges from one station to the next. One agent brought twenty-eight slaves to safety by pretending to lead a funeral procession. What appeared to be a serene scene on the outside might have been a bustling safe house inside. Some helpers were white; others were black. Some were Northerners; some, Southerners. To the escapers, what was important was that they were in the hands of men and women who believed in a common cause: that in a free society with democratic political and social institutions, human beings should never be considered another person's chattel property.

After hostilities began at Fort Sumter, South Carolina, slave escapers took on a new dimension. During the Revolution, hundreds of slaves had sought freedom by joining either the British or the Continental Army. In May 1861, Frederick Douglass recognized that the Civil War had broader implications than simply preserving the Union. He called on President Lincoln to use both escaped slaves and "free colored people" as a "liberating army, to march into the South and raise the banner of emancipation among those still in slavery."[38] Thousands of free black men in the North volunteered for service in the Union Army, but the government declined their offer. Tempers flared as some Union Army senior officers grew concerned about the thousands of fugitive slaves who were arriving as refugees behind Union lines. Writing from Hampton, Virginia, Gen. Benjamin F. Butler, USV, called them "contraband of war" and used them as laborers. Maj. Gen. John C. Frémont wanted runaways to join his ranks in Missouri as free soldiers, but President Lincoln, ever fearful that arming ex-slaves and free blacks would cause major dissention in the ranks, stopped that action dead in its tracks and dismissed Frémont from the Army.[39]

The situation began to change in 1862. Although it was a white man's war on the ground, at sea it was a different story. The Navy needed men fast, and with memories of the War of 1812 still fresh, the service permitted black sailors to enlist, although their rank was restricted. In the summer of 1862, Secretary of War Edwin M. Stanton authorized Gen. Rufus Stanton to recruit and train more than fifty thousand "contrabands" for labor and guard duty. In newly recaptured New Orleans, Major General Butler recruited the Corps D'Afrique, led by Pinckney Benton Stewart (a.k.a. Percy Bysshe Shelley Pinchback), as the first black combat troops of the Civil War. On September 11, 1862, General Stanton wrote, "I shall also have within ten days a regiment 1,000 strong of Nation [*sic*] Guards (Colored)."[40] A month later, the first Kansas Infantry Regiment began training at Fort Lincoln; at the same time, the First Regiment of South Carolina Volunteers (USCT) initiated raiding operations near Beaufort.

On December 24, 1862, in response to the raids, the president of the Confederacy, Jefferson Davis, issued Proclamation 111, which raised the stakes of battle considerably. Davis declared that former or runaway slaves captured under arms with the Union Army would be remanded to their respective states for sale or return to bondage; and that Union officers commanding black troops were guilty of leading an insurrection against the Confederacy and would be executed upon capture. Instead of discouraging the Union from fielding black troops, the proclamation provided just the challenge needed to increase the Army's size and fighting capability.

Soon after the Emancipation Proclamation went into effect in 1863, the country reaffirmed the war's purpose: to preserve the Union and end the institution of slavery once and for all. At the same time, the question raised was whether the black volunteers would fight. In May 1863, the War Department issued General Order 143, which directed the adjutant general of the Army, Maj. Gen. Lorenzo Thomas, USA, to begin training volunteer regiments known as United States Colored Troops (USCTs), both as infantry (USCI) and artillery units (USCA). Battles such as Milliken's Bend and Port Hudson in Louisiana, and Fort Wagner in South Carolina, proved the value of the USCTs as fighting forces. The Fort Wagner action has been particularly well remembered, not only in contemporary accounts but also in Edward Zwick's film *Glory* (1990), which immortalized the actions of the 54th Massachusetts Volunteer Infantry (USCI) and its dedicated leader, Col. Robert Gould Shaw, USV, of Boston. One USCT summed up the reason why these men took up arms when he said to his former mistress in Tennessee, "I ain't fightin' you, I'm fightin' to get free."[41]

By the end of October 1863, the Union Army had fifty-eight regiments of USCTs, with a total strength, including white officers, of 37,482 men.[42]

Despite the numbers and the great potential that this black army afforded the Union, some commanders refused to believe that this force could fight. On August 26, 1863, Abraham Lincoln confronted this misguided view and commented, "Some of the commanders of our armies in the field who have given us our most important successes, believe the emancipation policy, and the use of colored troops, constitute the heaviest blow yet dealt to the rebellion. . . . You say you will not fight to free negroes. Some of them seem willing to fight for you." [43] On December 7, 1863, reflecting the USCTs success in helping to turn the tide of battle, Lincoln declared, "The crisis which threatened to divide friends of the Union is past." [44]

At the conclusion of the Civil War, the Union Navy had integrated crews, and the Army had recruited 123,156 black soldiers in 120 infantry regiments, 12 heavy artillery regiments, 10 batteries of light artillery, and 7 cavalry regiments. Nearly 3,000 USCTs had been killed in 449 engagements, and more than 26,000 died from disease.[45] Some Confederate cavalry commanders, like Nathan Bedford Forrest who later led the Ku Klux Klan in the postwar period, were responsible for executing captured USCTs.[46] In accordance with Confederate Proclamation 111, after capture, some USCTs were reenslaved in their home states until the Confederacy surrendered. Others who had been free when they enlisted were sent to Confederate prison facilities like Andersonville, where they lived and died together with other Union POWs.

In slavery from the sixteenth to the nineteenth centuries, Africans defied their captors by revolting and escaping in increasing numbers. In 1852, Charles Sumner wrote in the *Liberator*, "They are among the heroes of our age." [47] As escapers, maroons, and fugitives, then as contrabands, and later as dedicated Union soldiers under fire on the battlefields of the Civil War, they broke the bonds their masters made. It is little wonder that bayonet charges against the Confederates were common among the USCTs; they took relatively few prisoners and gave as good as they got. Today, military grave markers near those battlefields note simply their names, units, and "USCT" in stone.

5

Acts of Pure Cussedness
Escapes in the Civil War

A prisoner of war who escapes may be shot, or otherwise killed in flight; but neither death nor any other punishment shall be inflicted on him for his attempt to escape, which the law of order does not consider a crime.

—General Order 100, *Instructions for the Government of Armies of the United States* (1863)

Committed escapers during the Civil War gave their behavior a name, "pure cussedness." Other POWs, both Union and Confederate, escaped because their sense of duty impelled them to return to the war, or because they believed that improper treatment by camp authorities would unquestionably result in their death. Confederate and Union officers like John Hunt Morgan and Thomas Rose were lionized in their own time for their daredevil escapes. Others remained nearly anonymous, buried in the huge bulk of narrative materials from the American Civil War.[1]

Union soldiers deeply lamented their capture and incarceration and often expressed it in song. George F. Root's "Tramp! Tramp! Tramp! or The Prisoner's Hope" expressed the Union prisoners' general melancholy:

So within the prison cell,
We are waiting for the day
That shall come to open wide the iron door,
And the hollow eye grows bright,
And the poor heart almost gay,
And we think of seeing home and friends once more.[2]

The Confederates despised the northern winters, not only because of the savage cold, but also because Union authorities denied them adequate food, clothing, and shelter to withstand it. Union prisoners could barely tolerate the South's summer heat and humidity, which generated diseases usually unknown in the North's more temperate climate. The Confederate postwar song, "Good Old Rebel," sung with gusto at meetings of the United Confederate Veterans, expressed more hostile sentiments:

> I followed old Mas' Robert for four years near about,
> Got wounded in three places, and starved at Point Lookout.
> I cotched the roomatism, a-camping in the snow,
> But I killed a chance o' Yankees, I'd like to kill some mo'.[3]

There were several who had their chance.

In December 1862, Gen. John Hunt Morgan, CSA, led twenty-four hundred cavalry raiders into his home state of Kentucky to attack railroad lines that supported Union military operations in Tennessee. In two weeks, Morgan's Christmas raid captured nearly two thousand Union soldiers and forced Union commanders to divert thousands of troops from the Tennessee front. A year later he did it again, riding furiously across Kentucky, and in July 1863, his cavalry raiders began to ravage regions of Ohio thought to have been immune from the rigors and terrors of front-line or hit-and-run cavalry guerrilla warfare. In a mad skirmish on July 26, 1863, however, the crafty Morgan and his men were surrounded and captured.

Union authorities considered Morgan and his command to be criminals and outlaws instead of regular POWs. Gen. Henry W. Halleck, USA, more a scholar than a soldier, realized that Morgan's way of fighting, political guerrilla warfare on a grand scale, seriously endangered the rules of war that existed at that time. Confederate officers, on the other hand, believed that raiding activities were in keeping with the military mission in general, and being held in civilian jails as criminals for the duration of the war was simply an outrage. Orders from Halleck to Gen. Ambrose Burnside, USA, sent Morgan and sixty-seven Confederate officers to the maximum security section of the Ohio State Penitentiary in Columbus. The others, about seventy Confederates, were incarcerated in Pennsylvania's massive walled prison, the Western Penitentiary in Pittsburgh.[4] Basil W. Duke, Morgan's brother-in-law, fellow POW, and the first of Morgan's many salutary biographers, later wrote, "It was not the apprehension or harsh treatment that was so horrible; it was the stifling sense of close cramped confinement." As far as Duke was concerned, "The dead weight of a huge stone prison seemed resting on our breasts."[5]

Although their treatment in the penitentiary was better than what others received in a Union military prison camp at the time, Morgan and a few of his raiders decided that nothing would keep them from an escape.

Gen. John Hunt Morgan, CSA. Union authorities sent Gen. John Hunt Morgan and sixty-seven other Confederate officers to the maximum security section of the Ohio State Penitentiary in Columbus. On the night of November 27, 1864, Morgan and six others broke out of their cell block after secretly digging through two feet of masonry with two table knives that they had obtained from sick comrades in the hospital. Courtesy of Macmillan

On the night of November 27, 1864, Morgan and six men broke out of their cell block after they secretly dug through two feet of masonry with two table knives given to them by sick comrades in the hospital. The small tunnel ended in the prison yard, and after they climbed over the outer prison walls, the men vanished into the darkness. With money provided to them from outside Southern sympathizers—Morgan's sister sent him cash hidden in books—he boldly boarded the Cincinnati train along with his escape partner, Capt. Thomas H. Hines, CSA. According to Hines, Morgan never lost either his sense of humor or his keen sense of irony. While he sat next to a Union major, Morgan noticed that the train was passing the Ohio State Penitentiary. The major turned to Morgan and said, "That's where the rebel General Morgan is now imprisoned."

"Indeed," said the general, "I hope they'll always keep him as safely as they have him now."[6]

After the breakout, two Confederate escapers were recaptured, but Morgan and the others left the train at Dayton, Ohio, and made their way back to Tennessee and a hero's welcome at home.[7] Meanwhile, Ohio Governor David Todd ordered the militia to search every house in Columbus and offered a $1,000 reward to anyone who could help recapture Morgan. Secretary of War Stanton put up an additional $5,000 from the federal treasury, and four separate investigations concluded that Morgan and his men had escaped without any direct outside aid.[8] Although Morgan's escape adventure became a legend in the Confederate South during his life, he died in a Union ambush at Greenville, Tennessee, the home of then Vice President Andrew Johnson.

Another escaper among the heroes of the Confederacy was Sgt. Berry Greenwood Benson, a Confederate sharpshooter and scout engaged in a host of battles from the first Manassas to Appomattox. After Benson's capture behind Union lines in 1864, he was charged with espionage, the punishment for which was summary execution. Benson recalled that he felt a good deal of alarm because, as he observed, "A trial by drum-head court-martial is a terrible ordeal. I realized that the case against me would be aggravated by certain suspicious circumstances which were likely to be brought out. I was tortured with anxiety, for I considered the chances of my being freed by the court of the charge of spying were but small."[9] Regarding his situation as critical, Benson began looking for a way to escape. He wrote, "If by any chance the court-martial were deferred till night, I would make a run for the woods, there being quite a forest on the other side of the road."[10] Apprehensions soon faded when another Confederate prisoner told Benson that he was regarded as a POW rather than a spy. His fear that the Union men intended to hang him was dispelled, and escape plans waited for another day.

Benson soon arrived at the large Point Lookout Union military prison, located on the tip of Maryland's southeastern peninsula, not far from Leonardtown in St. Mary's County, a distinctly Confederate-sympathizing region of the state. Security was strict, and camp conditions were terrible. At the time of Benson's arrival, there had been only about thirty-five successful escapes from Point Lookout.[11] On May 25, 1864, Benson slipped slowly and gently into the Chesapeake Bay, at first wading through the shallows and then swimming his way northwest. After a few exhausting miles, Benson saw what he thought were sharks gliding toward him from the deep water. The sharks may have been hallucinations brought on by his exhaustion, but real or imaginary, he had no desire to become a meal for a fish. At that moment, a land route south appeared preferable.

After working his way through Maryland on foot, Benson swam across the Potomac River as a shortcut to Virginia, and, like escapers before and after him, he took great risks to obtain food or help from residents along the way. He knew that Maryland and northern Virginia were hotly contested areas peopled by citizens caught in the middle of the Civil War. He also knew that it was unusual to see someone of military age on the loose without a recognizable uniform. Because he had no way of discerning who was loyal to what, deception and evasion became a way of life. While walking through the woods near Alexandria, Virginia, not far from Union-held Washington, Benson encountered two boys and told them that he was a deserter from Lee's army. They took him to the local miller, a New Jersey man who was the leader of a Union volunteer company that he had raised to counter local Confederate guerrillas. The deception failed. Benson had had the bad luck to encounter an armed unionist in Virginia who refused to believe his story. Benson was recaptured and arrived under guard at Old Capitol Prison in Washington on June 5, 1864. After Confederate Gen. Jubal Early frightened Washingtonians by a near attack on the city, Union prison authorities shipped Berry Benson, Confederate sergeant and sharpshooter, public enemy, POW, and a dangerous escaper, to the federal prison camp at Elmira, New York. With the lowest escape rate in the North, Elmira was one of the most secure POW camps in the entire federal prison system.[12] The Confederates called it "Hellmira."

Few prisoners escaped from Elmira; however, pure gritty deception paid off from time to time. One Confederate, Sgt. Maj. Joe Womack, used forged identity papers to get past the guards and walked out the front gate on October 26, 1864.[13] After Womack's departure, security was tightened, and Benson had to be more secretive about his plans for escape. He discovered that there were some inmates digging a tunnel. Swearing him to secrecy, the tunnelers admitted Benson to their escape community. After digging for two months, the group produced a tunnel that stretched more than sixty-six feet, and at four o'clock in the morning on October 6, 1864, Benson and nine other escapers crawled through it and left Elmira.

Free again, Benson made his way south through Pennsylvania to Baltimore, then to Leesburg, Virginia, with a combination of stealth, deception, luck, and cunning. He stole apples, clothes, and train rides on his way south. His persistence paid off in Virginia, where he met Col. John Singleton Mosby, CSA, and his 47th Virginia Cavalry known as the "Partisan Raiders." Benson knew then that he was safe and on his way back to his own unit. On Thursday, October 27, 1864, a Confederate picket halted Benson. Just after dark that day, Benson reported to Gen. Bradley T. Johnson, CSA, that he had escaped from Elmira prison and reported for duty. Benson returned to his regiment stationed near Petersburg, Virginia, and remained a dedicated Confederate soldier to the war's end. In April 1865, when hostilities came to a close, Berry Benson left Appomattox with the other Confederate soldiers in the Army of Northern Virginia and went home.[14]

In addition to Berry Benson, there were other Confederate POWs in Point Lookout who planned and executed a variety of escapes. Some enterprising prisoners left the camp by concealing themselves in barges and other boats. The Union guards found out about these efforts and recaptured most of them. Upon their recapture, most of these prisoners endured some kind of punishment; many hung by their thumbs for considerable lengths of time.[15] What these prisoners learned was the lesson that Point Lookout was a large camp that held thousands of Confederate POWs, and it was not easy to keep a secret.

Another Point Lookout prisoner who reported that secrets were difficult to keep was Sgt. James S. Wells, Company A, South Carolina Volunteers. Wells found himself in Point Lookout in 1864, a year for poor treatment of Confederate POWs in the North, and observed the futility of digging a tunnel even in the winter when security among the prisoners was lax. In his memoir he wrote bitterly:

> About the 10th of January our suffering had grown so intense that a party formed a plan for escape. It was a bold one in its conception and required men of determination and courage to undertake it. Captain Chears, a man about sixty years of age, and a member of a Virginia Cavalry Regiment, was placed in command. A tunnel was to be dug from Company A, 1st Division, to the fence, a distance of about twenty feet, and was commenced in a small tent. This work was extremely dangerous and had to be carried on with great caution. It was large enough for a man to crawl through. It was worked by detail, and as the dirt was dug out it was drawn to the mouth of the tunnel in an old haversack and distributed over the bottom of the tent.
>
> At last, it was complete, and the party was divided into squads of ten each. These squads were to make their exit on separate nights. After getting beyond the enclosure, each party was to choose its own mode of proceeding. The first party made the attempt. They were betrayed by a Sentinel, whom some of them had most foolishly bribed, as there was no necessity

for it. The alarm was given, and the prisoners, who had succeeded in getting out, had taken refuge behind the projecting banks of sand on the beach. As soon as the officers reached the spot, they called upon the prisoners to surrender, saying they would not be harmed. Major Patterson stood at the gate, and as each prisoner came up he deliberately fired at him. One was shot in the head, from the effect of which he never recovered, and the last account we had of him he was in a lunatic asylum. Another was badly shot in the shoulder and another in the abdomen, from which he died. The remaining seven managed to get into the camp again without being hurt, for which they could thank the darkness of the night. The tunnel was fired into several times, but no one was in it. Next day it was filled up and the men into whose tent it opened, confined in the guard house on bread and water for ten days. The shooting of these men was without any excuse whatever, as they had expressed a willingness to surrender, and were proceeding to do so; beside which, it is a recognized principle that a prisoner of war has a right to escape if he can, and the capturing party has no right to punish, but simply to remand him to proper custody.[16]

This event halted all thoughts of escaping from Point Lookout, at least for Wells's group, and they became more resigned to their fate. Fellow prisoner Luther B. Lake did not share this view.

Lake formed a small group of five prisoners who crawled as close to the deadline as possible. When the guards met and separated to search for the escapers, the group dashed for the Chesapeake Bay. Their escape took place on September 3, 1863, and like Benson's flight from Point Lookout, Lake's group had to swim through the Bay water and then make their way on foot, keeping near the shoreline. Later, still intact as an escape team, they encountered civilians, Confederate sympathizers in southern Maryland, who helped them along their way. After arriving at the Potomac River, the dividing line between Maryland and Virginia, they took a chance. They knew how to avoid towns like Leonardtown, Chaptico, Port Tobacco, and others where armed civilian Unionists often recaptured escaped Confederates and readily turned them over to federal military authorities. What they needed was a Southern-sympathizing Marylander who lived near the river's bank. By pure luck they found one, and after telling him that they were escaped Confederate soldiers, he agreed to help them cross.

By this time, Lake and the other escapers realized that they were about twenty-four miles south of Washington and could easily encounter Union forces without any warning. Lake recalled, "It was dark, and we were right in the Yankee camp." They had no idea where the sentinels were, but, being good scouts, they soon found the Orange and Alexandria railroad and thousands of campfires. According to Lake, "We succeeded in crossing between two [Union] camps' fires about twenty-five yards apart, and I am glad to say, no one halted us. We were so close to one guard I heard him cough." [17] In two days they reached the home of Lake's brother, the same place where the Yankees had captured them. Lake went upstairs, took two pistols, and rearmed himself as a soldier. He knew that he could not sleep there and risk recapture, so he and the group bedded down in a nearby cornfield. Soon they split up and went back to their original units. Lake returned to Company B, 8th Virginia Infantry, and after the war commented, "I never went to prison again, and I never surrendered at the end. No more Federal prison for me!" [18]

Escaping from trains that took POWs to prison camps was common during the Civil War. Decimus et Ultimus Barziza, a product of William and Mary College, practiced law in Texas before the war and became a Confederate infantry officer in 1861. Captured during the Battle of Gettysburg in 1863, Barziza escaped from a train when it stopped in Huntingdon, Pennsylvania. Using trains to escape was a good idea; they were faster and much more comfortable than walking. With his wit, luck, good humor, and an ability to speak with a distinct New England accent, Barziza convinced rural Pennsylvanians and other unsophisticated Northern residents that he was a discharged soldier from Maine on a business trip. Using this disguise to its maximum advantage, he traveled north and crossed the Canadian border. Later, he returned to Wilmington, North Carolina, aboard a blockade-runner. [19]

Another Confederate who used the train to escape was Joe Martin. When the train taking him to a prison camp stopped for wood, Martin saw a momentary opportunity to flee. Asking his guard if he could fill his canteen, Martin stepped from the train and descended to a small creek close by. While he was halfway to the creek, a bell sounded and the guard signaled for him to return to the train. Martin immediately concealed himself from the guard's view, but as the train began moving, he came out of hiding, removed his hat, and bowed toward the train. The guard, realizing that he lost his prisoner, returned the bow with equal courtesy. Without wasting any more time, Joe Martin went home.

At Camp Morton near Chicago, John George Dyess from Georgia made an unusual escape. He placed a gunpowder bomb in the stove that warmed the officers' barracks. The blast shattered the stove and blew out all the windows. No one was injured, and his only punishment was solitary confinement. A few days later, Dyess struck his guard on the chin, took his rifle, and escaped. He rejoined the Confederate Army of Gen. Joseph E. Johnson, CSA, and fought until the end of the war. [20]

Johnson's Island, a Union prison camp for Confederate officers on Lake Erie in northern Ohio, was a particularly dreary spot that steamed from heat and lake-effect humidity in the summer and became frigid and snowy in the winter. A group of three Confederate soldiers, captured in 1862, decided to scale the tall plank fence surrounding the prison camp. The escapers eluded their guards, whose gun shots not only missed them entirely but were dampened by the cover of a heavy autumn rain. Once out of the prison, the Confederates posed as travelers and purchased train tickets to Canada.

Although many Confederates, especially those from the Deep South, suffered badly from the cold winters in the North, the winter weather had advantages too. A Confederate Colonel Winston dug a tunnel with a pocket knife to the outer wall and then scaled it with a ladder he had made from his bedding. Using the frigid weather to his benefit, Winston chose a day when the temperature sank to well below zero and Lake Erie was iced over completely. After his solo breakout, Winston traveled cross-country for one mile to Ottawa County, Ohio, and then walked across Lake Erie to Canada, where Southern sympathizers booked passage for him down the St. Lawrence River to the Atlantic Ocean and finally home to Wilmington, North Carolina.

Other Confederate officers imprisoned at Johnson's Island also attempted tunnel escapes. One group failed to take into account how large one of their members was, and the tunnel opening proved to be too small for his massive body. Stuck in the hole, he cried out loudly for help. The Union guards obliged. Capt. Robert Cobb Kennedy tunneled out as well. Kennedy was a Georgian captured near Decatur, Alabama, and sent to Johnson's Island. Soon after his arrival, he succeeded in tunneling under a deep ditch along the parapets of the prison. After he emerged, Kennedy stole one of the officers' boats and rowed to shore opposite the island. Free from his Union captors, he made his way on foot and crossed from Buffalo, New York, into Canada, where he joined a band of exiled and escaped Confederates who devised an implausible raid into the United States to burn New York City. Kennedy was recaptured soon after he recrossed the border. Placed in irons, he was taken to New York, then tried and executed as a spy.[21]

When the tunnels at Johnson's Island were discovered and closed, Confederate officers tried ladders. Capt. T. Herbert Davis, CSA, was taken prisoner in 1862. Along with a small group of determined officers, he used a scaling ladder to go over the wooden walls. Another nonescaping but cooperative inmate removed the ladder after evening taps, about half past nine, and the men lowered themselves quietly down the wall using blankets knotted together. As escapers on the run from the Union Army, the officers crossed Lake Erie on the ice and reached the Canadian shore the following morning. At Montreal, they received funds for the trip back to Dixie from James P. Holcombe, Confederate States Commissioner. Davis's imprisonment and escape from Johnson's Island, however, took another fateful turn. After his return to Company B, 1st Virginia Infantry, he was taken prisoner in an encounter with Union forces at Sailor's Creek and returned to Johnson's Island. This time Captain Davis knew that the war was winding down, and instead of escape, he opted for quarantine and remained in prison until the war's end.[22]

Confederate navymen also abhorred POW life in prison. Capt. J. W. Alexander, CSN, the executive officer of the Confederate ironclad steamer *Atlanta,* was taken prisoner in June 1863, after a losing battle against Union monitors on the Savannah River. Alexander and several of his fellow *Atlanta* officers were taken to Fort Warren, a prison island about seven miles from Boston. Along with a small group, Alexander formed a plan to squeeze through a small hole in the fort's casement. According to Alexander's memoir, he found two openings called "musketry loopholes" that were more than six feet high and about two feet wide at the inside of the prison walls. One opening sloped, making it a very tight fit on the outside. Stripping off his clothes, Alexander discovered that he could just slide through. One by one, each man made his way through the loophole, downward into a dry ditch, and through the grass to a guarded sea wall. The escaping Confederates then observed that they could slip through the guard patrol if they made their moves when the sentries walked in opposite directions.

At first, Alexander's escapers were far too optimistic about their own strength, and their plan to swim had to be scrapped when they realized that they were too weak and the sea was too rough. After they decided to use a boat, they reversed course quietly and worked their way back to the prison compound. They told others about their new plan and route, and another Confederate naval officer, Lt. C. W. Reed, CSN, of the *Tacony,* suggested that there were two strong swimmers in the compound who could make it to one of the small surrounding islands, steal a boat, and return for Alexander and his three comrades: Lieutenants Reed and James Thurston (Marines) and a Kentucky political prisoner, Reed Sanders. The two sailors joined Alexander and Thurston and slipped quietly into the cold water for the long swim. Neither swimmer returned. Desperate to take advantage of the opportunity they had contrived,

Alexander and Thurston decided to chance the swim to the distant island themselves and, if successful, return for the other two. After very nearly being discovered by the sentries, both men tied their clothes to a floating target and pushed off.

Although it was August, the water was extremely cold, and the frailty caused by captivity's privations soon took its toll. Exhausted, both swimmers finally reached the shore and soon spied a small fishing craft. They cut the anchor cords and launched the boat. Their first chore was to pick up the others, but they had returned to the prison's safety and warmth. Alexander and Thurston sailed the area looking for food and fresh water. They came upon a suspicious waterman, but he accepted their story that they had lost their supplies while swimming. Deception often worked for Confederates in the North who could fake a Yankee accent. The waterman departed for shore and returned with some old clothes, tobacco, and brandy. Although the two escapers were grateful for the waterman's unwitting kindness, they knew that a speedy departure meant success, whereas dallying meant recapture.

After setting the course, Alexander fell asleep. When he awoke, he was shocked to see a small civilian boat searching the area. Hailed by the captain to come alongside, Alexander tried once more to spin his yarn about being lost, but the captain insisted on a search. Finding some Confederate money, the captain knew he had his quarry. Soon a Union revenue cutter appeared and collected Alexander and Thurston for a short trip to the Portland (Maine) county jail. For committed escapers on the run, county jails posed no real difficulties, and the prisoners immediately began looking for a way out. In the course of removing the iron bars and making their escape, Alexander and Thurston were seized by Union authorities and returned to Fort Warren. Although they never breached Fort Warren's walls again, Alexander and Thurston continued making escape attempts until their exchange at City Point, Virginia, on the James River.[23]

Great escapes, that is, large, well-organized breakouts, were not common during the Civil War, but a few did occur. One Confederate action was the takeover of the Union steamer *Maple Leaf* in 1863. Two groups of captured Confederate officers, one held in Fort Norfolk, the other transferred from New Orleans, had initially believed that they were being taken North for exchange, and they had all agreed not to resist their Union captors or try to escape in return for good treatment. In their view, right or wrong, they had a fair and legal agreement, if not a contract, with federal prison authorities: they felt a strong obligation to behave as prisoners in quarantine if the federals exchanged them as soon as possible. However, events, feelings, and the nature of the rising war psychosis during the Civil War made agreements such as this one very tentative. In many cases, temporary agreements failed as easily as they succeeded, depending on the policy affected by the course of the war on the battlefield or the whims of major authority figures. In this case, the Confederate POWs discovered that the *Maple Leaf* was not taking them to City Point, Virginia, for exchange, but to Fort Delaware—a large, old fort at the mouth of the Delaware River—to join thousands of Confederates, both officers and enlisted, who sat idling as POWs inside and outside the fort's great walls. Although their treatment had been relatively benign up to this point, the Confederates considered the federal intent so duplicitous, unreasonable, cruel, and mean-spirited that they regarded their contract as broken. As it turned out, this was enough for them to consider escape not only as a duty but also as a form of justified retribution.

On June 10, 1863, ninety-seven Confederate officers ranging from lieutenant to colonel, decided to act.[24] Capt. Emelius W. Fuller, CSN, devised the plan and organized its execution. Fuller had commanded the Confederate steamer *Queen of the West* until it was destroyed in action against Union warships on Grand Lake, Louisiana, in April 1863. Other plot leaders included Army Capt. Oliver Semmes, son of the famous Confederate Navy Capt. Raphael Semmes of the raider *Alabama*. The younger Semmes had commanded the Confederate gunboat *Diana,* and after a short action, had scuttled his ship to prevent Union forces from capturing it intact. Col. Allen Rufus Witt, CSA, of the 10th Arkansas Infantry, was captured on May 27, 1863, in action at Port Hudson, Louisiana, along with Capt. Eugene Holmes of Louisiana's Crescent Regiment. Henry W. Dale commanded the *Maple Leaf;* guarding the prisoners was 2d Lt. William E. Dorsey, USV, of the 3d Pennsylvania Heavy Artillery, assisted by Sgt. Thomas B. Burnie.[25] Dorsey's orders read, "Proceed in charge of certain Prisoners of War in the Steamer *Maple Leaf* to Fort Norfolk, Va., there to take on more Prisoners of War. He will then proceed with the same steamer to Fort Delaware, Delaware, and transfer the prisoners to the Commanding Officer of that Post."[26] Unexpected events prevented Second Lieutenant Dorsey from completing his mission.

In port, the prisoners were reasonably well guarded, but at sea, security loosened considerably. The Confederates were free to move around the ship almost at will, much to the delight of the plotting escapers. Captain Holmes made his way to the pilot house, where the ship's bell stood, and at 1730 hours sounded the prearranged call to action. The escapers overwhelmed the guards and seized their rifles; the ship was theirs.[27] Captain Fuller then took command.[28] After consulting with the other officers and discovering that the *Maple Leaf* carried a relatively small load of fuel, the escapers decided to sail south along the Virginia coast to a point near Cape Henry not far from shore.

There was considerable internal dissension among the Confederate officers as they reached their destination. Not all the prisoners aboard the *Maple Leaf* wanted to escape. About fifteen sick and wounded officers, including Captain Fuller, could not leave, no matter how much they wanted to. Others felt that they had given their word of honor in a parole agreement. They knew very well that their captors took these agreements very seriously, and that if they were recaptured after a parole-breaking escape, they could be tried and executed. In 1863, breaking a parole agreement was a capital offense. On the other hand, a number felt strongly that the federal authorities had already broken the agreement by sending them to the Union prison facility at Fort Delaware instead of to City Point for exchange. With these three positions firmly established among the Confederates, some decided to remain aboard the ship while others with no parole agreements chose to escape.

The Confederates encountered another problem: what to do with Captain Fuller? He had been instrumental in planning the escape, but he was too injured to leave. He had parole problems similar to the others. The answer was deception. The escaping group decided to act as if another officer had taken charge of the ship. Lt. Edward "Ned" McGowen, CSA, a Californian with a reputation for outrageous behavior in general and Confederate political activities in particular, proved to be the most believable choice. Fuller was an old man; McGowen was a young firebrand.[29] The escapers prepared a document for Union authorities telling them that they had taken over the ship, and McGowen signed it. On the evening of June 10, 1863, with the paperwork delivered both to the ship's captain and to Lieutenant Dorsey, seventy escapers lowered the ship's boats and went ashore in Confederate Virginia.

The *Maple Leaf* returned to Fort Monroe instead of steaming north to Fort Delaware. Captain Fuller, nearly an invalid, was in irons in a stateroom. The unfortunate Lieutenant Dorsey presented himself and reported the escape to Union Lt. Col. William H. Ludlow, the assistant inspector general and federal agent for POW exchanges.[30] One can only speculate about the degree of Ludlow's shock at what had happened and his wrath at Dorsey. He ordered cavalry units stationed in Norfolk and Suffolk, Virginia, to pursue the escaped prisoners. Ludlow next told Maj. Gen. John A. Dix, USA, commandant of the Department of Virginia and master of the Dix-Hill Cartel with the Confederates, what had taken place. As one can imagine, Dix was outraged and informed his immediate boss, Maj. Gen. Henry W. Halleck, USA, the Union Army's general in chief, that one of his junior officers had allowed a shipload of poorly guarded Confederate officers to escape from under his nose. One can only speculate about what President Lincoln thought, or actually said, when he heard the news.

To make matters even worse for Dix, Halleck, Ludlow, and, of course, for Lieutenant Dorsey, the popular press learned about the *Maple Leaf* escape, and poor Dorsey became the natural scapegoat. A few days later, the *Maple Leaf* sailed again for Fort Delaware with a full load of prisoners, but this time without Lieutenant Dorsey. After the Army charged him with dereliction of his guard duties, an outraged President Lincoln dismissed him from the Army in disgrace on June 20, 1863, without the benefit of a court-martial.[31] On April 1, 1864, the *Maple Leaf* met its own fate, when it struck a mine in St. John's River, Florida, and settled in the mud, never again to carry Confederate prisoners.

Ludlow's orders to pursue the prisoners reached Brig. Gen. Michael Corcoran, USV, of the 69th New York Militia. The colorful Corcoran, who had been a prisoner in Libby following his capture after the first Battle of Bull Run until his exchange in 1862, ordered Maj. James N. Wheelan, USV, stationed at South Mills, North Carolina, into the field to recapture the seventy escapers.[32] The escapers had other ideas and enjoyed some good fortune when they encountered a woman whose husband fought with the Confederate Army. She assisted them by providing a horse and cart and directions to the Dismal Swamp, where they hoped to contact the Confederate guerrilla Capt. Willis B. Sanderlin, whose help they needed for the next step in the journey.[33] More good fortune and help from the local people came their way, and they found Sanderlin.

The last stage of the plan was to break up the group into two parties, with a pair of escapers heading west toward Richmond while the others remained in hiding in rural Virginia. Proceeding slowly, the advancing pair reached their destination safely. Four days later, the other sixty-eight men arrived in Richmond by train. One escaper later recalled, "We entered the Confederate capital a dirty, fagged out, used up, but as happy a set of 'rebs' as ever wore the gray."[34] The curious spectators on the crowded Richmond thoroughfares might have mistaken them for wild men of the forest. Their unkempt hair, sun-browned faces, and tattered clothes gave proper evidence of a perilous journey, one that involved eleven railways, two boats, three stage coaches, several hired carriages, and four days of walking.[35]

Many other simple and complex escape experiences demonstrated the Confederate soldiers' rejection of the condition of captivity. These soldiers could count on little overt assistance from the Northern population, and for the most part depended on their ability to deceive civilian Unionists while on the run. For the Confederates incarcerated in Ohio, New York, Illinois, and other places farther from the Mason-Dixon Line, Canada was the "promised land." Confederates readily found sympathizers in that country, and, with their help and support for the Southern cause, the escapers made their way home, usually as passengers aboard blockade runners sailing south.

In the South, where most of the Civil War fighting took place, the situation was different. Although many escaped Union prisoners found their own lines by themselves, others received help from unexpected sources.

For Yankees on the run, Southern steel rails proved useless. Unlike the North, where industrial development required a vast rail system, the South's rail system was more oriented toward agricultural production and was thus small in comparison. During the war, the Confederacy used it exclusively for moving military supplies, troops, and large numbers of war prisoners. Civilian traffic was secondary, and Union escapers had little or no chance of being overlooked by watchful sentries or ignored by security-minded civilians. Union soldiers stripped of their money, clothes, and contacts, had to find other means. These means proved to be the South's slave population. Time and again the Union escapers received help from innumerable and often nameless slaves, their natural allies who provided food, shelter, protection, and directions to friendly lines, often at great risk to their own personal safety. Hannibal A. Johnson, a Union escaper from Columbia, South Carolina, remained on active duty for a year after the war and was pleased "to return some of the many favors and heroic acts of kindness done by the black men of the South." [36] If Southern steel rails proved useless to Union men, the human railway proved to be very effective.

Union prisoners at Andersonville, Georgia, had a difficult time escaping from the compound. The camp was too crowded to even hope that anyone could keep a secret for very long. Gossip mills about planned escapes worked overtime. Some prisoners tried to bribe their way out by giving guards money or Union brass buttons. Other prisoners attempted to dig tunnels in the soft sand but were thwarted by "tunnel traitors" who refused to keep silent.[37] Despite the lack of heavy wood readily available for shoring, Andrew J. Munn, Company A, 100th Regiment of the Ohio Volunteers, tried to dig a tunnel and suffered the effects of a camp snitch. Overall, the Confederates found and destroyed eighty-three tunnels in various stages of construction. Difficulties notwithstanding, many who really wanted to escape from a prison camp developed opportunities.

Although Munn's first escape attempt underground was foiled, he persisted in his efforts and left Andersonville permanently above ground from a work detail.[38] Munn's escape was not unique. Hiram E. Hardy of Vermont was among the 329 Union prisoners in Andersonville who managed to flee from work details and paroles. The 4th and 11th Vermont Volunteers had been ordered to tear up the track of the Weldon Railroad south of Petersburg, Virginia, on June 23, 1864, but while this work was going on, the Confederates attacked and captured seven hundred Union soldiers. Under Confederate guard, Hardy's group went first to Petersburg, then to Richmond by railroad. Their ultimate destination was the

Andersonville Prison, Georgia, 1865. Severe overcrowding of thousands of Union prisoners into a small area caused a breakdown of sanitary facilities, which resulted in the deaths of thousands of prisoners in just a few months. Lithograph by Anton Hohenstein, 1865. Courtesy of the National Archives

Pemberton building opposite the Libby officers' prison. As they marched through Richmond, they were greeted by streets lined with women and children who taunted them with epithets like "blue-bellied Yankees" and "Yankee sons of bitches." During a close search, everything of value was taken, and as they entered the Pemberton building, the name, command, and birthplace of each man were written down by Confederate officers.

Hardy's stay in Pemberton was brief. The Union prisoners were removed from Pemberton to Belle Island, near Richmond, kept there one week, and then sent to Lynchburg by rail. From there they marched to the prison at Danville, Virginia. By this time, the detachment numbered twenty-five hundred, guarded by about six hundred Confederate soldiers, who were distributed throughout the ranks so that about every fifth man on the march was an armed Confederate guard. During the march, one Union prisoner proposed to organize a mutiny and escape. His plan was to seize and disarm every guard at a given signal, which could easily have been done had there been unity of purpose and concert of action on the part of the prisoners. Since so many were afraid to act, the idea was scrapped. According to Hardy, had the men been aware of one quarter of what was in store for them at Andersonville from July 11 to November 3, 1864, then the requisite purpose and action would have been brought to bear. He wrote, "When I first entered the prison pen there were about thirty thousand confined there, mostly from the Army of the Potomac. . . . The horrors unnameable I witnessed, in some instances I think, would not be credited by my friends. Our poor fellows busied themselves about anything that could make them even for a moment forget their miseries." [39] Plans of escape were imagined by some prisoners and tunnels were dug, some without the least hope of success. According to Hardy, "One man dug a tunnel, and had actually succeeded in running it outside the stockade; but he worked too near the surface and the earth caved in and exposed him. . . . He took to his heels on emerging, but the hounds were sent after him; he was captured and brought back."

Knowing full well that death in the compound was more likely than coming through the experience alive, Hardy became involved in a plan to take over the entire camp. The idea was to tunnel from a point near the deadline to the inside of the Confederate fort, whose guns commanded the stockade. The strongest and ablest men among the prisoners were at a given moment to appear inside the fort, seize the guards who held it, take command of the prison, and reorganize the Union prisoners into military units in order to resume fighting. This complicated, large-scale operation was foiled, however, in Hardy's words, by "the treachery of one man more interested in his own welfare than in leaving Andersonville." In Hardy's view, the plan "redounded to the reputation of the American soldier for hazardous enterprise and lion like courage." With that plan betrayed to the Confederates, Hardy began tunneling once again, but that effort failed as well. The tunnel, large enough for the purpose, had actually been dug for the most part. The men had placed a tent over its mouth, and the dirt had been emptied into some old, useless walls. Men lay over the tunnel's mouth during the daytime. According to Hardy, "It was a glorious design, well planned, and sure to have been executed but for the treachery of one degraded man who sold the secret for a plug of tobacco."

Thousands of Union prisoners had died at Andersonville by the autumn of 1864. When the survivors were told that they were going to be transferred by train to the Confederate prison at Millen, Georgia, the time had come to leave Andersonville forever. On November 4, 1864, the Confederates began loading the POWs onto trains, about seventy to a car, packed so tightly that the men were forced to stand for the entire trip. Hardy and his fellow escapers made their way to the middle of the group and began cutting a hole in the bottom of the car. According to Hardy, "We took turns at the work, which was tedious in the extreme, we having only an old case knife to whittle away the hard pitch pine plank." Working during the daytime, the prisoners pulled the shavings into the car so that no one could discover what they were doing by the falling chips. It took them nearly half a day to cut a hole large enough to allow a person to slip through. By nightfall, they readied themselves for the escape.

Although the track was guarded, rain muffled the men's noise and darkness provided a shield. When the train stopped momentarily only a few miles from Millen, four Union escapers squeezed out the hole beneath the boxcar; then three more slipped out. Hardy's group kept still beside the track until the train moved on; the others darted for the blackness. They discovered that the car had stopped between two big fires that separated the guards. After the train went on, the men arose and saw a man coming along with a lantern. They quickly moved to the bank, about three feet high, until he passed. According to Hardy, "We started right away from the fires, desiring to get away from them as far and as fast as possible. We soon, in the intense darkness, ran against a log house; a small dog set up a yelping. When we left the cars we had nothing to eat, and we got nothing for two days, when we came across a solitary pumpkin which we devoured 'guts, seeds and all.'" Desperate with hunger, they were at the point of going boldly into the first house they saw; however, in a Georgia besieged by Gen. William T. Sherman and the Union Army, that would have been a foolish act. The Union had earned few friends among the civilians.

Despite their hunger, they carried on, traveling at night and hiding during the daytime. Then their luck changed. Met by slaves in rural Georgia, the escapers entered a POW form of the Underground Railroad. Provided with shelter, food, maps, and money, Hardy and his fellow POWs were guided north by slaves. The party finally reached friendly Union lines on November 19, 1864, sixteen days and 250 miles from Andersonville. Expressing his warmest appreciation, Hardy wrote, "I cannot close this narrative without expressing my gratitude to the colored people who rendered us such valuable assistance, often at the peril of their lives. Without their help, our escape would have been simply impossible."

Another Union soldier, William Wallace Hensley, captured in Mississippi by an Alabama infantry unit and interned first in Andersonville on April 21, 1864, was later transferred to Florence, South Carolina, from where he made an escape on February 2, 1865. With a small group of Irish Union prisoners, Hensley fled from Florence on his way to Union lines. To dodge Confederates and find food and directions, they sought out slaves during the night. Hensley wrote, "We would call on the Negroes of a night and call for something to eat and for information. We always found them very short for things to eat, but they always divided with us not charging anything, but we always paid them."[40] When an old slave rowed the escape party across a river, Hensley asked him how much he owed. He replied sternly, "Good Lord massa, I don't charge you anything."[41]

Confederate soldiers recaptured most of this escape group after it had traveled more than a hundred miles from Florence. It made little difference to Hensley that the war was nearly over and the Confederacy was paroling and exchanging their Union prisoners by the thousands. He knew that if he were recaptured, the standard punishment would await him. The time for standard punishment—hanging by the thumbs—was nearly over, however. Although he was recaptured, Hensley avoided punishment and finally arrived home in an exchange after a short stay at the Union hospital in Annapolis, Maryland.[42]

However daring were the train escapes from Andersonville and other prisons, digging tunnels was the best way to improve camp morale and created the organizational conditions necessary for great escapes. No greater tunnel escape took place than through the Yankee Tunnel at the

William Wallace Hensley, of Marion, Illinois, Union soldier, escaper in 1864, and survivor of Andersonville Prison. This photo was taken on May 8, 1901, his sixty-seventh birthday. Courtesy of William Crocken

Libby officers' prison in Richmond, where 109 Union officers escaped on the night of February 9, 1864. Forty-eight of these men succeeded in reaching the Union lines. It was dangerous, tedious work, accomplished only with discipline, dedication, and purpose. With great difficulty and enormous amounts of perseverance, men burrowed on all fours to loosen earth before it was carted back by the diggers and dispersed in the camp. Many prisoners recounted the act of tunneling with fondness. One Union prisoner recalled, "I fancied Adam must have crawled into paradise through a tunnel."[43] Another stated, "No doubt this was the universal experience, but the efforts were never relaxed. If the construction of tunnels failed to liberate the men, it at least furnished wholesome food for thought, and buoyed up their spirits with the hope which alone sustained the life of many a captive."[44]

Libby Prison, Richmond, Virginia. Lithograph by W. C. Schwartzburg, 1864. Courtesy of the National Archives

Leading the Yankee Tunnel effort was Thomas E. Rose, a native of Pittsburgh and a member of the 77th Pennsylvania Volunteer Infantry, a composite unit recruited from several western Pennsylvania counties. After his capture in 1863, Rose was sent to Libby, where early in January 1864, he organized a party of fourteen officers whose job was to begin the dig. One man always stood outside the work area, keeping watch for camp officials or interior guards who might stride through the area look-ing for anything unusual in the prison routine. First removing the floor-ing in the cook room and the bricks from the flue, the tunnelers then moved between the floor joists into the cellar under the end room that was used as the hospital. From that point the tunnelers continued through an opening near the northeast corner of the cellar, a space of about two feet by eighteen inches. The air grew fetid, and one officer had to stand at the tunnel opening to fan in fresh air with his hat. For three weeks groups of men scraped at the loose, wet soil with pen knives and some crude tools they had fabricated from supplies inside the prison. They concealed the earth and gravel they took out under straw and rubbish in the cellar.

Troubles befell the tunnelers as they neared completion of their shaft. The Yankee Tunnel ran for fifty-two feet, diminished to a tight sixteen inches, then widened to two feet in diameter at the exit. Rose's plan called for the diggers to link up with the Richmond sewer system; however, as they burrowed deeper and farther, they were confronted with sewer water that began to seep, then gush, into the tunnel. Although the diggers arose cold, wet, and smelling like sewer rats, they knew they had a good plan, but they had to make it better and considerably drier. As a solution, Rose decided to dig under the street alongside of the prison and surface in the yard of a warehouse across the street. At least it was a dry route. More important for the escapers' morale, there was a playful twist to their efforts: they were tunneling under the very noses of their captors.

On February 6, 1864, the escapers thought that they had gone far enough. As they began to dig upward toward the surface, they were horrified to hear the guards' voices. The hole was quickly plugged with old pants, then stuffed with straw. The escapers returned to their beds to regain some composure; shortly thereafter, they resumed their efforts. Surfacing once again, they saw that they were just clear enough for each

Col. Thomas E. Rose, USV, 77th Pennsylvania Volunteer Infantry, leader of the Yankee Tunnel in Libby Prison in Richmond. Courtesy of the Massachusetts Commandery Military Order of the Loyal Legion and the U.S. Army Military History Institute

escaper to make his own dash, so twenty-five officers emerged and took their leave of Libby Prison. The promised land was either the Union lines at Norfolk or Fort Monroe.

Posing as Confederate uniformed personnel, some Union escapers walked along the Richmond canal. Many Yankee Tunnel escapers, especially those traveling in groups, were quickly recaptured. One party of escapers stole a boat on what they thought was the James River. They followed the stream hoping to reach Hampton Roads, but instead they were traveling the Appomattox River toward Confederate lines. Realizing their mistake, they upset their craft and swam to shore for their lives. They were discovered the next morning by some Confederate soldiers nearly frozen to death.[45] Others hid in the Chickahominy swamps and were hunted down by dogs.

One who did not succeed was Col. Thomas Ellwood Rose himself. Only about two miles away from the Union lines, Rose abandoned precautions, thinking that he was safe from any further pursuit, and talked with two men who he thought were wearing Union uniforms. Unfortunately for Rose, they were Confederate scouts looking for escaped prisoners from Libby. A short scuffle ensued before a very unhappy Thomas Rose surrendered and was returned to prison. After his subsequent exchange, he returned to his unit and fought again, suffering a severe combat wound in Georgia. Rose, the mastermind of the Yankee Tunnel, survived his wound, mustered out of the Army in 1865 as a brevet brigadier general, and came home a hero.

After they returned to Libby, the recaptured officers received no unusual punishment, but the Confederate prison commandant, Maj. Richard Turner, CSA, made it clear to them that he would tolerate no more prison breaks by tunnels or any other means. He increased the number of roll calls to the point where most of the day was spent in counting and recounting. While keeping the prisoners distracted with head counts, Turner began conducting close room searches and managed to discover caches of sundry objects with cutting edges that could be used to dig more tunnels.[46] Although Colonel Rose and the Yankee Tunnel officers knew that working in large, secret groups produced significant results, failure was costly for everyone: the guards became surly; the commandant, whose position was always threatened by an escape, became more inquisitive about things out of place; the food rations diminished in quantity or quality; and suspicious or misbehaving prisoners were put into solitary confinement for long periods of time for the slightest offense. Boxes from home were no longer delivered but opened in the warehouse across the street, their contents pillaged at night. Recaptured escapers learned that their nonescaping comrades, as members of a captive community, had been treated as accomplices in the escape whether they had participated actively or passively cooperated. Thus the Yankee Tunnel experience taught valuable lessons applicable to future wartime escapers in general: escape challenged the notion that POWs were simply under a forced quarantine; the innocents were considered as guilty as the escapers; and, for the sake of a few, many suffered.

Sometimes, men crazed by fever, malnutrition, and disease attempted improbable and deceptive opportunity escapes. Although they ate about as well as the Confederate soldiers on the battle line, Union prisoners, who were more accustomed to a hardier diet of hardtack and beef, were given some uncooked bacon, a little tough beef, some raw cornmeal, and salt, fare that barely kept active soldiers alive. Hunger robbed men of their good sense, and these impromptu escapes failed. One Union captive, Robert Love, imprisoned at Belle Isle prison camp near Richmond, made a desperate rush past his guard and jumped into the James River. Although a number of Confederates fired at Love, he reached the other side unscathed, only to be met by his captors. Love was marched back to Belle Isle in chains and died shortly thereafter.

On the other hand, some unlikely escape plans yielded handsome rewards. One fortunate Union prisoner, John Bray, spent his time at the Pemberton prison factory trading clothes with his Confederate guards. In time, Bray had enough Confederate clothing to pass for a Confederate soldier. He simply held a blanket over his shoulders, and when he removed it, he was taken immediately for a Confederate soldier. Bray eventually returned to his unit and fought again. In the winter of 1864–65, James Hancock managed an escape from Castle Thunder, a prison for Union enlisted men in Richmond. Hancock pretended to be dead, and his live body was deposited in a coffin. The wagon carrying him to the cemetery had no tail, and Hancock slipped away into Richmond. The Confederates, knowing that Hancock was probably stalking around the city, found him at dinner in a hotel posing as a government contract man. However, he deceived his guards and made another escape. They finally caught up with the actor Hancock and delivered him back to the jail. The Confederates admired his nerve and perseverance and took no retribution. At the war's end, they set him free.[47]

Several Union single escapes were made from the prison at Salisbury, Virginia. Junius Browne, a war correspondent for the *New York Times,* escaped by making himself so familiar to his guards that when he visited the hospital, they let him through without having to show a pass. Along with a fellow inmate, Browne passed through the gate and hid in a nearby barn, and the *ad hoc* partnership made its way home. One group of prisoners in Salisbury was assigned to burial detail. One of the diggers was a ventriloquist, and as the men dropped dirt on the dead man's body, the ventriloquist threw his voice to make the dead man protest his own burial. The frightened guards scattered, and all the prisoners escaped. Other prisoners at Salisbury pricked their skin with red-hot needles and pretended to have smallpox. After being transferred to the hospital outside the stockade, the prisoners escaped.[48] In 1863, both Union and Confederate escapers were finally protected by the Union Army's General Order 100, *Instructions for the Government of Armies of the United States,* which stated, "A prisoner of war who escapes may be shot, or otherwise killed in flight; but neither death nor any other punishment shall be inflicted on him for his attempt to escape, which the law of order does not consider a crime." [49]

From 1863 to the end of the Civil War, escapers enjoyed a reasonable chance of success if they devised a means to leave the prison camp quickly and gain some distance from the search parties. In the Deep South, Union escapers consistently received help from slaves, who knew that the Union Army intended to free them. Generous with the scant rations they possessed for their own needs, they provided food, shelter, guides, boats, and anything else they could. Many slaves went far beyond passive assistance; they jeopardized their lives to help Union escapers by passing them along from one to another in a kind of *ad hoc* underground railroad, a practice that became common throughout the South. Union prisoners like Morris C. Foote, who escaped in 1864 from Camp Sorghum, Columbia, South Carolina, enjoyed such outside assistance when his turn came to find Union lines.[50]

Civil War POWs on both sides were never certain how or when to make their escape, yet many felt strongly that a try was worth the risk. Most soldiers endured the ordeal of being quarantined in a stockade, a converted armory, or a former fairground. Those who rejected the condition of captivity showed faith in their ability to escape and simultaneously developed those means that enabled escape to take place. Few escapers, Union or Confederate, enjoyed any real success if they depended solely on luck. Like their predecessors in the Revolution, they needed and often received direct help from others. When Confederates fled prisons in the North, soldiers like Berry Benson often used deception on their way south to Dixie, or, like Decimus et Ultimus Barziza and others, north to

Canada. Some Confederates relied on help from Southern sympathizers in contested areas or relatives who lived in the North, who provided money, maps, railroad timetables, clothes, and other items that escaping Confederates needed to make their way south. The *Maple Leaf* escapers fled quickly into contested regions of Virginia and found willing civilian accomplices who helped them locate Confederate partisan units. Working to the advantage of both Union and Confederate soldiers on the run were shared cultural characteristics. As evidenced by John Hunt Morgan's train trip, a Confederate escaper did not necessarily stand out in a Union crowd, nor did a Union escaper in a Confederate crowd.

With so much riding on escapes based on "pure cussedness," intolerable cruelty, and military duty, prisoners were willing to risk everything they had, including their lives, even if there was only the smallest hope for escape. Escaping soldiers from both sides may have looked hungry, dirty, and suspicious, but those characteristics were common to many soldiers at that time. Escapes on both sides ceased only when the war ended in April 1865. In the Great War some fifty years later, American prisoners devised more ways and means to break away from quarantine, not in Georgia, Ohio, New York, Maryland, Virginia, or the Carolinas but in a Europe torn apart by massive, modern, warring armies.

6

Homo Ludens:
Escape *De Luxe* in the Great War

The idea of war as a noble game of honor still lingered even in the dehumanized wars of today as an exchange of civilities with the enemy.

—Johan Huizinga (1944)

In the nineteenth and twentieth centuries, international agreements attempted to formalize the neutral status of POW quarantine. The Hague Conventions of 1899 and 1907 and the Geneva Conventions of 1929 and 1949 addressed some of the problems created by war and provided rules in law for the treatment of POWs.[1] The American Army adopted the Hague rules and superimposed them onto its 1914 version of the *Rules of Land Warfare.*[2] The *Rules* acted as a guideline for action by American soldiers toward their enemies and contained what was generally understood at the time as the POW code of behavior. They defined a POW as "an individual whom the enemy, upon capture, temporarily deprives of his personal liberty on account of his participation directly or indirectly in the hostilities, and who the laws of war prescribe shall be treated with certain considerations."[3] They forbade commanding officers from granting large-scale paroles to masses of surrendered troops in the field, and individual soldiers from giving parole to captured enemy soldiers without first obtaining proper authority. The *Rules* also reminded American soldiers that POWs were subject to the rules of the detaining power, not to the whims of individual enemy soldiers, and that escape remained serious business.

For prisoners in the Great War, a nonviolent escape or an escape in which there was no conspiracy among many prisoners to foment an insurrection or a rebellion against the captors, if followed by a recapture, was tantamount to being AWOL, or *Absent Without Official Leave,* and was treated relatively lightly. The American *Rules of Land Warfare* (1914), stated, "Escaped prisoners who are retaken before being able to rejoin their own army or before leaving the territory occupied by the army which captured them are liable to disciplinary punishment." These rules excluded the death sentence.[4] However, after an officer had given his word—parole—written or verbal, not to escape under specific circumstances, it became a crime to escape, often punishable by death. On the other hand, custom and tradition mandated that officers not on parole at least try to escape, knowing full well that a prisoner could be shot while escaping or, if recaptured, tried and punished by close or even solitary confinement for extended periods of time.[5]

Although a conspiracy to conduct an unarmed mass escape is different from an armed insurrection, captors feared them just the same. To quell camp rebellions at Andersonville, the Confederates kept several cannons aimed at the prison compound at all times. The Confederate *Maple Leaf* escape at sea became an armed insurrection and a mass escape at the same time. Col. Thomas Rose's Yankee Tunnel was an unarmed great escape. In both these last cases, after the prisoners broke out, the detaining side was forced to divert valuable combat troops to search for and recapture the escaped POWs. Although POWs may be unarmed, or minimally armed with home-made or obsolete weapons, a mass escape attempt or a camp rebellion puts both the conspirators and the innocent nonparticipants at risk. Furthermore, soldiers ordered to put down camp rebellions are notoriously impatient in dealing with prisoners in revolt.

For these reasons at least, conspiracies for the purpose of creating general uprisings and escapes have been dealt with harshly. Article 70 of the *Rules of Land Warfare* (1914) restated *General Order 100* (1863), Article 77: "If a conspiracy is discovered, the purpose of which is a united or general escape, the conspirators may be rigorously punished, even with death; and capital punishment may also be inflicted upon POWs who are found to have plotted rebellion against the authority of the captors, whether in union with fellow prisoners or other persons."[6] Although POWs have the right to attempt an escape, the sanctions against conspiring to organize an armed rebellion against camp authorities remain severe. Such severity surfaced thirty years later against the fifty unarmed British and Commonwealth prisoners from Stalag Luft III, whom the Gestapo executed illegally in 1944; rightly against the Japanese POWs who planned the prison revolts at Featherston, New Zealand, and Cowra, Australia, in 1944; and still later in the North Korean prison revolt against the Americans at Koje-Do in 1952.

During World War I, Allied and German airmen kept the notion of the chivalry of single combat alive in spite of a war with the highest technology available and nearly unlimited human destruction. Pilot and escaper Pat O'Brien commented that "the only chivalry in this war on the German side of the trenches has been displayed by the officers of the German Flying Corps."[7] In *Escapers All* (1932), J. R. Ackerley affirmed that German, British, Commonwealth, and American pilots engaged in a kind of single combat more akin to medieval duels than to technowar full of heavy ground artillery and mass infantry attacks against fortified trench lines. Whereas acts of chivalry were rare in the trenches, opposing airmen regularly showed one another a ceremonial respect and ritual courtesy practically unknown among the other combatants.[8]

Johan Huizinga commented that "the idea of war as a noble game of honor still lingered even in the dehumanized wars of today as an exchange of civilities with the enemy."[9] The nobility in what Huizinga called *Homo Ludens* required rule-oriented combat between equal titans. In effect, certain activities in war became a form of play. In World War I, these dangerous games began over the field of battle as pilots dueled each other in their Fokkers, Sopwith Camels, Nieuports, and Spads. For prisoners, these games continued in the prison camps, with escape one of the most competitive. For the pilots at least, without this unique form of interpersonal exchange, human conduct in war evolved into a state of mere butchery, as was the case in the trenches.[10]

What began ostensibly as quarantine captivities under the Hague Conventions of 1899 and 1907 evolved into duels of cat-and-mouse evasions of boredom. Looking back on life behind barbed wire during World War I, one British soldier, Wallace Ellison, stated, "I'm convinced that I was kept mentally fresh by the constant planning to effect my escape."[11] The alternative was unbearable monotony, what medical researchers called "barbed wire disease," which often prompted suicides. The American pilot and future popular author James Norman Hall wrote, "The monotony of the existence was hard to endure . . . ennui became boredom, or boredom ennui, whichever term is the more expressive for this disease in its aggravated form."[12]

The game's human motivations lay somewhere between the emotional low caused by defeat, capture, and the extreme boredom of living in a prison camp, and the incredible high caused by pulling something over on one's captors. Older generations of American soldiers had learned the art in earlier wars. The World War I generation learned it again, this time from French soldiers like Charles de Gaulle, who, following his capture in 1916, treated his escapes and recaptures as a sacred military duty, and from the many British POWs who viewed escape as a public school game of one-upmanship. Capt. Charles de Gaulle, a member of Colonel Pétain's 33d Regiment, fought at Verdun, where he was severely wounded and taken prisoner at Duoramont in 1916. During his captivity of two years and eight months, he made five unsuccessful attempts to escape and finally wound up at the Ingolstadt fortress for committed escapers. Capt. William Stephenson, a Canadian flyer who later became known as "Intrepid," one of England's unique millionaire superspies during World War II, flew the horrid Sopwith Camel during World War I. On July 28, 1918, as Stephenson broke up a German formation of Fokker D-VIIs, a French observer fired a burst of rounds into his airplane by accident and hit Stephenson in the leg. Left with no choice, Stephenson landed the Camel behind enemy lines, took another round in the leg, and surrendered. After several fumbling attempts, he learned how to prepare his exit in great detail, and finally escaped from a maximum security camp at Holzminden in October with the camp commandant's family portrait in his pocket.[13] Having models such as these, the pragmatic Americans, pilots and ground soldiers alike, took very little time to fashion their own escape commitments.

Following a shootdown, many pilots reported that their captors invited them to lunch in the opposing officers' mess, one that in all probability served the best food they received for the duration of their captivity. Regardless how formal the ceremonies between these knights of the air may have been, they ended when the pilots reached the enemy's permanent prison camps deep in Germany. Life became grim, and no ceremonial lunches were served. Food was inadequate and had to be supplemented by generous Red Cross parcels shipped from Switzerland. Prisoners froze in winter and roasted in the summer; guards became surly and mischievous; the only form of chivalry that remained open was the game of escape.

The first American POWs to escape from Germany were among those adventurers who refused to wait for the United States to enter the war and instead volunteered to fight with the Allied forces. Among the pilots, the escapers included Harold Willis, Everett Buckley, and Thomas Hitchcock, Jr. with the French, and Pat O'Brien with the Canadians in the British Royal Flying Corps. Escaping from prison camps or jumping from moving trains, these soldiers proved that escape, although hazardous at best, was possible. Buckley and Willis went south to Switzerland; the others managed to filter into neutral Holland.

Everett Buckley of Chicago served with the French Escadrille N-65 and was shot down during aerial combat over Dun-sur-Meuse on September 6,

1917. His aircraft turned upside down when it struck the ground, and he was a bit stunned at first. After Buckley's capture, he was taken to an old house in a nearby village for initial questioning by German intelligence officers. From there he was transported to the fortress of Montmédy, where he was kept in a cell for eighteen days, much of the time alone and fed exclusively on bread and water. After eighteen days' confinement in this fortress, he found that his treatment improved dramatically.

Removed to what the Allied officers called the "Microphone Hotel" at Karlsruhe, Buckley joined several English and French officers for his first good meal. Running his hand underneath the table at supper, he discovered a card on which was written, "Be careful, there is a dictaphone in the lamp."[14] Over the center table was a large hanging lamp, and upon investigation, he saw the dictaphone. The Germans believed in passive intelligence gathering, that is, in obtaining military information in an unthreatening manner. German intelligence felt that by placing Allied officers together in a room soon after capture and providing them with a good meal, they would relax, and their casual conversations would contain references to mutual experiences on the front. Creating such a homey situation, they believed, would also encourage prisoners to discuss personal matters that might yield valuable military information.

At the end of five days, Buckley was taken to the officers' prison camp near Karlsruhe, where he remained for six weeks. From Karlsruhe he was sent to Heuberg, at the entrance to the Black Forest, where he stayed for two months. During his captivity, Buckley attempted three escapes before eventual success. The first escape took place at Heuberg. He wrote, "I escaped from this camp by breaking through the fence. I managed to reach the frontier, but was caught just as I was going over. They sent me back to Heuberg where I was threatened several times with a bayonet because I refused to do road-making in an artillery fort. The presence of other prisoners at the time was the only thing that saved my life."

Since he could see Switzerland through the barbed-wire fence, a second attempt was inevitable. The second try took place at Donaueschingen, only a few days after Buckley was put to work on a farm. He recalled, "I ran about five kilometers when I came to the Danube and was unable to cross. Once more they caught me and sent me back to Heuberg. I was placed in prison for thirty-one days, where I was given two hundred grams of bread a day, with water, and a plate of soup every fifth day. They permitted me to go out and wash and get my drinking-water. At the termination of my prison sentence, I stayed ten days in the camp at Heuberg and was then sent to Varingenstadt on a farm." He remained on the farm for one day. After his punishment tour, he joined an *ad hoc* escape group that was ready to break out. According to Buckley, "That night I cut the bars out of a window and escaped with seven other prisoners. Although I managed to get as far as Bolhlege [sic], I was again caught by a sentry and sent back to Heuberg, which meant another thirty-one days in prison as before."

In July 1918, Buckley defied his captors one more time. After being sent to a farm he noticed a wooded hill on the edge of a field, a natural exit route. About three o'clock one afternoon, he saw an opportune moment and gradually worked his way toward the woods. He suddenly dropped his pitchfork and made a dash. According to Buckley, "My escape was discovered immediately and about twenty people joined in the chase. The guards were very much surprised and shot wild, which enabled me to reach cover safely. There I hid until things had quieted down a bit. Knowing that dogs would be used to follow my trail, I secured some wild garlic and thoroughly rubbed my boots with it. I then walked for six nights with nothing to eat but raw potatoes. I had previously provided myself with a map and a compass, which I had secreted on my person, and set my course for the Swiss frontier some seventy-five miles distant." From his previous attempts, Buckley knew the rules. He hid in the daytime and traveled only at night.

On the morning of July 27, 1918, Buckley arrived at a point near the Swiss border. Here he found three lines of guards and patrols with dogs pacing up and down between them. Crawling into a wheat field, he carefully studied the situation all day while preparing his plan to slip between the guards that night. His luck held; it was raining and very dark. He wrote:

> At half-past ten, I began my painful journey, crawling on my stomach. I tied my shoes about my neck so they would not scrape on any object, stuffed my handkerchief in my mouth so the dogs would not hear me breathe, and rubbed myself thoroughly with wild garlic so the dogs would not smell me. These preliminaries over, I wriggled along slowly and painfully until I saw the dim outline of the first sentry. I then worked away from this sentry until I could pass by him, and then wriggled along until I came in sight of the second sentry. By following this plan, I succeeded in getting by all three sentries. I then walked until I came to a signboard and found that I was in Ramsen in Switzerland.

The first people he met were two musicians. They took him to the military police who first questioned him and then took him to a train at Stein. Later he changed trains for Schaffhausen, where a French Swiss gave him a new suit of clothes, a pair of shoes, a cap, dinner, and a bed. On July 28, Buckley arrived in Bern, where the American Red Cross fitted him out with new clothing and gave him some money. He then returned to duty in France.

Thomas Hitchcock, Jr., of New York, was also a volunteer flier with the French. After his shootdown and capture, Hitchcock kept his compass hidden, hoarded food, and made plans to escape, but to no avail. His problem was one of opportunity. Finally, an occasion presented itself. During a transfer from the prison camp at Lechfeld to another camp, Hitchcock and two other prisoners were put under the charge of an elderly German guard, an obvious opportunity. They were traveling in an ordinary passenger coach, and as the train pulled into the station at the city of Ulm, Hitchcock realized that he had no map. His compass was not enough; he needed a map to make a successful escape. While the old guard slept, Hitchcock picked his pocket. Awakening, the guard reached for his map and found it missing. Knowing that it was now or never, Hitchcock rose from his seat, opened the door of the coach, and jumped out. The train began to move, and Hitchcock darted for the bushes close to the tracks. The old guard found himself in a serious dilemma: he had two other prisoners to guard and one in the bush. He cried out for his prisoner to return, but Hitchcock was already on his way. After the train left Ulm, Hitchcock walked seventy miles out of Germany and never saw an enemy soldier during his entire time on the road.[15]

Lt. Pat O'Brien, RFC, of Momence, Illinois, began flying in Chicago in 1912. In 1916, the United States conducted military operations in northern Mexico, and O'Brien joined the American Flying Corps. When it began to look as if the United States might remain neutral in World War I, O'Brien resigned and joined the Royal Flying Corps in Victoria, British Columbia. After initial cadet training, he arrived in France in May 1917, and joined one of the four British "scout" or fighter squadrons stationed about eighteen miles to the rear of the Ypres line. According to O'Brien, "You are expected to pick fights and not wait until they come to you!"[16] In O'Brien's case, the fight came sooner than he anticipated.

On August 17, 1917, a day of close calls, O'Brien flew his aircraft for the last time over enemy lines. German aircraft swarmed in anger against his squadron. Suddenly the worst happened; a hail of bullets splintered his instruments. A bullet pierced his upper lip, and he appeared doomed. His plane dove to the earth in a spinning nose dive, one that meant certain death for the pilot caught in its clutches. O'Brien eluded death, however; he woke up in a German field hospital, a POW on an operating table.

At least he was alive. When his condition improved somewhat, the Germans sent him to the officers' POW facility, a former civilian prison at Courtrai, Belgium, for temporary internment prior to his removal to a permanent POW camp inside Germany.

Few POWs remained in Belgium very long: Courtrai was just a holding tank. O'Brien discovered that there was talk of escape. What were the chances? They depended on the opportunities. Wild ideas were tossed about, ideas that never had the slightest chance of evolving into reality. One POW suggested that they disguise themselves as women. Bad idea: most of the British and Allied POWs were taller than Belgian or German women. Another POW suggested that the group steal a German Gotha bomber and fly it back to British lines. No chance. O'Brien dreamt at one point that he could hide out in a hangar, steal a German fighter aircraft, and fly it back to friendly lines. Bad idea: in time, the Allied POWs learned that German security was too tight for that kind of exploit. Trains, however, were another matter.

After three weeks in Courtrai, the Germans decided to transfer seven officers to the Strasbourg reprisal camp in German Alsace. It was felt that if POWs were kept there, then the Allies had to make the obvious decision to avoid bombing the town. O'Brien knew that if he made the trip, he was about to spend the rest of the war as a POW. No one in 1917 knew how long the war was going to last, but it was time to devise a real plan and establish a real commitment, for himself at least and for anyone else who wanted to come along. The "promised land" for Allied POWs in northern Germany or Belgium was neutral Holland, but the Dutch border was heavily guarded.

O'Brien had a compass as part of his flying gear, but he needed a decent map. After a clever deception enabled him to steal a map, he stashed some food in his knapsack and waited for the train trip south. Eight POWs climbed on a German troop train while the German officers checked the accompanying troops' weapons. O'Brien knew that this trip was his best chance. He wrote, "From the moment the train started on its way to Germany the thought kept coming to my head that unless I could make my escape before we reached that reprisal camp, I might as well make up my mind that the war was over." He wanted everyone to jump off the train, but the others refused. He recalled, "When I passed the idea on to my comrades, they turned it down." Nevertheless, he was determined to make the attempt. "The idea of remaining a prisoner of war indefinitely," he wrote, "went against my grain." After several fits and starts, O'Brien put his plan into action. Telling the guards that cigarette smoke bothered his throat, he opened the train's window. When the train slowed to about thirty miles an hour, he waited no longer. In an instant, O'Brien jumped up, shoved his feet and legs out of the window, dropped to the rail bed, and became a POW on the run.

His evasion was long and arduous. O'Brien walked from Germany to Luxembourg in nine days, using the North Star as his best navigational aid. He swam rivers and canals, avoided villages and civilians in general, and stole potatoes, vegetables, and clothes when he could. It took another nine days to walk from Luxembourg to Belgium. For the duration of the evasion, he hungered for a real meal, but concealment was more important. Desperate for something warm to eat, he finally asked some Belgian civilians for help and got it. In all, he spent eight weeks in Belgium, but he still had to cross the dangerous border to Holland. For that he needed more than a meal, he needed connections. His luck held. He knocked on the right door, a Flemish farmer who knew someone who helped to get escaped POWs through the border to Holland.

Unfortunately, O'Brien had run into an escape scam; this was not a partisan resistance line coordinated in Belgium and France from London, as were *Comet* and others in World War II, but one handled privately for money by entrepreneurial Belgian citizens, more an unscrupulous gang than a band of patriots. After he received a dummy Spanish passport, the Belgians told him the price. O'Brien was shocked. There would be no deal, but he kept the passport and left their company. He spent the next five days in an empty house, scavenging food from the garbage at night and hiding during the day. Deception again became necessary. On several occasions, O'Brien pretended to be a deaf mute. That cover worked well while he hid in cities or small towns because he could not speak Flemish, French, or German. He learned how to walk like a Belgian, and could saunter along the streets and roads without drawing any attention from the German occupation forces.

The way to the Belgian-Dutch border was short, but it was electrically wired and well guarded day and night. On November 19, 1917, O'Brien arrived at the border where he stopped to consider how to get across. Many of his initial ideas were bizarre. First, he thought of using a pole to vault himself over the wire. No, he was in no physical shape to do it. Stilts? This was not a circus act. Next he tried using a makeshift ladder and nearly electrocuted himself. The simplest and most obvious method suddenly came to him. Dig! "If I couldn't get over it," he wrote, "what was the matter in getting under it?" After digging furiously for two hours with the only tools available, his hands, O'Brien worked his way under the electrified fence and then under the outer fence to Holland. He had little notion about where he was or how to contact friendly forces. What was important was the fact that "I was out of the power of the Germans, and that was enough." More was to come, however, as King George V invited O'Brien for an audience. The king told the awestruck airman, "I fully appreciate all the service rendered us by Americans before the States entered the war." Later, O'Brien reflected, "When I first joined the Royal Flying Corps I never expected to see the inside of Buckingham Palace, much less to be received by the King."

After the United States entered the war in 1917, American pilots were taken prisoner regularly. Unknown to them, the Germans put them through the same stressful regimen they used against the other Allied POWs. Norman Archibald, reflecting upon his captivity after the war, wrote, "The morning was an eternity . . . arranging the bed, changing the table, placing a chair in a corner with the hope it might be overlooked, fiddling with the shutters, walking, walking . . . thinking and planning to escape." [17] Archibald was a keen observer. He realized, even as a POW in 1918, that Germany could not stand much more war. He saw that large quantities of supplies flowed into France and knew that the German civilian population was starving at home. He suspected, too, that the Allies were planning to mount a spring offensive in 1918, and the thought of a long captivity plagued him. He wondered, "When would the war end? What if Germany were not defeated?" A fellow prisoner responded, "I've heard that after eighteen months prisoners are exchanged." Archibald lamented, "Eighteen months? God! A year and a half in these holes . . . we won't be here." After deciding that an escape was problematical but possible, indeed their only salvation, they plotted a getaway. He wrote: "Escape! We must escape! No alternative; no other solution. Dreaming of freedom we whispered that if ever moved from here we must judge distances and watch for landmarks." [18] But their talk went in circles. "Escape, from here, was impossible . . . lingering looks towards France were tantalizing. Now hopeless, we were resigned to the present." [19] Archibald remained a POW until November 29, 1918, eighteen days after the Armistice, when he joined the first group of repatriated American POWs who boarded trains for Bern, Switzerland, the headquarters of the American Red Cross.

Lt. George Puryear, a trained lawyer from Memphis, Tennessee, was a member of the 95th Aero Squadron. After an air combat on July 26, 1918, he landed his airplane on what he assumed was friendly territory to take the surrender of the German pilot he had shot down. To his surprise, German soldiers arrived quickly and nabbed him. Rather than taking a surrender, the impetuous and cavalier Puryear was made a POW. He commented, "Never in my life have I felt so low as I did at that moment, and I hope I shall never feel it again." In response, Puryear became an escaper. He wrote, "People often ask me how one occupies the time shut up in a prisoner-of-war camp, and I answer that, as for myself, I spent most of my time planning and working to get away." [20]

Puryear was serious. Shortly after his capture, he and a French officer escaped from the Rastatt prison camp by climbing down ropes from their cells. After three days on the run, his French partner, Lt. André Conneau, misread their map and took the pair west instead of south toward Switzerland. With their escape supplies running out, they formulated a wild plan to go to an airdrome, steal a German airplane, and fly it back to Allied lines. Puryear wrote, "We had not gone very far when a German sentry stepped directly in front of us. If we had been in condition, we could have run . . . but being leg-weary . . . and exhausted, we did not attempt to run." [21] Tired, hungry, and sick with a severe cough from the cold, wet weather, Puryear and Conneau were readily recaptured and returned to Rastatt.

For his escape, Puryear spent five days in solitary confinement, then was sent to the officers' camp at Karlsruhe, where he met other escape-minded Americans, then on to Villingen in August 1918. With thirteen officers working in two four-man teams, one three-man team, and one partnership, the Villingen breakout on October 6, 1918, became the only great escape planned and executed by Americans in World War I. Of the officers in the plan, five actually got away: Harold Willis, Edouard Isaacs, Rowan Tucker, Blanchard Battle, and George Puryear. Battle and Tucker were both recaptured and returned to Villingen until repatriation; the other three kept on going.[22] Puryear avoided recapture and swam across the Rhine River to Switzerland near the town of Waldshut. In Berne, American authorities told him that he was the first American officer to escape. An American private arrived two days earlier.

Frank Savicki of Shenandoah, Pennsylvania, was the first American army private to escape from Germany to Switzerland. Captured at Château Thierry on July 13, 1918, Savicki was also taken to Rastatt where he received food, clothing, and some German money. Fifteen days later, the Germans transferred him to a farm near the Swiss border, where he observed that the war had taken a heavy toll upon the German civilian population in terms of starvation. Potatoes sold at one mark each. Horses became meat after they died, and general supplies were scarce.

Pvt. Frank Savicki, 4th Infantry, 3d Division, in World War I. Private Savicki was taken prisoner by Germans southeast of Château Thierry, south of the river Marne, on July 23, 1918. After two months and fifteen days in German hands, he escaped by fleeing across the Swiss border. Courtesy of the U.S. Army Military History Institute

On October 8, 1918, only a month before hostilities officially came to an end, Savicki escaped from the farm and arrived in Switzerland two days later. Other captured American soldiers and airmen followed suit.

Robert A. Anderson, a 1st lieutenant in the U.S. Air Service (Aviation Section of the Signal Corps), was assigned to the 40th RAF Squadron. In the course of his shootdown and subsequent capture on August 27, 1918, Anderson was wounded by a bullet below his left knee and shrapnel in his hip. After he received first aid from German medical personnel, Anderson was sent to a hospital in the large POW holding facility at Mons. From there he was taken to the large French prison at Fresnes, where he began planning his escape. Following his first attempt, Anderson was thrown into solitary confinement for fourteen days, where he was given only bread and *ersatz* (acorn) coffee.[23] Undeterred, Anderson bided his time; he had only to wait awhile before meeting and working with other like-minded POWs.

John Owen Donaldson, of Washington, D.C., was an Air Service pilot attached to the 32d RAF Squadron. He was shot down on September 21, 1918, while flying a combat patrol not far from Douai, where the Germans operated a large camp for recently captured POWs. After a short stay in Douai, Donaldson was taken to Condé, a holding facility for men being sent to Germany, a camp with the usual poor facilities: inadequate lodgings; blankets full of lice and fleas, known as "cooties" to the POWs; no heat, light, soap, or toilet facilities. After his first escape attempt and recapture, Donaldson, like Anderson, received the standard two-week sentence of solitary confinement on bread and water. British POWs, knowing that Donaldson would be considerably debilitated on that diet, managed to sneak food into his cell. Once released from confinement, he was transferred to Fresnes, where he again began looking for a way out. He met Anderson.

Lt. T. E. Tillinghast, a native of Westerly, Rhode Island, was captured on September 23, 1918, two miles southwest of Cambrai. After holding him only one night for questioning, the Germans shipped him to Fresnes, where he met the others. A team of five, consisting of Anderson, Donaldson, Tillinghast, Oscar Mandel, and a British NCO, escaped together by working their way through loose tiles on the roof, and at 10:00 P.M. on September 26, 1918, the escapers had reached the street. Mandel and the British NCO separated from the group and traveled to Brussels, where they were recaptured; Anderson, Donaldson, and Tillinghast crossed into neutral Holland at 2:00 A.M. on October 23, 1918, less than a month before the Armistice.[24]

The premier American escapers of World War I, who achieved some recognition for their partnership escape from the officers' camp at Villingen, were Harold B. Willis and Lt. Edouard Isaacs, USN. Willis was an adventurer and ambulance driver turned combat pilot who ended up serving as a pilot-sergeant in the American-French *Lafayette Escadrille,* and its only member to be captured by the Germans. After he was shot down over Verdun on March 1, 1917, he was sent first to Karlsruhe, then to the aviators' camps at Landshut and Gütersloh. Willis finally joined the other Americans at the officers' prison camp in Villingen, about fifty miles from the Swiss border, on July 9, 1918. At this time, the Spanish embassy in Berlin put considerable pressure on the Germans to incarcerate the Americans together, so they could receive mail and Red Cross packages.[25]

Willis was a committed natural escaper. He had taken part in two unsuccessful attempts before he was sent to Villingen, where he met Navy Lt. Edouard Isaacs (a.k.a. Izac), the only American naval officer taken prisoner at sea by a German submarine. Isaacs was serving as an officer on board the USS *President Lincoln,* when the German submarine *U-90* torpedoed it on May 31, 1918, during its return from Europe. Of the 715 officers, crew, and passengers, 26 were lost in the sinking; except for Isaacs and the fatalities, the rest were rescued from their lifeboats by two patrolling American destroyers, the USS *Warrington* and *Smith.* During the eleven days, from May 31 to June 11, 1918, that he spent aboard the *U-90,* he learned what he could about German submarine operations, observing, "I knew where the subs landed and how they landed."[26] Looking back, Isaacs recalled that he wanted desperately to relay this information to Adm. William S. Sims, USN, in London.

After first interning Isaacs in the zoological gardens at Karlsruhe, the Germans decided to move him to the officers' camp at Villingen. While his guards slept and the train slowed on the tracks to about thirty miles per hour, Isaacs seized an opportunity to jump through an open window, but injuries from landing on the steel rails prevented him from dashing into the surrounding woods. The train continued moving, but as soon as his guards realized what had happened, they pulled the emergency cord. When the train halted, the angry guards got off and promptly recaptured the injured Isaacs. After severely beating him, the guards delivered Isaacs to the commandant at Villingen, who told him bluntly that if he ever tried to escape again, he would be shot. For the escape attempt he was given two weeks of solitary confinement in his cell.[27] After he did his time, Isaacs was turned loose into the camp population, where he met Willis.

The Villingen POW camp was about fifty miles from the Swiss frontier. Discipline was strict but fair. Prisoners were confined in a small pen of huts, which afforded them no view of the outside, but they knew they were on the edge of the Black Forest. Willis, among others, thought about the odds of a successful breakout. According to Willis, "I should not get such a chance again so I determined to escape alone as soon as possible."[28] His first plan called for a solitary escape through a weak point he found in the barbed wire, but he encountered difficulties with some Russians. The Treaty of Brest-Litovsk ended the German-Russian war in 1917, and the Russian prisoners had split into two distinct groups: those who supported the czar and partisans of the revolutionary Bolsheviks. The czarist Russians remained friendly and loyal to the British, French, and American prisoners in the camp; the Bolsheviks,

Navy Lt. Edouard Isaacs (a.k.a. Izak), the only American naval officer taken prisoner at sea by a German submarine. Isaacs was serving on board the USS *President Lincoln* when the German submarine *U-90* torpedoed it on May 31, 1918. After his successful escape from the officers' camp in Villengen on October 6, 1918, Isaacs returned to duty and received the Medal of Honor. Courtesy of the U.S. Naval Historical Center however, often cooperated with the Germans in uncovering escape plans. Willis noted that some Bolsheviks overheard others talking about his plans and concluded that they gave him away. He recalled, "The day before I was off, the interior guard was doubled and a new wire fence was constructed at the place I had intended to use." [29]

After both Willis and Isaacs failed to escape on their first attempt, they pooled their determination, resources, and skills. Rather than merely contemplating what he wanted to do, Willis began collecting and hiding provisions and quietly gathering information about the best route to Switzerland. One of the French officers had hidden a map in the sole of his boot, and while the Frenchman kept watch, Willis laboriously copied the map for his own use. Soon after, the Americans discovered that the Germans planned to move the Russians to another camp, and it was this transfer that prompted the escape. Such an event meant that the Germans would search the camp closely for contraband, and the Americans knew that the German guards were precise and thorough. Months of preparations would be for nothing if the hoarded materials were suddenly discovered.

When the time was ripe, those who planned to escape made their move. In preparation for his role, Isaacs cut through the bars in the windows of the various rooms and constructed three bridges made of pine boards taken from the cases of food sent by the Red Cross. Isaacs knew that the Germans used dogs to pursue their escaping POWs. The solution to this problem was to spread ground black or red pepper around as the escapers left the compound on October 6, 1918. The dogs, in their enthusiasm for the hunt, sniffed the pepper deep into their nostrils, and even from a distance Isaacs and Willis heard the results. They knew that they had thrown the dogs off the trail.

After seven days and nights spent evading recapture, the two men approached the rushing currents of the Rhine River and realized that success meant a dangerous swim in piercingly cold water. Willis immersed himself first; Isaacs followed. Beginning in a feeder stream, they came to its confluence with the Rhine. First Isaacs:

> With a powerful blow the current struck me, and I was swept away toward the center of the river. . . . I made rapid progress until the center of the stream was reached. Then the fight began. . . . Mustering all my strength I made a final effort and succeeded in passing through the worst part of the center. But the exertion took the last of my strength; and although the shore loomed up less than thirty yards away, I could go no farther. So, turning over on my back I commended my soul to my God and closed my eyes. Instantly my feet touched the rocks.[30]

Willis's version of the story, however, contains more detail:

> We followed the bank. It was built into a stone parapet-embankment. A thick mist was curling up from the river, hiding the water. At several places I lowered Isaacs over the edge, but he could not see how far it was down or get a foothold, and it seemed a long way down. We seemed to be getting higher and higher above the river and the parapet embankment to be a sheer wall below us. We decided to make a detour back and find the stream we had crossed the night before at Havenstein. This would run down into the Rhine and must pass through a gap in the stone embankment. We moved with great caution.
>
> At last we came to the village and then the stream. We did the last hundred yards down the stream with such care that it took us two hours. At last we found a gentle slope, and crawling down that we stepped into the water. Our stream ran over a rocky bottom and was full of sand and stones. We had to be careful to make no mistakes. The noise of the water was a safeguard, but we must make not the slightest sound that might draw attention to us. Step by step we followed the stream. We passed under a railway bridge. Then we crept up a tunnel, and then along a second, where the stream, by a series of natural steps, reached the level of the Rhine. The water was terribly cold, but we hardly felt it, for we were heated up with nervous excitement. As there was certainly a sentry above us, we had to keep our bodies under water, and we did not leave the middle of the stream until a dark line showed us the junction of stream and river.
>
> In spite of the mist we could see the opposite bank, so there was no danger of losing our way. We dared not take off our clothes, as our white skins might be visible from above. Suddenly the current took me, and swept me rapidly out towards deep water. I managed to get off my fur-lined waistcoat, and then struck out. It was a nightmare. Although I swam with all my strength, the current continually swept me back towards the German shore. Realizing that I could make no progress with my trousers on, I managed to undo my belt buckle and slip one leg out with the aid of the other, kicking down with the free foot. That was a moment of anguish, while I swam with one hand when two were not sufficient. I nearly sank. My trousers clung to my feet. I felt myself drowning. Horrible! Of a sudden I managed to rid myself of the trousers that dragged me down, clutching me like dead hands, and my movements were free again. Swimming easily then, I touched the Swiss shore at about a mile below the spot we had entered the river and scrambled on to a sandy beach. Saved![31]

Swimming for their lives and losing track of each other, the officers arrived separately in Switzerland, suffering from cold and hunger, on Sunday, October 13, 1918. Both were emaciated, but Willis found a tavern and had several drinks to celebrate his escape. After their adventure, they found each other again, and Swiss farmers nursed them back to health with food, warmth, and drinks. The Swiss police delivered them both to the American ambassador in Bern.[32]

Returning to their own forces, Willis and Isaacs were surprised to learn that the war was rapidly coming to an end. Unlike the POWs in the World War II stalags, they had had no radios tuned into the BBC and thus depended on German propaganda newspapers and new prisoners for war information. Because they were so poorly informed, they had expected hostilities to continue well into 1919. Both men also found they had achieved near celebrity status. For his part in the escape, Willis received the French Croix de Guerre and returned briefly to combat flying duty.[33] Like Willis, Isaacs returned to duty less than a month before the Armistice, and he received the Medal of Honor. He retired from active naval service in 1921 as a result of the injuries he received from the guards after the first escape attempt. In 1936, he was elected to Congress where he served honorably until 1947. Isaacs died on January 18, 1990, at the age of 100.[34]

No less a committed escaper but one not so fortunate was Lt. Artemus L. Gates, USN. One of the Yale pilots flying Spads over Belgium, Gates was shot down, captured, and sent by train to the officers' prison camp in Villingen. As the train chugged slowly through a tunnel, Gates saw an opportunity to escape. He slipped through a window, hitting the ground hard. Regaining his composure, he ran into the woods as fast as he could. Among the items he carried with him were bits of food for traveling and a rudimentary map containing the railroad's route. Gates was determined to find Constance, the German town near the Swiss border, and he made his way there, bypassing towns, stealing food, and traveling at night. Finally, Gates reached the border crossing, but after so many days on foot in cold weather with very little food, he ran out of energy. At the German guardhouse, Gates surrendered, saying nothing. The kindly border guards noticed his fatigue and gave him some coffee and bread. Although they knew that they faced an unsuccessful escaper, they admired his grit and sent him back to Villingen without reproach or reprisal.[35]

In light of such escapades, the Germans tightened security. James Norman Hall found himself in the middle of what he called "Escape De Luxe" in his 1930 memoir. He wrote, "As time went on, the roll calls became more frequent, and they were even held at unexpected hours during the night, for various attempts at escape had been made, and some parties of prisoners had succeeded temporarily at least. At last, those of us who remained—although we had not lost hope—were so rigorously watched that any further break for the Swiss border, two hundred miles distant, seemed doomed to failure." [36] The war's cessation and the beginnings of a German civil war put an end to Hall's frustration.

At home, as the Bolshevik Revolution spread west from Russia into Germany, the German Army began to divide against itself. Upon the invitation of his noncommunist captors, Hall's pseudo-escape began on the morning of November 8, 1918, when the American pilots in the officers' prison castle at Landshut, Bavaria, learned that fighting had broken out in the streets of Munich. To Hall and others, Germany faced an imminent and vicious civil war. Three days later, the camp inspector, Herr Pastor, entered the compound and told them that an armistice had been signed. Hall's memoir describes the scene vividly. "The war is finished," Pastor said. One officer, Lt. Robert Browning, cried out, "Then let's get ready at once. In an hour's time we shall be on our way to Paris." Pastor responded by reminding Browning and Hall prophetically, "I said that an armistice had been signed, not that there is to be an immediate release of prisoners." Then he quipped, "It may be several months before you see Paris again."

Hall, Browning, and the other POWs pleaded with Pastor that four Allied airmen could do no harm traveling to Paris. After all, the war was over. What could prevent Pastor or the guards from leaving the gate open? Pastor understood their concern and offered them a fabulous deal. "You may go," he said. "I think it is best for you to make for the Swiss border, by way of Munich, Lindau, and Lake Constance. . . . I have wired a friend of mine, an artillery officer, at Lindau. He will meet you at the station." Hall and his comrades were thrilled, even euphoric, but Pastor reminded them to keep their heads and remain cautious. "Remember," he said, "this is an escape." Pastor added with the wisdom of age and experience, "Be circumspect and very self-effacing during this journey because everything is topsy-turvy in Bavaria."

The escape team heeded Pastor's instructions, and after three days of weaving their way through revolution-torn Bavaria, Lts. Jimmie Hall, Robert Browning, Charles Codman, and Henry Lewis of the U.S. Air Service were free men. After returning to France, Hall, a man who learned to fly an airplane before he learned to drive a car, wanted one last flight in his beloved Spad. He wrote, "For a time I gave myself up to the pure joy of flying, watching the tiny shadow of my Spad leaping from summit to summit of the cloudbreak below. There was no danger of ambush now, no need to scrutinize those peaks of curling, shifting vapor for the presence of enemies."

Later in life, James Norman Hall and his close friend, Charles Bernard Nordhoff, moved to Tahiti, where together they wrote the South Seas' trilogy, *Mutiny on the Bounty* (1932), *Men Against the Sea* (1934), and *Pitcairn's Island* (1934), three very different kinds of escape stories.

The last American prisoner to escape during the Great War was Pvt. Philip Rosen of New York's East Side, a member of the American 9th Infantry Regiment. Born in Budapest, Rosen emigrated from imperial Hungary and joined the U.S. Army within ten days of America's declaration of war on Germany in 1917. In captivity, Rosen, the only American among fifteen hundred French prisoners, traveled 130 miles on foot through Belgium and northern France until he reached a rail head. Like Hall, Rosen liberated himself from a German prison camp, except that Rosen did it on November 11, 1918, Armistice Day.

In November 1918, as hostilities ended in Europe, the American Expeditionary Force held approximately forty thousand war-weary German POWs. Rations were generous, and no one escaped. The war was over, and repatriation was imminent.[37] The United States held only 1,346 German servicemen at home, mostly interned merchant sailors.[38] From time to time, some of these Germans escaped across the Rio Grande River into a sympathetic Mexico, angered by recent quarrels with President Woodrow Wilson, Gen. John Pershing, and the U.S. Army. Since neither the German nor the American governments desired any publicity or controversy over these escapes, both sides kept quiet about them.[39]

Although professional officers did have a mandate to escape, it is generally assumed that World War I POWs lived in a state of enforced quarantine and that only a few attempted to escape when the chance arose. Edouard Isaacs called the Villingen escapers "live wires" and noted that many other Allied and American prisoners were more than content to sit out the war rather than to escape. "This lethargy," he noted, "was very disappointing to me."[40] This reluctance to leave the safety of confinement and return to life in harm's way was vividly depicted in comments made by Ralph E. Ellinwood, a civilian noncombatant ambulance driver who believed that the Germans were obligated to repatriate him within three months of his capture. In his postwar narrative, Ellinwood carefully evaluated the dangers and risks that he and his fellow prisoners opted not to take:

> We had one of the greatest chances of escape that night. We three Americans talked the situation over, and decided against an attempt. The proposed plan was to take what food we had and hide in the dugout under the

church on the hill above Mont Notre Dame. Once hidden there, the line would probably pass over us and we would be left in the rear of the Allied lines. But therein lay the danger. How soon would it pass over? Our food would only last for a few days and meantime the retreating Germans would use all the dugouts and the advancing Allies would clean them out with hand grenades.[41]

Physical dangers notwithstanding, Ellinwood understood that they had other problems too, subtle issues that finally ended any motivation to escape. "Being noncombatants," he wrote, "we could not be sure of our position, or our chances. We gave up the attempt, although several Frenchmen disappeared during the night. We knew well where they had gone, and we wished them good luck and godspeed!"[42] From Ellinwood's remarks, one can see that the prisoners understood that the Hague Convention prohibited the Germans from brutally retaliating against recaptured prisoners unless they committed a violent crime during the attempt. Quarantine was boring but safe.

Because their treatment in captivity was bearable, Allied prisoners in the Great War viewed escape as more of a ludic experience—a game played from ennui—than a risky action undertaken out of fear of personal annihilation. The Red Cross organizations in the United States, England, and France cared for prisoners' needs, thereby reducing the strains on an already overburdened German military and civilian supply system.

When an escape occurred, the Germans followed a standard procedure for locating and recapturing prisoners. German authorities searched the immediate area around a camp for several days and notified railway and police stations within a two-day walk that escaped prisoners were in the area. In general, however, the Germans depended heavily on civilians and civil servants to report strangers in the area, especially rag-tag, extremely hungry individuals struggling to hide themselves. Hunger, of course, took its toll, and many escapers simply surrendered to get something to eat or to recover from exposure to the elements. While on the run, each escaper was on his own, lacking the organized escape lines that would develop in occupied Europe during World War II.

J. R. Ackerley wrote, "If ever there is another great war, there will be no more prisoners—except in so far as nations can be imprisoned within the boundaries of their lands and dart about from end to end in their efforts to escape the poisons that fall from the sky.[43] Ackerley was wrong. In the next world war, from 1939 to 1945, opposing forces took fifteen million POWs of all nationalities. In 1939, the British War Office held consultations with selected escapers from World War I to formulate a plan to assist POWs in their escape and evasion efforts. Despite lukewarm support from some British traditional military authorities, the War Office created MI-9 for that purpose.[44] The Americans established MIS-X along the same lines. For most prisoners, World War II became the century's ultimate horror; captivity became a weapon rather than a respite, and the notion of quarantine faded in the dust of total war.

7

Home Run Kriegies
Escape and Evasion in Europe

After fifty-one days of outrunning and outswimming dogs and men, I made it back to my own outfit. This ordeal doesn't even show up on my service record.
—Leon Ballard (1989)

Allied POWs in the European theater called themselves "Kriegies," short for *Kriegsgefangene,* the German word for prisoner of war. In Europe, American forces totaled 3,607,302, of whom 93,941 became Kriegies. Only 1,121 died in captivity, mostly from wounds received in combat. The Americans called a successful POW escape a home run, a term derived from baseball, if it was a nonstop trip through occupied territory, or Germany itself, and a return to friendly forces, or possibly internment in a neutral county like Sweden or Switzerland. The first American home run hitter was "Shorty" Lee Gordon, who escaped from a freight car on the way to Stalag VIIIB in Poland in November 1943.[1] The highest ranking American officer to escape was Brig. Gen. Arthur W. Vanaman, who convinced a German officer to deliver him to Swiss authorities in 1945. Allied generals escaped too. For example, French Gen. Jean de Lattre de Tassigny, sentenced to ten years' imprisonment by the Vichy authorities in France, escaped from the Riom prison and fled to England in September 1943.[2] By war's end, 7,498 Americans, or roughly 8 percent of those captured, managed to escape from prison camps or evade their captors entirely. Nearly 300 American officers and 708 enlisted men escaped from European and North African prison camps; 2,666 officers and 2,987 enlisted men evaded capture completely and returned to their own lines.[3] According to MI-9, 28,349 British, Commonwealth, and Allied (Greek, Polish, French, Dutch, Czech, and Russian) soldiers escaped from prison camps or evaded capture in World War II (see Appendix 3: *World War II Allied Escapers and Evaders*).

The distinction between escaper and evader during World War II is fuzzy. Escapers were officially registered POWs, who were protected by the 1929 Geneva Convention. Pure evaders were never POWs; they were servicemen, airmen for the most part, who were shot down over enemy-held territory but were never captured. As such they remained active soldiers behind enemy lines. In their flight from captivity, some soldiers in both categories—escapers and evaders—became guerrillas, were sheltered by partisans, or used established escape lines. The distinction between the two thus lies in the term, not the experience. Legal status notwithstanding, both escapers and evaders found themselves on the run behind enemy lines.

Regulating the treatment of POWs, internees, and the sick and wounded was the work of the 1929 or Third Geneva Convention. This document, signed by forty-seven nations, contained some ninety-seven articles, and prior to the outbreak of European hostilities in 1939, all the belligerents were signatories except the Soviet Union. Stalin's reason for not signing rested on the Convention's assumption that war victims came under the protection of the Swiss-led International Commission of the Red Cross (ICRC). In Stalin's view, any outside or foreign influence and any connection to Geneva challenged his authority as dictator of the USSR. Stalin knew that Imperial Russia had signed and ratified the 1899 Hague Convention, but trusting the bourgeois capitalist Swiss to enforce the new POW provisions contained in 1929 Geneva Convention clashed with his belief in a closed socialist system. The Soviet leader refused to participate and denied access to any outsiders who wished to nose around the USSR's camps, especially in its Gulag system for political prisoners.

Stalin's authority and the USSR's sovereignty aside, the fact that the USSR ignored the POW provisions of the Geneva Convention complicated the situation and significantly affected the treatment of German and Allied POWs interned in Russia during World War II, and the millions of Displaced Persons (DPs) and postwar POWs, known as Disarmed Enemy Forces (DEFs), after it.[4] Japan was not a signatory either, although its representatives had signed the protocol in Geneva. Because the Convention's POW provisions were weaker than its own army regulations, the Japanese government failed to ratify it. For a regime that enveloped itself in militant Bushido, taking on an obligation to treat foreign POWs better than its own soldiers was unthinkable.

Participation in the Convention rules, especially those concerning food, clothing, shelter, labor, Red Cross inspections, and discipline, not only guaranteed belligerents' participation in the Golden Rule's reciprocal treatment theory, but also assured a high POW survival rate. Thus it comes as no surprise that American and British POWs were better treated in German captivity than the soldiers of many other nations because by the war's end, the United States held nearly a third of a million German prisoners, including such future noted postwar authors as Alfred Andersch, who had written letters home about the treatment, some of which had been published and had found a wide audience in Germany.[5] For German soldiers like Andersch, quarantine captivity became a welcome haven from war. As was true in the past, for escapers on all sides, captivity merely changed the battleground.

The 1929 Geneva Convention's escape provisions were quite simple and matched both the American *Rules of Land Warfare* (1863/1914/1940) and the Hague Convention (1899): escape was no crime and was punishable only by a short stint in solitary confinement.[6] As a result, POWs were not fearful of escaping, not only because they felt it was their duty to escape but also because they thought that they were safe from draconian punishments if they should be caught. As the fifty Commonwealth POWs in Stalag Luft III (Sagan, Silesia) and many fleeing evaders caught in covert European escape lines later discovered, however, light punishments ended in March 1944, when the Nazi politicos changed the rules and the Gestapo/SS entered the picture.

During World War II, American Kriegies were a minority behind the wire. British and Commonwealth forces had been "in the bag," as the British Kriegies' termed captivity, as early as 1940, when the German Army took nearly 50,000 British prisoners in France and another 30,000 in Greece and Crete a year later. By 1944, approximately 169,000 English and Commonwealth soldiers were held as POWs, and 6,039 escaped and made it back to England safely.[7] Based on its experience during World War I, British intelligence knew that POWs had powerful information-gathering potential. Disregarding the quarantine theory's premise that prisoners remain passive and await the end of the war, the British, and later the American, intelligence services, MI-9 and MIS-X, expanded their information-gathering and operational roles into German prison camps and marshaled that potential into finely honed organizations.

In London, MI-9 was organized around two primary missions: to act as a home base for POW intelligence gathering and to facilitate escapes by developing escape lines on the continent. MI-9's escape and intelligence-gathering activities rested on the understanding that the quarantine theory applied, by and large, only to the sick and wounded, and that healthy POWs, especially officers and noncommissioned officers, were obligated to keep up the fight. Although disarmed and in enemy hands, POWs considered the prison camp to be the new battleground, and most British POWs urged one another to continue acting like soldiers.

Responding to their traditional mandate to escape, eighteen British officers, led by Wing Comdr. Harry "Wings" Day, dug the first tunnel and escaped from the Dulag Luft (*Durchgangslager Luftwaffe*), the transit camp in Wetzlar for downed Allied airmen. The problem for escapers was not so much digging out as what to do after they emerged into a hostile wartime population. In time and with some experience, both the British MI-9 and the American MIS-X helped solve this problem.

The combined efforts of MI-9 and MIS-X produced active and productive "X" organizations throughout the German prison camp system.[8] Each committee consisted of a "Big X," to whom everyone involved in intelligence gathering and escape reported. Subordinate to "Big X" were the barracks subcommittees, whose duty it was to determine whether an escape proposal merited support. In most European camps, the rule was relatively simple: no escapes could be undertaken without permission from the "X" committee at both the barracks and the camp levels. According to Col. Delmar T. Spivey, USAF, one of the senior officers in Stalag Luft III, the "X" organization in general consisted of six major departments. *Tunnelers* organized the digging, while *Security* made sure that the others knew the location of all enemy camp personnel in the compound, especially during tunneling operations. *Tailoring* transformed clothes, burlap bags, blankets, and nearly any other source of cloth into escape clothing; *Maps and Compasses* created escape equipment; *Contact and Language* dealt with the Germans on a daily basis; and *Communications,* the most secretive of all, kept the camp informed about war news from the BBC and other sources, what Kriegies called intelligence or the "gen."[9]

The existence of an "X" organization first paid off when three British officers created a partnership, and in 1943, with "X's" blessing, completed the "Wooden Horse" escape. With cooperation from other prisoners who decoyed the guards with a vaulting horse, the enterprising young British prisoners tunneled under the barbed wire, left the camp, and made their way back to England.[10] In June 1943, Stalag Luft III's

"X" committee dressed two Kriegies in German uniforms. With the Kriegies posing as guards, twenty-five other POWs went first to the showers,
and then while others created a diversion, the group marched out the
main gate. Only one man made it north to Stettin; the others were
quickly recaptured.[11] By the time the Germans and the Allied Kriegies
evacuated Stalag Luft III in January 1945, more than two hundred sanctioned escape attempts had taken place.[12]

When escape attempts failed, and most did, both the Hague and the
Geneva Conventions permitted the captors to impose limited punishment
on the returned escapes. Alan Johnson, a former American sergeant and
Kriegie in Stalag Luft I (Barth, Mecklenburg), recalled that leaving the
camp was not a great problem. He observed, "If you made an escape and
lots of us did from time to time, you could get out of the camp, by tunneling or other methods. We would get out for three or four days or
nights, be on the town, loose, and no one could tell we were any different
from the Germans until you spoke, and if you didn't speak nobody caught
you. However, you had to eat. As soon as you ran out of the food you
carried, you looked around for other food, and stole it. Boy you were in
trouble!" Trouble meant time in solitary confinement, the "cooler," a
word so close to the German *Kühlschrank* for refrigerator that no Kriegie
or guard needed a translation. Johnson recalled what usually happened
to recaptured enlisted escapers in his camp, writing, "You got picked up
and hauled back, then you got put in solitary. It's pretty miserable torture
for some guys to sit there in solitary for two or three days, not talking,
not seeing anything or anybody. It didn't bother me too much because
I'm a solitary type anyway. Some guys, the gregarious type, they just
couldn't be more than an hour or two without company. Solitary would
drive them up a wall."[13] Jerry Sage, however, became known as the
"Cooler King" of Stalag Luft III because he spent so much time there.

In addition to stints in the cooler, the Germans placed some recaptured officers, mostly British and Commonwealth repeat offenders, in a
special officers' camp, Oflag IV C, Colditz Castle in Saxony, known to
the British as the "'bad boys' camp," or *Sonderlager* for unrepentant,
committed natural escapers. Built in 1014 as a home and fort for the kings
of Saxony, Colditz became a prison in 1800. In 1828, its dungeons were
constructed, and their bare, comfortless rooms were used to house the
insane.[14] Since the Germans knew they held wiley escapers at Colditz, they
assigned a much higher proportion of guards to prisoners there than they
did in the other POW camps. It was no easy matter to escape, but the

harder the challenge, the harder the POWs tried. The total number of Colditz escapers reached 130; of this number, 30 scored home runs, among them 14 French, 9 British, 6 Dutch, and 1 Pole.[15] One was Capt. Pat Reid.

In 1942, Reid, an Australian, escaped from Laufen, Oflag VII C. After his recapture, he earned a trip to Colditz Castle. Reid's own escape from Colditz began on foot, then continued by train through Munich and Ulm. Reid arrived within walking distance of the Swiss border, crossed, and finally made his way to safety. Reflecting on why he had become an escaper, Reid noted that as a boy he read popular books that taught him that escape was the "greatest sport in the world."

One of the main problems was determining whether all the conditions were right, or, if not, which ones could be ignored. An opportunity missed might not occur again for months or years, which made one eager to take it. Yet if conditions were adverse, or if the escaper misjudged the importance of certain aspects, then the escape was ruined and an opportunity was lost forever. To some captives, resignation to their status meant not physical but mental death through depression, even lunacy. According to Reid, the majority of Colditz prisoners escaped for self-preservation.[16]

As American airmen became Kriegies, the Germans learned that they too had committed natural escapers among their ranks. T. D. Cooke, for example, was more than a one-time tunneler. As a committed escaper he managed several escape attempts. Not too long after his capture, he jumped through a window thirty feet above the ground to a passing wagon and escaped. He was recaptured three weeks later. His second escape was through the tunnel under Stalag Luft IV (Grosstychow, Pomerania); this time he was loose for three months before recapture. To dig the tunnel, Cooke and his fellow prisoners in C Lager (Barracks C) of Stalag Luft IV used odd pieces of metal as digging tools and wooden slats from their bunks for the siding and overhead. Fans for ventilation were made from cans and bits of scrap metal. Sand removed from the tunnel was dispersed throughout the compound in trouser legs. The prisoners began their work at lockup and continued until dawn. Finally, the tunnel was finished and the escape got under way. Although the tunnelers burrowed their way outside the wire, a few even managing to escape temporarily, the fifty-foot tunnel was destined for failure. First, the Germans recaptured the escapers, and then the guards stumbled upon the tunnel itself. The Americans, however, had created a self-destructive device inside the tunnel in case it was detected. As three German guards entered the tunnel at its farthest point, the Americans, knowing their work had been discovered,

The main entrance to Oflag IV C, Colditz, Germany. This castle held Allied escapers from several nations: England, Australia, New Zealand, South Africa, France, Belgium, Poland, Canada, and the United States. Photo by George Newman

pulled the plug. Immediately, the entrance collapsed, destroying the tunnel as well as suffocating and entombing the guards. Because the camp authorities had no idea who was at fault, they took no reprisals. Instead, the Germans installed sophisticated listening devices, and the prisoners concluded that further escape attempts were too dangerous.[17]

The German Afrika Korps began transferring British and Commonwealth POWs to the Italians for safekeeping during the desert campaigns in 1941. By 1943, as the war progressed from North Africa to Sicily and then to Italy itself, the Italians held more than eighty thousand Allied POWs in northern Italy, distributed among seventy-two prison camps.[18] During this time, the Americans started to rub shoulders with the British, as they had in World War I, and learned that there was no lack of courage or desire to escape on the part of the British captives. One British officer, Rollo Price, captured in the desert with the 1st Battalion, South Wales Borderers, before the Battle of El Alamein, was held as a POW for fifteen months before he leaped from a moving train in an escape attempt. Loose in the Italian mountains and often sheltered by partisans and nuns, Price spent nine months on the run. Only a gunshot wound in the foot stopped him from making a successful escape.[19] Always impressed with the British sense of organization and desire to escape, David Westheimer, a POW in P.G. 21 and author of *Von Ryan's Express* (1964), commented that among the Americans, escape activities went on constantly and picked up with warmer weather. Westheimer recalled, "There were usually several tunnels going at the same time. Two of them eventually got beyond the wall but not far enough to be opened safely. The most elaborate tunnel began under the cookhouse steps. It was equipped with lanterns and a ventilator made out of cans. It was discovered by accident. . . . You don't open a tunnel until the escape attempt. We didn't have a successful escape from P.G. 21 the whole time I was there. Some prisoners got as far as the wall but never got over it." [20] The home runs took place later, when Italy became a no-man's land between the German defenders and the Allied invaders.

On June 7, 1943, before the Italians changed sides and declared war on Nazi Germany, the British prison organization in Chieti received orders from MI-9 not to attempt any large-scale breakouts. MI-9 feared possible mass Nazi and Fascist reprisals in the Italian camps, and it was clear to the British that all the POWs should wait for the coming Allied invasion. British senior ranking officers—SROs to the Americans and SBOs to the British—obeyed MI-9's orders and commanded all the POWs, under threat of court-martial, to wait patiently for liberation or further orders.[21] However, many Allied POWs, especially the Americans, grew angry at the possibility of missing a golden opportunity to leave on their own. In their opinion, the order was a mistake that could cost them their freedom. Some waited and obeyed; others, including many British, Commonwealth, and American prisoners, still fled the compounds when they could. Once at large, the escapers sought the Allied lines; many joined Italian antifascist partisans along the way.[22]

Along with David Westheimer, American infantry officers and enlisted men were captured in North Africa and transported to Italy. Westheimer's prison mate, Joseph S. Frelinghuysen, became an escaper the hard way. The apparent lack of adequate POW training among American troops in North Africa shocked Frelinghuysen's sense of military order. Shortly after his capture, Frelinghuysen was flown to Italy and interned at the Chieti prison camp. Observing his fellow prisoners, he thought they seemed disgruntled and were denying themselves the opportunity to become a resistance-oriented POW community. Whereas the British relied heavily on an escape organization for guidance, Frelinghuysen believed that the Americans depended chiefly on individual initiative, or close, even secretive, partnerships to find opportunities to escape. To him, the British who ran the camp understood captivity and cared far more for one another than did the Americans, who appeared to be disorganized and more or less on their own.

To the chagrin of some, many American prisoners liked it that way. Discipline was lax, and no one ordered their lives. For both groups, the individualists and the members of the tight captive communities, liberation by the Allies never came. Instead, stern German paratroopers arrived to replace the easy-going Italian guards, and thousands of POWs began the train trip to Germany. Frelinghuysen formed a hasty partnership with a German-speaking American Army officer, Capt. Richard Rossbach. They escaped Chieti together just in time and evaded recapture in the Italian Abruzzi mountains.[23]

After the Italians changed sides on September 8, 1943, twenty Americans avoided the German take-over of the Italian camp for sergeants at Sulmona in central Italy. Staff Sgt. Robert Blakeney quickly formed an *ad hoc* escape team that headed on its own for friendly lines. Earlier that summer, on August 16, 1943, Blakeney's bomber containing a ten-man air crew had been riddled with flak on a bombing raid over Foggia.[24] Blakeney recalled, "Our B-24 was badly shot up, and we tried to get to Sicily but were forced to make a crash landing on a beach in Reggio, Calabria." The B-24 Liberator had no flaps to slow it down when it came in for a landing at 140 miles per hour. When the front end of the bomber hit the beach, there were two explosions followed by fire. The aircraft broke up, and five men were killed instantly; of the five who survived, two were badly hurt and burned. Stunned and injured, the survivors were forced to remain close to the crash site. Italian soldiers captured them easily and took them into town for interrogation. They were then put on a train for Bari, where they joined members of other air crews. Italian authorities separated the officers and enlisted men, with the officers transported by train to stalags in Germany, while the enlisted men were sent to the Italian prison camp at Sulmona. When they arrived at Sulmona, they were greeted by three thousand to four thousand other POWs: English, French, and Canadians, many of whom had been captured at Tobruk, Dunkirk, and other places several years before. The camp routine was dull, but in late September 1943, the captives were jolted by rumors that Italy had capitulated.

With both Italian and German guards at the camp, the situation could easily have turned explosive as the conflict between the two countries escalated. An English colonel in the "X" committee told the Yanks that POWs were not to escape without his permission. At the same time, a German officer warned another prisoner that anyone attempting to escape risked being shot. These admonitions did not deter Blakeney, whose opportunity arose when he and his prison mate, John M. Hess of Uniontown, Pennsylvania, took an evening walk around the camp to pass the time. As they circled the camp, they noticed that fewer Italian guards were posted, particularly at the gate houses. Keeping this strange situation in mind, they continued their nightly exercise. Then on a night in late September, they saw that the gate was open. Returning to their barracks, Blakeney and Hess told the other POWs about this incredible sight. According to Blakeney, "There was no hesitation by anyone. We casually approached the gate, opened it more, and then we all ran as fast as we could. Within three to four minutes we heard gunfire, but we all had run three-minute miles by that time. We learned later that several English soldiers had followed us out." Once out of the camp, the group met in a vineyard, split up into two-man partnerships, and headed into the mountains that surrounded Sulmona. There they began the elusive life of escapers.

Moving only at night, they ate raw potatoes, stole tomatoes, and proceeded south toward Allied lines. Like so many escapers in Italy, Blakeney and his partner needed help and obtained it from rural, antifascist

S. Sgt. Robert Blakeney, USAAF, June 1943. After the Italian government's capitulation on September 8, 1943, twenty Americans avoided the German takeover and headed on their own for friendly lines. The odyssey lasted for twenty-five days until they met Canadian soldiers on patrol. Blakeney received the Silver Star and other decorations for the escape and was just twenty years old when it happened. Courtesy of Robert Blakeney

Italian families. He recalled, "We finally saw an isolated house, and we were very hungry. We watched the house and the area for a few hours; saw only a man and his wife, then approached them for something to eat. We had hot goat's milk cheese (first time), and it was great. They gave us some bread to take with us. We were doing well until we came on to the fig trees. They were the most delicious figs in the world."

Refreshed and well fed, they continued their trek south. Distrustful of the local inhabitants, they avoided populated areas by leapfrogging from farm to farm. Finally, however, they encountered a friendly farmer whose son had emigrated to Chicago and served in the American Army. The old man gave them some cheese, bread, a chicken, and a safe place to rest for several days. From experience, British and American escapers had learned that the poorer the house, the more likely it was that assistance would be forthcoming, despite the threat of death imposed on those who helped Allied escapers on the run.[25] After this respite, Blakeney and Hess continued southward for several days. Coming upon another farmhouse, they watched it for several hours, then asked a woman for some well water. To their horror, the woman screamed in Italian, "Tedeschi!" (Germans!) Blakeney looked up and saw several German soldiers on patrol nearby. Surprisingly, the Germans ignored them, and their odyssey continued. They proceeded south until they came to another farmhouse, where they met a patrol of Canadian soldiers. After twenty-five days of escape and evasion behind enemy lines, Blakeney and Hess were free men.[26]

In southern Italy, fighting raged between the Germans and the Allies as the German Army slowly retreated north. The Americans attacked the beaches of Anzio, but their advance ground to a halt. During the fierce fighting around Villa Crocetta near Anzio, the Germans kept taking and retaking the town. On May 27–28, 1943, Warren Fencl's infantry unit engaged heavy enemy forces, and by the morning of the 28th his unit pulled back again. In the fighting, Sergeant Fencl and his squad were left to fend for themselves. He recalled, "We smashed our weapons on the rocks, and we hid. But an eagle-eyed German saw us, and as they say in Hawaii, 'All pua [finished].' We stood up with our hands on our heads waiting to be shot. What a feeling. It felt like my whole insides drained out, and I saw no tomorrow. It was time to die."

No one died. An English-speaking German sergeant took them all prisoner, and they were subjected to a week's interrogation. Then on June 16, 1943, Fencl's squad looked up and saw an American P-51 Mustang approaching on a strafe and low-level bombing attack. The German soldiers ran for cover, while Fencl and the other prisoners remained caught in the middle. After the firing and bombing had ceased, the group stepped over the rubble that had once been the interrogation office. Two trucks were parked nearby, waiting for their drivers. The time for escape was at hand. According to Fencl, "I stood there and looked at the barnyard and felt my insides return. One of the P-51s was circling overhead, so we waved thanks. He waved his wings and left. The last man out found two cartons of Camel cigarettes and passed them around. He opened a pack and we took one and he said, 'Let's let up, light up, load up and let out!'"

Without waiting for further instructions, they jumped in the trucks and traveled the bumpy dirt road to the southeast. When they reached a highway, they encountered a German convoy. "The Germans looked at us," wrote Fencl, "some waved, and some took a second look, then we waved back." Then one of the trucks ran out of gas, but the resourceful Kriegies loaded everyone into the remaining truck for what proved to be the last leg of their short journey. When they finally met the Americans, however, their elation turned to shock at the greeting they received. Fencl recalled, "We were sure glad to see them until they pointed their weapons at us and said: 'We were prisoners; we were German infiltrators!' We were taken back to their prisoner of war holding camp until proven otherwise. Again we gave our name, rank and serial number and a Master Sergeant took our fingerprints."[27]

Planning a mass escape in the heart of enemy territory was another matter. With stealth, a high degree of organization, and closely guarded cooperation among the participants, sixty-five RAF officers tunneled under the wire of Oflag VII B at Eichstätt, Bavaria, on June 3, 1943. Despite these precautions, the escapers failed to reach Switzerland, and all were recaptured promptly with the help of troops, Hitler Youth, and the Home Guard. One unexpected outcome of this escape was that the Bavarian police learned how to identify strangers in their midst.[28]

Most Allied POWs waited behind barbed wire far from neutral Switzerland, somewhere in the German states of Pomerania, Silesia, Brandenburg, and Saxony. Thus part of the preparations focused on improvising civilian clothes made from uniforms and creating false German documents in order to facilitate the use of the German railway system. Some escapers even fabricated their own versions of German uniforms. Wearing dog tags as their only form of military identification, the Allied escapers considered themselves in uniform and conforming to the rules; the Gestapo considered them soldiers in civilian clothes, or partisans.

Since partisans were viewed as no better than spies, most armies traditionally punished them harshly. During the Civil War, for example, the Union Army shot or hanged nonuniformed Confederate partisans shortly after capture. To clarify the partisan situation and to help distinguish soldiers from civilian partisans, the 1929 Geneva Convention required all soldiers to wear uniforms with visible markings of rank; unfortunately, nothing was said about what escaped prisoners should or should not wear. According to historian Alfred M. de Zayas, partisans, especially the Russian partisan armies and British commandos who led partisan groups in Greece, Yugoslavia, and France, not only were a huge military threat to the German war and supply effort but also posed serious legal difficulties in the face of the 1929 Geneva Convention's uniform identification requirements.[29] In light of these problems, Hitler issued a new directive that formally linked partisans with escapers and punished both with execution. In part his directive read:

> To all prisoners of war! The escape from prison camps is no longer a sport! Germany has always held to the Hague Convention and only punished recaptured prisoners of war with minor disciplinary punishments. Germany is determined to safeguard her homeland, and especially her war industry and provisional centres for the fighting fronts. Therefore it has become necessary to create strictly forbidden zones, called death zones, in which all unauthorized trespassers will be shot on sight. Escaping prisoners of war entering such death zones will certainly lose their lives. They are in constant danger of being mistaken for enemy agents or sabotage groups. All police and military guards have been given the most strict orders to shoot on sight all suspected persons.[30]

Although this document was posted in every POW camp in Germany, British, Commonwealth, and American POWs defied these threats and continued operating their escape activities in the "X" organizations.

A bitter lesson was learned after the mass breakout from Stalag Luft III on March 24, 1944. Led by a South African, Roger Bushell ("Big X"), and an Englishman, Harry "Wings" Day, the Sagan escape was the most meticulously planned mass exodus from a prison camp in the military history of the twentieth century, and changed the meaning of escape for the remainder of World War II. In *The Great Escape* (1950), Paul Brickhill described "X" as an organization that employed more than six hundred Kriegies working as diggers, forgers, lookouts, and dirt haulers. Bushell was a veteran tunneler, who, along with eighteen other RAF officers, had dug his way out of the Dulag Luft in the summer of 1941. Although he nearly scored a home run on his first try, he was recaptured only a few yards from the Swiss border.[31] As a result, Bushell became a condemned man long before the Sagan escape and knew beforehand that recapture would bring about his immediate execution.

Prior to the great escape, the Kriegies dug more than a hundred tunnels under Stalag Luft III, but the "ferrets," the German Air Force sergeants responsible for seeking out tunnels and tunnelers, destroyed them all. In 1943 and 1944, the Kriegies dug three active tunnels, Tom, Dick, and Harry, each about thirty feet deep and three hundred feet long, heading under the wire by three different routes. When Tom and Dick were discovered, Bushell directed the organization toward Harry. Planning was extensive, especially for the use of maps, compasses, and German

money. Garden tools were generally available for digging, and the Kriegies stole or bartered for the electrical wiring they needed for lights. The
group found plenty of bed slats to shore the tunnel from cave-ins. In all,
the audacious "X" committee planned to take two hundred prisoners
through Harry into the Silesian countryside.

Luck, as always, played a significant role in this escape. The American
and British officers initially lived together in Stalag Luft III, and the two
groups cooperated in all phases of the breakout preparations until, by a
stroke of bad luck, the German camp authority decided to separate them
shortly before the escape date. So many American airmen had arrived
from the fierce combat in Italy and the escalating air war over Europe
that the North Compound had grown too small to accommodate them
all properly. The Americans reluctantly departed for the newly constructed South and Center Compounds while the British kept on digging.
Two hundred men readied themselves, but the tunnelers' bad luck continued, for when they broke the surface, they were short of the woods
and nearly in full view of the guards. Bushell had to make a quick decision: close the tunnel, give up, or leave as planned. Because the forgers
had already dated the travel papers, they had no choice. Only eighty of

Stalag Luft III, Sagan. This photo illustrates the kind of miniature railway the tunnelers
constructed to remove dirt from tunnel Harry prior to the Great Escape in 1944.
By permission of the German Bundesarchiv Koblenz #95141135:35

those involved in the plot actually got out of Harry; seventy-six, including Day and Bushell, made it to the woods while four others were halted at gunpoint at the tunnel's exit.

The seventy-six escaped POWs became the objects of a huge manhunt. Only three men—two Norwegians and a Dutchman, Bram Vanderstock—were able to blend into the European landscape and return to England. The others were recaptured in less than two weeks.[32] The fate of the Stalag Luft III escapers became clouded in controversy after the SS/Gestapo executed fifty recaptured officers, including Bushell, in March and April 1944. As a result of these murders, the senior ranking American officers in Stalag Luft III forbade any more escape attempts from the American South Compound, even those in progress.

One took Gestapo dictates seriously, especially in 1944 when they came from Hitler himself. In July 1944, Alfred Jodl noted in his diary that a warning had gone out to all the POW camps that anyone who broke out faced a death sentence.[33] Some escapers were returned to Stalag Luft III; others were put into special camps like Colditz for committed escapers; and some were sent to the dreaded Nazi concentration camps. By October 1944, most Kriegies knew that the rules had changed.[34] Internally, the traditional German armed forces were humiliated when the SS took control of the 4.75 million POWs in Germany, at least on paper. Committed escapers, like Wing Comdr. Harry "Wings" Day, as well as evaders captured by the Gestapo, were sent to SS concentration camps and temporarily stripped of their POW status.[35]

Life in a concentration camp differed considerably from that in a POW camp. Status as a POW was vitally important to Kriegies because the International Red Cross Commission in Geneva, Switzerland, served as their Protecting Power and vigorously enforced the 1929 Geneva Convention. Loss of that status was catastrophic. The SS exercised complete and exclusive control over everyone in its charge. Although the SS created an elaborate system of identification in its concentration camps, it reduced all its prisoners from the status of human beings with natural and legal rights to the nonstatus of political captives or *Häftling*. As Elie Wiesel from Hungary and Primo Levi from Italy so eloquently demonstrated in their Holocaust survivor narratives, the SS could do anything to anyone with impunity. Yet Wiesel later noted that inmates encouraged escapes despite the retributions.[36]

Even in the rigid environment of a death camp, some civilian and military prisoners revolted and escaped. At the small Struthof-Natzweiler concentration camp in the Vosges Mountains outside Strasbourg, one

Frenchman disguised himself as the feared camp commandant, stole his car, and drove out the front gate with formal salutes from the guards. Success followed this escaper when he joined the French Resistance in Alsace. At Auschwitz, 747 prisoners tried to escape and 377 were successful, mostly those in working parties sent outside the camp. Recapture by the SS in this instance could mean only one thing, execution. The lovers' partnership established by Mala Zimetbaum and Edward Galinski was one example.

Mala Zimetbaum was barely twenty years old in 1944 when she fell in love with Edward Galinski, a Polish political prisoner. Because Zimetbaum was fluent in several languages, she served her captors as a messenger and interpreter, a job that gave her the run of Auschwitz. The pair bribed an SS guard to supply them with a uniform and a pass so that Galinski could pose as a guard with a prisoner in tow. The deception succeeded, and the two lovers escaped the death camp. Two weeks later, the SS recaptured the couple and condemned them to death by public hanging. Galinski stepped onto the gallows first and shouted "Long live Poland" before he dropped to his death. Zimetbaum had other ideas. Before the guards could hang her, she pulled out a razor blade and slit her wrists, spraying her executioners with her blood.[37]

After the SS murdered 250,000 political prisoners, mostly civilian Jews, at Sobibor, Poland, the civilians organized themselves into an escape committee and joined with Russian POWs in the largest civilian mass escape of World War II. Theirs was the greatest escape of them all. On October 14, 1943, the inmates revolted in a bloody camp uprising that freed three hundred of the six hundred people in Sobibor.[38]

Unlike Bushell, after Wing Commander Day was recaptured, he was sent to the huge Sachsenhausen concentration camp at Oranienburg, just outside Berlin. Within a day of his arrival, Day and a few others held in the same hut started to dig a tunnel to escape. After ten days of furious work, they fled with only a compass to guide them west. Even though Day was recaptured again and returned to Sachsenhausen, his luck continued to hold. Because the police recaptured Day, not the SS, the SS was embarrassed by this escape. Sachsenhausen served as the SS headquarters for all concentration camp activities throughout Germany and the occupied countries, and Day had tunneled out under their very noses. As punishment, Day and the others were taken to the inner *Straflager,* or punishment barracks, and chained in their individual cells. In April 1945, as the Russian Army began to pound Berlin, the POWs were moved south to join other noted prisoners near the Swiss border. There they were rescued by an American patrol.[39]

Records of the 8th Air Force Historical Association show that the Gestapo placed eighty-two American fliers in concentration camps for four months. By 1944, the interservice rivalry in the German armed services was intense. The Wehrmacht was retreating on the eastern front; the Luftwaffe was unable to prevent Allied bombers from devastating the German homeland; and more submarines were being destroyed at sea than could be replaced. The SS field units, the *Waffen SS,* and the *Sicherheitsdienst* or Security Services that operated the concentration camp system, were intact. As it was still protective of its turf concerning Allied POWs in its care, the nearly wingless Luftwaffe rescued many but not all POWs from the SS and returned them to Geneva Convention-abiding POW camps. All told, 147 American soldiers, mostly recaptured escapers and newly captured evaders, were imprisoned by the SS.[40]

By April and May 1945, although the concentration camps had become an inflammatory issue, Supreme Headquarters Allied Expeditionary Force (SHAEF) was too busy repatriating the thousands of POWs who were flowing back to friendly lines to take particular note of the situation. At this point, the types of captivity mattered less than the state of being free from it. As the hostilities ended, however, the British turned their attention to the matter of the great escape from Stalag Luft III and its consequences. Still impassioned by the Gestapo's outrageous execution of fifty officers, British military authorities exercised their own form of retributive justice. After a successful manhunt for the murderers, British military courts tried and later hanged fourteen Gestapo members.[41] The innocent, however, suffered along with the guilty. Life after the war for kindly and just Col. Friedrich Wilhelm von Lindeiner-Wildau, the camp's commandant in March 1944, changed for the worse as well. Before the escape, he had asked the Allied senior officers to cease escape activities, warning them that the Gestapo had entered the picture and that death threats had been made against recaptured escapers.[42] Colonel von Lindeiner's revulsion toward SS terror tactics was so great that had the SS forced him to shoot prisoners in the camp, he vowed to take his own life in protest. After the escape, he was court-martialed for dereliction of duty. His problems did not end there for when the war finally ended, he was held and interrogated by the British for two years as a war crimes witness. His house in Berlin was completely destroyed, and when he tried to go home to his Silesian estate, he discovered that Silesia was Poland,

and his estate had been confiscated by the state. Remembering the old Roman proverb "Woe to the vanquished," Colonel von Lindeiner felt dishonored by popular accounts of the escape and in 1953, he wrote, "Not only have I had to take humiliation as a German officer and Junker from my own side, and then impoverishment, but also this defamation from those we tried to be decent to."[43]

After D-Day, June 6, 1944, the tide of war turned against German forces on the ground in France. After a summer and autumn of intense fighting, the Germans withdrew toward their own border in order to regroup, rearm, and introduce seasoned east-front *Waffen SS* forces to counterattack the Allies in Belgium. During the Battle of the Bulge in the Ardennes, fought between December 16 and 25, 1944, the *Waffen SS* attacked in force, battering the frozen Americans and taking 23,554 prisoners. For many, captivity was short but deadly; for 81 Malmèdy prisoners, members of B Battery, 285th Field Artillery Observation Battalion, the brief captivity ended in death by execution in an open field. During the ensuing chaos, 20 Americans escaped into the surrounding woods. Of the 81 bodies discovered, 41 showed evidence of pistol shots to the head.[44]

By the winter and spring of 1945, many captured soldiers believed that World War II was about to end. Listening to homemade radios, the old-hand POWs heard the latest war news from the BBC. In Germany, they witnessed a worsening of conditions in the camps and were presented with greater opportunities for individual and small group escapes. One American, captured in December 1944 during the Battle of the Bulge, found himself in an escaper's dilemma during the pandemonium at the war's end. He recalled that someone had cut the wires in the compound, noting, "I guess it was maybe April or May, and once again I couldn't get anybody to go with me, and I broke through. I didn't have to use any tools; the wire was broken. About two days later, I came across an American tank group that almost killed me. I found out in the matter of a few hours that I was far too weak to keep up with them, to even stay with them, so they put me in a jeep and took me back to some makeshift hospital and fattened me up for a few days."[45] This war's-end escape from Moosburg in western Germany was typical of those Kriegies who were tired of being confined and fearful that the special SS killing teams were about to murder them outright.

By January 1945, the Russians had advanced the eastern front closer to the Reich, forcing the Germany Army and Air Force to abandon their prison camps and march the Kriegies west from the eastern stalags. With thousands of new Kriegies arriving from the evacuated eastern camps, the already full western camps became dangerously overcrowded, and the Germans discovered the impossibility of guarding, feeding, and housing them in accordance with the 1929 Geneva Convention. Many thousands remained in place, knowing a sure thing when they saw it, and awaited liberation and repatriation. On the other hand, as the situation deteriorated and organization broke down, many individuals and partners escaped from the camps and made their way to friendly lines. Exactly how many Allied POWs made impromptu escapes in April and May 1945 remains unclear.

Although most escaped Kriegies headed west, some headed east toward the Russians, who sent 5,241 American POWs home from the Black Sea port of Odessa. Of those who headed east, 2,500 Allied escapers, or one in seven, made their way to Odessa on their own with the help of Polish and Russian citizens. One Kriegie, Mike Enfros of Toluca Lake, California, wrote, "I escaped Stalag 2B [Hammerstein, Pomerania] when the Germans evacuated the camp." Later he spent about a hundred days largely in hiding, and after reaching the Russians, he ended up leaving Odessa aboard a Texaco oil tanker.[46] In January 1944, Thomas E. Lawson and his partner Eddie Wiergacz escaped from a work detail outside Oflag 64 (Altburgund) near Szubin, Poland. They hid in a farmhouse at first, then contacted a friendly Russian captain who was on a forward patrol nearby. The captain advised the pair to head to the Russian lines about a mile to the rear. After joining the Russians, they returned to Oflag 64 and found it in Russian hands. Wiergacz spoke Polish, and Lawson had several cartons of Lucky Strike cigarettes for trading, so together they set out for Moscow via Warsaw and Minsk. Bartering for food along the way, Lawson and Wiergacz found Russian civilians to be both friendly and helpful. Eventually they began to encounter other escaped Kriegies, and soon they were traveling by train to Odessa, from which they sailed on a British ship for home.[47]

Others in the eastern stalags had no desire to head east. Initially liberated by the Red Army, many American Kriegies discovered that instead of being returned to their own lines, sometimes only a few miles away, they were about to be sent east to Odessa for return to the United States by ship. Such POW exchange agreements reached by world leaders far away made no sense to them; in their view, a new form of captivity was merely replacing the old one. The Soviets were not only political and military allies throughout the war, they were also fellow prisoners who suffered immeasurably in the German stalags. Why the Red Army would want to hold Allied POWs in a camp they despised when they could be returned to their own lines by a short truck or plane ride was beyond comprehension.

What the Kriegies did not know was that the politics of the Cold War were beginning, and many POWs had unwittingly become the initial currency. Stalin wanted his Soviet citizens back, willingly or through forced repatriation if necessary. As roughly defined at the Yalta Conference, "citizen" meant any Soviet soldier captured by the Germans or any emigré held by the Allies who opposed the communist political framework of the Soviet Union. Stalin and his military intelligence service, the NKVD, a precursor of the KGB, were especially interested in recovering the forty-one thousand anticommunists and their families who had fought with the Germans. Anticommunist ethnic groups, particularly Cossacks, Ukrainians, and czarist Russians, had fought the Red Army for decades, and the unique opportunity to oppose the Stalinist regime in German uniforms with German weapons and logistic support had proved attractive to those willing to use any means of overturning Stalinism at home. In eastern Europe, retribution became a word with teeth. Tito of Yugoslavia received twenty-six thousand Croats who fought Serbians and the Allies in Yugoslavia. The fate of Russians who fought Russians and of Croats who fought other Yugoslavians was sealed at the Yalta Conference when the Allied powers agreed to return all citizens to their countries of origin, whether they wanted to return or not. The policy of forced repatriation began.[48]

In April and May 1945, while these complicated political maneuvers were taking place around them, thousands of American Kriegies and Allied POWs sat in their camps waiting for their own repatriation. Some waited in vain. When units of the Red Army overran Stalag III B (Furstenburg an der Oder) in eastern Germany, they mistook the Americans for Hungarians and opened fire, killing some fifty American prisoners and wounding several hundred others.[49] Some POWs in other camps, realizing their precarious situation, seized the opportunity to escape. At a point along the Elbe River separating the American and Red armies, a truck driven by black GIs smashed through Russian barriers and reached the American lines. As a result, the Russians announced that escape west was a political crime punishable by up to six months of civil internment.[50]

At the international political level, allies were quickly becoming enemies. In 1945, some Kriegies, called "exfiltrators," escaped from the Russians and made their way back to American lines, which, in some cases, were only a short distance away. Others idled away their time in their old camps or were transported to Odessa for the trip home in accordance with the agreements made between the Russians and the other Allied powers at Yalta and Potsdam. Indeed, some may have been lost without a trace; war has always taken some soldiers to its macabre bosom. According to a postwar study conducted by Dr. Paul Cole, the Russians liberated 28,662 American POWs from German camps. Cole suggested that only 280 were not repatriated. However, some anti-Russian, bargaining-chip, post-war research contradicted Cole by suggesting that the 1945 American pre-Cold War agenda set the POWs up for the nightmare of massive abandonment. The bargaining-chip theory suggests that in 1945, Stalin ordered the Red Army to seize and hold more than fifty-thousand Allied POWs for political ransom, and that the United States and other Allied governments knew it.[51] Although the bargaining-chip position was disputed by official U.S. government intelligence circles, the Defense Intelligence Agency continues to conduct active searches in Russia for traces of American POWs from World War II, Korea, the Cold War, and Vietnam.[52]

As the Russians received their own POWs back from camps in Germany, Austria, and England, as well as those Russians captured in German uniform who were incarcerated in the United States, many liberated Kriegies returned home under orders not to discuss their experiences in Russian hands. What the Soviets did with their own returned POWs, especially those repatriated against their will, engendered another controversy. In the Stalinist world, being a POW was a crime against the state. In Graz, Austria, for example, a memorial commemorates hundreds of Russian POWs whom the Red Army liberated from German captivity and then executed in the street. In like manner, many former Russian or Ukrainian soldiers who fought with the Germans were executed shortly after they stepped from the ships, trucks, or trains that brought them back to Judenburg, Austria. After learning their likely fate, some anticommunist Russians, many who were not Soviet citizens, committed suicide rather than be delivered into the hands of the NKVD. In the Soviet Union, the GUPVI system for POWs and the Gulag system for political prisoners and state criminals were full of Wehrmacht prisoners who were forced to rebuild a devastated Soviet Union. Most of the Germans and Austrians were released in 1947 and 1954. As far as the Red Army POWs were concerned, a few went home after repatriation, but unknown numbers of others, kept for years in the German stalags and concentration camps, disappeared into the Soviet Gulags for the specious crime of "anti-Soviet behavior."[53]

Exact numerical counts of evasions vary, but the American Air Force Escape and Evasion Society believes that they numbered somewhere between 6,000 and 7,000 airmen, approximately 25 percent of whom were captured along the way.[54] MI-9's figures are lower. They show that 1,022 British and Commonwealth officers and 3,645 enlisted men (Other Ranks) as well as 2,676 American officers and 3,010 enlisted men, evaded capture. The problem with these figures is that they reflect only the official numbers of those officers and enlisted men whose return was facilitated by uninterrupted escape lines and could be calculated by British intelligence. One American who evaded capture without anyone's help wrote, "After fifty-one days of outrunning and outswimming dogs and men, I made it back to my own outfit. This ordeal doesn't even show up on my service record."[55]

During and after the war, American MIS-X made no distinction between escapers and evaders in its figures, citing a total of 12,000 who returned during hostilities. Allied figures for both escape and evasion came to 35,190, about the size of a full infantry division, which in itself shows how effectively a well-organized, highly dedicated, clandestine operation can function.[56] From 1940 to 1942, most evaders were soldiers caught behind enemy lines; from 1942 to France's liberation in 1944, they were generally Allied airmen shot down in occupied France, Holland, Belgium, Italy, and the Balkans. Before they flew combat missions over Europe, however, the pilots and crew were briefed on the existence of escape lines. Embedded in the murky world of active espionage, resistance, and deception was what George Watt, a veteran of the Lincoln Brigade in the Spanish Civil War, called "a war within a war."[57]

In using escape lines, the trick was to make contact with the Resistance, which was linked directly with MI-9 in London. The main MI-9 evasion route, code-named *Comet,* was handled by Colditz escaper Airey Neave. One must keep in mind, however, that escape lines were formed and operated by civilian resisters, for the most part, not by professional Allied intelligence personnel. The success of a line was due to the dedication of its operators. Unarmed, practically defenseless, and always vulnerable, the British, Commonwealth, and American fliers were at the mercy of these volunteers, who knew that their own capture usually meant death for the men and condemnation to a concentration camp for the women.[58] The cost was high. In *Saturday at M. I. 9* (1969), Airey Neave recalled that more than four thousand civilians from France, Belgium, and Holland participated in the escape lines, and more than five hundred were arrested and shot, or died in concentration camps.[59]

From London, Neave centralized his efforts first in Brussels, where *Comet* picked up men on the run in Belgium and Holland. From Brussels, the route went directly through Paris and carried evaders south through occupied and unoccupied France to the Spanish border, where Spanish antifascist partisans took them to Madrid for a few days and finally to the British naval base at Gibraltar. Rather than taking some escapers and evaders south through the French provinces, a Canadian line called *Shelburne,* operated by Sgt. Maj. Lucien Dumais, generally received escapers and evaders in Paris and sent them directly across the English Channel to Falmouth. Such was the case with the first American escaper, Lee Gordon, who fled from captivity, evaded his captors by joining *Shelburne,* and crossed the Channel to England. A third and smaller line took evaders from Rouen, Amiens, and Lille through Paris, south to Marseilles or Toulouse in France, and then either across the Spanish border to Madrid or by sea to Gibraltar.[60]

Evasion required special grit from everyone involved. If airmen who were shot down landed relatively safely and avoided early capture, they were taken in by Belgian, Dutch, and French Resistance operatives, who tended to their immediate needs and prepared them for a trip on an updated version of the American Underground Railroad. Although they may have resembled Europeans, the American evaders found that simple American habits like walking with a bounce or a shuffle, holding a knife and fork improperly, wearing a hat tilted, or holding a cigarette in public gave them away immediately. Evaders learned European ways from risk-takers like Maurice Quillien in France, who recalled his problems getting clothes for downed flyers. "Some of them ended up with trousers and sleeves that were much too short," he noted.[61] Because it was easy for English-speaking Gestapo agents to pose as Englishmen or Americans, which happened often, the Resistance workers were always careful to test evaders' true identities. If American evaders had no knowledge of professional football and baseball teams, screen celebrities, or comic strips, they could be mistaken for Gestapo penetrators and shot. After their identities were verified, evaders then received civilian clothes and some rudimentary lessons in everyday European mannerisms before beginning their journey. Such was the dangerous life they shared with their friends in the Resistance.

In *Comet,* Allied evaders were generally known as "parcels," and the objective was to move them along swiftly and safely, much like the mail, from one station to another to England. Each line in Italy, Belgium, France, and Spain in the west, along with the secret lines in the Balkans, Hungary, and Rumania, was complex and extremely dangerous. George Watt passed through the line and vividly remembered the waiting. According to Watt, it became "increasingly unbearable," and he recalled an old soldier's song he had learned from the British battalion in Spain that kept running through his mind:

> Waiting, waiting, waiting
> always fucking well waiting,
> waiting in the morning,
> waiting at night.
> God send the day
> when we'll fucking well
> wait no more.[62]

Americans commonly characterize their military experiences by the expression "Hurry up and wait"; patience has never been an American virtue. Learning it was a chore.

With *Comet* and the other lines operating successfully in the north, MI-9 took control of an unusual line in Rome that was operated by a bizarre Irishman known as the "Vatican Pimpernel," an eccentric Roman Catholic priest, Rt. Rev. Msgr. Hugh O'Flaherty. In 1943, MI-9 appointed a British Army lieutenant colonel, Sam Derry, then a major and a good Anglican who had been taken prisoner in North Africa by the Afrika Korps, to act as the official British liaison. Derry escaped from an Italian train near Rome and received orders to render official British assistance to what O'Flaherty was doing on his own initiative.

If ever a perfect "Pimpernel" came to the rescue of prisoners in need of help or on the run, it was Hugh O'Flaherty. Having lived in Rome for many years before the war broke out, O'Flaherty had many Italian friends who hid Allied escapers and evaders from the omnipresent Gestapo. The Monsignor cryptically called himself "the superior" and often toured Italian POW camps in search of missing men. According to Derry, whose cover was as a Roman Catholic priest with the new name of Pat, Monsignor O'Flaherty's favorite hideout was an apartment directly behind SS headquarters in Rome. "Faith," O'Flaherty once chortled to Derry, "they'll not look under their noses." [63] He was a smart gambler who played his cards well. In nine months, O'Flaherty's makeshift line cared for 3,925 Allied evader-escapers, including 2,591 British, 185 Americans, and 615 others. Only 122 were recaptured by the Gestapo, and just 6 were shot in Rome and the surrounding region.[64] As a true humanitarian, Monsignor O'Flaherty's concern extended to all prisoners in difficult circumstances. After Rome's liberation, he approached Gen. Mark Clark to make certain that German prisoners were well treated. Later, he flew to South Africa to inspect the conditions of thousands of Italian POWs and visited Jewish refugees in Jerusalem. O'Flaherty testified on behalf of several Italian collaborators and managed to convert and baptize his old Gestapo nemesis, SS Col. Herbert Kappler, after the Allies jailed him in Rome for war crimes.[65]

Although the number of escape and evasion experiences totaled well into the thousands during World War II, very few could have succeeded without some kind of outside help. Monsignor O'Flaherty, the "Vatican Pimpernel," was only one of the many persons who risked and often sacrificed their lives in the service of escapers, evaders, and prisoners held by all the countries at war in Europe and Africa. In recognition of his service, the U.S. Congress awarded Monsignor O'Flaherty America's highest civilian honor, the Medal of Freedom; the British government bestowed the Commander of the British Empire on him; and the Italian government granted him a pension for life. Monsignor O'Flaherty accepted the first two awards but refused the pension. When the war was over, he went back to his position as the Notary of the Holy Office in the Vatican until 1960, when he finally returned to Ireland, where he died quietly and peacefully in 1963.[66]

For Allied servicemen and civilian internees held by the Imperial Japanese Army throughout the Pacific region, there were no pimpernels. MI-9 and MIS-X were virtually powerless; there were no established underground escape lines; and partisan activities were minimal except for the isolated American operations in the Philippines. Prisoners of war and internees found themselves alone, cut off from the outside world, and fighting for survival in the jaws of one of the most extraordinary kinds of captivity ever known. For these captives the stakes of resistance and escape escalated to a new dimension. The prison camp became the arena for a bitter contest between wills, one in which the captors' determination was pitted against the prisoners' values, courage, and tolerance for unsurpassed human cruelty.

Survival in the Pacific
Escape from Militant Bushido

There was talk of escape, but escape brought seemingly insurmountable problems
because we, as caucasians, stood out in the world of yellow men.

—Joseph Petak (1991)

On February 19, 1942, President Franklin D. Roosevelt
signed Executive Order 9066. Using the precedent established by Abraham Lincoln's many proclamations against political prisoners during the
Civil War, as marginally legal as they turned out to be, the United States
Army imprisoned more than 110,000 innocent Japanese Americans, both
citizens and legal aliens, in a vast system of internment camps. Never
before had so many innocent American citizens been surrounded by
barbed wire in their own country. Gerald Ford finally revoked Executive
Order 9066 formally over thirty years later. Much as the USCTs had done
after their escapes from slavery before and during the Civil War, young
second-generation Japanese Americans, known as the Nisei, found a way
to escape their civilian confinement. While parents and family members
sat in the camps, they joined the Army.

Altogether, 33,000 Nisei volunteers were formed into two units on February 1, 1943: the 442d Regimental Combat Team from the West Coast
and the 100th Infantry Battalion from Hawaii. They were divided almost
equally between Europe and the Pacific, and their record, again like the
USCTs nearly a century before, is impressive. There was never a question
that toughness and determination characterized the Nisei units in the
American Army, and in the combat areas, the Nisei soldiers took their
motto, "Go for Broke," very seriously. Although at home, in the American popular press, these soldiers were often characterized stereotypically
as "our Japs," in Italy and France, the 442d earned the reputation of being

America's toughest ground soldiers. As Alan R. Bosworth pointed out in *America's Concentration Camps* (1968), they went for broke and suffered a 314 percent loss of the unit's original strength—more than 9,486 casualties—and became the most decorated combat team in the history of the U.S. Army.[1] In the Pacific, many served as combat interpreters and constantly ran the risk of being killed by their own troops. Frank Fugita was captured and became a POW; Iva Ikuko Toguri d'Aquino, an American student stranded in Japan in 1941, became a civilian internee. After the war, Fugita went home; Iva d'Aquino was charged with treason and convicted of being "Tokyo Rose."[2] Neither prisoner escaped from their captivities; they knew better.

In the Pacific theater, problems escalated considerably. Early victories of the Imperial Japanese Army yielded a large number of Allied prisoners and internees, and despite its discipline in the field, the Japanese Army's behavior against its prisoners devolved into outrageous forms of treatment. Squalid prison camps holding approximately 140,000 American and Allied POWs were spread throughout Asia, including Manchuria, Korea, China, Indonesia, Burma, Thailand, Singapore, Hong Kong, Indochina, Formosa (Taiwan), the Philippines, and Japan itself. Official "X" committees were formed in the camps, but there was little contact with MI-9 in London and MIS-X in Washington. Escape from most of these facilities, the jungle camps in particular, presented unique problems, and escape from camps in Japan was virtually impossible.

The British did form two escape organizations in Asia: the British Army Aid Group (BAAG), under the singular leadership of Australian Lt. Col. Leslie Ride, and (Ground Service) GS I(e) under Lt. Col. Robin Ridgeway. Ride had escaped from Hong Kong in 1942, by wearing civilian clothes and walking out the front gate of the prison. During the course of the war, BAAG worked closely with the Chinese communists to assist whatever escapes there were in the South China/Hong Kong area, and from time to time aided evaders and American fliers. In September 1943, the U.S. Air Force formed the Air Ground Aid Service (AGAS), the American equivalent of BAAG, to assist in the recovery of Allied evaders.[3] But despite these attempts, nothing proved very successful, and never before had such a large and varied group of POWs been so isolated from the outside world.

In the Japanese POW system, many camps were relatively removed from friendly but terrified populations, but not all. Proximity meant little, however, because few American, British, or Commonwealth POWs could speak the native languages, and if escapes were successful at first, long distances—much of which consisted of jungles and oceans—separated escapers from friendly lines. Partisan and guerrilla units helped Allied escapers, especially in the Philippines, Indochina, and China, but their numbers were small and contact was particularly difficult. Recaptures, with few exceptions, met with catastrophic results: public executions by shooting, beheading, or some lethal combination designed to humiliate the victims and create mortal terror in the remaining prisoners. Relatively few Allied POWs decided on escape as a means of self-liberation compared to the more sophisticated and, in many cases, highly organized escape activities in Europe. Even in the worst quarantine conditions that POWs suffered in the twentieth century, most Allied prisoners focused on their personal survival. They worked, starved, suffered, and sat it out.

The Japanese did not begin the twentieth century as draconian captors. The radical change in Japanese military attitudes and behavior toward prisoners of war in World War II occurred in part as the result of cultural retribution for European double-dealing in the early part of the century. Originally issued as *Japanese Army Regulations for Handling Prisoners of War* in February 1904, *Army Instruction No. 22*, Article 2 of the General Rules, stated, "Prisoners of war shall be treated with a spirit of goodwill and shall never be subjected to cruelties or humiliation."[4] From 1904 until 1945, a deteriorating series of events proved fateful.

After stunning victories during the Russo-Japanese War in 1904 and 1905, the Japanese took considerable numbers of Russian prisoners and treated them well. At Port Arthur, several Russian medical officers were astonished at how kind the Japanese were toward the sick in the naval barracks. The Russian Red Cross confirmed these reports: "Since the surrender, the whole attitude of the Japanese Army toward us has been exactly the same as if it were dictated by the fundamental values of European civilization . . . there has been nothing lacking on any point in the treatment by the Japanese medical staff of our sick and wounded."[5] What astounded the Russian doctors and the British observers who reported on Japanese behavior was that the Japanese Army was indeed a full participant in the Hague Conventions and acted accordingly in good faith.

The Russians, on the other hand, had trouble keeping up their end of the agreement. It became apparent that they had wildly inflated views of their own prowess and suffered their losses badly. In Japanese captivity, Russian officers complained bitterly about trivial matters instead of supporting the general welfare of their men, and the Russian commander in chief, General Kuropatkin, openly admitted that he had difficulty restraining his troops from killing their prisoners or any wounded Japanese they found.[6] In effect, the Russian Army set aside the traditional Golden Rule in favor of mistreating Japanese wounded, sick, and healthy POWs while foolishly expecting the Japanese soldiers to be one-sided humanitarians. How inconsistent it must have appeared during the Russo-Japanese War to discover Russians killing Japanese prisoners, including the sick and wounded, when the Czar of Russia himself led the movement to establish rules of war for the entire international community. What Europeans created for the world on paper was one thing; what they did in battle and after it was another.

Japan had signed and ratified the Hague Conventions, the international standard that regulated combatants' behavior in World War I, and the Imperial Japanese Army treated German prisoners taken in the Pacific very well.[7] Following the Great War, however, the culture of Japan changed. The country was seized by men consumed with the idea that they must militarize the entire nation in order to eliminate political, economic, and social dependence on European values. Beginning with children in elementary school, they set a goal of creating a society that thought in terms of conformity, collateral value assessment, and hierarchical decision-making.[8] As historian Philip A. Towle pointed out, the Japanese military elite no longer felt the need to satisfy Western standards.[9] The traditional Bushido warrior code, incorporated in the *Imperial Rescript to Soldiers and Sailors* (1882), spoke of dedication to the emperor, personal courtesy and health, truthfulness, obedience, frugality, and honor that regulated traditional Japanese knights or Samurai.[10] Twentieth-century militant Bushido hardened the traditional code, steeped in Buddhist cultural backgrounds, into a distinctly national ethos and began to filter it into non-military culture.

Radically different from the cultural trends present in nineteenth-century Europe, Japan's drive toward conformity in a military society contrasted significantly with Europe's liberal notions of regulating individuals, and by extension national, behavior through the power of law. Whereas Europeans who gathered at The Hague in the Netherlands in 1899 thought in terms of mitigating the horrors of war for individuals and possibly outlawing war in general, the militant Japanese officer corps began to see war as a means to achieve a new kind of cultural destiny. By the 1920s, Japan and Europe were headed in different directions. Japan had evolved into a quasi-military state, whereas most of Europe had tired of war and sought ways to end it. In the 1930s, the forces of national socialism in Germany and fascism in Italy followed Japan's example and led the world into the most devastating total war in human history.

The pivotal period for Japan was the Meiji era from 1868 to 1912. Named after the emperor who assumed the throne in 1868, this period witnessed an end to Japan's unique form of feudalism and partially westernized its culture in only forty years. The emperor introduced a constitution in 1868, and then the government divided the country into new political subdivisions rather than the traditional confederation of small kingdoms. With a strong central government in place in 1872, Meiji introduced universal conscription and deprived the influential professional military of its power and class status. Although most Samurai, Japan's feudal and knightly class, accepted the emperor's orders, some believed that he was ill-advised. In 1887, led by Saigo, one of the staunchest supporters of imperial restoration, a group of Samurai revolted. Saigo failed. By 1905, after a solid victory over Imperial Russia on the eve of World War I, Japan had modernized, industrialized, and evolved into a world military power to be reckoned with.[11]

Events that followed World War I showed conclusively that the European colonial powers were not ready to deal with Japan as an equal. After the Allies denuded Germany of its colonies in the Pacific following the Versailles Treaty in 1919, militarily powerful Western nations, encumbered with a false sense of cultural superiority over Asia and its peoples, created an expansive colonial system in Japan's back yard. During the Versailles meetings in France, the Japanese delegation wanted Western nations to insert a racial-equality clause in the Covenant of the League of Nations. Western nations ignored the request, arousing bitterness among those Japanese officers who had lived through Meiji, defeated the Russians, and fought on the side of the Allies against the European Central Powers.[12]

To these men, westernization meant something. Japan's post-war imperial gains made at Versailles were substantial, including some important German colonies and trading concessions in the Pacific region; however, something equally important was missing, full equality with the nations of the West.[13] When the colonizing nations refused to take the Japanese request seriously, the prominent political luminaries in the Imperial Japanese Army and Navy took offense. Military leaders began to oust civilians from government, and by the 1930s a decidedly militant Japanese officer corps controlled most governmental decision-making. Bitter feelings toward European and American political snobbishness and blatant racism regenerated Japanese political xenophobia, which, in turn, produced a unique form of Japanese cultural isolation and dramatically exalted notions of sociocultural superiority. Meiji acted first to transform

Japan's government from a feudal system to a constitutional monarchy, and the spirit of traditional Bushido, once the distinctive mark of honor among the Samurai, became thoroughly militarized and descended on the nation from top to bottom. As a cult stressing obedience to the emperor and possessing an overwhelming sense of moral superiority, militant Bushido developed as a very real spirit of Japanese regional destiny to lead Asia in the creation of a distinctly Asian empire.[14] In the name of the Emperor, the stage was set for Japanese aggression, war, and, ultimately, war crimes.

The Japanese called their new empire the Greater East Asia Co-Prosperity Sphere, and war became the means to achieve it. With Korea firmly in place as a Japanese colony in 1905, Manchuria to Korea's north became the first target in 1931, as imperial Japanese militarists began flexing their muscles. China, Britain, Canada, Australia, New Zealand, Burma, Thailand, the Philippines, and the United States discovered that when Japan acted as a world military power, it became expansive, belligerent, and dangerous. Militant Bushido also took a terrible toll on outsiders, especially those men and women who became prisoners of war. Rather than showing justice, sincerity, self-control, and honor, all values that formed the basis of the traditional *Rescript to Soldiers and Sailors* (1882) and the benign *Japanese Army Regulations for Handling Prisoners of War* (1904), the Imperial Japanese Army adopted the prescriptive *Military Field Code* in 1941. This unbending document required absolute obedience to superiors from generals to privates: total conformity in all military and personal matters; an understanding and complete acceptance of Japan's military and moral superiority; and suicide in place of an honorable surrender.

As captors who believed that surrender was an act of shame and disgrace to all soldiers of all nations, the Imperial Japanese Army became draconian and inflicted numerous forms of cruelty upon hundreds of thousands of Allied POWs and innocent Asian civilians in the name of cultural superiority on one hand and empire-building on the other. Laurens Van der Post suggested in his critical analysis, *The Night of the New Moon* (1985), that the "Japanese were themselves the puppets of immense personal forces," and "they truly did not know what they were doing."[15] Blending his own POW experience with what he knew about Japanese monoculture, Van der Post developed the theory of chaotic revenge to explain what happened to Allied POWs and internees in the Pacific. According to Van der Post's view of militant Bushido, Allied POWs were not understood or treated as human beings because the Japanese detested them to the point where their very existence aroused excessive personal hatred. According to the chaotic revenge theory, the desire for personal revenge against nineteenth- and twentieth-century European assumptions of superiority became a duty of every Japanese soldier. Instead of being just soldiers in captivity, Allied POWs and internees became symbols of a Western imperial past that used military, social, and economic power to bend the lives and spirits of the peoples of Asia to their inflexible will.[16]

Few prisoners who suffered at the hands of the Japanese disagreed with the first part of Van der Post's evaluation; however, the second part—that the Japanese as captors did not know what they were doing—presented a problem, and many took issue with his conclusion. Although it is true that the Japanese hated the European colonization of Asia, their own racial policy backfired, as was manifested in China, the Philippines, Thailand, and Indonesia. By freely using brutality toward all its prisoners and internees, the Japanese showed that the propaganda line, "Asia for Asians," meant Japan only. In his explanation of chaotic revenge, Van der Post created a large chasm between his views and the reflections of thousands of other prisoners in Japanese captivity who understood the burden of internationalized racism firsthand.

The torturous circumstances that made death imminent and reflected the attitudes of militant Bushido began in China and were later directed particularly against the Americans and Filipinos held in the Philippines, the British and Commonwealth POWs along the Burma-Siam Railway, and the Dutch in Java.[17] More than 61,000 POWs were marched to Burma and Thailand to labor on the railway. Nearly half were British; the others included 18,000 Dutch, 13,000 Australians, and 650 Americans, 320 of whom came from the 2d Battalion, 131st Field Artillery Regiment of the Texas National Guard, captured in the Dutch East Indies. The other Americans were sailors who survived the sinking of the cruiser USS *Houston* after the battle of Sunda Strait near Java on March 1, 1942.[18] Their problem stemmed from the fact that they were not experts in cultural analysis but ordinary soldiers and sailors who had become powerless victims of revenge-seeking captors. They had no idea why their guards, Korean or Japanese, were so cruel, why they struck one another, why or how they could be subjected to the unreasonable Japanese *Military Field Code* (1941), which was a far cry from the Hague Convention (1899) and the 1929 Geneva Convention, which regulated treatment for prisoners of war, the sick and wounded, and civilians.[19]

In the Allied POW view, Articles 46 and 47 of the 1929 Geneva Convention regulated punishments in general, and Article 51 regulated punishment for escapes. It read: "Attempted escape, even if it is a repetition of the offense, shall not be considered as an aggravating circumstance in case the prisoner of war should be given over to the courts on account of crimes or offenses against persons or property committed in the course of that attempt. After an attempted or accomplished escape, the comrades of the person escaping who assisted in the escape may incur only disciplinary punishment on this account."[20] Although they knew that as POWs they were subject to the laws, regulations, and orders in force in the Imperial Japanese Army, they believed that there were limits to their captors' absolutism. They were wrong. Even toward the war's end, when normally a losing side treats its POWs better as defeat closes in, the opposite was true for the Japanese. Executions continued until the Emperor ordered the army to cease hostilities. To these thousands of victims, the Japanese evolved from an enigma on one hand to the dramatis personae of a gigantic immortality play on the other.

In his memoir, Joseph A. Petak wrote, "There was talk of escape, but escape brought seemingly insurmountable problems because we, as caucasians, stood out in the world of yellow men."[21] John Durnford, a British junior officer captured in Singapore in 1942, remarked that his group of POWs rejected escapes for several reasons: the jungle terrain presented a physical and geographical impossibility even for the region's natives; recaptured escapers were all executed in public, and corporal punishments were levied against the sick who were already dying from neglect; and survival itself came to absorb the spiritual and physical energies of everyone.[22] Durnford wrote, "A voice with strong compulsion was urging me to escape at once and get home. Every minute it seemed to threaten to split myself from me. To escape? To die? I don't know."[23]

As Durnford pointed out, the stakes were too high and the probability of success was too low. One day in 1943, the Japanese marched thousands of British prisoners in Singapore from Changi to the Selarang Barracks, where they faced the difficult task of having to sign their escape rights away with the movement of a pen. Having seen the dreadful consequences of failed escapes and recaptures, these men knew that execution not only awaited them but also awaited anyone who helped them, and possibly innocent comrades as well. Eric Lomax, a signal officer from Scotland imprisoned in Singapore, remembered being forced to sign a document that said, "I, the undersigned, solemnly swear on my honour that I will not, under any circumstances, attempt an escape."[24] Forsaking escape, many of the Death Railways' survivors returned to the quarantine of desolate prison camps to wait for liberation.

Changi was not the only place where the Imperial Japanese Army concentrated Allied POWs from several countries. Comdr. C. D. Smith, USNR, was imprisoned in Shanghai, China, shortly after the United States joined the war in December 1941. Because Smith had worked as a merchant mariner, later as a Yangtze River pilot, he spoke Chinese and understood Japanese reasonably well. After his capture, he underwent a sham trial for war crimes and received a prison sentence. With Comdr. John B. Wolley, RN, and Corp. Jerold B. Storey, USMC, Smith formed a small group to escape Ward Road Prison in Shanghai. While preparing for the escape, Smith received some significant outside help, initially from a friend who threw saws into the prison to cut the prison bars, and later from Chinese citizens and soldiers who opposed the Japanese occupation. Smith knew Shanghai very well, a stroke of good luck that enabled the group to navigate its way to the outskirts of the city and increase its evading room. Since Smith was able to communicate with both communist and nationalist Chinese soldiers on the way north from Shanghai to the American lines, the group eventually reached Chungking.

Most of the Americans captured in April and May 1942 surrendered in the Philippines. The Americans on the Bataan peninsula, Luzon, surrendered in April, while thousands hurried in near panic eight miles by sea to the island fortress of Corregidor. Facing a defeated American Army holed up on the "Rock," as the soldiers called it, the Japanese Army issued a "Proclamation to the Defenders of Corregidor Island." It read: "If you continue to resist, the Japanese Forces will by every possible means destroy Corregidor Island and annihilate your forces relentlessly to the last man. This is your final chance to cease resistance. Further resistance is completely useless. You, dear soldiers, take it into consideration and give up your arms and stop resistance at once." [25] When Corregidor fell to the Japanese Army on May 7, 1942, eleven thousand American and Filipino prisoners were herded into an area about the size of two city blocks, with Japanese guards posted around them. Edgar D. Whitcomb, an Army Air Force bombardier-navigator, prisoner of war, and future escaper, recalled, "People began to die in increasing numbers, and it looked as if we would all die if things continued as they were." [26]

Escape from an island? It was a long swim, and the only place to go was back to occupied Bataan. On May 22, 1942, 2d Lt. Edgar D. Whitcomb and Capt. William Harris, USMC, left Corregidor by sea. [27] Both men swam the eight miles from Corregidor to the occupied Bataan peninsula. Whitcomb recalled: "It was about 8:30 P.M. when we lowered ourselves into the water to start swimming. There I stopped for a moment to kiss the old Rock good-bye. . . . It was only two or three miles across from Corregidor back to Bataan at the closest point, and it should have been possible to swim the distance in a few hours if things went well. Both Bill and I had a lot of confidence in our swimming because we had been practicing every day, just off the shore from the prison camp on the opposite side of the island. The water was cool, and it felt good to the body."[28] During the long swim to the far shore, the two men drank fresh rainwater while large waves bobbed them about and slowed their progress. From time to time one swimmer lost sight of the other. Night set in, and still they swam on. Fish nipped at their arms and legs, but the sharks kept their distance. Weary from the swim, Whitcomb and Harris saw the distant outline of a large Japanese barge standing next to the shoreline dotted with trees. "Without a word," he wrote, "we turned and headed for the shore, which offered much better security for us than the Japanese barge." About twenty feet from shore, they came upon some large rocks. According to Whitcomb, "Like two sea monsters emerging from the water, we struggled our way across the rocks and onto the shore." Then, realizing that they had exhausted themselves, both men dropped into a clump of bushes and slept. "When we awoke," commented Whitcomb, "the sun was low in the western sky. We were free."[29]

The two escapers separated, and Whitcomb decided that deception was the best means to save his life. He joined a group of civilians, changed his identity for what he considered to be the war's duration, and fooled the Japanese into believing he was a civilian internee. His masquerade proved to be effective and useful. Disguised as a civilian, Whitcomb was exchanged and returned to the United States on the Swedish ship, the SS *Gripsholm*. It was not until the war's end that he convinced the Army Air Force that he wanted another combat assignment in the Pacific, where he had been captured in 1942. In 1945, at his own insistence, Whitcomb returned to flight duty in the Philippines.[30]

Captured with the American forces in the Philippines in 1941–42 were more than 45,000 members of the Philippine Commonwealth Army, many of whom were regular soldiers in the American Army and were known as the Philippine Scouts. Together with the Americans, more than 78,000 Filipinos faced surrender to the Imperial Japanese Army in April 1942. Approximately 3,000 soldiers escaped to Corregidor, while 75,000 marched to Camp O'Donnell with the Americans. Many Filipinos were quickly released by the Japanese, but about 45,000 Filipinos and 9,300 Americans served together in captivity. Some, however, decided to risk execution and defy the Japanese. As escapers, the Filipino soldiers blended perfectly into their own human terrain. For example, Larry L. Pangan, a master sergeant in the Carabao Division commanded by Brig. Gen. Maxim Lough, managed to escape from a work detail in November 1942.[31] Manuel D. Bananga was a member of Troop E, 26th Cavalry. After his unit was defeated on Bataan, he left by boat on April 7, 1942, for fortress Corregidor, where he fought with the 4th Marines until May 6. Wounded and taken prisoner, Bananga found himself first in Bilibid Prison in Manila, then in Capas, then in Camp O'Donnell. Bananga's luck held. He managed to get himself released from a field hospital, and then he headed north into the mountains. When the American forces landed in Lingayen Gulf in January 1945, he reported for duty.

Other Filipino escapers like Exequiel Cruz Laquian, Company D, 2d Battalion, Banal Regiment, became guerrillas for the duration. Captured as a guerrilla and headed for certain execution, Laquian escaped when his captors allowed him to go to the latrine along the Pasig River. With sirens glaring and searchlights illuminating the water, he swam downstream and eventually rejoined his unit. Eleuterio Maquinana, a corporal in Company L, 57th Infantry, surrendered with his unit on April 9, 1942. He escaped, went south about three hundred miles to his home, and fought against the Japanese Army as a guerrilla until liberation.[32] In spite of the Japanese policy of Asia for Asians, captured Filipinos were considered to be American mercenaries and received no better treatment than the Americans. In many cases, it was far worse.

In 1942, three Naval Reserve ensigns walked out the front gate of Cabanatuan prison camp on the Philippine island of Luzon on the day they arrived. The three ensigns had no outside help, became lost in the jungle, and decided to turn themselves in. Because they had not been present for the issuance of orders from Cabanatuan's Japanese prison administration, upon their return they were forced merely to detail their experience before the other prisoners. They suffered only the mildest punishment. According to Steven Mellnik, after their jungle ordeal they looked pretty good, much better in fact than the other POWs in camp.[33] One Mexican-American passed as a Filipino and escaped from the prison hospital. Upon learning that his squad was marked for execution because of his escape, he returned voluntarily. Although he was hounded and beaten, he survived the retribution.

Despite Japan's refusal to ratify the 1929 Geneva Convention, the Japanese government established a Prisoner of War Bureau in December 1941, charged with handling POW matters. Like the Soviet Union in Europe, Japan still had the Hague Convention to abide by as well as its own internal regulations, the *Japanese Army Regulations for Handling Prisoners of War* (1904), initially benign enough on paper to resemble the practice of traditional rather than militant Bushido. Actual practice in accordance with the *Military Field Code* (1941) was different from the strict guidelines on paper. Rumors of POW mistreatment began to filter back to the United States in late 1942, mostly from evaders who managed to avoid capture and sail in open boats to Australia. Secretary of State Cordell Hull responded by sending diplomatic notes to the Japanese, while the neutral Swedish liner *Gripsholm* continued to bring Red Cross packages to Japan.[34] Hull's notes meant little, and the American POWs received no mail or Red Cross packages until 1943. Even then, most of the Red Cross packages were pilfered before the POWs received them.

As early as 1942, the Japanese camp commandants addressed the escape problem by threatening to establish a ten-for-one retributive escape and execution policy. To discourage individual, partnership, and small group escapes, they set up a form of mass reprisals against the innocent, one that affirmed a vital aspect of the Japanese military ethos: collateral or joint responsibility for each soldier's actions in a primary military unit. Forming "Blood Brother" groups, or what the prisoners called "shooting squads," the Japanese camp authorities held groups of ten prisoners responsible for a possible escape by any member of the group. If one or several members of a "shooting squad" escaped, those left behind were to be executed.[35] Threats turned to reality one day on Luzon when the Japanese guards, without revealing their purpose, asked Theodore Biggers for ten men as volunteers after one man escaped from a work detail. The guards shot all ten in front of the other prisoners.[36]

Knowing that some Americans devised escape plans regardless of the risks and severe punishments, the Japanese Army needed some device to legitimize its policy of severe retributive actions. The solution was an amendment to its *Prisoner of War Regulations* on March 9, 1943, that permitted recaptured Allied escapers to be legally punished in the same way as its own deserters. The amendment read, "The leader of a group of persons who have acted together in effecting an escape shall be subject to either death, or imprisonment for a minimum of ten years. The other persons involved shall be subject to either the death penalty or a minimum imprisonment of one year."[37]

In spite of the order, on October 25, 1943, two enlisted men, Pvts. Oscar B. Brown and Robert Lee Pease, escaped from the Davao Penal Colony on Mindanao.[38] While pretending to work on a rice paddy dike, the Americans, along with a Filipino convict, killed a guard and made a clean getaway. However, the fate of three junior officers who attempted another escape revealed what the new order really meant. As the three men crawled along the ditch in the dark to get through the wire surrounding the camp, they were stumbled upon by an unsuspecting prisoner. One of the officers rose and began fighting with the meddler. As a second escaper jumped to his feet, and he too began to berate the stumbler for intentionally ruining the escape. A nearby guard overheard the word "escape" spoken once too often, and the Americans were seized and severely beaten. The three men were then marched to a site in full view of the camp with their hands tied and pulled over their heads and their bodies bent forward to ease the pressure on their arms. The men were beaten once again and endured this torture for forty-eight hours, until the guards shot two and beheaded one.[39]

Because individual escapes grew riskier for the groups of ten, the shooting squad became the natural breeding ground for the formation of *ad hoc* escape organizations. Several requirements existed before anyone could be brought into such a group. Each member had to be fully committed to escape and to accept the reality that one mistake could cost the lives of the entire group. Each member needed to accept a job within an organizational hierarchy based on skill in an area of expertise rather than on rank alone. Each member needed to remain healthy enough in camp to be able to make an arduous journey, and no one outside the group, even close friends, could know about the escape. Inside the camp, it was crucial to develop friendships with someone who had connections in the regional community. Outside help, especially during the evasion phase, was also vital. If one link was weak or missing, the entire escape plan became useless.

There were two major breakouts from the Davao Penal Colony, abbreviated to *Dapecol* by soldiers, on the southern Philippine island of Mindanao. The first one took place in 1943, the other a year later. The initial group consisted of twelve men: officers Melvin H. McCoy (Navy); Stephen M. Mellnik (Army); William E. Dyess, Leo A. Boelens, and Samuel Grashio (Army Air Corps); A. C. "Shifty" Shofner, Michael Dobervich, and Jack Hawkins (Marines); and two Army sergeants, R. B. Spielman and Paul Marshall.[40] Accompanied by two Filipino convicts who acted as guides through the jungle, this group planned and executed the only organized American escape from Japanese captivity in World War II. Although the group had not been a shooting squad before the escape, the members came together slowly in secret meetings within the confines of Davao. Such secrecy was critical. Dyess remembered the story of the American soldier and his Filipino friend who planned a breakout from the Negros Island camp. They told their plans to one person too many, and the Japanese found their little store of supplies. This evidence of intended escape resulted in the beheadings of both men.[41]

If complete secrecy was the first requirement, a full commitment to leave the camp was the second. Others included skills in survival and navigation, physical stamina to make the journey, and an individual understanding that recapture would most probably result in some form of brutal execution. The POWs were mindful of how Colonel Mori, camp commandant at Cabanatuan, had dealt with recaptured escapers. When an unsuccessful group of three had been returned, the men were tied naked to the barbed-wire fence and beaten with sticks until they collapsed unconscious. Their tormentors revived them with water and beat them again. After three days, one was beheaded and two were shot by a firing squad in a scenario reminiscent of the Davao escapers. Although some who fled were allowed to live, their lives were made miserable. One soldier was beaten and penned like an animal in a small wooden cage; he soon went insane.[42]

Retaliation against nonescapers continued to present problems. Although members of the group worried about possible reprisals, they decided that the Davao camp was a likely prospect for an escape, possibly more so than any other camp in the Japanese system. For example, Samuel Grashio recalled that one of the redeeming features of Davao, compared with Cabanatuan, was that supervision was relatively lax. Japanese patrols controlled all the regional roads, and it became obvious that the Japanese believed that the jungle was impassable. As a result, they refrained from watching the eastern and northern sides of the camp with any care and did not assign guards to every work detail.[43] The commandant, Major Maeda, was an honorable man, nothing like Cabanatuan's Mori, and the group believed that he preferred some form of group punishment other than vicious reprisals.

At first, the group planned to steal a Filipino banca outrigger and sail to Australia, but they needed a navigator. The choice was Melvin H. McCoy, an Annapolis-trained, experienced naval officer who had carefully hidden his nautical navigation books from the Japanese after capture. The group developed a convergence plan that took several groups of three men each out of the camp in successive stages. Passing the sentries as usual, they attracted little attention. According to Hawkins, "We marched up to the guard and halted and saluted."[44] The guard counted the men and let them continue on what had become a normal plowing detail. Instead of proceeding to work, they plunged through the banana grove to a thicket, grabbed some equipment stored during work details days before, and hurried to the edge of the jungle. As planned, the men waited there for their two Filipino guides, Ben and Victor. Only seconds before Hawkins and the others gave up hope, Ben and Victor arrived. Hawkins recalled, "Silently we shouldered our packs and struck off in Indian file on the muddy trail with Ben and Victor in the lead." Hawkins confessed that at this point in the escape, euphoria overwhelmed him. "Plunging deeper into the dark shadows of the dripping jungle, I felt a surging exultation. I was free!"[45]

Hawkins soon learned that the Philippine jungles on Mindanao were uninviting places for strangers. The breakout began on April 4, 1943, at around ten o'clock in the morning. With swamps, mountains, swollen rivers, and endless soaking rain, backpacking through a tropical rain forest tested the strength of the hardiest. For a group of American and Filipino escapers weakened by the physical and emotional strains of battle, surrender, a death march, and then captivity itself, each obstacle seemed insurmountable. Muddy swamps sucked down their feet and legs, and sharp, high grasses knifed their bare skin. Steamy heat soaked the men with sweat, claiming valuable body water and precious calories, and swarms of flies were constant companions. The escapers drank from hanging vines, while thorns scraped and punctured their bodies. Although fatigued almost beyond endurance, they made about a hundred yards an hour. Then they met the bees. Dyess recalled with some horror, "They were the biggest brutes I ever saw. Their hive must have been in the log near the spot where Victor built the fire. When two of them hit me in the back simultaneously, I thought I had been stabbed. I fell forward across the log and covered my head with my hands. About a dozen bees had a try at me as I found later when I picked their stingers out of my shirt. Bob was stung a dozen times before he plunged into the water. No one escaped. The bees raised hell more than half an hour, then left us."[46] After the bees, the group felt pains on their legs, chests, and arms from leeches. Lacking proper medicines, the men had only two remedies available: burning them off with a lighted cigarette or rubbing tobacco into the sores. Both were unpleasant. The destination, however, was always more important than the obstacles, and the group was determined to make contact with Filipino guerrillas, who continued the fight against the Imperial Japanese Army.

After several days spent navigating the trail north, the group found Kapungagen, a seemingly abandoned Filipino village. A small party left the group to investigate; the others waited. Upon the scouting party's return, all the escapers experienced another euphoric moment; the village was not abandoned, it was the home of Filipino guerrillas. They met and joined Lt. Col. Wendell W. Fertig's partisan army and became soldiers again before leaving the Philippines. According to Dyess, "Within a few hours we got our orders. They brought with them a thrill that blotted out the misery of the past. We were fighting men once more."[47] After fleeing from Davao and spending time with Fertig's Mindanao guerrilla command, most members of the escape team fled the Philippines to Australia by submarine and eventually reached the United States.[48]

Back in Davao, camp authorities discovered the escape. The camp commandant sent eighty-five soldiers into the jungle in search of the escapers. Unsuccessful in their mission, the patrol stumbled upon some luckless Filipinos instead and shot them in reprisal for the escape. As predicted, the Japanese seized each escaper's respective shooting squad; however, Hawkins's evaluation of Colonel Maeda's response proved correct. An officer more committed to traditional than to militant Bushido, Maeda executed no one. Instead, camp rations, already at a critical level to sustain life, were reduced, and the guards became more security-conscious. The most unusual reprisal came when the camp authority arrested some prisoners and forced them to undergo fifteen- or thirty-day periods of "meditation," during which time they were supposed to ponder the sins and crimes of the escapers.[49]

The second Davao escape took place on March 27, 1944. Less skillfully planned, it was a more opportunistic and violent episode than the earlier incident. Led by two survivors of the Bataan Death March, Army Capt. Mark M. Wohlfeld and 1st Lt. Hadley C. Watson, the plan called for the lightly guarded escape team to go to a point near the jungle's edge, where they would put themselves in a position to attack and kill the guards with shovels.[50] After several false starts, Watson began the escape roughly according to plan. He assaulted and killed his guard with a shovel. Marvin H. Campbell disabled a Japanese corporal, grabbed his rifle, and killed another guard. The remaining guards then scattered in a mass panic. In the midst of the chaotic shootout, Wohlfeld attacked the guard nearest him and ran for his life. Caught in the mud of a bog, the angered and stunned guard took aim with his rifle and fired, grazing Wohlfeld in the side. In spite of his slight wound, Wohlfeld again attacked the guard, this time viciously packing mud in his face and pushing him underwater to make sure he was dead. Years later, Wohlfeld wrote that his escape was "more or less a spontaneous affair. The actual

Maj. Mark Wohlfeld, USA. Major Wohlfeld led the second Davao escape on March 27, 1944. Members of the escape party eventually found Lt. Col. Wendell W. Fertig's partisan army and became soldiers again before leaving the Philippines. In December 1944, Wohlfeld refused repatriation, waived a promotion, and joined 1st Cavalry Division's fight through the islands of Leyte and Luzon. Courtesy of Carl Nash

fight at the squash field took less than sixty seconds, but once it was started it couldn't be stopped." [51] Completely alone, Wohlfeld ran into the jungle as fast as he could.

Of the eleven POWs who marched from Davao that morning, eight escaped. Wohlfeld had separated from the others during the breakout and wandered around the Mindanao jungle alone. After dodging Japanese patrols and picking swamp leeches from his skin for four days, Wohlfeld discovered to his horror that he was still only a short distance from Davao. Without outside help from friendly Filipino villagers, he knew that recapture was only a matter of time. Close to despair, he encountered a group of natives on a spear-fishing expedition. With his hands held high in the air, he faced a man pointing a spear at his head and cried, "Friend! Amigo! American!"[52] The Filipinos were friendly and gave him rice and bananas before taking him to their village. As their honored guest, the weary and hungry Wohlfeld had a banquet and some much-needed rest. With the help of a young girl who served as an interpreter, he discovered that there were American and Filipino guerrillas fighting in Mindanao and he asked for guides to take him there.

After several days' march through the jungle, Wohlfeld's party heard the command "Halt," given in English.[53] On April 1, 1944, much as Hawkins, Dyess, Grashio, and the others had done less than a year earlier, he stood face to face with Colonel Fertig's Mindanao guerrillas. Not only was he free, he discovered that friendly villagers had also rescued Watson and most of the others, including Army Lts. James D. Haburn and James McClure. Andrew T. Bukovinsky and Marvin H. Campbell joined Fertig's guerrilla forces operating in the western Mindanao region of Zamboanga.[54] Wohlfeld became Fertig's division chief of staff until October 1944, when American troops landed on Leyte. Wanting to rejoin the regular forces, he commandeered a Filipino banca outrigger and a small crew to sail north on a fourteen-day journey to Dinagat Island, Leyte, where his journey ended. As an escaped POW, Wohlfeld had the right to go home to a promotion and possibly a desk job to finish the war comfortably. Instead, Wohlfeld waived the promotion and in December 1944, joined the 1st Cavalry Division in its fight through Leyte, then from Luzon to Manila and through old Fort McKinley, and finally into the surrounding mountains.[55]

Too many obstacles cluttered the pathway for escape in Asia. Although some American prisoners planned or simply seized opportunities to escape from Davao, other camps in the Pacific were far more secure. Some were positioned in areas too remote for any hope of success; others in Japan offered no possibility for escape at all. Even toward the war's end, when more recently taken and briefly held American prisoners began to return to Allied lines in Burma from Japanese camps, they appeared to the attacking British troops to be in horrible condition. In his memoir *Quartered Safe Out Here* (1992), Scotsman George MacDonald Fraser commented on a day in 1945, when an American escaped from a camp near Rangoon and wandered into his position. Fraser wrote, "He was in a fair old state, and when the master-gyppo (sergeant) put porridge and a fried breakfast in front of him he burst into tears, and, according to an eye-witness, buried his head in the bosom of the nearest soldier and kept repeating 'Oh, boys, boys!' while they assured him he was awreet noo."[56] The effect of witnessing the happiness of escape thrilled the Scotsmen; at the same time, their hatred for the Japanese grew considerably.

When the world discovered what had happened along the Kwai River in Thailand, in the Philippines, Java, and many other POW sites, the desire for retribution became nearly uncontrollable and impervious to time's healing process. By 1945, 25,600 Americans had been taken prisoner of war in the Pacific. More than 22,000 surrendered in the Philippines in 1942; 1,555 surrendered after the Japanese invasion of Wake Island in December 1941; and 400 were taken alive in Guam as well as 200 in China. By 1945, 10,650 American POWs had died in captivity, and 14,950 were eventually liberated.[57] The American death rate peaked at 45 percent of the prisoner population, and thousands of Allied POWs aboard the unmarked "Hell Ships" en route to Japan drowned after the ships were unknowingly torpedoed by American submarines. The Allies suffered even greater numbers of captures and deaths than the Americans. The Japanese captured 22,400 Australians, nearly half of whom, about 13,000, worked on the Burma-Siam Railway, the "Death Railway," until 1943, along with 61,000 other POWs. The number of dead on the railway became appalling: 2,650 Australians died working on the line, along with 10,000 Dutch, British, Americans, and Canadians. To increase the labor pool beyond the available prisoners, the Japanese Army conscripted more than 70,000 Thai and Malay civilians, most of whom died from starvation, neglect, and murder.[58]

As Van der Post pointed out, one paradox of World War II in the Pacific was that the Japanese flouted the Golden Rule. When the war's progress worsened for the Japanese, POW treatment deteriorated as well. Malnutrition was never a temporary issue; at one thousand or fewer calories a day, starvation was certain. In spite of initial official disbelief in Washington, the American government accepted the escapers' debriefs, and by May 1945, the surgeon general ordered all transport commanders who brought repatriated prisoners home to feed them very lightly.[59] Most POWs weighed less than one hundred pounds when they returned to Allied control, and prisoners recalled almost universally that in camp they were forced to grow their own food.

Until escapers provided eye-witness evidence, the War Department was not terribly anxious to publicize rumors of atrocities in the Asian prison camps. By 1944, after the American military services debriefed their respective escapers and discovered what had really happened to American and Allied prisoners in Japanese captivity, policies began to change, and a new spirit of resolve for total victory against Japan gained considerable momentum. Part of that resolve centered on the use of escapers to publicize the graphic descriptions of Japanese camps that first appeared in intelligence reports issued by the Office of the Provost Marshal General in 1944 and 1945.[60] By 1944, escapers were permitted to go public with their stories.

After attaining freedom, many escapers developed a strong political agenda: they felt a need to bear witness to the horrors of Japanese captivity while the war continued. Jack Hawkins wrote, "We believed that if we were successful in returning to our own forces, our revelation to the world of the barbarous Japanese treatment of prisoners in the Philippines would bring the pressure of world opinion to bear upon Japan and might result in a general improvement in the lot of all the prisoners of war in Japanese hands."[61] Sam Grashio, for example, put together a radio show in Hollywood that described the Bataan Death March, complete with sound effects of men being tortured and killed. Published escape narratives filled with war propaganda from Pacific captivity began to arrive in the nation's bookstores at the same time. William E. Dyess's *The Dyess Story* (1944) appeared first and enjoyed wide circulation among U.S. citizens anxious to discover what happened to their lost army in the Philippines. Dyess had suffered the worst of the Bataan Death March, and his narrative was especially graphic in its descriptions of atrocities committed on Bataan, at Camp O'Donnell, and later in the Davao Penal Colony. In the same year, Melvin McCoy and Steven Mellnik's joint narrative *Ten Escape from Togo* (1944) followed Dyess's lead and described Japanese atrocities in significant detail.

These narratives did their work well and served as powerful propaganda to continue the war against Japan. They aroused an American wartime public that had believed that its soldiers who were captured in 1942 were patiently waiting for liberation under the care of an international law-abiding Imperial Japanese Army. Simultaneously shocked and horrified, the American public, Congress, and the military services reacted with a desire for severe retribution. The price that the Japanese nation paid for adopting militant Bushido and practicing brutality against Allied prisoners of war was heavy. In 1945, it came in part through the use of atomic bombs against Hiroshima and Nagasaki.[62] After the war, the call for retributive justice came through military tribunals.

Although the atomic bomb and its possible long-term effects were hotly debated issues, the retributive justice brought to bear against war criminals was not questioned. Beginning in 1945 and lasting through

1948, the Allied international community called for military courts to seek legal accounting against those Japanese officers and enlisted men who directly affected the fate of prisoners in the Pacific. Killing unarmed POWs, internees, and innocent civilians became an internationally recognized war crime.[63] The U.S. Army sought evidence and sent Graves Registration units to Bataan and Corregidor, where they used surrendered Japanese soldiers to dig up American bodies for reburial in the Manila military cemetery. In a letter home to Pottsville, Pennsylvania, Martin O'Hara, brother of author John O'Hara, reported that the executed soldiers were hastily buried where they fell. He wrote with a tone common for the time: "I'm here on the 'Rock' with a platoon digging up dead G.I.'s (Jap P.W. labor) and sending them to our cemetery in Manila for a decent burial, and, Walter, do I work the ass off the sons-of-bitches. When we finish here we are going to disinter the victims (that we can find) along the 'Bataan Death March.' We have 1,800 sons-of-heaven here who failed their Emperor."[64]

In 1946, the Americans tried and executed Gens. Masarahu Homma and Tomayuki Yamashita, along with Col. Seiichi Ohto, chief of the secret police, and fifteen others in the Philippines, for the Bataan Death March and POW treatment. O'Hara wrote, "My job is to process them before they are executed. There are eighteen Japs awaiting execution here including Lt. General Masarahu Homma, what a morbid looking bunch of bastards they are."[65] Most were ignominiously hanged. General Homma was shot by a firing squad. O'Hara knew the executioner, who told him that General Homma and Lt. Gen. Hikotara Tajima shouted "Banzai" before they died.[66] Although doubts have surfaced among contemporary scholars concerning the validity of these trials and the need for executions, Martin O'Hara was satisfied that justice was done.[67]

For the generations who came after the American GIs, Australian Diggers, British Tommies, and all the Western internees and civilians who suffered so terribly at the hands of the Imperial Japanese Army, these experiences may be more easily ignored or forgotten than remembered. For former POWs whose memories contain individualized living images of these events, however, the issue has not been resolved. The old wounds still hurt as the long-range effects of the prison camp diseases continue to take their toll in human suffering. Medical and psychological studies concur with the health care community's belief and the Veterans' Administration's acceptance that the captivity experience in the Pacific was outrageous. As a result, Allied POW veterans' organizations in Britain, Canada, Australia and New Zealand, and the United States have sought for years to bring suit against the Japanese government in the World Court, citing Article 131 of the 1949 Geneva Convention: "No High Contracting Party shall be allowed to absolve itself or any other High Contracting Party of any liability incurred by itself or by any other High Contracting Party. . . ." In effect, the surviving veterans believe that the ill-treatment they received as POWs during World War II created severe illnesses for most, early deaths for some, and enduring cases of post traumatic stress disorder for all.[68]

The drama of the Asian holocaust continued during the summer of 1995, when several British veterans of the Death Railway told their story honestly and frankly to a Japanese court. Formal governmental apologies to those who suffered needless cruelty from their captors meant very little to these men; the ability to remind an entire nation publicly about their suffering meant a great deal. Because of these men's actions, a nearly disbelieving Japanese public, long removed from the tragic horrors that took place during World War II, heard about them for the first time.[69] As far as these veterans were concerned, they did their moral duty to those who died needlessly as POWs in Japanese hands. On the other hand, chances remain virtually nonexistent that any modern government will continue to bear the cost of or the guilt for the sins of previous generations.[70] In the postwar world, guilt began to turn inward, as new voices emerging from the ashes of war blamed the soldier-prisoners for their own mistreatment rather than their culpable captors.

Tigers
The Will to Escape in Korea

We guessed we were in for it. Perhaps the war was going bad for their side. Perhaps we had been rebels. Perhaps we had served their purpose, whatever it was, there was something in the air. . . . We were tense; now the guards would not even let us go to the toilet.

—Rubin Townsend (1990)

Beginning in 1950, the United States ordered 1,319,000 service personnel to participate in what evolved from a so-called "Police Action" into the Korean War. Forces of the United Nations, including South Koreans, Americans, British, Commonwealth nations, Greeks, French, and Turks, fought against the military and political forces of North Korea and the Chinese People's Volunteers on nearly the full length of the Korean peninsula from 1950 until an armistice between the warring parties stopped the fighting in the summer of 1953. The war cost the United States approximately $70 billion, and in the fighting, American military forces lost nearly 37,000 dead from combat and other reasons.[1] For a country still recovering from World War II's price tag of more than $560 billion and 350,000 dead, the action in Korea was expensive not only in dollars but also in human terms, especially for POWs. Atrocities were commonplace, and the number of prisoners mounted as the fighting intensified: 7,140 American servicemen were known to have been captured; 2,701 prisoners died in captivity; and 4,418 were returned to United Nations control at the end of hostilities in 1953.[2]

For the Americans as well as other United Nations troops, captivity at the hands of the North Koreans paralleled captivity at the hands of the Japanese during World War II. The weather often played a role in the deaths. After a capture in the winter, the communist North Koreans commonly removed the prisoners' heavy clothes and combat boots and then forced them to march barefoot in the coldest weather. Frostbite became a major problem almost immediately. The average food ration was one rice ball per day with little or no water. On the marches, prisoners were often paraded through Korean towns and displayed as criminals in front of the local populace. Any prisoner unable to continue marching because of exhaustion, frostbite, illness, or wounds received in battle was executed on the spot.

In addition to the individual executions common on the marches, American and United Nations prisoners suffered and died from malnutrition, dysentery, pneumonia, wounds, and ill-treatment by the North Korean guards. Mass executions took place from time to time. One very lucky American, Army Pfc. John Valdor, told a *Newsweek* correspondent how the North Koreans massacred his group of prisoners:

> They told us they were taking us to chow. They took us out in groups of twenty-five or thirty. They walked us up a hill behind some bushes and told us to sit on the ground. Before we knew what was happening, they opened up on us with rifles and burp guns. The fellows were screaming and crying and the guards were laughing as they shot into us. I was shot in the left arm and I lay down on my face and played dead. When we were all down, they went around clubbing us with rifle butts. Anyone who moved or made a noise was shot through the head. We got away after the guards left us for dead. We got away from the scene as far as we could make it and then hid in the hills all night, all day yesterday, and last night. This morning we heard someone yelling in American. It was the airborne guys. I was never so glad to see anyone.[3]

In all, more than a thousand United Nations soldiers died or disappeared without a trace on the Korean death marches.[4] For these heavily guarded prisoners, escape was particularly difficult; either they were bound for the prison camps north along the Yalu River or they met death along the way. Nevertheless, with a keen understanding of the realities of the extreme cruelty inflicted on Allied POWs in the Pacific theater during World War II and fearing certain death in enemy hands, American and United Nations POWs began to escape.

A young Marine, Pvt. Charles Martin Kaylor, found himself sitting on the line in North Korea when news of his dependency discharge came through. On November 28, 1950, his term of enlistment was up, and for him the war was over, or so he thought.[5] His unit, the 1st Marine Division, and the Army's 7th Infantry Division were moving north for an assault on the Chosin Reservoir. Directed to headquarters for evacuation to the rear, Kaylor hitched a ride on the lead truck of a five-truck convoy for a seventy-mile trip south. Although local Koreans attempted to tell the American soldiers the news, little did he know that the Chinese had decided to counterattack that day. As the convoy worked its way south, the lead truck encountered an enemy roadblock and smashed into it headlong. Firing began, and the chaos of battle wrapped itself around him and the other men in the convoy. With its tires blown out from hand-grenade shrapnel, Kaylor's truck swerved into a ditch. Driver and gunner ran for the nearby woods; Kaylor was alone. A grenade exploded near him and he fell to the ground unconscious.

When Kaylor awoke, he was wounded and a prisoner of the Chinese People's Volunteers. His captors frisked him and took his parka. The convoy survivors were then forced to walk to a Korean village, where Kaylor's interrogator told him that his destination was first China and, ultimately, home. During an eleven-day walk north in ever-increasing cold, the small group met more prisoners at the village of Kanggye near the Yalu River. Interrogations continued, and the Marines were told they could go home if they gave the Chinese the information they wanted. Although they exaggerated and lied about force locations and troop strengths, the Marines satisfied their captors, who informed them that release was imminent. After loading the prisoners onto trucks, the Chinese took nineteen of them south to the Imjin River area, where the release went awry and the escape began.

The Chinese were concerned that the new United Nations offensive might result in the wounding or death of the prisoners. As artillery whistled through the air, forcing their captors to huddle in foxholes, the nineteen men seized the opportunity and dashed away. Instead of finding friendly forces, however, the group ran into more Chinese. One of the Marines spoke the language and explained to their new captors that they were all released POWs making their way back to their own lines. The Chinese front-line soldiers thought this an unlikely story at best, and it looked to the Americans as if a summary execution, theirs, was about to take place. The Marines saw no option short of attack. Not only were they clearly escapers confronting recapture on the battle line, but they were also soldiers again.

After a brief but successful fight with the Chinese, the escapers decided to wait in a nearby Korean village. More luck smiled on them when they encountered a friendly Korean who told them to sit tight while he tried to get word to the Americans. As they waited, they looked outside and saw a small, single-engine L-19 spotter aircraft flying overhead. The quick-thinking Marines then cut the wallpaper into strips and spelled out

"POW 19 Rescue." The L-19 pilot knew that this could be a trick to lure him into a trap, so he dropped the short message, "Come out to the letters so you can be counted."[6] Confirming that indeed nineteen American prisoners were holed up below, the pilot sent for tanks. On May 25, 1951, the escaped Marines saw the armored cavalry coming to their rescue.

In January 1951, Army Sgt. Rubin Townsend found himself under fire from the Chinese, along with eighty-five fellow soldiers of the U.S. Army 2d Division. The Chinese attacked aggressively, each time forcing the Americans to withdraw farther and farther up the hill. The assault continued late into the night. Suddenly there was the dazzling flash of a concussion grenade, and Townsend fell unconscious. When he came to, he saw Chinese and captured American soldiers standing over him. He was a prisoner. Marched to the rear in the snow, Townsend and the others were sent to small huts to rest. Fed only bowls of millet, a mixture of grain and corn, and some hot water if they were lucky, many of the Americans collapsed from extreme hunger during the course of the march. The wounded fared even worse, and most died en route north. Dysentery also set in, and the situation looked bleak indeed.

As the group trudged north, Townsend saw his first opportunity to escape. Noting that no guards were around as they crossed a small bridge, Townsend and two other prisoners jumped down into the snow. He wrote, "I kept falling and trying to keep my feet down, or at least I hoped they were down. As I hit the snow I could hear one man land to my left and one to my right. From the fall from the bridge we must have burrowed into the snow seven to eight feet. All I knew was [that] it was over my head. The snow had broken the long fall, and we were lucky not to have hit anything on our way down like a tree, rock, or anything like that."[7] The escaping Americans discovered an old hut in the mountains and hid there while seeking to regain their strength. They knew it was a long trip to friendly lines through unfriendly territory. The task of fording rivers and streams in mid-winter Korea and leapfrogging from hut to hut in the mountains was daunting, yet they pressed on.

Unfortunately, the fleeing escapers visited one hut too many. The warmth felt too good, and they lingered too long. Shots rang out, and the men realized that they were surrounded again. According to Townsend, "We were in a hell of a spot. As the firing ceased we talked in a low tone and tried to make plans. We stood no chance trying to run out the back as there were fifty yards to the tree line or bush. We would have been shot to hell. We talked, and determined that we would have to give up or be shot. We all agreed it would be better to surrender and try to escape again rather than be killed or wounded." [8] Resolute and defenseless, they surrendered and became prisoners once again. They never revealed the fact that they were escaped POWs; instead, they said they had simply become lost and were hunting for their unit.

Townsend, a committed natural escaper, continued to look for new ways out. Now firmly in Chinese captivity, he again marched north. This time he knew what to expect in terms of treatment but not in terms of the Chinese program of POW political indoctrination.[9] Soon the three escapers became separated, and Townsend was on his own again.

Assigned to a new group of captives, Townsend heard from some South Korean prisoners, rightly or wrongly, that the North Koreans intended to shoot them. Although the Chinese, not the North Koreans, controlled the Americans, Townsend considered it a good possibility. The guards had grown surly and began punching the South Koreans before they were taken away from the Americans. To Townsend and the others, the South Koreans were undoubtedly headed for execution. The Americans' sixth sense told them that they were next. The guards now distanced themselves from their charges and isolated them as well. Townsend found an old sickle and hid it. He later wrote, "We guessed we were in for it. Perhaps the war was going bad for their side. Perhaps we had been rebels. Perhaps we had served their purposes, whatever it was, there was something in the air. Perhaps the South Korean's warning was correct. We were tense; now the guards would not even let us go to the toilet." [10]

The men agreed that time was running out. They needed to make a break fast. Townsend took the sickle from its hiding place in the grass roof. Another American grasped a stone from under a grass mat. The plan, much like Hannah Dustan's centuries ago, was simple enough: kill the sleeping guards, take their weapons, and disappear into the mountains as fast as possible. Townsend described the assault:

> I inched my way to the door like a cat and could not even hear the other two who were doing the same thing. As I stood near the door I could hear him [a guard they called "Guess Who"] breathing. I saw the others poised beside the rear door. There we stood; our lives were on a string, and we knew it. I said, "Go." I reached out and grabbed "Guess Who" by the hair and cut his throat with the sickle. I heard a thump, like a melon being crushed, and knew the others had done their job. I took his weapon and just leaned him on the wall as he had been. We wasted no time and slipped very quietly toward the mountain.[11]

Armed with weapons and having some experience with evading recapture, Townsend's small group of three escapers again leapfrogged from hut to hut in search of food. At one point, they engaged and defeated a small enemy patrol, taking its rifles, ammunition, and food. Crossing a bridge, they encountered an enemy force of about twenty soldiers and exchanged fire for about an hour. Townsend turned to his fellow escapers, but found that they had disappeared. He was alone again.

Townsend recalled the pact the men had made before attempting the escape. Each man had felt it was important that someone return to friendly lines, not only to save his own life but also to bear witness to the catastrophic treatment inflicted on those in captivity. Remembering the pact, Townsend's choice was clear. He jumped from the bridge into the cold water and began swimming downstream. On shore once again, he resumed his journey, traveling without a weapon. Townsend climbed yet another mountain, found a hole, and slept before continuing south. Hearing the blasts of artillery, he counted the seconds between the explosions and figured that he was at least six very dangerous miles from friendly lines. He slipped around the enemy units at night, and heading in the direction of the artillery, he spotted some friendly troops. "There was no doubt in my mind they were South Korean soldiers," he wrote. Townsend stood up and cried out, "American! American!" His ordeal was over.[12]

During the Korean War, hostile fire, air combat, and malfunctions brought down 1,690 Air Force personnel behind enemy lines. Of this number, 1,180 fliers survived combat actions in which their aircraft were lost. The Air Rescue Service, first developed in World War II, evolved into Search and Rescue (SAR) and, with the help of newly developed rescue helicopters, reached 175 airmen soon after they parachuted to safety. The rest were captured and became either POWs or World War II–style evaders who avoided capture and made their way back to friendly lines. Three such evaders were Col. Albert W. Schinz, Lt. Clinton D. Summersill, who walked forty miles in the snow and lost his feet to frostbite during the Korean winter, and Capt. Donald S. Thomas, the "Caveman," who avoided capture by holing up in dugouts and caves. In their virtually incredible evasions, each officer not only showed determination in the face of overwhelming odds, but also developed *ad hoc* evasion schemes that worked. Schinz managed to devise a large "May Day" ("M'Aidez" or "Help Me") signal for aircraft flying over his position; Summersill struck up a friendship with Christian South Koreans who delivered him to an outpost of the 5th ROK (Republic of Korea) Division; and Thomas's friendly relations with Christian North Koreans resulted in their help in hiding him from the communists searching for a dangerous enemy on the loose.[13]

After being shot down in 1950, Air Force Capt. William D. Locke, along with Lt. Alexander Makarounis and Sgt. Takeshi Kumagai, became POWs and barely survived a 160-mile death march. Then opportunity knocked. The North Korean Army suffered reversals in the battle against United Nations forces and began to retreat. Not wanting prisoners to slow their march but not wanting to shoot them either, they deposited their American prisoners in Pyongyang to await further developments. The alert prisoners then devised a small opportunistic escape. Aided by some friendly North Koreans, they managed to hide under the floor of a schoolhouse, where they waited until United Nations forces advanced to their position.[14]

Air Force pilot Capt. Ward Millar, author of *Valley of the Shadow* (1955), broke his ankles upon bailout and a hard parachute landing. Evasion was not a possibility. After his capture by the Chinese, he spent three months in relatively tame medical captivity. Millar knew that when he was fit, the Chinese planned to send him to a POW camp somewhere in North Korea. Thus he stalled as long as he could by lying to his interrogators about his mission and general knowledge of military matters. He learned some Chinese and Korean, bartered with his captors for food and medicines, and managed to survive the initial weeks in ankle and leg casts. After Millar's broken ankles healed to the point where he enjoyed some mobility, he seized the opportunity to hobble out of a Chinese field hospital. With the help of a defecting North Korean, Millar signaled a friendly aircraft, and both men were rescued. These adventures not only reflected well on the downed Air Force pilots themselves, but also on the North Korean civilians, who, like the radical preachers in England during the American Revolution, delivered their escaped prisoners to friendly hands at great risk to their personal safety. Few escaper-evaders in the Revolution, Civil War, World War II, or Korea reached their own lines safely without this sort of outside help.

In April 1951, Air Force observation pilot Melvin J. Shadduck found himself caught in a canyon with an airplane full of holes from ground fire. After landing his dying aircraft, Shadduck, hampered by an injured arm and hand, attempted to evade capture, but six Chinese soldiers found him and took him prisoner. Shadduck believed that he was in danger of being shot at once, but by 1951, the Chinese knew that POWs were valuable as bargaining chips with the United Nations and as possible converts to their way of thinking. Both motivations yielded some positive results. Whereas the North Koreans often executed many of their prisoners soon after capture, the Chinese kept their United Nations POWs alive.

In his first escape attempt, Shadduck tried unsuccessfully to walk toward United Nations' lines. He had only gone about seventy-five feet when his captors stopped him, turned him around, and took him back to the officer in charge of their unit. Still in the front lines, Shadduck managed to duck American strafing attacks, but knowing that the allies were nearby, he recalled thinking, "I must make a break for it." [15] But Shadduck's wounds worsened, and he decided he would have to wait. The Chinese soldiers brought Shadduck to a bunker-laden valley that doubled as a small field hospital, where a doctor administered first aid to his burned hand. Additional air attacks on the facility continued because the Chinese never used red crosses to mark field hospitals, and United Nations aircraft had no idea that they were attacking a medical area. At the hospital Shadduck met his first political commissar, an English-speaking interrogator, and he took the opportunity to ask why the Chinese refused to display the red crosses. The interrogator responded ironically, "Because then they would know we were here." Shadduck missed the irony; to him the answer was nonsensical, Shadduck's condition suddenly deteriorated. His hand and arm became infected, and his fever rose; in spite of his condition, or perhaps because of it, he looked again for another way to escape, but this time nature failed him. Spring rains soaked the region, and Shadduck decided to stay put.

What bothered Shadduck the most was the poor medical care he received from his captors. He knew that he might suffer death in captivity if his wounds were not treated properly. He again considered escape, especially when he discovered that he was only about forty miles north of Seoul, which meant that he could reach friendly lines in two days. Still, the best tactic, he decided, was to remain as invisible as possible, but this proved impossible as the Chinese soldiers crowded around him to look at the second hand on his watch and to take his ballpoint pen. When the unit was later ordered north to China, Shadduck was told to "hike." This really frightened the airman. China meant permanence, a captivity with no end, a life sentence. It was his worst day in captivity. His fear mounted until it reached the point where he considered stealing a MIG and flying to the United Nations lines.

Shadduck's fears were finally allayed. His unit went north, but he was left with those who remained in the south, near the Imjin River. Later, he joined some American prisoners taken from the 3d Division, who were in far worse shape than he was. As the senior ranking officer in the group, Shadduck now shouldered the responsibility for five other prisoners. The group was diverse, composed of Joe, a sergeant who hated the Chinese; a

Turkish soldier who spoke neither English nor Chinese; Bill, a young Army private; Dave from Tennessee; and Jim, another very young but seriously wounded soldier. Each day a Chinese soldier brought small bags of millet, but he refused to give the group any water. Shadduck searched the compound for a water pail, found one, and drew some dirty water from a nearby well. He knew that the water was poisonous, and that it was capable of incapacitating them all if they drank it immediately. To solve the problem, Shadduck scrounged some sticks and a few burning coals and started a fire to boil the water. Together, the group learned to survive by boiling water, improvising survival materials, and helping each other stay free of the lice that infected the camp. For Jim, these efforts were fruitless. He died.

Shadduck realized that survival under these circumstances was questionable at best and resolved not only to escape but to initiate a rescue. He learned that at one point the trail leading from the compound crossed a highway, and he believed that if he could get there undetected, he would enjoy a fair chance of a successful escape. He told his comrades that if he made it back to United Nations lines, his first task would be to organize a raid with sufficient forces to rescue the others. They were both hopeful and skeptical. Fortunately for Shadduck, the Chinese were accustomed to seeing him walking around the compound. When he made his move, he walked to the bluff where he usually dumped refuse, then kept on going to the closest escape line, the Imjin River.

Arriving at its banks, Shadduck found the river swollen with spring rains and impassable. He then decided to work his way along a trail that paralleled the river; there he caught sight of a Chinese or possibly a North Korean outpost. Terrified of being recaptured and having to abandon his pledge to his men, Shadduck skirted the outpost long after the guards fell asleep. He kept close to the Imjin's bank so that the river's noise would muffle his own. In the darkness he came upon a small boat, which at first glance appeared to be perfect for the crossing. He climbed in and began to row to the other side, but the river was too powerful and held him in its swirling clutches. Frustrated and angry, he decided that being by himself in a small skiff in the middle of the Imjin River was not the best way to remain undetected and alive. He resolved to continue by using stealth and returned to the shoreline to resume his journey on land.

Shadduck's fortunes changed for the better when he found outside help. He met a young Korean boy who took him to his family, who in turn fed and warmed him. Like other escapers in other wars, Shadduck found that he had to depend on the kindness of the local country people for his survival. With cultural insurance—he spoke Japanese—Shadduck was able to communicate with ease. Korea had been a Japanese colony from 1905 until the end of World War II, and many Koreans spoke Japanese. After getting some sleep, Shadduck and the boy started out but were nearly captured when they came too close to a Chinese infantry unit. Later, the boy rushed to Shadduck with the good news, "Americans. Americans. Come. Come." Wary of another false alarm, Shadduck and the boy carefully approached the United Nations troops and discovered that they were Greeks on patrol with the U.S. 7th Cavalry. His ordeal of thirty-four days in captivity was far from over, however.

As soon as he reached the United Nations lines, Shadduck reported that he had left other prisoners behind waiting for rescue. Being an airman, Shadduck thought immediately of a helicopter rescue and an air assault, but those tactics would have to wait for the next war—in Vietnam. He was with the Army now, and the colonel said, "We'll do it with tanks." With combat air cover searching for Shadduck's earlier marker signal, "6 PW," the tanks rumbled into the POW area, and under enemy fire, the remaining Americans and the Turk were loaded into the vehicles and taken away. The wounded POWs were soon transferred to waiting helicopters that took them to hospitals. For them it was a good day; Shadduck had kept his promise.

Shadduck, Millar, Locke, Kaylor, Townsend, and others escaped in contested areas, where friendly United Nations forces were within reach. However, escape from Chinese prison camps situated well behind the lines in North Korea proved impossible, even for the most determined committed natural escapers. Although most of the Yalu camps lacked barbed-wire enclosures, if the inmates managed an escape, there was no place to go. The region was sparsely populated, the weather and terrain were hostile, and the chances of finding friendly or defecting North Koreans were nil. Even without heavy barbed-wire fences, security was tight, and the Chinese and North Koreans had positioned their camps so that anyone determined enough, or foolish enough, to leave would be easily recaptured. James Young remembered what happened to several American escapers. "When the prisoners were recaptured they were sent to the prison for six months to a year."[16] Infantry Sgt. Lloyd Pate also described the efforts of some who tried but failed. Like others, he observed that it was relatively easy to leave a camp, but difficult from then on. When an escape occurred, the Chinese first searched the immediate vicinity and then put out an alarm. Because there was a reward for every prisoner they brought back, the North Koreans kept their eyes open. One American POW gave Pate his personal papers and pictures to hold in case he died during a partnership escape with another POW. After four days on the run, both prisoners were recaptured, and, according to Pate, when they were brought back, the Chinese "beat the hell out of them." [17]

As in both world wars and again in Korea, Americans were part of a larger international force. The United Nations Command and the corresponding community of war prisoners consisted of men from South Korea, France, Turkey, Greece, England, and the British Commonwealth nations, including Canada, Australia, and New Zealand. Despite the large numbers of prisoners, committed escapers found one another and began planning escapes. Among the British POWs, the most determined but luckless escaper was Capt. Anthony Farrar-Hockley, a member of the British 29th Independent Infantry Brigade Group, Gloucestershire Regiment.

Captured on April 25, 1951, when the Chinese surrounded and defeated the Gloucesters near the Imjin River, Captain Farrar-Hockley baited the Chinese much as Wing Comdr. Douglas Bader had baited the Germans five years earlier.[18] A British POW, Rifleman Pvt. Leonard Jones, 1st Battalion of the Royal Ulster Rifles, remembered one such incident: "Captain Farrar-Hockley of the Gloucesters gave us all a fright when he told one of the Chinese who had pulled him into line to 'keep his filthy hands off the King's uniform.'"[19] Completely shocked by the insolence of a fellow prisoner, Jones fully expected to be shot. The Chinese guards did nothing, however, and Private Jones remained alive.

From his capture in 1951 until his release in 1953, Farrar-Hockley attempted five escapes. In his *Edge of the Sword* (1954), he recalled that shortly after his capture he broached the issue, noting, "The night would surely bring a good opportunity, and we must be ready for it." As he looked around, Farrar-Hockley realized that other British prisoners were thinking the same thing, even considering the possibility of overpowering the Chinese guards. Knowing that such an attempt would be suicidal, the British Gloucesters decided to wait for a more opportune moment. Farrar-Hockley commented, "We were learning the first lesson of captivity."[20]

Farrar-Hockley's first real escape came when he quietly slid into the waters of the Imjin River shortly after his capture. The prisoners, under guard, had been marched only a short distance from the point where they had been taken, but night was descending quickly. As the group reached the shoreline, Farrar-Hockley saw that opportunity knocked. With binoculars still around his neck and in full combat uniform, he decided to take the risk and jumped in. Although nearly drowning in the swift current, he swam on. Finally feeling sand underneath his boots once more, he waded out of the river and crawled slowly into the night. Fatigue gripped him, so he found a spot on the bank where he could sleep. The next day he returned to his capture point, then wandered from village to village until he came face to face with a North Korean soldier, who pointed a pistol at his chest. Farrar-Hockley knew beyond a shadow of a doubt that he was recaptured.

While he was still held close to United Nations lines, Captain Farrar-Hockley joined a small group and made a second escape with three other prisoners. With hopes of reaching friendly lines, they crept from the prison village in the dead of night. On the trail, they met a friendly Korean who gave them food and tobacco. They hid in a hut, but North Korean soldiers sought them out. Farrar-Hockley scrambled for cover, but concealment was useless. "The box in front of me crashed to the ground," he wrote. Then it "was removed and splintered by another mighty kick, and I lay exposed in the full light of the torch."

In his third escape, Farrar-Hockley decided to use a tunnel to leave the prison compound at Namchon-jom village. After he squeezed through the tunnel's exit, he felt alone but exhilarated, recalling, "The night air smelt of freedom and filled my veins with fire!" Quickly and deliberately he headed into the nearby mountains and made for the Yellow Sea. Fifteen difficult days passed before he had his first glimpse of the Pacific Ocean. But to escape he needed a boat, and the only way to secure one was to convince a North Korean civilian to take him south. Again, fate did not permit Capt. Anthony Farrar-Hockley to remain a free man. As he entered one side of a cornfield, a squad of Chinese soldiers entered the other side. The Chinese soldiers recaptured him in short order.

His fourth escape involved three others who disappeared through a hole in the wall of a shack. "Neither shots nor other sounds of alarm reached us as we crossed the main Chinam-po highway and left the interrogation center behind a hill—free men once more." The team climbed into the mountains and leapfrogged North Korean villages, heading once more for the sea. They were about to descend into a village when the enemy struck. Farrar-Hockley heard the sound of a round being rammed into the chamber of a rifle and saw a civilian North Korean sentry standing about twenty-five yards away. It was too late to run. As the guard led him to a village hut, Farrar-Hockley decided to try deception by attempting to convince the man that he was a Russian. The ruse almost worked until a Russian-speaking North Korean police captain entered the hut, and Farrar-Hockley instantly knew that the game was up. He was a prisoner yet again. This time Farrar-Hockley was taken to the Central Police Headquarters in Pyongyang and then to a secure prison camp.

Up until this time, Farrar-Hockley had not been forced to walk hundreds of miles in the winter snow as had the Americans in 1950 and 1951, nor had he been subjected to North Korean atrocities like the Suncheon Tunnel Massacre. He had been too busy escaping to become a victim of atrocities or subject to the politics of captivity in the Korean War. As the United Nations POWs in North Korea became aware of the peace talks in 1952, committed escapers like Farrar-Hockley found themselves forced to hold back. However, on August 4, 1952, after another round of fruitless negotiations in Panmunjom, Farrar-Hockley decided that the time was right for another escape attempt. He formed another small group, and his fifth attempt was on. According to the plan, three men were to go to the latrine and keep on walking, but again bad luck struck. The men were discovered and arrested. Farrar-Hockley faced his interrogator, who raved, "You have conspired to make men escape. . . . You have used your former rank to order men to disobey the regulations." For punishment he sat alone for three days in solitary confinement in a North Korean police station. After his return to the prison community, he planned another escape, but an unidentified compound snitch informed the Chinese of the group's intentions. The escape attempt was shelved.

Although Capt. Anthony Farrar-Hockley was never successful in his escape attempts, he never ceased trying. According to Farrar-Hockley, he played a hardball, real-life version of Snakes and Ladders, a game of escape in which the player, near the moment of success, suffers a radical change in luck that takes him back into captivity. After playing his own escape cards too many times, he decided to accept quarantine and wait with thousands of other United Nations POWs in Korea for formal repatriation in 1953. Nevertheless, Sir Anthony Farrar-Hockley proved beyond doubt that he was a committed natural escaper, someone the Americans affectionately referred to as a "tiger."

By 1953, United Nations POWs felt more like political prisoners than traditional POWs. In captivity in North Korea, United Nations and American POWs were punished not so much for what they did but for what they represented.[21] Indignity replaced the traditional enemy of the POWs, boredom. The war itself bounced back and forth along the 38th Parallel in a stalemate, and soldiers were killing one another for small bits of land, nothing more. Talk of an armistice made sense, and in the northern prison

camps, political indoctrination sessions and impossible camp rules confounded any ideas the men may have harbored about escape. Senior ranking officers found themselves in solitary confinement, and the desire of
the camp authority to create doubts in the minds of the POWs became
the top priority. Little did the POWs know that much of the dialogue
among the Chinese, the North Koreans, and the United Nations representatives centered on POW issues in both parts of warring Korea.[22]

Two years after hostilities ended, Ward Millar's *Valley of the Shadow*
(1955) and Clay Blair's *Beyond Courage* (1955) appeared as laudatory
memoirs of committed escapers and evaders. More to the point, both
books attacked the emerging popular beliefs that American prisoners
craved quarantine, confessed to committing bogus war crimes, and collaborated with their captors against each other. As postwar investigations
revealed, some did collaborate; however, other POWs, including American pilots and United Nations prisoners like Captain Farrar-Hockley,
resisted their captors to the best of their abilities and displayed the will, if
not the mandate, to escape. One reason for this mentality was the fact
that a large number of military personnel in Korea had also served during
World War II. As a result, many United Nations soldiers were as escape-
minded in Korea as the Allied prisoners had been in the German stalags.
Although the rules changed slightly when the 1949 Geneva Convention
supplanted the rules set in 1929, the Korean situation showed that political captivity had replaced the traditional notions of quarantine. As
Allied POWs discovered in Asia during World War II, international law
meant very little when captors had other agendas to follow.

During the Korean War, hard-resisting POWs, including many committed natural escapers, were called tigers by their peers and reactionar-
ies by the North Koreans and Chinese. After capture and on the death
marches they looked for ways out as soon as possible. In prison camps
they were persons of such fierce independence, high self-esteem, and
stubborn convictions that they thwarted all enemy efforts to mold their
thinking. According to Albert D. Biderman, tigers were the tough guys,
not always advanced in rank but with chests full of medals for valor. In
Korea, and later in Vietnam, where careerism and personnel manage-
ment often replaced martial spirit in the American military services,
the qualities that made for outright heroism and individual resource
were not always congruent with those that made for successful military
careers. Tigers rarely distinguished themselves at cocktail parties; rather,
they saved their energies for the field of battle.[23] While less aggressive

prisoners needed incidents of cruelty to generate the will to escape, tigers often had that will at the time they were captured. They never needed another code to keep; they had two already: the mandates in the 1929 and 1949 Geneva Conventions that required all prisoners of war to give only name, rank, and serial number; and one built into their individual and collective personalities, what the American soldier-escapers of the Civil War had called "pure cussedness."

As a people schooled in practical individualism, Americans have long behaved more as dissenters than as obedient followers, especially when dealing with one another. Writing in 1835, Alexis de Tocqueville once praised American soldiers for their revulsion toward blind obedience. "The state of [American] society," according to de Tocqueville, "does not prepare them for it, and the nation might be in danger of losing its natural advantages if it sought artificially to acquire advantages of this particular kind."[24] On the other hand, de Tocqueville envisioned neither the cruelty imposed on prisoners, as was the case in Korea, nor the kind of political warfare aimed at dramatically changing soldiers' basic attitudes, especially toward one another.

The American military services recognized that political conscience became more important in the Cold War than it had been during World War II. A middle ground was essential, because a political act or statement made in a prison camp remains radically different from individual political acts undertaken at home. Prisoners do not represent themselves; they act as direct representatives of their government and military services engaged in public warfare. After Korea, the American government decided that something had to be done so that its soldiers, more accustomed to the rule of law, could better understand what was expected of them. The lessons learned from Korean captivity in general implied that future hostilities in the Cold War would contain strong political issues for soldiers to come to terms with, from capture to repatriation. Politics, although central to statesmen who ask a nation's youth to fight, generally remains foreign to free-thinking professional and often conscripted soldiers who fight primarily for each other rather than for grand causes.

At home, Americans began to raise questions about why some of their POWs in Korea publicly revealed they had begun to see the war from the enemy's viewpoint. Following the general repatriation in 1953, the military services investigated 565 such cases and processed 192 for collaboration. More worrisome still was the fact that twenty-one Americans and one British Marine defected to the Chinese. Two books then appeared, further rocking both the Pentagon and the White House: *Shall Brothers*

Be, published in 1952 by the Chinese People's Committee for World Peace, and *Thinking Soldiers,* in 1955, two years after the defections. The authors of the latter, progressive POWs Andrew M. Condron, Richard Cordon, and Lawrence V. Sullivan, claimed they were well treated and had decided to defect in order to promote world peace.[25] Was American society in so much disarray that its citizens in uniform could not resist the pressures of hostile political interrogators in a prison camp?

Along with numerous articles in popular magazines describing "brainwashing," Eugene Kinkead offered his vision of social decay in *Every War But One* (1959). Kinkead argued that because no one escaped and scored a home run from a North Korean or Chinese prison camp, American POWs had acceded to enemy pressures for quarantine, cooperation, and docility. On the other hand, Albert D. Biderman pointed out that American prisoners made forty-six escape attempts from North Korean camps, with six escaping parties apprehended at rendezvous points. Biderman concluded, "Our confidence in the perfectibility of man should not be undermined by one-sided attention toward imperfections. Instances of self-sacrificing devotion to ideals in exceptionally trying circumstances are a primary source of this confidence." [26]

In the face of very difficult circumstances in Korea, most Americans hung tough, and they hung together much as they had done in previous wars, including World War II. One example of unusual self-sacrifice was the remarkable story of Navy Lt. (jg) John K. Koelsch, whose actions as a prisoner of war won him the Medal of Honor. On July 3, 1951, while flying a helicopter rescue mission, Koelsch was shot down. After evading the North Koreans for three days on the ground, he was taken prisoner. Shortly thereafter, he began demanding medical attention for his fellow prisoners. The North Koreans paid little attention and sent him to a prison camp. Although he suffered from malnutrition, Koelsch continued to demand better treatment for others, and during interrogations refused to give any information other than name, rank, and serial number. More mistreatment followed, and Koelsch died from malnutrition on October 16, 1951.[27] Another example of self-sacrifice was Father Emil Kapaun, the Catholic chaplain of the 1st U.S. Cavalry. His uncanny genius for scrounging and an unqualified devotion to the camp's suffering POWs wore him out. Dysentery and a severe blood clot killed him.[28]

The 1949 Geneva Convention's mandates served the internationally recognized purpose of ameliorating the hazards of war for individuals, especially POWs and other protected personnel. The *Rules of Land Warfare* (FM 27-10, 1947) regulated how American forces treated their own

POWs in the field. Although only one out of every twenty-three American POWs was ever suspected of any misconduct, the secretary of defense ordered a complete review of American POW policy. As a result, the U.S. military services issued Order 207 in 1953, an early version of the Code of Conduct which stated that American soldiers are duty-bound to try to escape.[29] Also in 1953, the secretary of defense created an Advisory Committee on Prisoners of War, and its 1955 formal report contended that the "Armed Forces come from a cross-section of the national population," and "the record seems fine indeed." However, in regard to the POW experience, the armed services needed something that bound prisoners together into a POW community through a "unified and purposeful standard of conduct."[30]

In 1954, a year before the report was formally published, with Lieutenant Koelsch's actions in mind, President Dwight D. Eisenhower issued Executive Order 10631, prescribing the Code of Conduct for Members of the Armed Forces of the United States.[31] The President's Executive Order stated, "Every member of the Armed Forces of the United States is expected to measure up to the standards emphasized in the Code of Conduct."[32] It read:

1. I am an American fighting man. I serve in the forces which guard my country and our way of life. I am prepared to give my life in their defense.

2. I will never surrender of my own free will. If in command I will never surrender my men while they still have the means to resist.

3. If I am captured I will continue to resist by all means available. I will make every effort to escape and aid others to escape. I will not accept parole nor special favors from the enemy.

4. If I become a prisoner of war, I will keep faith with my fellow prisoners. I will give no information or take part in any action which might be harmful to my comrades. If I am senior, I will take command. If not, I will obey the lawful orders of those appointed over me and will back them up in every way.

5. When questioned, should I become a prisoner of war, I am bound to give only name, rank and service number and date of birth. I will evade answering further questions to the utmost of my ability. I will make no oral or written statements disloyal to my country and its allies or harmful to their cause.

6. I will never forget that I am an American fighting man, responsible

for my actions, and dedicated to the principles which make my country free. I will trust in my God and the United States of America.

In 1988, the Code was updated and rewritten in degenderized language, assuming that women might become POWs and subject to its precepts. However, Article 3, "I will make every effort to escape and aid others to escape," remained unchanged. After three centuries of military experience, the American military services recognized that in captivity, the fight continued, and according to the Advisory Committee, "When the use of weapons is denied, the mental and moral 'will to resist' must be kept alive in every prisoner."[33] Thus the duty of every member of the captive community became demonstrably clear: to continue to resist up to and including escape. The principle behind this article lessens the need for camp tigers like Captain Farrar-Hockley or Melvyn Shadduck, although in reality, they will surface and provide leadership when unusual circumstances call for it.

Not only did the American POWs learn something from their British counterparts in World Wars I and II, and again in Korea, the American military services took the lesson one step further. By creating a code simple enough for everyone to understand, the American armed services recognized the need to formalize ideals in order for POWs to share the risks in enemy captivity equitably. Questions remained, however, concerning the degree to which the Code served to regulate what prisoners actually did in captivity. Only another war with an extended POW experience accomplished that task adequately. Ten years later, the Vietnam War tested its validity, legality, range of interpretations, and ultimately its effectiveness for American POWs. As was the case in Korea, the captors denied their prisoners the benefits of the Geneva Convention, and with only the Code of Conduct serving as a guideline for POW behavior, the long war in Vietnam became not only a war of attrition and a military endurance match, it became a difficult test of faith.

10

Free from the Jungle Camps
Escape in Laos and Vietnam

The moment I committed myself to escape I gave up that firm grip on life. I knew that as soon as we were on the other side of that fence and into the jungle, the rest would be up to us.

—Dieter Dengler (1979)

Escapes from enemy hands in Indochina began during World War II shortly after the fall of the Philippines to the Imperial Japanese Army. On June 27, 1942, a little more than a month after the final surrender of American forces in the Philippines, five Americans—Capt. R. S. Fralik, 1st Lt. Maurice G. Hughett, and Sgts. Gordon V. Stoddard, Charles W. Held, and I.A.W. White—all Air Force men, washed ashore in Vichy French Indochina after narrowly escaping from the Philippines by boat. First spotted by a lighthouse keeper and later turned over to the French occupation army, the Americans soon became the wards of the *Kempei Tei,* the feared Japanese secret military police. In prison, they joined two British Royal Artillery Bombardiers (corporals), G. Baxter and B. Cassidy, two antiaircraft gun personnel who had escaped together on the night of June 8, 1942. After traveling about thirty miles, the British partnership was recaptured and turned over to the *Kempei Tei.* After spending several weeks in silent solitary confinement and suffering harsh interrogations together, the Americans were released and entered prison with the other Allied POWs. Baxter and Cassidy were beheaded in July.[1]

For some Allied prisoners, the stay in Saigon was relatively short. Many found themselves herded quickly into unmarked naval transport ships for the dangerous voyage to Japan, while others remained in Saigon for several years. Not all were content to remain in quarantine captivity. Basil Bancroft, a black South African, developed contacts in Saigon and acquired a phony ID card that showed him to be a citizen of Martinique. He disappeared into Saigon's bustling streets, while Paddy Purcell, an Irishman in the British Army, slipped away entirely and faded into the Vietnamese landscape. After Purcell's success in 1944, one of the Americans, 1st Lt. Maurice Hughett, a native of Dallas who was always known as "Tex," decided to make his own escape.

According to Douglas Cotton, a fellow prisoner in the Saigon prison compound along the docks near the Saigon River, "Hughett was never allowed out of the camp, but he managed to get out at night and developed his own contacts." On his return trips from town, he often brought medical supplies back to the camp, and during his secretive interludes in Saigon, he developed some friendly relationships with various French nationals. Hughett was also a member of a small regular working party at a Japanese transit camp based at a former French school. According to Cotton, "By this time he had acquired a white civilian type shirt and a pair of chino shorts and brown shoes, and more importantly, a Vietnam style sun helmet. During the midday meal break he would quietly disappear for a time. We believed that he met contacts. . . . Dressed as he was, he could easily pass for a civilian French national." [2] He was told that an escape could be arranged, and on Christmas night of 1944, "Tex" Hughett disappeared into the hands of the French. Hughett wrote, "A Mme. Audibert and friend took me by auto about 100 miles north to a coffee plantation where we spent the night. I was in the rear floorboards covered by rugs. Two French lieutenants arrived by auto with a French uniform for me and we drove to the coast where we spent the night. The next day we drove to Tourane [Da Nang]. I was wined and dined by the French military there. Ironically, a lieutenant there had turned us over to the Japanese almost three years before. They apologized profusely for that episode." [3] Later, Hughett went with the French to the Dong Hoi air base and then by aircraft to the Plain of Jars in Laos. Once in Laos he became a guerrilla and continued the war against the Japanese until July 1945, when he received orders from American headquarters to cease guerrilla operations.

Twenty years later, American combatants replaced the French in Indochina. For the Americans, the opposition changed from the Japanese to the communist Vietnamese, and Allied soldiers again found ways out of captivity. If one considers the length of American military involvement in the Vietnam War, from 1960 to 1973, and the number of soldiers who served in that country, about 2.5 million, it is a wonder that so few fell into enemy hands. Although there were indeed several large battles between 1965 and the Tet Offensive in 1968, none was ever lost either to the Vietcong or to the North Vietnamese Army on a scale analogous to the French defeat at Dien Bien Phu in 1954. Although no large numbers of prisoners were ever taken at any one time, the war's combat losses became a slow grind of downed airmen and ground soldiers overrun on their battlefields or outposts. Because of the aggressive flying of MEDEVAC helicopters and SAR aircraft, combat infantrymen or "grunts" as they called themselves, as well as the riverine sailors in Vietnam, knew that they could be in a hospital shortly after being wounded or rescued soon after a shootdown.

Beginning in World War II, each service, especially the Navy and Air Force, developed and conducted extensive and very dangerous Search and Rescue (SAR) operations for their downed fliers and shipwrecked sailors. Each service understood that replacing experienced pilots and aircrew was expensive. Aircrew morale—the feelings of well-being and belonging—was at stake for airmen fighting over inhospitable terrain, and it was important for them to know that there was at least a chance of rescue after a shootdown, no matter how slim the odds.[4] Both unarmed MEDEVAC and SAR personnel earned respect and admiration from their helpless clients. One of those clients was Air Force Lt. Col. Iceal E. Hambleton, whose rescue operation became the most complicated SAR mission in Air Force history.

Hambleton's remarkable experience on the ground and the Air Force's SAR mission became the seeds for William C. Anderson's adventure novel *Bat-21* (1980) and a popular film with the same title in 1990.[5] In April 1972, Hambleton's aircraft, an EB-66 electronics warfare plane, was hit by an enemy surface-to-air missile immediately south of the DMZ (Demilitarized Zone) between North and South Vietnam. A working Air Force Forward Air Controller (FAC) pilot, Capt. J. D. Kempton, flying a twin-engine OV-10 Bronco, spotted Hambleton while he was still floating down to earth in his parachute and called in close air support to clear the ground and protect Hambleton from early capture. Kempton summoned SAR helicopters, two UH-1B Cobra gunships, and two UH-1H troop-carrying "Slicks." As they made their approach to rescue Hambleton, they were attacked by the North Vietnamese, who shot down one helicopter and damaged another so badly that the force retired, leaving Hambleton on the ground to fend for himself. New FACs arrived from the air base at Da Nang to relieve Kempton, one of whom, Capt. William Henderson, was shot down and taken prisoner after he had evaded the enemy forces for eight hours. The North Vietnamese took Henderson to Hanoi and put him into solitary confinement for several months before they allowed him to enter the American POW community.[6]

Disregarding the obvious dangers, other FACs arrived and continued to direct air strikes around Hambleton in an attempt to clear the way for another SAR rescue mission. The second SAR effort also failed, and the Americans lost a large HH-53 helicopter, known in Vietnam as a "Jolly Green Giant," and its crew. Hambleton's rescue was becoming expensive. It was possible that by 1972 the North Vietnamese understood American radio and teletype codes; certainly their radio intercept personnel understood English. What saved Hambleton was his passion for golf. He phrased his radio transmissions to successive FACs in golf terminology, something foreign to his enemies even if they understood standard English. He tramped from one "fairway" to another until finally a team rescued him on April 14, 1972.[7]

Captured American soldiers considering escape faced camp conditions in South Vietnam that presented several challenges. Sometimes double and triple canopy jungle covered the makeshift compounds, making them difficult, if not impossible, to see from the air. The Vietcong and the Laotian Pathet Lao were wise enough to place their camps far from friendly lines or government outposts. The POWs were usually much too debilitated from arduous journeys over unknown terrain to escape early in captivity. For the few who did escape, the civilian population—some terrified by the Vietcong's ability to harass them, some Vietcong supporters—rarely assisted anyone. Americans were very conspicuous. Compared to Vietnamese, Cambodians, and Laotians, they are noticeably large people. Americans seldom understood the Vietnamese language and had little knowledge of Indochinese taboos and values. These general factors combined to make evasion following an escape in Indochina extremely difficult.[8] Despite the odds and the measures taken by the captors to conceal their prison facilities, some POWs took the escape gamble anyway.

First to escape were Lt. Charles F. Klusmann and Lt. (jg) Dieter Dengler, two naval aviators shot down and captured in Laos. On June 6, 1964, Klusmann flew from the USS *Kitty Hawk* to photograph Pathet Lao installations in central Laos between Khang Khay and Ban Ban, a dangerous area about twenty miles from the North Vietnamese border known as "Lead Alley" because of the heavy concentration of antiaircraft fire.[9] As Klusmann was flying low passes to take clear photographs, his aircraft, an RF-8A, was hit, and after the aircraft ignited, Klusmann bailed out. His wingman, transmitting as "Corktip 32," remained flying overhead and acted as a relay for Klusmann's emergency ground-to-air calls for help. First to respond was an Air America C-123 cargo plane that arrived when Klusmann's wingman had to leave. Temporarily in charge of the rescue effort, the Air America plane called for more help, and an Air America U-10 arrived, along with two helicopters. Within an hour these circling airplanes sighted Klusmann and attempted to make a rescue, but it was not to be. The Pathet Lao lay in wait for the rescue helicopters, attacked them, and made rescue far too dangerous.[10]

Following his capture by the Pathet Lao, Klusmann remained with them for eighty-six days of solitary confinement. After being coerced into signing a propaganda document denouncing U.S. government policies in Southeast Asia, Klusmann was integrated into a small prison-camp population of Laotians and Thais. He formed an *ad hoc* escape alliance with five other prisoners, and the group left the prison camp together on August 21, 1964, by crawling under the wire of a stockade. Klusmann evaded recapture in the jungle for three days until, luckily, he found a friendly Meo village.

Following Klusmann's repatriation, naval authorities and the press showed interest in Pathet Lao allegations that he had signed statements favorable to the communist cause. The Navy acknowledged that he had made statements in captivity but denied the Pathet Lao's allegations that Klusmann had been a cooperative prisoner. Various newspaper reports suggested that Klusmann received outright help from the guards. The *New York Times,* for example, reported that anticommunist guerrilla soldiers belonging to the Meo tribe's Gen. Vang Pao bribed his guards. Another report from Vientiane stated that Klusmann talked five of his guards into fleeing with him.[11] In the end, although the Navy honored his escape, it remained tight-lipped about the details. Vice Adm. Bernard A. Clarey, USN, deputy commander in chief of the United States Pacific Forces, said, "The whole fleet is proud of your initiative in getting away on your own." [12] Remaining true to the Code of Conduct and the Geneva Convention, Klusmann had signed a prepared document only under extreme duress, an act that became part of the common experience of most POWs in Southeast Asia in the years to come.[13]

Dieter Dengler was a German immigrant to the United States who, as a boy, hid from American bombs during World War II. While flying a mission over Laos on February 1, 1966, he was shot down, and after being held for five months, he escaped into the Laotian jungle on June 30. Dengler successfully evaded his pursuers and was rescued on July 20, 1966.

While in captivity, he was appalled by conditions at the prison camp, particularly the lack of food. The only protein he and the other prisoners saw in several weeks was a bucketful of tadpoles that one of the guards had caught. According to Dengler, "He had mashed the little wigglers into a slimy mess and even though we were used to eating stinking dead rats and maggots, mashed tadpoles were hard to swallow, literally and figuratively."[14] Too weak to make a long jungle trip, he wondered whether his small group had the strength to escape, much less to travel even a mile after a breakout. He commented, "We lay silently in our hut most of the day because talking took too much energy."

Disease compounded Dengler's problems in the camp. He recalled that he was chained to one of the Thais who had a bad case of dysentery, noting, "He defecated continuously, fouling the floor and bedding nearby. Sitting there with him in the corner, dizzy from his sick fumes, and my hands spotted with his feces, I was beginning to go crazy. The waste lying around everywhere attracted the rats and ants. We were too weak to catch the rats for food, and the ants became the true torment of the jungle, surpassing even the leeches and mosquitoes." With the choice becoming more and more obvious, Dengler began thinking not so much about the Code of Conduct, or even about his desperate desire to escape, but instead, like Barbara Leininger during the French and Indian War, he thought about the likelihood of his own death in captivity and interpreted Grotius's doctrine of intolerable cruelty in light of his situation. Escape was no game here; Dengler had to escape or most probably would die at the hands of his captors.

The small group led by Dengler began making plans. Their scheme called for Dengler to steal a machete, hide it, and then dig it up again at the appointed time without being detected. The next steps called for gathering clothing suitable for the jungle and assembling rations. When all the preparations were completed, the time came to act. On the night before the escape, the members of the group were nervous but determined. Everything looked normal, but as the guards busied themselves with the daily camp routine, Dengler discovered that two of them were missing. The escape had to be postponed.

On the next day the men readied themselves again. According to Dengler, "Morning came and we readied ourselves for the escape in near silence. We divided the rice and changed our clothes once more." When the escape began, he reflected, "The moment I committed myself to escape I gave up that firm grip on life. I knew that as soon as we were on the other side of that fence and into the jungle, the rest would be up to us." All the guards were present this time, and Dengler watched where they placed their weapons because the plan called for the team to take over the camp with or without a shootout. In any case, they needed to steal the guns. Dengler wrote, "Like a cat, I jumped up to the porch on the guards' hut. . . . There were two Chinese weapons leaning against the wall. Then I spotted an American M-1 in the far corner. I looked out through the front entrance of the hut and realized I was standing in full view of the kitchen, about a hundred feet away. I jerked myself back against the wall, and when no one was looking, I jumped across the open doorway to the M-1 on the other side." Armed, Dengler then stole a full ammunition belt and two more rifles for the Thais in the group. So far, everything had gone according to plan, but suddenly a firefight broke out between the guards and the escapers. Their plans had to change. Dengler recalled, "Screaming and yelling filled the air. Someone was shooting wildly in my direction, and I wondered what had happened to the other guys, especially Gene [Lebrun], who was supposed to be covering me from the hut. I seemed to be all alone, out in the open. Only three feet away, Moron [a guard] was coming on at a full gallop, his machete cocked high over his head. I fired from the hip point-blank into him. The force of the blast hung him in the air, his machete still raised, and then spun him backwards to the ground." As blood gushed from the guard's wounds, Dengler stood over him in disbelief. What one bullet could do! Screams came from guards and prisoners alike. Dengler shot another guard. They were running in all directions, and he opened up at the fleeing forms. One man dropped, and Dengler reloaded his rifle. Another guard tried to run into the jungle. Dengler shot again. The man fell, then rose from the ground, holding one arm as he disappeared into the thick growth. "Then suddenly," wrote Dengler, "everything was eerily quiet."

The time had come for the escapers to leave the familiarity of the camp and enter the uncertain environment of the Laotian jungle. Faced with a problem nearly identical to that faced by the Davao escapers in Mindinao (Philippines) during World War II, they had to find their way along a trail rife with leeches and worms in search of food and water. Dengler reflected, "The jungle canopy above us separated from time to time and as I glanced up now and then at the millions of stars above, I wondered if anyone back home sensed that I was now a free man." The obstacles became secondary even though the trail presented innumerable hazards to the escape party. Dengler recalled, "The going got steep and rough and we frequently slipped and fell. The ground ripped my bare feet and my clothes snagged constantly on branches and thorns. I didn't know who was in front of me and who was behind. Fatigue had struck us all dumb." After finding some water and resting, Dengler and the others noticed a C-130 aircraft circling the area. To them, making contact was the key to success. It was the morning of June 30, 1966, their first morning as free men in more than five months.

As in many escapes, the initial plan was an *ad hoc* patchwork of diverse interests temporarily stitched together by necessity. As escaper-evaders on the loose, however, the former captives no longer had the need for close cooperation, and the group decided to split up. The three Americans went one way and the Thais went another, never to meet again. The Americans, Dieter Dengler, Gene Lebrun, and Duane Martin, an Air Force helicopter pilot, remained together at first. Then Lebrun disappeared into the jungle and was lost forever, and Martin was killed by enemy soldiers during a chase. Dengler knew that the Vietcong soldiers were also searching for him.

As the sole survivor, Dengler made his way to a point where he would be visible to American pilots flying overhead. Exhausted from the journey, he prepared his mind for death; instead, he saw American rescue helicopters rushing toward him. A huge SAR "Jolly Green Giant" put on its brakes about two hundred feet above him and let down the tree-penetrator. Fumbling with excitement and nervousness, Dengler finally grabbed it and ascended into the belly of the waiting helicopter. After his repatriation and recovery from his wounds, Dengler told his story to Congress and the *Saturday Evening Post,* and thirteen years later he wrote his thriller-memoir, *Escape from Laos* (1979), for the general public.[15] The Navy awarded him the Navy Cross for extraordinary heroism during the escape of June 30, 1966. The citation reads in part, "Lieutenant (jg) Dengler, keenly aware of the hazardous nature of the escape attempt, boldly initiated the operation and contributed to its success. When an unplanned situation developed while the escape operation was being executed, he reacted with the highest degree of valor and gallantry." [16]

As the war heated into an international conflagration, Americans began to escape from the Vietcong in South Vietnam. Captured in a Vietcong raid on a Special Forces camp on November 24, 1963, Army Sfc. Isaac Camacho remained a prisoner of war for two years. The American prisoners soon discovered the fear of what Holocaust victims called "selection," being randomly chosen to die for no apparent reason as a symbolic act of reprisal for acts far beyond one's reach or responsibility. Camacho and the others learned that the Vietcong executed two Americans for what the South Vietnamese government did. For example, in 1965, Nguyen Kao Ky's government executed Nguyen Van Troi, a committed Vietcong political cadre, in Saigon's busy downtown marketplace.[17] The National Liberation Front announced that it had killed

Army Sgt. Harold C. Bennett in reprisal for Troi's execution. On Sunday, September 26, 1965, the Front broadcast over Liberation Radio that it had executed Army Capt. Humbert "Rocky" Versace and Sgt. Kenneth Roraback, both innocent POWs, as further acts of retaliation and reprisal.[18] There was no Geneva Convention in the jungle.

Isaac Camacho refused to wait his turn for execution. Instead, he escaped from the Vietcong on July 13, 1965. Within days he was home with his family in El Paso, Texas. In a UPI interview, Camacho revealed his experiences with interrogations and forced confessions. That the popular media immediately called them "brainwashing" was reminiscent of the Korean problem twelve years before. Even after two years in captivity, Camacho remained resistant to his captors' propaganda, and when asked at home to make some personal comments, he unexpectedly attacked critics of the war. President Lyndon Johnson responded to Camacho's words in public, and on September 4, 1965, the Army presented him with the Silver and Bronze Stars. To add some hometown flavor, after naming him grand marshal of the Fiesta de Las Flores parade, the city of El Paso declared the celebration to be "Sergeant Isaac Camacho Day."[19] Isaac Camacho, soldier and escaper, became a public hero, and the Army later promoted him to the rank of captain.

The Vietcong captured two Marines in May 1968, Sgt. James S. Dodson on May 6 and Lance Cpl. Walter W. Eckes, four days later. Dodson was helping local Vietnamese harvest their rice when six Vietcong soldiers approached him from behind and struck him unconscious. When he regained his senses, Dodson found himself trussed up and barefoot for a trip through the jungle. The Vietcong soldiers led Dodson through communist-controlled areas, and, paradoxically, Vietnamese civilians gathered along the way to offer him water, candy, cigarettes, and bananas. When the party arrived at a recently bombed-out hamlet, angry Vietnamese civilians showed Dodson their teeth, until the communist village chief dispersed them. Turning to Dodson, he said in English, "The Vietnamese don't kill their prisoners."

Dodson arrived at a temporary prison camp on what the Marines called "V.C. Mountain," about twenty miles southwest of Da Nang, where he met fifteen South Vietnamese Army prisoners and Lance Corporal Eckes.[20] Eckes had been hitchhiking back to his unit when men whom he thought were three amiable Vietnamese strolled up to him at a road junction. Eckes then saw the rifle pointed at him and knew he was a prisoner. After tying him like Dodson, the Vietcong led him along jungle pathways through heavily damaged, communist-held hamlets to "V. C.

Mountain." A few days later, the Vietcong brought Dodson into the camp at the end of a rope, and the two Americans began what became a conventional form of political captivity in South Vietnam. Interrogations got under way in earnest, and their captors told Dodson and Eckes to fill out personal information papers with much more data than the Geneva Convention required. The two Americans refused to cooperate at this juncture, not knowing that the Vietcong were patient in this regard. Soon after the noon meals, about two o'clock, the prisoners read communist propaganda under the supervision of the camp's chief and political officer. Later, at five o'clock, they listened to a half-hour English-language radio program from Hanoi.[21]

Unknown to their captors, Dodson and Eckes formed an escape partnership. Both men considered the Code of Conduct's mandate to escape as their personal duty; opportunity alone dictated when and how. A second element entered into the decision as well: the unbridled fear of a lengthy incarceration. Time came for the move from "V. C. Mountain" to a more secure, permanent prison camp deeper in communist territory. Dodson and Eckes were told that they were being taken to Cambodia for release, but both men doubted their captors' word and feared a long march to North Vietnam. One evening on the trail, while the two Americans and their guards sat in a semi-circle eating supper, Dodson and Eckes noticed that the Vietcong soldiers stacked their rifles against a nearby tree. Suddenly Dodson jumped up, grabbed two carbines, and threw one to Eckes. The escape was on. Aware of the immediate danger, the guards ran away, abandoning their equipment and arms. Dodson and Eckes then turned around and marched toward the Marine base at Da Nang. After four days of making their way through the thorny brush embedded in the thick Vietnamese mountainous terrain, they heard a VC search party passing close by. Not wanting to be recaptured, they used the terrain for concealment, and the danger passed. After forty-six days of captivity, the escapers reached a South Vietnamese Army camp, and their ordeal came to an end on June 20, 1966.[22]

Army Special Forces 1st Lt. James N. Rowe found himself advising South Vietnamese forces in the Mekong Delta in 1963. After a Vietcong ambush and a futile firefight, he was captured and imprisoned in the dense U Minh forest, where he learned about his captors' philosophy: if they could control his mind, his body followed suit. The interrogator, Mr. Ba, a man Rowe called "Plato," told him, "The ultimate goal is to help me correct my errors and become a better person."[23] Rowe had a different agenda, what he called KISS, an acronym for "keep it simple, stupid."

He kept it simple, played for time every day, and as an opportunist, he watched for the right time to escape. It took five years for the right time to present itself, and in the meantime Rowe learned how to survive as a prisoner in the jungle camps.

Rowe gave in when it was necessary and learned how to resist when he had to. His captors gave him what they said was a Red Cross Index Data Card, but Rowe refused to fill it in. His interrogator knew the Geneva Convention as well as Rowe did, and knew too that the Vietcong's version asked for more military information than the standard Red Cross capture card. Mr. Ba responded to Rowe's refusal by saying, "The Red Cross is a tool of the imperialist aggressors and the Front does not recognize them." Reflecting on his own sense of law, Rowe wrote: "I knew that there was protection for a prisoner of war that forbade forcing him to make statements to be used as propaganda, forbade physical or mental coercion to create an environment which was so oppressive that a man would violate his beliefs and honor to escape it. But what good was this protection when it wasn't recognized by your captors? There was a churning knot of real fear in my stomach."

Without the Red Cross connection and with the Vietcong's rejection of the 1949 Geneva Convention for the Protection of Prisoners of War in 1964, Rowe knew not only that he was on his own, but also that his captors held the power of life and death without any international supervision whatsoever. Physical resistance was worthless; his life, like that of so many prisoners before and after him, hung on the whim of the captor. He heard from his guard, "You are a prisoner . . . no longer a soldier. Each prisoner should be responsible for himself to the Front. You must no longer feel responsible to your government which has sent you to die in Vietnam." In effect, Rowe observed that the rules for his captivity regressed to those of the Middle Ages, and that his captors were trying to exploit his weaknesses, his desire to live, his dependence on others for strength, and his personal anxieties in order to attack the loyalties that he had formed before captivity. In 1967, one Vietcong defector who had encountered Rowe in the jungle camps called him, "Mr. Trouble," because he had made several escape attempts and remained utterly defiant and, in the defector's words, "stubborn, sneaky, and very smart." [24]

In camp, much like the prisoners of the Korean War, Rowe became a student. The Vietcong ridiculed the American Code of Conduct as a useless piece of paper, and the major portion of his lessons addressed thought control and his captors' understanding of the duty of the POW before, during, and after release. In spite of his political lessons, diseases, and near encounters with death, he planned and attempted several escapes.

As his captivity dragged on from 1963 through 1968, Rowe kept up his improvised tale to the Vietcong that he was merely an ordinary advisor to the South Vietnamese. He knew that if his captors discovered his actual Special Forces mission in South Vietnam, his execution would be a certainty. He wrote, "I knew of their dual standard of 'justice': anyone who opposed them was an 'enemy of the people' and therefore subject to death in any fashion the Vietcong executioner chose; whereas those who supported them—whether they were soldiers, political cadre indoctrinating all those under their control, terrorists bombing and killing innocent people, or simply peasants who happened to live in a Vietcong-controlled zone and either willingly or unwillingly aided the revolution—all were 'patriots.' Any harm to them was considered a 'crime against the people.' " Rowe's crime was that he was a Special Forces officer, and after the Vietcong finally discovered his secret, they condemned him to death. All that was left was Rowe's march to the place of trial, condemnation, and execution.

On December 31, 1968, after five years in captivity, James N. Rowe liberated himself. The Vietcong received orders to take Rowe to Zone Headquarters. As Rowe's party marched through the jungle, it was attacked by American B-52 aircraft. In the confusion caused by the heavy bombing, the guards became disoriented, and the group dispersed. Rowe and his guard, whom he called "Porky," slogged through the middle of a cattail field, up to their thighs in muddy water. As the American helicopters swarmed overhead, Rowe waved. Once or twice the two men had to crouch as the light observation helicopters made firing and spotting passes. Nearby, a group of Vietcong soldiers returned the Americans' fire, were fired upon themselves, and died in action.

Porky and Rowe took more precautions against being spotted from the air. As they cleared a path by tunneling through the heavy tangle of reeds and brush, Rowe observed that his guard was more concerned about hiding from the helicopters than guarding his condemned prisoner. At one point, Porky made a fatal error and left his position open to Rowe's watchful, opportunistic eye. Rowe described how he turned the tables on his guard when he became entangled in the brush. He said, "I reached forward and tripped the flange release at the rear of the magazine, feeling the click as the catch dropped loose. Porky straightened up seconds later, and as he stepped forward into the tunnel he had made, the magazine of ammunition dropped unnoticed into the water. I stepped on it as I passed, grinding it into the mud."

Although he still had the two grenades, the guard now carried an empty weapon. With Porky's weapon useless, Rowe prepared to make his second move. The pair traveled another hundred meters when Porky stopped and looked for his weapon. Seeing that the magazine had disappeared, he glanced knowingly at the ever-circling helicopters. Rowe noticed that his lips twisted in "an almost embarrassed grin." The odds had evened up, and Rowe found his energy level rising. "The factors of morale and determination," wrote Rowe, "gave me a reservoir from which to draw."

As the helicopters persisted in their area search, Rowe and Porky continued their evasion through the high grass. Rowe finally seized the moment. He assaulted and killed his guard, becoming a free man, but he still had work to do. The helicopters were very close; all he had to do was signal them. He stood in the clear and waved his mosquito net and handkerchief. Soon a Cobra gunship rolled in, joined by a second. Rowe thought, "They've seen me! I'm OK, they've seen me!" He was exuberant and waved frantically, trying to encourage them to hurry. But the Cobra pilots at low attack altitude at first believed that the man on the ground waving a handkerchief was a Vietcong soldier merely baiting them to fly in dangerously close, a tactic often used by the Vietcong to shoot down American gunships. The gunship pilots quite rightly became very cautious and nearly began firing. Rowe wrote, "Up in the Cobras—I learned later—the radio crackled into life. 'There's a VC down there in the open. . . .' From the other ship came the reply, 'Gun him!'" Rowe's luck held; the veteran pilots and crews of B Troop, 7th Armored Regiment, 1st Cavalry Division, the "Dutch Masters," held their fire.

Rowe watched with emotional abandon as a helicopter circled wide above him, then lined up for a low pass. All the while, he continued to wave his net frantically, making sure that the pilots kept him in their line of sight. His persistence paid off when the door-gunner in amazement saw Rowe's dark beard—a sure sign of an American soldier—and alerted his pilot. When the aircraft landed, Rowe wrote, "I dove onto the cool metal flooring and heard myself shouting, 'Go! Go!'"

After his escape, Rowe helped to revamp the Army's Survival School curriculum, wrote his book, and used his experience to prepare other soldiers for political rather than military captivity in South Vietnam. After he retired from the Army, Rowe returned briefly to active duty as a counter-insurgency specialist stationed in the Philippines. On April 21, 1989, a member of an assassination squad of the Philippine Liberation Army shot and killed him near his office in downtown Manila.[25]

The Vietcong captured Marine Lance Cpls. Steven D. Nelson and Michael R. Roha during an attack on the outpost at Phu Loc on January 7, 1968. They were fifteen miles northwest of Da Nang, not very far but far enough. During captivity, both Marines were paraded through nearby villages, on display in propaganda events. On the nineteenth day of captivity, the two Marines noticed that one guard slept soundly while another left for food. Alone and nearly unguarded for a few moments, Nelson and Roha seized the moment and fled into the jungle; twenty-four hours later, on January 22, 1968, a week before the Tet Offensive changed the fundamental nature of the war both in Vietnam and in America, they found safety behind their own lines.

On June 21, 1968, another Marine, Cpl. Don Fisher, stood perimeter watch on top of Hill 819 near Ca Lu, a spot below the DMZ near the contentious border between North and South Vietnam. North Vietnamese soldiers infiltrated the position, took him prisoner, and tied him to a tree with vines. Thinking that their prisoner was tied securely, the weary North Vietnamese soldiers bedded down for a rest. As his captors slept, Fisher worked his way free from the vines and crept into the darkness of the night-time jungle. When morning broke, Fisher made his way back to his unit.

Sgt. Buddy Wright of D Company, 1st Battalion, 22d Infantry, was captured on September 22, 1968. His North Vietnamese captors then led him into Cambodia. On the morning of his fifth day in captivity, Wright freed himself from the ropes that bound him and dashed into the surrounding jungle. After the alarm sounded, the North Vietnamese set out determined to recapture their quarry, and Wright spent several days playing cat-and-mouse, evading recapture. Wright eventually realized that although he had eluded his captors with some success, he was traveling west, deeper into Cambodia. He turned around and headed east again toward the South Vietnamese border. Weakened from his flight through the jungle, Wright reentered South Vietnam, where he encountered a friendly South Vietnamese soldier who led him to an outpost. On October 6, 1968, he took a short helicopter ride to friendly lines.[26]

Most American officers and enlisted men in Southeast Asia took the 1949 Geneva Convention, the Uniform Code of Military Justice, and the Code of Conduct very seriously. Military policy required each service member to carry a Geneva Convention card, and the curriculum in basic and survival training required them to memorize Article III of the Code:

"If I am captured . . . I will make every effort to escape and aid others to escape." Following the Code, many POWs in Vietnam, both in the North and South, attempted to escape and assisted others in their efforts. Of the 766 known POWs in the Vietnam War, 22 American military prisoners, about 3 percent, made successful escapes from the bamboo camps in South Vietnam, and 2 escaped from Laos (see Appendix 5: *American Escapers in South Vietnam*).[27]

One can only speculate on why the American media neglected most of the escapers during hostilities in South Vietnam. Only two, James N. Rowe and Dieter Dengler, published narratives about their escapes. Rowe's *Five Years to Freedom* (1971) appeared after the U.S. government had declared its policy of Vietnamization as well as its intention to withdraw from the war. Dengler's *Escape from Laos* (1979) was published several years after the communist victory. Along with Charles Klusmann, Isaac Camacho, James Dodson, and Walter Eckes, both Rowe and Dengler received wide media attention shortly after their escapes. Other escapers received very little publicity. At home, the military services silenced the public ballyhoo about escapers for fear that such publicity, especially when discussing individual heroics against the Vietcong, harmed rather than helped those who remained behind the wire.[28]

At the time few people in the United States other than American civilian and military intelligence officers knew that the traditional Golden Rule had become severely tarnished in the North. As the Vietnam War heated up in the South and as more American forces were deployed, losses mounted. Increasing numbers of prisoners, mostly airmen from the Air Force and Navy, were taken in air operations against the North. Of the 766 POWs taken, only 591 American prisoners left Hanoi in 1973. These numbers were small, both in the North and the South, when compared with 130,201 Americans taken during World War II and 7,140 in Korea.[29] Numbers are meaningless, however, when other forces were at work, especially forces that influenced the thinking of the general public in the midst of an escalating war that it understood very little about. Newspaper and magazine human-interest stories about escaped prisoners in the South, such as Klusmann, Dengler, Camacho, and Rowe, portrayed them as war heroes and found a ready audience at home. Since the North Vietnamese subscribed to every major American newspaper and magazine, and often used them as propaganda devices against their prisoners, the escapes undoubtedly brought down their wrath upon those who remained behind, especially those prisoners held in the North.

Beginning in 1964, North Vietnam had endured bombing attacks against military targets around Hanoi. To the North Vietnamese in Hanoi, Haiphong, Vinh, and other areas where American aircraft found targets, the air war began to resemble World War II. To the POWs' chagrin, the response resembled that of World War II as well. After the Doolittle raid on Tokyo in 1942, the Japanese declared unilaterally that the downed American fliers were to be treated as war criminals rather than protected POWs under international law. Japanese military authorities tried the Americans in sham war crimes trials and executed several. Like the Japanese, the North Vietnamese considered American air attacks against any military target in the homeland a war crime, and the American prisoners became "pirates" in a hostile new world.

In August 1966, with sentiment in the United States still supporting the war, two North Vietnamese officials called press conferences in Prague and Beijing to announce their country's position that captured American airmen were war criminals who had forfeited all claims to protection. Hanoi's legal position was based on its decision to invoke its exception to the American-sponsored Article 85 of the 1949 Geneva Convention and promised large-scale, international public trials.[30] In response to Hanoi's actions, President Johnson tried to maneuver the United States and North Vietnam into a negotiating position by calling on the neutral International Commission of the Red Cross (ICRC) for help. The ICRC was powerless to intercede because as early as 1964, Hanoi refused to allow its representatives to enter North Vietnam for the traditional purpose of protecting POWs and inspecting the prison camps. The result was tragic. The American POWs were alone, left to the whim of their captors and the shifting fortunes of a very long war.

The war-crime accusations finally culminated in the public humiliation of American POWs on July 6, 1966, when the North Vietnamese paraded them through downtown Hanoi in handcuffs amid angry crowds of civilians. Individually and as a group, the Americans looked gaunt and dejected, and the American media reported that they resembled the American POWs during the Korean War.[31] Ralph Gaither wrote that "July 6, 1966, was one of the blackest days of my captivity." [32] James B. Stockdale remembered the event and later commented that they were simply caught like "rabbits in a briar patch." [33]

What may have served as a morale booster for the North Vietnamese at home offended the noncommunist international community, much of which had been at least minimally friendly toward the North Vietnamese in their battle with the mighty United States. To many in the international community, this degrading treatment of American POWs in Hanoi flew in the face of the 1949 Geneva Convention and reversed North Vietnam's aura of valiant underdogs. Then too, by allowing the American public to see its prisoners paraded helplessly on television, Ho Chi Minh's government took a huge risk not only of angering an already frustrated Lyndon Johnson but also of generating a sense of public outrage among Americans, as well as support for the war. Although many people were deeply angered, it was not enough to change the course of events. Instead, a paradox surfaced during and after the Vietnam War in terms of how American society perceived its soldiers and POWs in general and its escapers in particular.

Two new POW images arose: prisoners as helpless victims of the fortunes of war and as battling underdogs. The good soldiers were the POWs. Others, from generals to grunts, who in previous wars had been painted as democratic heroes by such popular war correspondents as Ernie Pyle and Marguerite Higgins, became villains in the Vietnam War. This happened at the same time as the American press corps in Saigon began to depict members of the military services as dangerous pariahs who rejected the values of freedom and democracy held so dear by American society. Tired of rehashing the daily military briefings, termed "the 5 o'clock follies," the press corps not only turned openly hostile toward the war and government policies, but also ultimately toward the soldiers who were ordered to fight it. In the press's view, truth had become the first casualty of the war, especially when the press's freedom had been curtailed and it was being transformed into an arm of the government.

War news during this period became a form of propaganda and exercised psychological control over the mood at home, abroad, and in enemy territory.[34] As propaganda for their cause, North Vietnam had wanted the world press to portray an image of defeated, weak, and guilty war criminals running for their lives through the streets of Hanoi. The North Vietnamese effort backfired, however, because the tragically bizarre images actually conveyed the three dramatic elements of what Rupert Wilkinson called "dynamic toughness": that Americans faced their enemy captors squarely; that they took care of themselves and others in captivity; and that they could "take it" by standing up to adversity. Thus, during and after the Vietnam War, prisoners assumed more prominence than in any previous wars. For the first time in America's military experience, POWs became widely acclaimed public heroes even while they were still held captive.

At home, the Vietnam War posed a strategic dilemma. South Vietnam's strength was based not on its own determination for victory, or on political stability, but on military commitments made by the United States and a few other SEATO allies. The United States had little or no will to win, but it had an inordinate fear of losing, which resulted in great discrepancies between what the American military said it did and what actually occurred in the field. Journalists called these inconsistencies the "credibility gap." Army historian Harry G. Summers, Jr. went one step further. He suggested that the Army encountered troubles both with the euphemisms used to hide the horrors of war and with public perceptions of American cold-bloodedness—progress defined only as body counts—which then deeply offended the media people trying to report the war honestly and inflamed their strong sense of idealism. The effect, according to Summers, was that official military war reporting became offensive to the American people.[35] Historian Jonathan Schell concluded that since the government and the military sought to evade public scrutiny, the press turned to the antiwar movement for news. The military was humiliated in print, and dissent became more important to the media than the battles.[36]

Lyndon Johnson, a masterful press-manipulator in domestic politics, abhorred the negative press coverage of the war. His successor, Richard Nixon, who hated the press in general, commented that the negative portrayal of the behavior of soldiers in the field in Vietnam actually contributed to changing the course of the war. By the 1970s, coverage of the war had so saturated American television, newspapers, and magazines that people had tired of its reality. After the press broke the My Lai story and informed the American people and the world that members of C Company, 1st Platoon, 1st Battalion, 20th Infantry of the Americal Division, had committed a serious war crime, Nixon charged that the media were more friendly to the enemies than to the Allies. There is some truth in Nixon's statement. From the start of open hostilities in 1961 through 1964, the American press seldom reported the political murders of South Vietnamese committed by the North Vietnamese or the Vietcong. According to Roger Hillsman, from 1961 to 1964, the Vietcong kidnapped 28,504 individuals and assassinated 6,587 Vietnamese civilians. Later, some reports did focus on the discovery of the bodies of thousands of South Vietnamese civilians who had been murdered with their hands tied behind their back in Hue by a communist cadre during Tet of 1968. Nevertheless, the American war crime at My Lai became an icon for the war; North Vietnamese and Vietnamese war crimes went virtually unnoticed except by the South Vietnamese.[37]

While the press painted returning soldiers as blood-lusting villains, not heroes, the paradox is that the prisoners of the Vietnam War were viewed in a favorable light. During World War II, POWs had received short shrift in the popular press, and they were branded as "brainwashed" collaborators after Korea. In 1973, the Vietnam POWs were cast by the press as classic stand-up victim-heroes. The repatriation, known as Operation Homecoming, was saturated with press coverage. The entire nation watched the POWs step from Air Force transport aircraft and heard prominent personalities like Jeremiah Denton and Richard Stratton speak briefly at the microphones. These men expressed their thanks to a nation whose spirit had changed radically while they had fought their personal war in prison. The escapers, those men who had rejected the condition of captivity, faded into the wake of time and events left by those who returned from Hanoi.

Conditions in North Vietnam were similar but not identical to those in North Korea. Although the Hoa Lo (the Oven) prison sat in downtown Hanoi, many of the other camps in the North Vietnamese prison system were isolated from population centers. With no hopes of any outside help, the American POWs were vulnerable. In the camps, most were malnourished and weakened by harsh treatment. Unlike the MIS-X operations during World War II, intelligence services in the United States found themselves unable to establish anything but the barest contact with the Hanoi insiders. Except for occasional letters to and from wives and families, the camp authorities denied the Americans access to the Red Cross and any other recognized neutral humanitarian service. The POWs were stranded, dominated by the camp authority on one hand and answerable to their senior officers for upholding the Code of Conduct on the other. Somewhere in between sat a small cadre of escapers who made their presence felt.

Although a number of POWs succeeded in escaping in South Vietnam and Laos, no one scored a home run from the prison facilities in North Vietnam. Yet some Americans defied the odds, gained permission from the senior officers in camp, and at great risk to themselves and others broke out of their confinement. There were at least six committed escapers in North Vietnam: Lance P. Sijan and George E. Day, who made individual escapes; George Coker and George McKnight, who escaped together in 1967; and John Dramesi, who first attempted a lone escape through enemy territory, and who, in 1969, created a tragic partnership with Edwin Atterberry in Hanoi. Sijan and Dramesi were what Biderman called tigers, or what Aleksandr Solzhenitsyn called committed natural escapers. George Day may have been a tiger at first, but events and circumstances tamed his instincts after the North Vietnamese put him into the American POW community. Dramesi remained a tiger throughout his captivity and made life miserable for some prisoners and often for himself. Day and Dramesi lived through their captivities; Sijan and Atterberry died.

Capt. Lance Sijan, USAF, was shot down on November 9, 1967, and was captured by North Vietnamese soldiers after forty-six days of evasion in the jungle.[38] After spending several days in a prison compound, Sijan escaped, but within a few hours he was recaptured and beaten severely. As he lay nearly unconscious, he asked his cell mates about the chances of escaping again. Combining three values—duty to his office, rejection of the condition of captivity, and a total commitment to the Code of Conduct—Sijan began digging into the earthen floor intent on escaping despite having pneumonia. After several attempts and recaptures, Sijan, the committed natural escaper, died in Hanoi on January 22, 1968.[39] President Gerald R. Ford awarded Sijan a posthumous Medal of Honor after all the POWs returned, some of whom knew what had happened to Sijan. The citation read in part:

> After being captured by North Vietnamese soldiers, Capt. Sijan was taken to a holding point for subsequent transfer to a prisoner of war camp. In his emaciated and crippled condition, he overpowered one of his guards and crawled into the jungle, only to be recaptured after several hours. He was then transferred to another prison camp where he was kept in solitary confinement and interrogated at length. During interrogation, he was severely tortured; however, he did not divulge any information to his captors. Capt. Sijan lapsed into delirium and was placed in the care of another prisoner. During his intermittent periods of consciousness until his death, he never complained of his physical condition and, on several occasions, spoke of future escape attempts.[40]

Shot down on August 26, 1967, during his sixty-seventh combat mission, an attack on a surface-to-air missile site, Maj. George Day, USAF, was taken prisoner by members of a North Vietnamese local militia. He thought of escape early and wanted to be the first American out of North Vietnam. He initially feigned extreme internal injuries so that his captors would not hang him upside down or bind him too tight; however, the next morning a guard entered his hut and told him that a jeep had arrived to take him to Hanoi. Knowing that Hanoi meant permanent captivity, Day decided that the time was ripe for an escape south, about forty land miles to the border and, hopefully, friendly lines. Although his broken arm was in a splint, Day worked himself free, and on September 1, 1967, he crawled away from his underground cell.[41] On the escape trail for seven days, evading the enemy as best he could, Day tried without success to signal aircraft flying overhead. On the eighth day of his evasion, he crossed the Ben Hai River that separates North and South Vietnam. On the ninth day, as he tried to gather some food, he heard a Vietnamese cutting wood. When he looked up, he was confronted by a young man holding a Russian AK-47 assault rifle. Day later wrote, "It was the blackest moment in my life; two miles from the Marine Corps camp of Con Thien, South Vietnam, perhaps six or eight miles south of the DMZ [Demilitarized Zone] I was captured."[42] Four weeks later, Day joined hundreds of other Americans at Hoa Lo Prison in Hanoi. Although Day did not escape again, he became a ranking member of the hard-resisters in the Hanoi prison system. After his release on March 14, 1973, he received the Medal of Honor from Congress for "conspicuous gallantry and intrepidity at the risk of his life above and beyond the call of duty."[43]

The earliest partnership escape from the prison system in North Vietnam took place on October 12, 1967, when Air Force Capt. George McKnight and Navy Lt. (jg) George T. Coker broke out of the "Dirty Bird Annex" on the north side of Hanoi. After the downtown run in Hanoi in 1966, the Americans suffered countless rounds of quizzes and torture sessions coupled with the demoralizing thought of endless captivity. Since the POWs understood the Code of Conduct's mandate to resist and escape, the stage was set for some prisoners to break out. As part of Hanoi's rigorous POW purge in the fall of 1967, Coker and McKnight, two hard-resisters, were placed in handcuffs and put in solitary confinement. After two weeks they learned how to pick both the handcuff and the cell locks. McKnight could see Hanoi from his cell and learned, more or less, where they were. The Red River, the only real pathway available to them, was nearby. Remembering Article 3 of the Code of Conduct—"If I am captured I will continue to resist by all means available. I will make every effort to escape and aid others to escape"—they decided to formulate a plan. As Adm. James B. Stockdale wrote:

> They just decided to fill up on water before they left, make it to the river, swim down it by night, and bury themselves in its muddy bank by day. They figured on a two-knot current and, both being good swimmers and having a knowledge of the local geography, thought they would be at the river's mouth after three or four nights of swimming. There they would overpower the crew of a sailboat and head for the U.S. Navy's Seventh

Fleet. All in all, they figured on an eight-day trip to the navy ships. They would drink polluted river water as necessary and live off the land for food, and figured they wouldn't get really sick till they got where they were going.[44]

On the night of October 12, 1967, Coker and McKnight broke out of their cells, climbed over the walls, and crept through Hanoi's streets until they arrived at the Red River's bank at a point very close to the Paul Daumer Bridge. The long swim began with a five-knot downstream current that they used to swim and float fifteen miles from Hanoi toward the South China Sea. Both men knew that they had to hide and rest during the day, so they crawled into a mudbank, but early the next morning, on October 13, 1967, an old woman and a young fisherman startled them and called the local militia. Coker and McKnight were recaptured after only twelve hours and fifteen miles on the run. Thinking about the odds of making his escape, Coker wrote, "I think a realistic appraisal of the odds against escape should be given. There have been too many hero movies about escapes that blow this out of proportion. You should not say, 'If I have a 25% chance, I'll go.' It is really absurd to anticipate even a 2% chance of escape. If you come up with a 1 in 1,000 chance of success it is pretty good." [45] To judge by these remarks, the Camp Authority in Hanoi needed Solzhenitsyn's window bars set in cement, barbed wire, towers, fences, reinforced barriers, ambushes, booby traps, and meat-fed grey dogs to keep Coker a prisoner.

According to Stockdale, Coker and McKnight were not ill-treated after they came back. The North Vietnamese put them into close confinement with heavy irons. Then they placed the two officers in solitary confinement in "Alcatraz," along with the other hard-resisters.[46] It was also clear that the Hanoi prisoners expected no outside help from a very hostile Vietnamese civilian population; the only escape line was the Red River to the South China Sea and the American Seventh Fleet. Escape might not be practical under these circumstances, but practicality means little to tigerish natural escapers.

Capt. John A. Dramesi, USAF, was born and raised in South Philadelphia's tough neighborhoods, and fell into the mold created by men like Berry Benson in the Civil War, whose escapes were more defiant "pure cussedness" than cautious practicality. His F-105D was shot down on April 2, 1967, and although rescue aircraft circled overhead, he was taken prisoner by two North Vietnamese militiamen with rifles and a young boy with a machete.[47] Knowing that he was on his way to Hanoi's prison system, Dramesi was taken first to a bamboo hut that acted as a temporary cell. Trussed up like an animal ready for slaughter, a torture the Hanoi prisoners called the "Ropes," Dramesi was quizzed about military matters and was given some initial political indoctrination. A few days later, he worked his way out of the hut on his hands and knees and remained on the run until discovered by an old man who signaled a nearby road gang to make the capture. Dramesi's first escape came to an end when his civilian captors turned him over to the military. He went to Hanoi after all, but he never stopped seeking out escape opportunities.

By 1969, Dramesi had formed a partnership with Edwin Atterberry of Dallas, Texas, and on May 10 of that year they struck out together for the Red River. Before their escape from the "Zoo," one of the outlying camps in the North Vietnamese system, the two men planned what they called the "Party" well in advance. In *Code of Honor* (1976) Dramesi recalled, "None of the plans were written down because of the guards' weekly inspections." In the planning stage they began putting aside bits of wire, glass, string, and other useful items; they also stole clothing that could conceal their identities as they traveled the Red River to the sea, much like Coker and McKnight's plan two years earlier. "Ed had stolen a burlap bag," wrote Dramesi, "one of the peanut bags, and I managed to hide two baskets and a bamboo carrying-pole during the confusion of serving the evening meal. These props were the perfect things necessary to complete our disguises." To prepare themselves physically, they exercised by running around their cells in little circles every day. Mental preparations included developing a story in common, which would say that they escaped to avoid certain torture and miserable conditions. According to Dramesi, "I knew that the North Vietnamese would not accept the real reason men are willing to gamble with life—to be free."

When the time for the escape arrived, their fellow POWs had second thoughts, many considering the likelihood of dangerous reprisals. Others thought about home and family and the possibility that they would not be with them again. What had been a barracks-level escape organization dwindled into a "party" of two. For Dramesi and Atterberry, the escape was a commitment, and they intended to go, as Coker noted earlier in his post-captivity reflection, within their own measure of risk.

Luck, as always no small ingredient in any escape, worked against Dramesi and Atterberry. After an uneventful departure, they began to run into trouble. As Dramesi recalled, on the outskirts of a town called Cu Loc, a villager approached who identified the ragged Americans as probable prisoners on the run. The old man quickly ran one way while Dramesi and Atterberry ran the other way. The escapers took refuge in a church, but by morning they knew that recapture was imminent. Dramesi wrote:

> It was a clear, beautiful day to be free. As the sun rose, groups of fifteen to seventeen men and women, all armed with rifles and Russian AK-47 machine guns, moved past us, searching the nearby fields. If only we were just a little farther out. We were so close to Hanoi that it was easy to organize these large search parties. It seemed like hours had drifted by, but I realized I had completely lost track of time. Finally, one group invaded the churchyard. They tore down the barricades and searched inside the church. They were gathering to leave when one of them, perhaps as a reluctant afterthought, decided to crawl into our brambled thicket. The young soldier was no more than three feet away when he cocked his .45 automatic pistol and let out a yell. It sounded like a hundred guns were cocked on command.

The major in command of the unit was very proud as he surveyed the two recaptured escapers standing there in mud-spattered black pyjamas. Back inside the walls of the Zoo, before being separated, Atterberry shook Dramesi's hand and said quietly, "We tried."

While Dramesi and Atterberry were preparing for their escape, similar thoughts spread among the other POWs in Hanoi. Fellow prisoner Charlie Plumb recalled the fierce temptation to break out on the spur of the moment when the opportunity presented itself. Plumb and his cell mate had made some escape preparations such as hoarding food, loosening the bars on the windows, and creating disguises. An opportunity did present itself on Saturday night, May 10, 1969, when the Vietnamese reduced the guard patrol to a skeleton crew. According to Plumb, this action prompted countless fantasies about leaving Hanoi behind forever. However, remembering SRO Robinson Risner's and James Stockdale's wise directives that no one should attempt another escape without outside help, Plumb had second thoughts and decided against it. He recalled, "Discretion set up too many obstacles. We couldn't let emotion outrun reason." [48] Then the entire cell block in the Annex and the Zoo came alive with tapping.

Because of Dramesi and Atterberry's escape, the North Vietnamese camp authorities took heavy reprisals, and interrogators tortured both men to the limits of their endurance. Commenting on the Dramesi-Atterberry torture session after their recapture, Stockdale wrote, "Dramesi was worked over heavily and cried out, and he could hear Atterberry over in cell 5 doing the same." [49] The Vietnamese put Dramesi in irons for thirty-two days and administered the "Ropes," or strappado, fifteen times. Edwin Atterberry died in torture; so too did James J. Connell, a POW not associated with the escape at all.⁵⁰ Although most prisoners had no prior knowledge of the escape, the camp authorities were convinced that the entire POW community had acted in consort with Dramesi and Atterberry. Twenty-five men at the Zoo were beaten until their backs and buttocks were a solid mass of blood. One prisoner's finger was severed. Ten were put in irons together for six months, with the right leg of one man shackled to the left leg of the next. According to Plumb, "After that we didn't think much about escape—not that it would be impossible but that the aftermath for the remaining prisoners would be too horrible. We would wait until all of us were safely home before we told our story." ⁵¹

The reprisals against the other prisoners in the system were so great during the summer of 1969 that the entire Hanoi POW organization nearly came to an end. Future escapes that developed on the inside were off; the costs were too high. Reintegrated into the POW community, John Dramesi abandoned escapes but remained a hard-resister during the rest of his time in Hanoi. After repatriation, he dedicated his narrative *Code of Honor* (1975) to his friend and fellow committed escaper Edwin Atterberry. Nevertheless, feelings among some of the surviving Hanoi POW veterans remain strongly divided on the entire Dramesi-Atterberry issue.

From 1970 to 1973, the Hanoi prisoners learned to sit tight, survive, and wait for something to happen beyond the prison walls. Toward the close of the war, events outside Hanoi affected escape plans as much as or more than any actions within the camps. Outside action began in 1970 when a combined Army-Air Force special warfare team planned and executed the Son Tay prison raid. Although the camp was empty and the raid failed to rescue anyone, it made the North Vietnamese feel more vulnerable. As a result, they brought all the American POWs into Hanoi from the outlying camps; stopped the beatings, leg irons, strappado, and extreme isolation; and began treating the prisoners more humanely. On a grander scale, the Son Tay raid introduced a new version of the Golden Rule: given the outrageous conditions in the Hanoi prison system, the United States was prepared to respond. Two more years passed before outside efforts again affected conditions for the POWs.

Without interservice organizations like MIS-X or MI-9 to assist escapes or gather military information inside the North Vietnamese prison system, naval intelligence developed an escape plan on its own. First, some contact was established with the POWs inside Hanoi. Next, a coordinated breakout was planned, which would take place sometime between May 29 and June 19, 1972, with the escapers again attempting to navigate down the only natural escape line they had, the fast-moving Red

River, from Hanoi to its mouth at the South China Sea. The Navy developed an elaborate rescue plan, Operation Thunderhead, which included a primary rescue helicopter flying steady SAR patrol missions and placing SEALs (Sea Air Land) and UDT (Underwater Demolition Team) personnel offshore in a submarine, the USS *Grayback*. One of the mission planners, Edwin L. Towers, commented, "I couldn't help feeling that if there were reasons to justify sticking my neck out, Operation Thunderhead was it!" [52]

As a rescuer, Towers commiserated with the POWs. His imagination ignited feelings of resolve, along with frustration and anger. He wrote, "Just fifty miles away was a hostile land which held hundreds of Americans captive. It concerned me that once having escaped from a POW camp, our men would have to navigate down sixty miles of river before we could even have an opportunity to assist them. If only the communications were better, so we could coordinate the escape and rescue efforts simultaneously." [53] Unfortunately, the SEALs made enemy contact too soon and lost men. The Navy, believing that the mission had been compromised, then canceled the escape-rescue. Towers was bitterly disappointed. "I would have gladly risked my life," he wrote, "by flying up the Red River to Hanoi in order to extract these men and so would the other crewmen." [54] For the Hanoi prisoners, liberation would come only through diplomatic activities in Paris.

By late 1972, peace talks promised an end to hostilities, and thoughts of escapes from the rigidly monitored confines of the Hanoi Hilton and from other prison camps in North Vietnam were largely abandoned. The 1973 Paris Peace Accords between the United States, the Democratic Republic of Vietnam, the National Liberation Front, and the Government of South Vietnam brought a temporary halt to the war and returned 651 Americans from the region. In April 1975, the North Vietnamese Army invaded and defeated South Vietnam. By 1976, Vietnam had become one country, the Socialist Republic of Vietnam, and the United States imposed a trade embargo, insisting that the lingering and complicated issue of the 2,453 missing Americans had to be resolved. [55] Only Marine Pvt. Robert Garwood emerged after the hostilities, an escape of sorts, following a custody that lasted from 1965 to 1979. [56]

In 1978, Garwood managed to make several trips to the Victory Hotel in Hanoi, where he posed as a foreign worker buying cigarettes and liquor. One night he saw a group of middle-aged Westerners sitting in a corner speaking English. After so many years of speaking only Vietnamese, Garwood's English had faded. He wrote, "I am an American in

Vietnam. Are you interested?" [57] He then rolled the note as tightly as he could and asked one of the Westerners for a cigarette. After a short conversation, he put the note in the man's lap. The man was indeed interested and began the process of facilitating his release. When asked what was important by a Vietnamese colonel prior to his release, Garwood responded, "Only my freedom." [58] The Garwood captivity had continued long after hostilities ceased, but in spite of its length, the Marine Corps prosecuted and found him guilty of collaboration and physical mistreatment of other prisoners. He lost all his back pay, about $140,000, and left the Marine Corps without a cent. Escape in Garwood's case was costly. [59]

Even when the war was over, tragedies continued for thousands of Vietnamese. Shortly after the end of the hostilities, the North Vietnamese communists established political reeducation camps that combined hard labor with political indoctrination. Former members of the Army of Vietnam (ARVN) were ordered to these camps in short order, and the North Vietnamese initially told them that their incarceration would last for about two weeks, depending on their former rank. In camp, they discovered to their horror that the sentences were open-ended, and they were subject to the whims of their new captors. One refugee, Mr. Tanh, had escaped from North Vietnam in 1955 after the Viet Minh's victory over the French. As a young Catholic boy, he had experienced communist reeducation firsthand; as an adult, Tanh served as a soldier on the losing side in a long and bitter war. Both experiences taught him what the North Vietnamese communists were about to do.

During the war, Tanh became a junior officer in the South Vietnamese Army and was a schoolteacher in Saigon when the city fell in 1975. He explained that after the NVA/PAVN victory, the North Vietnamese authorities ordered all former ARVN officers to report for transportation to a reeducation camp. After reporting, he received food, mosquito netting, and clothing. Loaded on trucks, these new prisoners moved from Saigon west to Tay Ninh, where they built their own camp. The food ration was rice and salt only, with no medicine, sugar, or vegetables other than what they grew themselves. All contact with the outside, including letters from the family, was forbidden at first, until the camp authorities realized that families sent food to the prisoners. Fearful, most men stayed in their camps and obeyed orders; the escapers were executed in front of the other prisoners or taken out at night and shot. Work consisted of clearing minefields, and the new prisoners at first suffered heavy casualties. After the tenth month in camp, the authorities finally permitted some visitors. By 1978, Tanh had become a seasoned prisoner and realized that his captivity might be endless. He realized, too, that the camp authority released its captives either randomly or in accordance with the party affiliation of their relatives. Finally, his turn came for release. Forced to leave his wife and children behind, Tanh fled Ho Chi Minh City (Saigon) for the coastal city of Vung Tau by boat. His family also escaped and joined him in Australia.[60]

Another generation followed Tanh's, one born during the war but barely able to remember either the events or the ravages of the war itself. Whereas the Americans tried to escape as duty to their offices and the Code of Conduct or as a rejection of the conditions of captivity, Vietnamese refugees often escaped from what they considered a cruel political regime in the aftermath of the Vietnam War. Mr. Bach, born in 1972 and a college student in the United States in 1993, explained why he escaped: "My country was a prison that lacked all human rights. The word 'Freedom' never existed and the individual will was horribly suppressed. Day by day I lived under the Communist rule, suffering and becoming thirsty for freedom. At the age of sixteen my parents planned to have me escape Vietnam, hoping to find a country that offered freedom and education. Leaving all my childhood behind, I fled Vietnam by boat."[61]

In the Asian refugee communities in the United States, Australia, and the other countries that accepted them, Bach's story is the norm. By the 1980s, conditions in the SRV forced other Vietnamese, Cambodians, and Laotians to escape because of religious or racial persecution, as was the case with the ethnic Chinese-Vietnamese in 1978, or because of old war-related vendettas against the Hmong tribesmen. They were forced to leave their homes and sometimes their families and often found themselves reimprisoned in refugee camps in Thailand, Hong Kong, the Philippines, or Malaysia. The fortunate ones like Pin Yathay, who escaped from the Khmer Rouge's reign of terror in Cambodia, emigrated to France.[62] Others went to the United States, Canada, Australia, Britain, France, and many other countries in the space of a few years.

What links the Vietnam experience for the Americans and the South Vietnamese is that imprisonment became more radically political than military. Nearly without exception, the Asian expatriate refugees yearn for the beauties and comforts of home and wait patiently for the time when they can return with impunity. In February 1994, nearly twenty years after all these events, the U.S. government lifted its trade embargo against the Socialist Republic of Vietnam. The last prisoner was transferred out of Hoa Lo on March 16, 1994, because a Singapore firm began to transform the facility from a prison into the five-star Horizon Hanoi Hotel, with nine stories and two hundred rooms. Even twenty-five years later, the odd politics of the Vietnam War loom in the background. Inside the complex, the SRV is reserving 2,500 square meters for a prison museum.[63]

The divisive issues of the Vietnam War, much like those of the Civil War a century before it, have lasting appeal for veterans, scholars, poets, and journalists. The most enduring issue surrounding American captivity in North Vietnam remains the individual and collective response to the Code of Conduct. There is little doubt that Article 3, the mandate to resist and escape, became contentious in Hanoi.[64] Most pilots and aircrew shot down over North Vietnam before 1970 followed the Code to the degree that they could in their circumstances. Supported in this effort by the examples of hard-resisting senior officers like James B. Stockdale, Jeremiah Denton, Robinson Risner, Eugene McDaniel, Howard Rutledge, and others who suffered terribly, the younger prisoners often found substance and meaning in the application of the Code's simple philosophy. Stockdale explained that they had to accept torture, but they had to gauge it so that the torture meant something. It was never solely a question of the ends justifying the means; the Hanoi prisoners often suffered greatly under torture before they "rolled over" and gave the interrogators what they wanted. Then they had to "fall back" and forgive one another for divulging code-breaking information, and then "bounce back" for another round. As a result of this sort of suffering over a period of years, the Code meant more than its rule-book quality; it began to represent an icon of community solidarity among the prisoners.

The Code of Conduct mentions no consequences for violating American military law under the Uniformed Code of Military Justice. Comdr. Richard Stratton, USN, whose famous bow and monotone confession pleased his captors at first, but embarrassed them later, contended that the individual could withstand only so much torture before being made to confess anything. Resisting a torturer to the best of one's ability was the objective, not resisting to the point of total self-sacrifice at any single instance. Stratton suggested that the Cold War prisoner should attempt to save his mind and body in order to continue the fight over the long haul rather than give in to one's primal instincts to resist at all costs. Most important, Stratton, along with many of his prisoner colleagues, maintained that the greatest good for the greatest number of prisoners in a POW community begins with tolerance of failure, endures through forgiveness of others' weaknesses, limits resistance to what is absolutely necessary, and maintains strong links with the captive community at large.[65]

Keeping the Code meant keeping the faith, one that opposed the agenda of a political adversary who knew the Code too.

Many prisoners suffered reprisals because of the escape attempts, but when attempts were sanctioned by the senior ranking officers in the prison system, then the others, begrudgingly or not, endured the reprisals. Thus the Code of Conduct, as the prisoners in North Vietnam discovered, acts as both a guideline for ethical behavior and a pointer toward a set of hard and fast laws that regulate POW behavior. That the Code's practitioners must be practical and thoughtful at the same time became common sense. Escaping or assisting a fellow prisoner to escape may defy an individual's common sense to survive as comfortably as possible, but in the long run may give a community of prisoners the best chance of survival with dignity.[66]

If one reflects on the likes of escapers like Gustavus Conyngham in the Revolution, Thomas Rose, John Hunt Morgan, and Berry Benson in the Civil War, and the thousands of escapers in the world wars, Korea, and Vietnam, with or without a formal Code of Conduct, it becomes clear that military prisoners of war will try to escape or help others to escape captivity as part of their prescribed duty in a prison camp. At a POW studies conference sponsored by the Defense Force Institute at the Australian Defense Force Academy in May 1994, a distinguished Australian Army lieutenant colonel was asked why Australian forces have no Code of Conduct for POWs. "We don't need one," he responded.[67] If one considers that so many British and Commonwealth soldiers escaped in the twentieth century's wars, he was correct. On the other hand, culture counts, and the Americans see the problem through a different, more legalistic lens than the British or the Australians, even today.

Although the military services had their mandate to escape embedded in a strong set of ethics, other Americans had no code to keep at all, namely, civilian war correspondents in Vietnam and the civilian hostages who were taken during the Middle East crises. With nothing more as a backdrop than a sense of urgency, a firm belief in innocence, and strong personal ethics, they generated the will to defy their captors. Two escaped in Beirut.

11

The Pseudo-Wars
Civilian Hostages and Escapers

It was as if the whole nation had been blindfolded and hog-tied, hauled through the streets of a strange city with people taunting them in a foreign tongue.
—Steven Roberts (1980)

One powerful legacy of the Vietnam War was America's heightened concern for its military prisoners in enemy hands. Less attention was paid to civilians, mostly correspondents who became prisoners in Southeast Asia, forty-six of whom died or were listed as missing by 1975. With an abiding concern for their own, the newsmen created a Missing Correspondents File, and men like Tim Page and Wally Burgess found ways to continue their respective searches for friends and colleagues. Among the missing was Errol Flynn's son Sean, who wandered into Cambodia looking for a story in 1973. The Vietcong captured him and his cameraman. Flynn was determined to report the war rather than become a part of it and tried twice to escape his captors. Sometime in November or December 1973, Flynn's luck ran out. According to Wally Burgess, an Australian who discovered Flynn's fate through an interview with an eyewitness in Cambodia, on Flynn's third attempt, Vietcong guards shot him in the back.[1] His remains have not been recovered, but the tradition of civilians leaving their captors, or attempting to, continues.

Six years after Operation Homecoming, the return of the Americans from North and South Vietnam, the spectre of captivity descended yet again upon Americans in government service. On November 4, 1979, a large group of Iranian students, under the public scrutiny of the Ayatollah Khomeini, broke away from a demonstration and marched toward the American embassy in Tehran. In the beginning, about 450 students planned a three- to five-day sit-in, but events overtook intentions. Sparked by the United States' admission of the exiled Shah for medical treatment, the participants' anger flamed into outrage, and the sit-in became a siege.[2]

The Carter administration's failure to free the hostages by any means available soon led to a loss of national pride and a sense of universal humiliation at a time when American military capability was ebbing and the country's morale was still recovering from the Vietnam debacle. During the Iran crisis, Americans were affronted by the punishment propaganda broadcast on the evening news, but they had little knowledge of the long-standing religious and political hatreds that had erupted in Iran, and no realization that these hatreds could possibly affect them directly. That the Shah had close ties with the U.S. State Department, the Pentagon, and the intelligence community was of no importance to the average citizen in the United States. The national mood turned ugly when the news reported that Iranian religious fanatics had begun to execute members of the Shah's regime in public, and there was grave concern that American hostages would be murdered in a similar manner. In a way reminiscent of the Korean and Vietnam wars, the pseudo-wars in Iran and Beirut had begun to place a stranglehold around America's throat. Journalist Steven Roberts observed, "It was as if the whole nation had been blindfolded and hog-tied, hauled through the streets of a strange city with people taunting them in a foreign tongue."[3]

Instead of ordering military action, President Carter, like Sam Houston in Texas more than a century before, tried to negotiate a solution rather than involve the country in another foreign incursion for the sake of fifty-three civilian diplomats and Marine embassy guards. War-weary Americans had no taste for interventionism, instead developing a national preoccupation with symbols, including yellow ribbons and candlelight vigils.[4] Although the United States was not at war with Iran, President Carter knew that as commander in chief of America's armed forces, he could order a rescue mission without the consent of Congress, if he believed that the long-range benefits of a success might compensate for the high risk of failure. Under enormous pressure to do something, President Carter initiated a raid against Tehran on April 24, 1980.[5] Cyrus Vance, then the secretary of state, opposed the mission so vehemently that he threatened to resign if it was carried out. The operation began despite Vance's concerns. After a helicopter collided with a C-130 transport aircraft in the desert, leaving eight men dead, the president aborted the mission. Though no fault could ever be found in the raiders' courage or dedication, the failed rescue mission became another symbol of failure for Americans in the Middle East. It was not to be the last.

Because of the close confinement, heavy security, and constant press attention, no one escaped from the Iranians. None of the preconditions for wartime escapes existed in Tehran. After 444 days, on January 20, 1981, the eve of Ronald Reagan's presidency, the Islamic revolutionaries released the fifty-two hostages. Iran won the contest but became an international outlaw, and Reagan soon discovered that he had to address another Iran-inspired hostage crisis in Lebanon. In the 1980s, more than fifty Western nationals, all civilians except for Lt. Col. William Higgins, USMC, on duty with the United Nations, were kidnapped and held hostage. The world knew Terry Waite, a distinguished Englishman who represented the Anglican Church in Lebanon and eventually became a hostage himself; the eighteen Americans held in Beirut began their ordeals in anonymity but became familiar names and personalities as time went on.

American involvement in Lebanon in the 1980s related to the Lebanese civil war, which began in April 1975 and ended officially in October 1990.[6] The American captivity experience in Lebanon began with several abductions in June 1982 and ended with Terry Anderson's homecoming in December 1991. Of the seventeen American hostages, three died in captivity, one was rescued, eleven were released, and two escaped. Many kidnapped Americans were targeted directly and grabbed near their homes or offices as they were entering or leaving. Several hostages, however, were either taken by accident because they resembled an intended target or grabbed because they identified themselves as Americans to the wrong people.

The methods of capture fell into three broad categories: (1) the hostage was taken from the street and forced into a getaway car; (2) the hostage was cut off while traveling in a car and forced from the vehicle at gunpoint into a getaway car; and (3) in the most ingenious method, the hostage was tricked into compliance and easily led away. The most common method of abducting human targets from the street was by hitting them over the head to daze them and then forcing them into a car at gunpoint. As kidnappers whisked away their quarry, friends, relatives, and bystanders often watched the scene in horror, unable to help the victims for fear of endangering their own lives. Regardless of the method, kidnapped Americans were seldom released very quickly. A few were considered worthless to their captors and were released after several hours, but such events were rare and appeared to be the work of independent operators not connected with the radical Hezbollah.

The first American kidnapped in the 1980s, now seldom remembered, was David Dodge, acting president of the American University of Beirut

(AUB). Dodge's abduction—as he walked from his office on July 19, 1982—was claimed by Islamic Amal as an act of retaliation for the kidnapping of three Iranian diplomats. The second victim, Frank Regier, an engineering professor at AUB, was grabbed when he ventured into the dangerous streets of West Beirut. He wanted to find a friend and tell him about plans to evacuate Americans by helicopter.[7] Regier was taken on February 10, 1984, supposedly to secure the release of the seventeen Shi'ites convicted of Kuwait bombings in December 1983. Three of the bombers had been sentenced to death. One was the brother-in-law of Imad Mugniyeh; another was his cousin. As Regier sat in captivity, the world learned that family ties ran deep in Lebanon. Mugniyeh wanted his relatives released.

Using the same capture methods, kidnappers took the Cable News Network (CNN) Beirut Bureau Chief Jerry Levin on March 7, CIA Station Chief William Buckley on March 16, and the Reverend Benjamin Weir, a Presbyterian minister, on May 8. As Weir struggled with his captors, his wife Carol screamed in vain for help. Like the four Americans before him, Weir became a captive of the Islamic Jihad. About the capture of Peter Kilburn, very little was known except that he disappeared from the AUB campus on December 3, 1984. Unlike that of the other hostages, the motivating force behind Kilburn's abduction appeared to be financial rather than political. Rumors began circulating almost immediately that a hostage was up for sale to the highest bidder. Like the Barbary pirates of old, Peter Kilburn's captors hoped to reap a financial reward—ransom—from their American hostage.

A little more than a month later, and eight months after Weir's capture, the second Christian cleric, Father Lawrence Martin Jenco, was seized. Jenco was taken captive on January 8, 1985, on his way to work, and his kidnapping appears to have been a mistake. Stationed in Lebanon as the new director of the humanitarian Catholic Relief Services, Jenco had been in Lebanon for less than a year. In fact, his kidnappers believed that they had taken Jenco's predecessor, Joseph Curtin. The kidnappers were stunned to find that they had the wrong man. However, he was an American, and after several hours of hushed conversation, Jenco was given the bad news that any American was fine. According to Larry Pintak, a well-dressed man approached the bound priest who was still not blindfolded and looked him directly in the eye. "Father," he said softly, "I am so sorry."[8]

Terry Anderson, the chief Middle East correspondent for the Associated Press, was next. On March 16, 1985, Anderson was seized as he returned from his regular Saturday morning tennis match with photographer Don Mell. Anderson had interviewed Shi'ite spiritual leader Sheik Mohammed Hussein Fadlallah the day before. On May 28, David Jacobsen, the director of the American University of Beirut Medical Center, was kidnapped as he walked across the street from his apartment to his office. This was another possible case of mistaken identity, as Jacobsen believed he was mistaken for Einer Larson, the AUB controller. Accused of being a CIA spy, Jacobsen was questioned at length about frequent visits to New York, as well as about the finances and faculty associated with AUB.[9]

On June 9, 1985, a second form of capture began to be used against the Americans when Thomas Sutherland, acting dean of the College of Agriculture and Food Sciences, was snatched. Returning to the AUB campus after his arrival from the United States, Sutherland was seized about two blocks from the airport. His car was cut off, and at gunpoint he was moved to a getaway car. Sutherland's driver was powerless to stop the abduction or follow the kidnappers because they shot out the tires of his vehicle. In 1986, three more Americans were taken hostage. On September 12, Joseph Cicippio, assistant controller of the AUB Medical Center, was kidnapped from his apartment on the AUB campus three days after Frank Reed, the director of a private school in West Beirut, was seized. On October 21, Edward Tracy, an author and book salesman, was abducted from a sidewalk cafe. Tracy's kidnapping marked a change in the methods used to steal Americans, and the few who remained in the city exercised far more caution than their unlucky colleagues.

Although kidnapping became more difficult, even the best security measures were overcome by determined captors. On January 24, 1987, in what may have been the most cleverly planned of all the abductions, four Beirut University professors were convinced by several men impersonating Lebanese Internal Security officers to participate in a hostage-taking demonstration. As their startled colleagues looked on, the captors led their hostages away. The newest hostages were Mithileshwar Singh, an Indian with American residency; Americans Jesse Turner, a visiting professor of mathematics and computer science; Alan Steen, a journalism professor; and Robert Polhill, assistant professor of business. The final two American hostages seized in Lebanon were journalist Charles Glass, a former Beirut correspondent, and Lt. Col. William Higgins, USMC, a United Nations peacekeeper. Both were riding in vehicles that were cut off and forced to stop. Glass's capture occurred in the southern suburbs of Beirut. Glass was initially reluctant to leave the car to join the friends with whom he had been riding, but a loaded Russian assault rifle (AK-

47) pushed in his face through an open window persuaded Glass that cooperation was his only choice. On the other hand, Higgins, alone at the time of his capture, left little evidence about how he was forced to leave his vehicle for a one-way trip into captivity. Driving the second car in a two-car convoy, Colonel Higgins disappeared after the lead car turned a corner. The lead driver realized what happened when he returned to find Higgins's car abandoned at the side of the road. For both men, the hostage experience degenerated into unspeakable horrors: Glass was badly tortured; Higgins died in 1989.

Captivity in Beirut had a routine all its own. There were no prison camps. The hostages were kept alone or in small groups, and were frequently moved from hideout to hideout to prevent a rescue attempt and to protect them from the hazards of civil strife. The methods of transfer were unique in Lebanon. Generally the hostages were bound before being hidden in a car or truck for transport, although the Lebanese captors occasionally resorted to more creative measures to keep the hostages passive or hidden from view. At times they wrapped their victims mummy-like in plastic packaging tape, leaving only their noses free so that they could breathe. According to *Time* correspondent David Aikman, the hostage "was placed in the trunk of a car or quite often in a secret compartment built under the bed of the truck and bolted in." [10]

The captors also lied to their captives in order to bind them mentally during the removals. David Jacobsen described two instances in which the hostages were told that they were being released and consequently were docile while being led to a waiting vehicle and moved to their next prison. [11] Terry Anderson described one of his transfers: "Once they dressed me in a chador [the head-to-toe veil worn by religious Muslim women] and put those little round spot Band-Aids on my eyes, and then they put the sunglasses on. Well, the Band-Aids came loose, and with the prescription sunglasses on, I could see perfectly well. So I was sitting in the back of the car with a guard sitting next to me, just kind of peering around." [12] With or without the packaging tape or curious disguises, all the hostages were moved several times during their captivities. Their prison landscapes ranged from the slums of West Beirut, to the city of Baalbeck in the Shi'ite controlled Bekaa Valley east of Beirut, to southern Lebanon.

The general health of the hostages declined as their captivities lengthened because of frequent beatings and unsanitary living conditions. Although books, a radio, and sometimes even a television and videos were supplied, they arrived inconsistently and were readily removed. Day to day and month to month, the hostages amused themselves and often thought up clever ways to do so. Reverend Weir, for example, looked for religious themes in his surroundings. He wrote, "An electric wire hanging from the ceiling seemed like three fingers. I could see a hand and an arm reaching downward. . . . Here was God reaching toward me . . . two white circles near the ceiling . . . the ears of God . . . a hook of reinforcing rod had been bent out of the concrete form before pouring, forming almost a closed ellipse. The eye of God."[13] Held in solitary confinement after his Lebanese friends were released, Charles Glass focused on his family and thoughts of escape. Alan Steen shared stories with his colleagues about his experiences backpacking and camping alone in the Alaskan wilderness. Terry Anderson fashioned many items from whatever was at hand, making rosaries, playing cards, French language flash cards, and even a chess set from pieces of tin foil. According to *Newsweek* reporter Larry Martz, Anderson's prison writings were voluminous, including a collection of thirty-two poems.[14]

The captivity experience varied for each of the hostages. For some, it was an endless battle with solitary confinement, while others had the companionship and community of fellow hostages. In either case, captivity was a long, exceedingly boring experience, with lines of communication formed, whenever possible, among the prisoners themselves, between the prisoners and their guards, and, from time to time, with the outside. The community of captives became very important to all the men held in Lebanon, and they kept their fellow cell mates' spirits up with lively discussions when they were housed together. However, even when they were separated, often in solitary confinement, they found ways to communicate. Terry Anderson taught and communicated with his companions— David Jacobsen, Benjamin Weir, Martin Jenco, Thomas Sutherland, Frank Reed, and Terry Waite—by a kind of sign language and tap code, one tap A, two taps B, and on to twenty-six taps, Z. Although it was very cumbersome and time-consuming, the tapping reinforced the spirit of their companionship and helped the hostages to survive frequent abuse from the guards. It also eased their endless boredom and allowed them to ignore their squalid surroundings.

Although some received more punishment than others, all the hostages were beaten at one time or another. Jacobsen reported that he received a particularly brutal beating from his captors after they forced him to make a video announcing the "execution" of William Buckley. He sent his condolences to Buckley's wife and children, not realizing that Buckley was a bachelor.[15] Of all the captives, Buckley appears to have had the most difficult time. Gordon Thomas reported that the CIA received three videos from Buckley's captors. One reportedly showed him being tortured, and the last video provided a disturbing picture: "He [Buckley] appeared to have lost between fifty and sixty pounds. . . . There were further signs of bruising from the injections [drugs were reportedly used in his interrogations]; his eyes continued to display the effect from being hooded." [16] Although some hostages were left with psychological wounds, which are less visible, many suffered from permanent physical or neurological damage, which acts as a constant reminder of their captivity experience.

Most of these hostages looked for a means of escape, but only two succeeded in fleeing from their prison and evading their captors long enough to reach safety. Jerry Levin escaped on February 14, 1985, after eleven and one-half months of solitary confinement. Six weeks earlier, having moved to a new cell, he had looked out the window and recognized where he was. He knew his way if he could somehow free himself from the chains he wore twenty-three hours and fifty minutes of the day.

During the evening of February 13, after he had been brought back from the toilet, he found that his guard had improperly refastened his chains. When midnight finally came he slipped free, opened the window, and stepped out onto the second floor balcony. Using his blankets as a rope, Levin slid to the ground, and, shoeless, he raced down the mountain, trying to avoid lights and barking dogs. Finally reaching the bottom, he hid under a truck until he was spotted by a Syrian soldier. Levin tried to persuade the Syrians to return for the other Americans he believed were also being held, but they refused.[17] Levin felt that his captors may have facilitated his escape because his wife, Sis, had actively campaigned for his release, meeting with Amal leader Nabil Berri immediately after he was taken and spending several weeks in Syria speaking to government officials, including Foreign Minister Farouk Al Sharaa. Whether the Lebanese facilitated his escape or not, after Levin's flight the remaining American hostages were immediately moved to a different location. When Father Jenco was finally released, he asked Levin why he did not return for him. Levin replied that he had tried but that the Syrians had refused to listen.

David Jacobsen, Frank Reed, and Alan Steen all actively sought opportunities and means of escape. Although his cell mates were angry with him for putting them in danger, Jacobsen was never able to proceed very far with his plans, so his captors never knew his intentions and he was never punished. Reed and Steen, however, were caught and severely punished. Responding to Robert Ajemian's questions concerning his life in captivity, Reed explained why he tried to escape twice, saying, "I've always been dogged and independent-minded. Sometimes my fellow hostages pleaded with me to take books or special treatment. The way I saw it, privileges from the guards only reinforced their hold over us. I tried hard to get into their consciences, to make them feel guilty. Sometimes that invited harsh treatment. Even then, when they beat me, I was determined never to cry out." [18]

Reed's first escape attempt involved standing on a stool to reach the keys that the guards had inadvertently left in the door. At the second door, however, he was unable to reach the keys. Returning to his cell, Reed tried unsuccessfully to close the door behind him to disguise his attempt. When his guards found it open the next morning, Reed was beaten, losing partial hearing in his right ear, and had live wires attached to his fingers. Four days later, Reed tried again. This time he hoped to overpower his guard, but he discovered that he was too weak. Again he was punished. After his release, medical examinations showed that he had been systematically poisoned with arsenic, which in small doses acts as a depressant.[19] Steen was able to progress further. He actually broke free from prison, only to be returned to his captors by local residents. As punishment, he was severely beaten and had several fillings knocked out of his teeth.

The last hostage to make an escape was Charles Glass. By August 17, 1987, Glass had had enough of being a hostage and began writing notes on scraps of paper. Using his own blood as ink and offering a $10,000 reward to anyone willing to help him, Glass managed to send out nine notes. When his guards discovered two of the notes, they moved him to a new cell, where they chained him to the wall. Because the guards were afraid the neighbors might hear the rattle of Glass's wrist chain, they taped it, leaving only two links open for the lock. Glass moved the tape on one of the links to give himself an extra link, so that it was loose enough to slip off. He needed eighteen links to slip the chain from his ankle, but the guards kept it locked tightly on fourteen links. Looking down, Glass determined that he could tie the links together with thread from his blindfold, using rust from the chain as a disguise. After a week, Glass thought that he had the problem solved; however, the guard broke the thread and he was back to seventeen links. Several weeks later, the guard accidentally left him with the necessary eighteen links after his morning bathroom visit, and Glass knew that his opportunity was at hand. Wanting to be left alone, Glass feigned illness for most of the day. He slipped out of his chains and fled the apartment late that evening. Adding insult to injury, Glass locked up his abductors and dashed for the open streets. Pretending to be a Canadian, he convinced an unsuspecting couple to take him to the Summerland Hotel, where he contacted some Lebanese friends. His captivity and escape came to an end when he was taken into custody by the Syrian Army.[20]

Although all the hostages hoped to be rescued by outside forces, only Frank Regier was. After Jerry Levin was kidnapped, his wife, Sis, paid a visit to the leader of the Shi'ite Amal, Nabil Berri, who assured her that his force was doing everything in its power to secure Levin's release. Children were enlisted to spy in West Beirut with hope of finding out where Levin was being held. Berri thought they had found him, but when Amal raided the apartment on April 15, 1984, they found Frank Regier and a French hostage, Christian Joubert, instead. Most news reports at the time covered the secrecy of the raid's plan by stating that the children playing outside had heard English being spoken and thought that they saw Western men being held captive. The cover story insisted that the children told their parents, who then told the Amal militia. With some good fortune, no one died in the raid, and Regier and Joubert were delighted to be free.

Three Americans died in captivity in Lebanon: William Buckley, Peter Kilburn, and Lieutenant Colonel Higgins. On October 4, 1985, the Shi'ite Revolutionary Justice Organization claimed that it had executed William Buckley. He actually died on June 3 in a cubicle next to David Jacobsen, Martin Jenco, and Benjamin Weir. The other hostages heard Buckley's condition worsen steadily through the month of May, and as he became more delirious, they begged their captors to take him to a doctor or a hospital. The guards refused and decided to stop giving him fluids. One guard claimed that this was the proper care for the kind of pneumonia caused by torture and the unsanitary conditions that the hostages had to endure. The U.S. government recovered Buckley's remains in Beirut on December 27, 1991, and he was buried in Arlington National Cemetery. Peter Kilburn was sold to a pro-Libyan, Abu Nidal faction for $1 million and executed, along with two British citizens, on April 17, 1986, in retaliation for the earlier American bombing attack on Libya. His body was returned to the United States for burial. After Kilburn's execution, President Reagan reportedly stated that the remaining American hostages, Anderson, Jacobsen, Jenco, and Sutherland, were worth $30 million in order to outbid a $10 million offer from Colonel Qaddafi of Libya. The Organization of the Oppressed of the Earth claimed that it had hanged Lieutenant Colonel Higgins on July 31, 1989, in retaliation for the kidnapping of Sheik Abdul Kareem Obeid by Israeli forces. Although there is speculation that Higgins may have died earlier, including claims by some factions of Hezbollah that he had received a fatal electric shock during a torture session in April 1989, no conclusive evidence concerning his death has ever been revealed. The U.S. government recovered his body in Lebanon, and he was buried with other Marines at Quantico National Cemetery.

Twelve American hostages were released by their captors after varying lengths of captivity. David Dodge was released on July 21, 1983, after only one year, and there were some hopes that additional releases would be forthcoming. Hope turned to despair when on December 12, 1983, terrorists calling themselves al-Dawa, "The Call," detonated six bombs in Kuwait in a ninety-minute terror spree. Targets included the American and French embassies, and the terrorists killed six people. Eighteen Shi'ite suspects were arrested, and seventeen were convicted, including fourteen Iraqis and three Lebanese. The Reverend Benjamin Weir was released on September 14, 1985, after sixteen months in captivity, bringing with him the demands from the kidnappers for the release of the al-Dawa bombers. Father Martin Jenco was released on July 26, 1986, after eighteen months, and David Jacobsen was freed on November 2, 1986, after seventeen months as a hostage.

The releases of Weir, Jenco, and Jacobsen were soon linked to a complicated and secret sale of military weapons to Iran by Israel, referred to as Iran-gate, an event that later developed into the Iran-Contra scandal in the United States. In March 1983, the U.S. Congress passed the Boland Amendment, which prohibited the military services and the CIA from selling weapons to the Nicaraguan Contras. To circumvent this restriction, the White House and the National Security Agency sought to use intermediaries in Britain and Israel to sell arms and replacement parts to the Iranians, with the profits from these sales going to provide direct help to the Contras. By so doing, the letter of the law would be obeyed, they thought.

The administration and the intelligence community knew that the Iranians were behind the hostage-taking activities in the Middle East. When the lid blew off this cauldron of international arms intrigue, hearings on the hostages-for-money and arms deals took place in Congress, and American intelligence operatives like Lt. Col. Oliver North made the headlines. It became obvious that North and others attempted to bypass the letter and spirit of the law in order to placate the Iranians and help the Contras. From the hostages' point of view, the restrictions imposed by the Boland Amendment and North's difficulties with Congress multiplied the hazards involved in trying to devise a plan to free anyone. At the same time, the international kidnappers seized the moment and announced that they had no intention of freeing any more hostages until their demands had been met. As a result of the Iran-Contra scandal and all the public attention it received in the United States, those remaining in captivity in Beirut waited four more years for freedom.

On April 22, 1990, Robert Polhill was released after thirty-nine months as a hostage, and Frank Reed was freed on April 30 after nearly forty-four months. The deal was reportedly arranged with the help of Syria, but immediately after the release of Polhill and Reed, the House of Representatives passed a nonbinding resolution, approved by the Senate, that recognized a united Jerusalem as the capital of Israel. This political act by the U.S. Congress ended hopes for the release of any more American hostages. However, in August 1991, United Nations Secretary-General Javier Pérez de Cuéllar received a letter from the Islamic Jihad that promised the release of the rest of the Western hostages if he made "a personal endeavor, within a comprehensive solution, to secure the release of all detainees throughout the world."[21] For the remaining hostages who undoubtedly considered themselves pawns in the deadly game of Middle East politics, prospects for release had definitely improved.

On August 11, 1991, Edward Tracy was released after sixty-nine months in captivity. One month later, Israel released fifty-one prisoners and the bodies of nine Arab guerrillas. On October 21, 1991, Jesse Turner was freed. On the same day Israel released fifteen Lebanese detainees. As a result, Thomas Sutherland was let go on November 18, and on December 1, twenty-five more Lebanese prisoners held by the Israeli-controlled South Lebanon army were released. Joseph Cicippio was released on December 2, and Alan Steen, on December 3. The hostage crisis finally came to an end when the longest-held American hostage in Lebanon, Terry Anderson, was released on December 4, 1991.

Although in the West religion enjoys less political value now than it did in the past, in the Middle East, politics is defined by religion. The idea of trading hostages for a political purpose gained considerable strength when the hostage-takers in the 1980s sought the release of Lebanese Shi'ites held in Kuwait and the release of Lebanese and Palestinian Shi'ites held in South Lebanon and Israel. The American government was expected to put pressure on its Israeli and Arab allies to release these prisoners. With more than a touch of irony, the men held in Kuwait for the al-Dawa bombings were set free when Iraq invaded Kuwait, and Imad Mughni-yeh's relatives were eventually able to make their way back to Lebanon. The Kuwaiti prisoner problem was a cost the United States did not have to pay, but there is some question whether it could have paid even if it had wanted to.

Looking back, there is little doubt that the hostage crises in Iran and Lebanon were both extended captivity experiences that had a profound impact upon the American nation as a whole. Iran clearly showed the United States that a small nation can impose its will on a large one by taking hostages, exposing them to the international media, and exploiting basic human concerns for their welfare and safety. In order to bring about an Islamic revolution in Lebanon, the leaders of the Hezbollah movement concluded that foreign interests needed to be eliminated. By committing terrorist acts against the United States, the leaders of Hezbollah hoped to remove any influence that strongly supported the moderate government friendly with the West.

Terror and hostage-taking were part of Hezbollah's religious war against the United States. Ayatollah Khomeini's labeling of America as the "Great Satan" when he came to power in Iran was the beginning. He knew that the American government preferred to talk rather than fight another war, and he played that card as long as he could. When the military services attempted a raid that failed, frustrated Americans at home considered it an exercise in feeble planning and interservice bumbling. The people of the United States felt embarrassed, and its war veterans became so furious with President Carter, one of the most peace-oriented chief executives in American history since Thomas Jefferson, that he lost his incumbent presidency to Ronald Reagan in 1980.

After the hostage events in Iran, the mood of the country began to shift from a trend toward universal pacifism to a more militant stance, as exemplified by calls for a stronger defense policy. In spite of the poor appetite for meddling in other countries' internal affairs in the aftermath of the Vietnam War, Americans began looking for political candidates who took a more assertive stand in world affairs. Although Americans admired President Carter's honesty, concern for human rights, and passion for world peace, they looked to a more traditionally conservative leader to help America regain the respect of the international community. Ronald Reagan became America's choice for eight years, and policies began to change. Although President Reagan campaigned openly to rebuild an American military force greatly reduced during the Carter administration, the rhetoric came to an end with key mistakes made in the Middle East.

The American military services, with the possible exceptions of the garrison forces in Korea, Germany during the Cold War, and Bosnia, have never been exceptional international peacekeepers in the contemporary sense. Neither the U.S. Army nor the Marine Corps is a trained police force. With nineteenth-century-like naïveté, the Reagan administration believed, wrongly, that the mere presence of the Marines on the ground and a battleship at sea would generate enough fear and respect to force opposing sides to negotiate a settlement within the framework of a reasonable compromise. Instead, the American peacekeepers became prime targets, and on October 23, 1983, Hezbollah killed more than two hundred Marines in one fanatical suicide attack. The survivors' faces reflected bitterness as they pulled dead Marines from the wreckage, and the news services accurately reported that America had not witnessed that number of dead soldiers at any one time and place since Vietnam.

The Vietnam experience taught the American government and its military services many valuable lessons that proved applicable in the Gulf War in 1991. Tactics and weapons aside, the government learned that it first had to secure the support of the people through their representatives in Congress before it committed Americans to the field of battle. This view was enunciated by Harry G. Summers, Jr., who wrote convincingly that it was an obvious error to commit the Army without first obtaining the commitment of the American people, especially when there was likelihood of prolonged combat in a limited war that could produce large numbers of casualties.[22]

The hostage crises in the Middle East during the 1980s taught different but equally applicable lessons to foreign policymakers of the 1990s. The most valuable lesson learned is a reconsideration of Emmerich de Vattel's dictum in his *Law of Nations* (1758) that a third party should not become willingly committed to another's civil war, because both parties embroiled in the war are equally alien to the third party; instead, the best approach is to offer assistance to re-establish peace.[23]

The second lesson, which is a harsh one for Western nations struggling with their own internal cultural conflicts, is that much of the world makes war for reasons beyond the comprehension of the traditional nation-states. When the Cold War came to an end in 1989, the world sought relief from the old imperialisms, capitalist and socialist. As journalist Robert Kaplan pointed out, something else was happening as well. Future peacekeeping, no matter how moral or well-intentioned, would not work where religious and ethno-tribal concerns are generating new kinds of civil warfare for which the large nation-states remain ill-prepared.

Instead of enjoying economic and social progress in this new era, many countries are degenerating into ungovernable ethno-religious entities that are as yet undefined in the world political arena. In a world in which the two Cold War superpowers no longer divide the globe into two clearly defined blocs with the Third World competing for the attention of both, Americans have learned that the notion of a peace dividend is pure folly. What has transpired is the unexpected reemergence of older and vastly more brutal kinds of racial, ethnic, and religious conflicts. In Kaplan's view, cultures, not countries, are now battling one another for control of their respective turfs.

In cultural wars, neither individual countries nor the United Nations can impose political will on radical groups by the simple presence of their troops in camouflage uniforms and carrying unloaded rifles. Both Karl von Clausewitz's traditional view of war as "politics by other means" and Hugo Grotius's concept of *jus gentium,* the law of nations, are becoming marginalized, because both assume that armies represent the interests of sovereign nation-states. The events of the 1990s strongly suggest that the entire concept of nation-states is in trouble, as the former Third World cultures fight civil wars in protracted, low-intensity conflicts. Criminals, once in the backwater of international relations, have surfaced with high-tech weapons and, in some cases, very sophisticated electronic intelligence and communication services. According to Kaplan, war and crime will become virtually indistinguishable in the twenty-first century.[24]

Noted political scientist Simon W. Duke, who has written extensively on warfare, weaponry, and security, as well as on why nation-states make war on one another in a modern age, commented that the powerful nations of the past are steadily becoming static cultural dinosaurs whose security depends more on the comfort of weapons of mass destruction than on the character of their people and the courage of their convictions.[25] Given the status quo, international behavior grows worse, not better, in an age of high-tech weapons and low-tech belief systems. Events may prove Kaplan and Duke wrong and new solutions may be found, but Duke's view that culture plays a more important role than hardware and Kaplan's pessimism about crime's victory in ethno-religious wars may be the most sobering evaluations offered for the present.

With government proving to be ineffective in solving the political conflicts that caused the hostage crises, a new force emerged at home: hostage families became outspoken political activists who demonstrated quite convincingly that despite all the rhetoric, the American government had done very little to help their loved ones held captive in the Middle East. This was a new phenomenon in the 1970s, but it was also inevitable in a world influenced, if not dominated, by world news services like the Cable News Network (CNN), Independent News Network (INN), and other services that not only sought out and exploited war news for the sake of human interest, but also continued to report armed hostilities like football games or soap operas. Night after night, the entanglements of governments, hostages, and captors penetrated family living rooms around the world, much like the POW conflict during the Vietnam War. Americans watched as sickly victims paraded in front of cameras to recite canned messages, plead for personal relief, and demand political policy changes from the government, all of this, of course, without any intervention from the International Red Cross.

The hostage-taking experience thus generated a new kind of propaganda war, in which women like Peggy Say and Sis Levin became fully committed combatants. Say and Levin traveled worldwide to seek help from representatives of friends and foes alike. The hostage families learned from the Vietnam experience that silence breeds only inactivity from a timid government. Exhibiting the determination of a Father Hugh O'Flaherty and the members of escape lines in previous wars, the women left few stones unturned in their efforts to free *their* hostages. At home, feelings of helplessness manifested themselves, and symbols such as wreaths and yellow ribbons, the "folk assemblage of war," began to signify, if not replace, practical political policy and human resolve in the United States.[26]

If the hostage-takers could use the media effectively in their struggle against the West, then Say and Levin could do likewise against the hostage-takers. Peggy Say's and Peter Knobler's *Forgotten: A Sister's Struggle to Save Terry Anderson, America's Longest-Held Hostage* (1991) told of her struggle to free her younger brother, Terry Anderson, from captivity in Beirut, and in 1992, after Anderson's release, *Life* reporter Edward Barnes published "The Last Hostage," in which Say described her emotions after her long struggle.[27] Anderson's memoir *Den of Lions* appeared in 1993. Sis Levin's *Beirut Diary: A Husband Held Hostage and a Wife Determined to Set Him Free* (1989) narrated her struggle to understand the situation in Lebanon and free her escaper husband, journalist Jerry Levin. The Reverend Benjamin Weir and his wife narrated similar experiences in *Hostage Bound: Hostage Free* (1987). In *Holding On* (1990), Sunnie Mann recounted her experiences while trying to free her hostage husband Jackie Mann, held in solitary confinement in Beirut for two years.

Mann had been an RAF fighter pilot during World War II and was shot down six times. After the war, he relocated to Beirut, where he lived for forty years until his abduction.[28] Brian Keenan published his narrative *An Evil Cradling* in 1992; a year later, John McCarthy and Jill Morrell published their joint memoir *Some Other Rainbow*.

With the return of the last hostages from Iran and Beirut, America's twentieth-century experience with hostage-taking ended for the time being. During their captivity, the hostages received considerable attention from the American news and, later, entertainment media. For example, Peter Jennings probed the motivation of terrorists in *Hostage, An Endless Terror,* broadcast on ABC in 1978. The show focused on six incidents that occurred in the 1970s in which victims were seized and used as political pawns, and then depicted the psychological impacts of these events as seen through the eyes of the surviving captives. As Pierre Salinger noted in *America Held Hostage* (1981), if nothing else, the Iran hostage crisis heightened public awareness about the perils of captivity and taught Americans once again how to deal with the frustrations of being unable to free their fellow citizens. Nevertheless, when the ex-hostages arrived in Algiers on the first leg of their journey home from Iran on February 2, 1981, they flashed victory signs, clenched their fists, and shouted, "Thank You! We made it!" During a thirty-five minute reception inside the airport terminal, responding to reporters' questions, one hostage replied with characteristic POW understatement, "It's good to be out of Khomeini land." [29]

Because of the barrage of news in the media, public sensibilities had become somewhat deadened to events unfolding in Lebanon. Thus few ex-hostages wrote narratives of their experiences. However, Rocky Sickmann's *Iran Hostage: A Personal Diary* (1982) and Charles Scott's *Pieces of the Game* (1984) were the exceptions. Finally, the American hostage struggle, which began in June 1982, ended in December 1991 with Terry Anderson's release. In the midst of these events, Army reservist Kurt Carlson published his narrative, *One American Must Die: A Hostage's Personal Account of the Hijacking of Flight 847* (1986), recalling his experiences aboard the hijacked TWA Flight 847 and being held hostage in Beirut by Shi'ite terrorists.[30]

Shortly after his escape in 1986, Jerry Levin, along with his wife Sis and Herbert Bodman, made a recording, *Lebanon: Emblem of Captivity; Forgotten Hostages*. On one side of the record, Levin and Bodman discussed Lebanon as an emblem of cultural and political captivity, a country in which Christianity shares an uneasy balance with a growing Muslim population. On the other side, Levin and his wife discussed their view that the hostages were merely pawns in a battle of silence and pride waged by American and Middle Eastern participants.[31] In 1992, Home Box Office and David Wheatley made the impressive television docudrama *Hostage,* a show that examined resistance themes already treated effectively in previous military films. Like so many prior captivity films, Wheatley's film depicted how a prison community divided against itself while uniting against its captors.

Making heavy use of television news footage, Wheatley focused on the kidnapping and captivity experiences of British hostage John McCarthy and Irish hostage Brian Keenan, and dramatized how toward the end of their captivity, they were held with American hostages Terry Anderson, Thomas Sutherland, and Frank Reed. Although no military code of conduct influenced the civilian hostages' desire to escape, the endless captivity, the beatings, executions, torture, and numerous uncomfortable transfers certainly constituted another distinct application of Hugo Grotius's description of intolerable cruelty.

The hostage crises of the 1970s and 1980s wrote another chapter in America's book on captivity experiences. Taking American and other Western hostages for political purposes still goes on. In India, the militants of Al Faran, one of the thirty Islamic groups fighting to win Kashmir's independence, took five prisoners in 1995 and continued to demand ransom in 1996. One hostage, Norwegian Christian Ostroe, was beheaded; the others, including American Donald Hutchings, remain in captivity.[32] In these pseudo-wars of the few against the many, the end seems to justify the means for all sides.[33]

12

Escape by Other Means
Prison Raids and Raiders

When we realized that there was no one in the compound, I had the most horrible feeling of my life.

—George Petri (1970)

A raid is a small-scale military operation designed to penetrate hostile territory swiftly in order to secure information, release POWs, confuse the enemy, or destroy enemy installations behind the lines. It ends with a planned withdrawal upon completion of the assigned task.[1] From the colonial wars to the hostage crises, most American raids have been daring, carefully planned, military operations consisting of special volunteer soldiers organized into small units. In the past, it was often the luck of the draw that determined who went on a raid and who stayed behind. In modern wars, the needs of a raid demand more from soldiers, sailors, and airmen than they did in the past, and these individuals train for special operations in a variety of commando skills—stealth and deception, hand-to-hand fighting, guerrilla tactics, and the use of special weapons not normally used by standard fighting soldiers—long before they ever make an assault.[2]

During the Revolution, each side wanted its prisoners back. In America, George Washington wanted to recover his seamen from the poisonous British prison hulks and developed an active exchange policy. Because the British presence in the colonies was simply too strong, especially in New York, no plans for raids developed. After Gen. John Burgoyne's surrender to the American Gen. Horatio Gates at Saratoga, New York, in 1777, the two generals formulated surrender terms—the Convention—for thousands of British, Hessian, and Loyalist POWs without the advice or consent of the Continental Congress.[3] Unhappy with Gates's cordial leniency toward Burgoyne, the Continental Congress ordered the Convention prisoners, consisting of 2,442 British, 2,198 Hessians, 1,100 Canadians, 598 sick and wounded, 12 staff officers including Burgoyne and the Hessian general von Riedesel, 6 members of the British Parliament, and 300 American deserters, to march from place to place throughout the colonies, because it feared that General Cornwallis's large force might free them through a mass raid. Had that taken place, and had Burgoyne's force been released again for duty against the Continental Army, General Washington's meager forces would have faced inevitable defeat. The Battle of Yorktown and Cornwallis's surrender in 1781 ended that fear and the major eastern land hostilities in the first Anglo-American war.[4]

In England, despite Benjamin Franklin's diplomatic and humanitarian efforts from Paris, no exchange policy developed between the British and the Americans that worked very well. Part of the problem involved the French, who refused to grant Franklin a safe port for exchanges. All the while, American naval prisoners were regarded as traitors and enjoyed no rights of exchange. Knowing this, John Paul Jones took action. At sea, he always made it his business to take as many prisoners as possible for exchange. Once, he devised a bizarre plan to kidnap the Earl of Selkirk from his estate on St. Mary's Isle and hold him as ransom for the American POWs in England. True to his plan, Jones raided the island in April 1778, but he discovered that the earl was away. Rather than taking any prisoners or hostages, Jones permitted his men to take the family silver instead. Remorseful because he had allowed the theft of personal property, Jones later arranged a meeting with the countess to return her silverware.[5] By 1779, small POW exchanges had begun; the number of escapes had increased; and the need for hostage-taking and prison raids had subsided.

Between the end of the American Revolution in 1783 and 1815, there were several confrontations between the United States and other nations, like France (1798–1800), which for the most part were fought at sea. When Thomas Jefferson began his presidency in 1801, the war against the Barbary pirates of Tripoli broke out. The Bashaw, the appointed leader of Tripoli, and other Turkish leaders believed that unless they had a peace treaty with a foreign country, they were at war with it. Tribute was the price for immunity.[6] Many individual unarmed American merchant ships were taken captive, but events turned warlike when the Tripolians took the new frigate *Philadelphia* on October 22, 1800. After working furiously to get his ship off an unmarked barrier in the harbor, Capt. William Bainbridge, USN, concluded that the task was impossible and surrendered the *Philadelphia* and its crew. After looting the ship, the Tripolians took Bainbridge and 307 American prisoners.

On February 6, 1802, Congress authorized the Navy to protect ships and seamen from any more hostile boarding and captive-taking. In response to the *Philadelphia*'s capture, on September 12, 1803, President Jefferson sent Capt. Edward Preble, USN, a former prisoner in the British prison hulk *Jersey* during the Revolution, to sail the USS *Constitution* into the Mediterranean Sea in order to destroy the *Philadelphia* and free the prisoners. On the night of February 16, 1804, Preble ordered Lt. Stephen Decatur, Jr. and some hand-picked volunteers—nine officers including Decatur, James Lawrence, Charles Morris, David Porter, and Thomas Macdonough, plus fifty sailors and eight Marines—to board the *Philadelphia,* set it on fire, and scuttle it.[7]

The first steps involved deception and stealth. After Preble captured a Tripolian ship, the *Mastico,* and rechristened it the *Intrepid,* Decatur and his raiders sailed it into the harbor under British merchant colors. As the Americans came alongside the *Philadelphia,* the Tripolian prize crew hailed them and asked their business. The American pilot, a Sicilian volunteer named Salvador Catalano, explained that the ship had troubles and needed some help. As Decatur tied the *Intrepid* alongside the *Philadelphia,* some of the Tripolian crew realized that this was a raid and raised the alarm. Fighting broke out on deck. The Americans, who were well rehearsed in their duties, defeated the Tripolian prize crew, then scattered quickly and placed their explosive charges in the proper spots. Blasts rocked the *Philadelphia* as the charges blew the ship apart, and as the raiders scampered back into the *Intrepid* for departure, flames licked the *Philadelphia*'s sides and masts.

Decatur and the entire party, having completed one of the most daring raids in American naval history, returned to Preble after only thirty minutes aboard the *Philadelphia.* Shortly thereafter, Preble entered Tripoli harbor, destroyed the shipping, and shelled the city. As an act of military and political intimidation, the Decatur raid tipped the balance of power in favor of the United States. In August 1804, the American fleet, about one thousand officers and men, hoping to free the American POWs and defeat the Bashaw's forces, conducted several unsuccessful frontal assaults against the city of Tripoli. The Marines, led by William Eaton, the shady American consul in Tripoli, then decided to conduct an end-run through the desert to the town of Derna. After the Marines captured the city and defeated its defenders, the Bashaw sued for peace, freed the captives, and signed a treaty on June 3, 1805, that renounced his policy of tribute for peace.[8]

By 1815, after more naval actions against the Barbary powers, especially Tripoli, the American Navy evolved into a mature force that represented the political will of the United States. Decatur planned and executed treaties of peace in the name of the president and returned American prisoners from Algiers, Tunis, and Tripoli. The long-term result of these coordinated land and naval raids, executed with the courage of a Decatur, was to establish the precedent for small unit attacks against politically lucrative targets, including prison raids to recover soldiers and sailors from enemy hands in times of war.

During the Civil War, the Confederate Army more often used its cavalry as an independently operating, semi-uniformed force of partisans against outposts and trains than against prison camps. One of the most notable tactical firebrands of the Civil War, prewar Virginia lawyer John Singleton Mosby, joined the Confederate Army as a private soldier. On February 17, 1862, after he fought at the Battle of Bull Run with cavalryman J.E.B. Stuart, Mosby was commissioned a lieutenant in the Confederate cavalry. Like John Hunt Morgan and Nathan Bedford Forrest, Mosby understood war differently from traditional army officers. He had no formal military training in any service academy or military school and grew impatient with soldiering-as-usual in the Confederate Army. Like other innovative cavalrymen, Mosby knew that there was real value in raiding federal outposts. Stuart agreed, and in 1862 with fifteen men, Mosby formed the 43d Battalion, Virginia Cavalry, commonly known as the Partisan Raiders.

Highly mobile, self-sufficient, and expendable, Mosby's Partisan Raiders hit and ran where and when they wished. Planned targets and targets of opportunity were always small and vulnerable, and Mosby rarely attacked without a reasonable chance of success. In Virginia, he forced Union commanders to watch their rear and flanks. Col. Percy Wyndham, USV, a British officer serving with the Union Army, despised Mosby's unorthodox tactics and called him a horse thief. Because Mosby's tactics were feared and many Union commanders abhorred all forms of guerrilla warfare, some of his men were executed as war criminals. After Mosby hanged several of George Armstrong Custer's cavalrymen in reprisal, the Partisan Raiders and other Confederate cavalrymen enjoyed the same rights as other prisoners captured by federal forces in the field.

John Singleton Mosby, along with John Hunt Morgan, Nathan Bedford Forest, and especially the outlaw Charles William Quantrill, gave

Lt. John Singleton Mosby, commanding officer of the Partisan Raiders in Virginia, 1862–65. Courtesy of the National Archives

the Confederate cavalry a bad name. Instead of being the mounted arm of the infantry, much as J.E.B. Stuart's force was for Robert E. Lee, they often assumed the role of independent partisans fighting for themselves as irregulars. Mosby's Partisan Raiders operated in Virginia as irregulars; Morgan's raid into Ohio landed him in the state penitentiary for crimes against the state; and Nathan Bedford Forrest's infamous attack against Fort Pillow, where his men murdered captured black Union soldiers in cold blood, darkened his personal reputation for life. As a result of these activities, the troops suffered for the crimes of their officers. B. F. Nelson, a Confederate cavalryman, was interrogated following his capture in 1864. From what he saw happening around him, he feared for his life. Many years later, Nelson recalled, "Fifteen of our names were called, ten of whom were executed at daylight. In ten days time, the same performance was repeated and continued until more than thirty men were taken out and shot. Then to our great relief, we were sent to Camp Douglas, Chicago. It was finally decided that we were prisoners of war rather than guerrillas."[9] For members of paramilitary units who fought as partisans, the penalty after capture was death, until the 1949 Geneva Convention legitimized these activities and granted partisans the status of real soldiers worthy of POW treatment.[10]

Among the partisan Confederate cavalrymen, Quantrill's men were undoubtedly the worst. In the name of the Confederacy, but really for their own wealth, they committed outrageous acts, including theft and murder against unarmed civilians. Consequently, they were branded as outlaws even in wartime. In 1865, after formal hostilities ended in Virginia, Quantrill took thirty raiders into Kentucky and was mortally wounded in action on May 10, 1865, on a farm outside Wakerfield. Then something curious happened. Quantrill may have been brutal in war, but near death he found religion. After a bullet destroyed his spine and caused fatal internal bleeding, he received the Last Rites of the Catholic Church. Wounded, dying, and totally helpless, William Clarke Quantrill lay at the mercy of his bitter enemies. Instead of defiling him as an act of revenge, the Union troops put him on a wagon and took him to a Louisville military hospital, where he lingered until June 6, when he finally died.[11]

After the Civil War, some of Quantrill's men, including Jesse and Frank James and the Younger Brothers, formed outlaw gangs, became civil criminals, and continued raiding for money. The romantic Robin Hood image of stealing from the rich and giving to the poor that these outlaws mythologized, transformed serious violent crimes into popular, if not populist, political acts. The well-known "Ballad of Jesse James" remembered that:

Jesse James was a lad who killed many a man.
He robbed the Glendale train.
He stole from the rich and he gave to the poor,
With a hand and a heart and a brain.[12]

With the exception of Jesse James's older brother Frank, more a soldier than a criminal who surrendered to federal authorities rather than live constantly on the run, the Quantrill-trained James and Younger gangs were hunted down and destroyed.

Prison raids conducted by small forces during the Civil War aimed at freeing relatively large numbers of POWs for future combat duty. The poorly planned Union Kilpatrick-Dahlgren Raid, which took place from February 28 through March 4, 1864, proved to be a disaster in several respects. The raiders aimed at liberating the numerous Union prisoners in Richmond by approaching the city from two different directions.

Gen. Judson Kilpatrick, finding the defenses too strong, decided not to attack; Col. Ulric Dahlgren was thus trapped and killed, and ninety-two Union raiders were captured. Papers found on Dahlgren's body revealed a controversial plot to capture Jefferson Davis and burn Richmond.[13] In response, the Confederates tightened their security and decided to move their Union prisoners deeper into the South. They settled on a site far from the fighting in rural Sumter County, Georgia, near the tiny village of Anderson, where thousands of enlisted Union POWs were to die from disease and malnutrition during the fateful summer and autumn of 1864.

During the midsummer of 1864, Confederate agent Jacob Thompson worked in Canada and developed a plan to gain Confederate control of the Great Lakes by raiding cities and towns along their shores. Thompson needed men, and part of his plan to build a northern force included striking the Confederate officers' prison camp at Johnson's Island on Lake Erie, as well as Camp Douglas, the large enlisted men's prison facility near Chicago. Thompson's raiders intended to board the Union armed steamer *Michigan,* which defended Lake Erie, and overpower the crew. At the same time, Confederate officers, all prisoners on Johnson's Island, were prepared to overwhelm the camp guard force as soon as a cannon ball from the *Michigan* arched over their quarters. However, Thompson failed to take control of the vessel, and the entire scheme, although it served as a morale booster for the Confederate captives, failed.[14]

While on his rampage through Georgia in late July 1864, Gen. William T. Sherman, USA, decided to liberate the Union prisoners at Andersonville. To accomplish this task, Sherman sent Maj. Gen. George Stoneman, USA, with a 2,050-man cavalry corps to attack the prison. Like a number of other raids on prison camps, this one was a failure. The Stoneman force was just too small and the odds too great. Stoneman and his entire unit were surrounded by Confederates and forced to surrender, making Stoneman the highest ranking Union officer taken into captivity during the Civil War.[15] News of the raid boosted morale among the Union prisoners in Andersonville, but despite General Sherman's close proximity, they had to wait for removal to other Confederate prisons and subsequent prisoner exchange. Sherman was not ready to sacrifice another senior general for the sake of POWs. He had plenty of troops, and Union POWs were, after all, expendable.

In World War I, as R. C. Sherriff's play *Journey's End* (1928) pointed out, raiding parties were constantly seeking prisoners. In small bands, German and Allied soldiers quietly approached the other side's trenches, skirmished, and returned with their respective prizes.[16] Because each side maintained trenches and walls of extraordinary fire power, no large prison raids were ever attempted, even when opposing armies were relatively close by. The situation changed during World War II, however, because that war generated vast numbers of POW, internment, and concentration camps, which presented a target-rich environment. Never in the history of mankind had so many people been held captive in so many places at one time.

Opportunities for conducting successful prison raids did not really exist until 1944–45, when Allied forces began to tighten the noose around Germany and Japan. In Europe, two major raids were planned, but only one was attempted. The first plan was a side effect of problems that surfaced inside Oflag 64, a large girls' school converted into a prison camp for Allied officers about 150 miles northwest of Warsaw, near Szubin, Poland. Two American officers had become ill and were given appointments to visit a doctor in a nearby village. As they walked along the sidewalk under guard, they were suddenly ordered by the camp's security officer to walk in the street. The Americans refused, saying that under the provisions of the Geneva Convention they were not to be demeaned or humiliated. The security officer then charged them with criminal behavior and demanded the death penalty. Although the Americans were acquitted, other prisoners grew concerned that their lives might be threatened by surprise armed assaults by SS death squads.

Realizing that danger existed in Oflag 64, MIS-X devised a rescue plan. To resolve the most pressing problem, MIS-X sent small caliber weapons to the officers under cover. If the enemy assaulted the POWs, they would at least have weapons to defend themselves. Thirty men were then selected from among volunteers in the 101st Airborne Division for a low-level jump to attack and secure the guard house. The third phase of the plan called for twenty converted B-17 bombers to land close to the camp and evacuate the prisoners. To launch the raid, BBC radio was ordered to broadcast "Give me liberty or give me death"; meanwhile, the escape committee planned some preparatory mayhem inside the camp. After all the preparations were completed, the American Army's highest levels scrapped the raid when a large German column entered the Szubin region.[17] As Generals Stoneman and Sherman had learned eighty years before, the risk of catastrophic failure became too great to recover a relatively small number of POWs.

On March 27, 1945, elements of the 10th Armored Infantry Battalion and B Company of the 37th Tank Battalion conducted the raid that came closest to succeeding in Germany. It was a long-range armored thrust designed to liberate Oflag XIII B, the officers' prison camp on a hill overlooking the city of Hammelburg, Bavaria, about sixty miles east of the American lines. Gen. George S. Patton ordered the raid; Col. Creighton Abrams, who later replaced Gen. William C. Westmoreland as commanding general of the Military Assistance Command in Vietnam (MACV), selected the raiders. The officers of this force designed the operation, calling it Task Force Baum after its commanding officer, Maj. Abe Baum.[18]

Patton's motivation for ordering the raid was both military and personal. Militarily, a successful raid would surely dramatize Patton's aggressiveness, build the Third Army's confidence, and reinforce America's trust that notable military field commanders would take the risks necessary to free American POWs. Patton believed that a good plan violently executed now was always better than a perfect plan next week. The Hammelburg plan called for Task Force Baum to advance farther into enemy territory than military opportunity, the current tactics of land warfare, or the need for morale-building at home reasonably required.

On the personal side, Oflag XIII B housed a prisoner of some importance, General Patton's son-in-law, Lt. Col. John K. Waters. While in his original unit, the 1st Armored Regiment, 1st Armored Division, Lieutenant Colonel Waters had distinguished himself as a promising officer. After his capture in North Africa in 1943, he showed himself to be a natural leader. In January 1945, he marched more than three hundred miles in the cold rain and wet snow in the "Black March," from Oflag 64 in Szubin (Altbergund), Poland, to Parchim, Germany. During the march, he assumed the position of executive officer of a group of more than eight hundred Allied prisoners and made sure that most of them stayed on their feet. In early March 1945, the weary survivors, near death from exposure, starvation, and ill health, arrived in Hammelburg, a POW camp that held mostly Russians.

The Hammelburg raid began at Aschaffenburg, a small city south of Frankfurt am Main, and drove east. The German High Command mistakenly believed that the thrust consisted of Patton's main force units, not the small Task Force Baum. Hauptmann (Captain) Richard Koehl's antitank unit was in Schweinfurt, about twenty miles east of the Americans, when he received orders to intercept the raiding force at Hammelburg.[19] Commanding a group of German mobile tank destroyers, Koehl intercepted and destroyed some of the advancing American armor. The surviving units turned south toward Hammelburg. Arriving at the edge of the prison camp, Major Baum erroneously ordered his tanks and light infantry to charge. Inside the camp, the commandant surrendered his command to the American senior ranking officer. Lieutenant Colonel Waters had attempted to contact the American tankers outside the camp, but he received a hip wound that forced him into a military field hospital.

The Americans continued their advance on the compound, and it looked as if they had won the day. The German flag came down, and a crude American flag went up. For a little while, the Hammelburg POW camp was liberated, and the raid was a stunning success. The scene reminded Major Baum of New Year's Eve in Times Square: the liberated prisoners, flushed with joy, enthusiasm, and a longing for freedom, rushed him and his small raiding force. Then events turned sour. Baum believed that he was raiding a small camp housing a few hundred prisoners. Instead, the Hammelburg officers' compound contained fifteen hundred relatively disorganized, weak, hungry, and debilitated Serbian, Russian, and American POWs, fearful of the dangers of war and aching for a different kind of life. To some, the raid looked like a window of opportunity for a way out. They were wrong.

For most Hammelburg prisoners, the sequence of chaotic events turned into catastrophe. Waters was nowhere to be found, and Major Baum considered heading back to American lines. Before he could gather his forces for an orderly withdrawal, however, the fortunes of war quickly turned against him. Hundreds of Kriegies had jumped on the tanks for the easy ride back to American lines, but they soon discovered the perilous position they were in. Task Force Baum was surrounded, and some vehicles had already exhausted their fuel supplies. The German defenders in the region, mostly combat engineers, were expert in the use of the *Panzerfaust,* a rocket-propelled antitank shape-charge that stopped the American tanks in their tracks and killed a number of passengers and crew. Sensing that the raid was dissolving into a disastrous free-for-all, some prisoners escaped from the camp. Norman Fruman, one of the temporarily liberated American officers, wrote, "A few of us decided to risk making it back to American lines fifty miles away on our own."[20] However, Fruman, like many others who broke out during the Hammelburg raid, was quickly recaptured by patrolling German infantrymen.

As remnants of the American raiders and prisoner-passengers rolled into the town of Reussenberg, the German attack began and finally stopped the American exit from Hammelburg in every direction. Tanks were hit and became incinerators. Infantry dispersed and casualties mounted. For the Americans, the German ambush at Reussenberg was the end of the trail. The officers and men of Task Force Baum who survived the mission surrendered and became POWs themselves in the prison camp that they had briefly liberated. A few men returned to American lines. One was T. Sgt. Charles O. Graham, a 10th Armored Infantry Battalion assault-gun platoon leader who escaped capture, evaded the Germans, and became the first man to tell Third Army headquarters what had happened.

The Hammelburg raiders had left the American lines on March 26, 1945, with 53 vehicles and 294 men. Everything was destroyed; nearly all the men were either killed or captured, and the unit was erased from the command's operational chart. Oflag XIII B Hammelburg was finally liberated on April 6, 1945, by the 14th Armored Division of the American Seventh Army. General Patton's personal physician, Maj. Charles Odum, rushed into the camp to find Lieutenant Colonel Waters in the hospital. "Funny meeting you here," quipped Waters. "We've been worried about you, Johnny," replied Odum.[21] When the press later asked him about the Hammelburg action, General Patton told reporters that the raid was a diversionary tactic devised to trick the German command into thinking that a larger force existed than actually did. In his journal, published posthumously by the *Saturday Evening Post* in August 1948, George Patton wrote, "I know of no error I made except that of failing to send a combat command to Hammelburg."[22]

In late 1942, the Japanese evacuated Camp O'Donnell, the end point of the Bataan Death March on the Philippine island of Luzon. Prior to transferring the POWs to prison and work camps in Japan, Formosa, Thailand, and Korea, the Japanese sent six thousand American POWs to the nearby Cabanatuan camp. By 1945, Cabanatuan's prison population was considerably reduced and contained only some civilian internees and a relatively small contingent of military POWs, who subsisted for years on almost nothing. Cabanatuan was not large by European standards, but it was surrounded by three rows of barbed-wire fence, eight feet high and four feet wide, with three guard towers twenty feet high and machine gun pits. All the buildings in camp were constructed of wood, bamboo, and nipa palm. Outside the wire, the Japanese constructed several metal sheds for a motor pool.[23]

On the night of January 30, 1945, the American 6th Ranger Battalion, led by Lt. Col. Henry Mucci, with the help of Filipino guerrillas and the Alamo Scouts, made a deep penetration behind enemy lines and struck the Cabanatuan prison camp. A dawn reveille formation was interrupted by the Rangers, who shot as they charged, wiping out the Japanese guards

U.S. Marines liberated from Cabanatuan. Proudly wearing Marine uniforms for the first time in three years, sixteen U.S. Marines liberated from the Japanese prison camp at Cabanatuan, near Manila, pose with the commander who rescued them. With the help of Filipino guerrillas and the Alamo Scouts, Lt. Col. Henry Mucci (first row, third from left) led the American 6th Ranger Battalion against Cabanatuan and liberated 516 prisoners on the night of January 30, 1945. Official U.S. Marine Corps photograph by Pfc. Jack Lartz, courtesy of the U.S. Army Historical Center

before they could kill the prisoners.[24] The results of the raid were encouraging: the Rangers had inflicted considerable losses on the Japanese and liberated 516 prisoners. Casualties included one American civilian prisoner who suffered a heart attack at the prison gate during the raid, another who was left behind by accident, and two soldiers killed in action in the raid. A month later, on February 23, 1945, the 1st Battalion, 511th Parachute Infantry Regiment, and other elements of the 11th Airborne Division jumped behind enemy lines to free 2,122 American and Allied internees imprisoned and nearly starved to death at the Los Baños camp at Laguna. These two raids were the most spectacular and successful POW recovery operations in American military history. Other Japanese POW and large internment camps were liberated by invading armies and sometimes by guerrilla units. Speaking about the Cabanatuan raid,

Gen. Douglas MacArthur, a theater commander who knew what to say to the press most of the time, commented, "No other incident of the campaign has given me such personal satisfaction."[25]

During the Korean War, there were no large prison camp raids behind enemy lines like those against Hammelburg, Cabanatuan, and Los Banõs. Instead, small unit raids took place that recovered handfuls of displaced escapers who found themselves near the battle lines. Like Melvin Shadduck's tank assault to rescue his fellow POWs, when United Nations combat units battled North Korean or Chinese units, they occasionally found abandoned POWs. Richard Crow, an American prisoner of the North Koreans, had this experience while he and others were on a twenty-day march. What appeared to him to be a raid on the morning of September 28, 1950, saved his life. According to Crow, "The North Koreans took out eleven South Koreans and shot them. Later that morning the [North Koreans] tied up ten Americans. We thought they would be shot, but a North Korean officer came running in and ordered them untied. Then the North Koreans took off. A short while later United Nations troops liberated us. The North Koreans left all the prisoners behind when they hurriedly evacuated the town. Soon the American 1st Cavalry poured in the town."[26]

Richard Crow and other United Nations prisoners freed in this manner were taken first to field hospitals and then flown to Pusan. The next stop was Japan, where the United States had established a recuperation camp exclusively for prisoners freed in Korea. On the battlefield, the advance-retreat nature of Korean combat changed front lines regularly. Some sectors resembled the trench warfare late in the Civil War and World War I; in other sectors, what was the rear yesterday became the front line today, and vice versa. After the first armistice talks in 1951, large prison raids above the 38th Parallel jeopardized future negotiations.

In the Vietnam War, the Americans learned again that no single operation was more difficult to accomplish than a prison raid. Raiders knew from experiences in World War II and Korea that success was possible but elusive, but it was difficult to develop intelligence that showed conclusively that prisoners were actually present at the target. In 1966 and 1967, when Col. Francis Kelly commanded the Army 5th Special Forces Group, the rescue of prisoners became a major objective. Several enemy prison camps were overrun, but the Vietcong followed a policy of moving their prisoners frequently and had standing orders to kill them during a raid.[27] According to Benjamin F. Schemmer, the participating American military services operating in Vietnam—Army, Navy, Coast Guard, Marines, and

Air Force—mounted ninety-one prison raids between 1966 and 1970, most of which were documented in unit diaries and after-action reports. Of this number, twenty succeeded in rescuing 318 South Vietnamese soldiers, 60 civilians from Vietcong prison camps, and 1 American, Army Sp. 4c. Larry D. Aikens. Freed on July 10, 1969, Aikens died in an American hospital fifteen days later of wounds he had received shortly before his rescue.[28]

Few combat experiences survive as well in a soldier's memory as raids. One experienced Army raider on his second Vietnam tour in 1968 served as a member of a Long Range Reconnaissance Patrol (LRRP) and expressed both the determination and the corresponding frustration that he experienced when his raid in the Bong Son area in the An Lao Valley failed (see Appendix 1: *Oral History Formats*). One of the teams had discovered a battalion-size North Vietnamese Army base camp in the jungle. Inside that base camp was a sixty-foot long bamboo cage which held POWs. After the group brought that intelligence out, a Special Forces Team with LRRPs went in and planted some sophisticated listening devices alongside the main trail. The raider wrote: "My team was given a mission in late August of 1968 to penetrate the area, infiltrating the base camp, determine if POWs were being kept there, and get them out if confirmed that there were any being held. After we were inserted by chopper, going was very difficult because the jungle had been sprayed with defoliant. Noise security was difficult to maintain because the movement through the dry and brittle jungle would break the foliage, making a lot of noise. It was a necessity to move very slow so as to make no noise going in."

They made it to the base camp undetected, but then things went terribly wrong. The raider continued, "I stopped the team and went back to check on the listening devices to see if they had been disturbed. One of my team was a South Vietnamese Airborne Ranger who had been with the previous team who had planted the devices. Either the NVA had known of the devices' locations or else I stepped on one of the devices which also had been booby-trapped. Something detonated, and I was blown up into the air about fifty to sixty feet and down into a ravine. The South Vietnamese ARVN [soldier] was also wounded."[29] When he landed down the hill from the team, he was severely wounded. The team's location was compromised by the explosion, and the mission collapsed.

After successful raids or successful escapes, the intelligence gained from former prisoners revealed that the Vietcong were smart captors and regularly moved all their prisoners from camp to camp. The problem became how to catch the Vietcong while they were moving their prisoners, a dangerous situation because the guards were armed and ready to shoot the POWs. It was better to surprise them in camp, if possible. David Beville, a member of the Marine Force Reconnaissance Team in 1967–68, described his experiences raiding POW camps. Preparing for the raid, the Marines dropped the team a day's march from the suspected prison camp site in Laos. The plan called for a surprise raid on the camp, using two raiding teams. One would reconnoiter the camp, and if prisoners were sighted, the assault group would attack. "When we hit the camp, we knew they were supposed to be there. Our job was supposed to be looking at it to see how many we could see, and then they were going to bring in other teams." The Marine raiders were dismayed at what they discovered: "We were about twenty miles into Laos when we hit that camp, and I still think they knew we were coming. No fires. They had been gone two, maybe three days. When we went in, there was nobody there except some dead Americans they had tortured." [30] Finding the aftermath of murders in Vietcong prison camps was shocking but common if the raiders arrived before the evidence could be hidden or removed.

Some raiders went into Laos, off-limits to regular combat forces, and were bound to secrecy. However, raiding and rescue missions into Laos and Cambodia were commonplace throughout the Vietnam War. In addition to attack missions, small, lightly armed, special intelligence-gathering units attempted to place themselves in main thoroughfares like the Ho Chi Minh Trail. They watched for troop movements, any physical signs of POWs being shipped north, or POWs being removed from one prison camp to another. This kind of intelligence-gathering operation was critical and consisted of looking at and listening to enemy activities, and not shooting until time and circumstance favored the raiders.

In Vietnam, intelligence data concerning location and activities of American prisoners were coded BRIGHTLIGHT and received immediate teletype priority and nearly instant response. In Saigon, MACV established the Joint Prisoner Recovery Center (JPRC) solely to react to BRIGHT-LIGHT messages from any source. [31] An entire force of American Special Warfare personnel was on call from the Mekong Delta in the South to the Demilitarized Zone in the North, including the Marine Corps' Force Reconnaissance units, Army Special Forces, and the Navy SEAL (Sea Air Land) Teams (1 and 2 in Vietnam). SEAL platoons were small, elite, well-trained units consisting of fourteen men, who were skilled at naval unconventional warfare. South Vietnamese special warfare units included their own SEALS, Kit Carson Scouts (KCS), and the Province Reconnaissance Units (PRUs) with American advisors.[32] The PRUs in Vinh Binh Province in the Mekong Delta participated in one BRIGHTLIGHT operation that released fifty-one South Vietnamese prisoners, some of whom had been in captivity for five years.[33] On February 19, 1971, the Army's Rangers mounted an assault on a reported Vietcong prison compound that supposedly held six Americans. Helicopters first sprayed the target area with tear gas in order to immobilize the enemy in the compound; then the Rangers repelled from the assault helicopters to attack the camp. After they swept the area, they found nothing, and as Shelby L. Stanton noted, it was another "frustrating example of attempted prisoner recovery operations, where the Rangers might have achieved success if given accurate prison information."[34]

No raid in Vietnam, large or small, failed because of a lack of American training, dedication, motivation, or expertise. Failures were primarily due to the Vietcong's skillful use of evasive tactics and the American problem of developing immediate, real-time intelligence. The Vietcong tactic of moving prisoners frequently prevented the Americans from developing delicately detailed intelligence around which to coordinate missions. Internally, too many things went wrong for the Americans. Intelligence was too old; missions were compromised when too many people knew what a raiding unit intended to do; and, in the case of Vietnam in general, direction and supervision of BRIGHTLIGHT operations took place at high command levels positioned a considerable distance from the target.

After many unsuccessful rescue operations during the Vietnam War, the most exacting full-fledged prison raid was planned and executed in enemy territory in 1970. As early as 1966, the Air Force realized that it was losing significant numbers of pilots over North Vietnam. Ranking military officers joined forces with the intelligence community—the Central Intelligence Agency, Defense Intelligence Agency, and National Security Agency—to initiate a show of force against the North Vietnamese, doubling as a real effort to free Americans from enemy hands. After extensive preparations and despite bad weather, on November 21, 1970, Col. Arthur "Bull" Simons, USA, led the raiders on the first centrally planned American strike against a prison in North Vietnam, Son Tay.

One HH-3 and five HH-53 helicopters carried fifty Special Warfare soldiers to the prison camp by air. After landing, the raiders scrambled around the camp for twenty-seven minutes looking for American prisoners. None was present. Although American intelligence had suspected that the American POWs had been removed from Son Tay, it was too late to stop the raid. American intelligence used a North Vietnamese spy, "Alfred," a senior Hanoi official, to procure a head count of the American prisoners in Son Tay. Sometime before the raid, he had reported that there were no American prisoners in Son Tay because they had been moved to "Dogpatch," the Dong Hoi Prison Camp near the Chinese border.[35] On the ground, the raiders smashed doors, searched cells, and entered into a brief combat with enemy soldiers on the site. Finding an empty camp, they boarded the escape aircraft and left. After the raiders returned to base, 1st Lt. George Petri commented, "When we realized that there was no one in the compound, I had the most horrible feeling of my life."[36]

In spite of its failure, the Son Tay raid had several positive effects. First, the North Vietnamese realized that outlying camps were vulnerable to American assaults and began to move prisoners to Hanoi. This meant that American POWs were able to interact with other captives, which lessened their sense of isolation. In addition, inside the POW community itself, the raid served as a powerful morale booster. Few narratives fail to mention the effects of Son Tay inside the compounds. After repatriation, 320 prisoners were asked to take part in a survey conducted by the Monroe Corporation. Responding to questions concerning what aided their morale during their long captivity, most former Hanoi POWs commented that the Son Tay raid played a significant role.[37] Looking back on the raid, one former POW, Marine Corps Gun. Sgt. John A. Deering, wrote, "Soon after Son Tay we were transported to downtown Hanoi's Plantation Gardens, where we learned of the rescue attempt from new captives via intricate inner communications. Unlike before, we developed a means of communication and a chain of command. That in itself kept a lot of us going."[38] At home, feelings were different.

The humanitarian aspect of the Son Tay raid was ignored by many editors and television commentators, who decried the resumption of large-scale bombing over North Vietnam. Antiwar activists also condemned the raid. However, military communities, especially the POW families, understood that Son Tay was as much a humanitarian act as a purely military operation.[39] Despite the raid's failure to recover any prisoners, the families believed that the government and the military services in general were beginning to show enough courage and determination to respond to reliable information concerning the outrageous North Vietnamese mistreatment of their family members in captivity.

Frustrated with negotiations with the North Vietnamese to end hostilities in 1972, the American Joint Chiefs of Staff proposed that a force consisting of 3.5 divisions, about 57,500 men, deploy solely to rescue the

Americans in Hanoi. The plan called for simultaneous airborne, amphibious, and air mobile strikes to surround Hanoi with American troops. Small Special Forces teams planned to seize Hoa Lo (the "Hanoi Hilton"), the Plantation, and the outlying camps. Although the plan was ambitious, the tactical problem, that more raiders might die than there were POWs, proved nearly insurmountable. The political and social problems, however, were even greater. By 1972, had the Americans invaded North Vietnam for any reason, chaos would have erupted inside the United States, already war-weary and dangerously divided, if not on the brink of furious civil strife, over Vietnam. The Joint Chiefs of Staff finally scrapped the plan and never issued the alert. Nonetheless, all the forces were in place and ready to go had President Richard M. Nixon ordered the Pentagon to initiate the operation.[40]

In April 1975, eight more Americans were taken prisoner: five missionaries, the six-year-old daughter of a missionary couple, an American consular official, and the chief provincial advisor for the State Department's Agency for International Development, who were held for five months before release.[41] On May 12, 1975, shortly after Saigon's fall to the North Vietnamese Army, the SS *Mayaguez,* an American merchant ship on a cruise from Hong Kong to Sattahip, Thailand, was seized by hostile Cambodian forces in international waters off the Wai Islands in the Gulf of Siam. The captors forced the ship to proceed to Tang Island, about thirty-five miles off the coast of Kompong Som, and to remain at anchor.[42] The crew was put on a captured Thai fishing boat and later picked up by an American destroyer.

Perhaps military activities should have ended there, but President Gerald Ford instructed the Navy and Marine Corps to react to the seizure of the *Mayaguez,* and launch a joint rescue operation. On Thursday, May 15, 1975, forty-eight Marines boarded the ship and found it deserted. At the same time, the Marines attacked Koh Tang Island, where they took heavy fire from Cambodian communist forces on the island. One helicopter carrying thirteen Marines and crew dropped into the sea twenty yards from the beach, killing everybody on board; two other helicopters were shot down as well. To recover one old, rusty merchant ship, the United States lost fifteen Marines dead, three missing, and fifty wounded, in addition to twenty-three men killed in a helicopter crash in Thailand.[43]

Some raiding activities continued even after the end of formal hostilities in Vietnam. American intelligence officers developed hearsay reports that some American prisoners were being held as slaves in a camp near Nhommarath, Laos. Aerial photographs taken in December 1980, showed a building surrounded by a wall and what looked to be the number "52" and the letter "K" stamped into a farm plot outside. American pilots had been told to use "K" as an emergency distress signal during the war, and some analysts believed that this signal represented an individual's or possibly a group's attempt to signal aircraft flying over the region. The Americans decided to act.

According to Thomas W. Lippman, writing for the *Washington Post,* the government feared political backlash and ordered the Central Intelligence Agency to use only indigenous personnel to investigate the scene. Following the probe, officials concluded there was no doubt that a prison camp existed, most likely a small reeducation work camp for former members of the defeated Royal Lao Army; however, there was no evidence to suggest that the Pathet Lao kept any Americans there.[44] Believing that there were Americans in enemy hands in Laos, retired Army Col. James "Bo" Gritz launched a short-lived raid, Operation Lazarus, on November 27, 1982, eleven years after the war was over.

Gritz recruited Charles J. Patterson, a former Special Forces soldier, as his second in command. As the mission's errors unfolded, it became evident that Lazarus was not to rise from his grave, and Patterson parted company with Gritz. Patterson explained the rationale for the raid as he understood it:

> It is assumed, due to delicate diplomatic relations between the United States, Thailand and Laos, the U.S. Government cannot commit official assets until positive proof of U.S. POW presence is provided. It is assumed, once such a determination has been made, the U. S. Government will follow the President's [Reagan's] stated policy to do whatever is required to return the POWs to U.S. control. The Thai Government can only look the other way due to their policy of providing sanctuary for Free Laos. It is assumed the Free Guerrilla Forces can approach POW locations and access them by force if desired. It is also assumed that the underground auxiliary forces are adequate to support such a tactical operation and act as an evasion mechanism, should aerial support be denied in evacuating POWs to safety once liberated. It is assumed that the U.S. Government will tacitly allow the operation.[45]

These were incorrect assumptions. The raiders had no legal mandate to search for American prisoners in Laos without that country's prior permission. A raid is an act of war, and in 1982, the United States had no desire to resume any warlike activities in Southeast Asia for any reason. As Patterson and Tipton pointed out, a surprise raid by American military forces is one thing; an unsupported, private, independent operation raid is another.[46]

In the end, Operation Lazarus consisting of four American civilians and fifteen indigenous Laotians, turned out to be both a "mission impossible" for the raiders and a political embarrassment to the United States. Without any discernible permission from or connections to the American government, the team entered Laos illegally by crossing the Mekong River from Thailand. The team became lost, the raiders grew discouraged, and they were lucky to escape with their lives. After Gritz and the others returned to Thailand, they were arrested and briefly jailed in Bangkok. Gritz should have known that no private citizen can start a war, with its implications of mass death and general destruction, by attempting to free a small number of hostages or prisoners. What may take place in fiction or in the movies has to be divorced from events in real life. Confusing the two means only trouble. Operation Lazarus, for example, became the background for Ted Kotcheff's film *Uncommon Valor* (1983). In the film, the prisoners were rescued; however, fiction and fantasy are not related to international, public, or military law. Eleven years after the war in Vietnam ended, the government and people of the United States were in no mood to resume hostilities in Southeast Asia.[47]

Raiding, like captivity itself, took its place in folklore long before it ever appeared as a recognized form of military operation. One German legend and three traditional Scottish border ballads serve as examples. Near the town of Hopsten in northwestern Germany sometime after the crusades, armed men raided a castle in Vennhausen and kidnapped the lord's only daughter. They took her to a local monastery on a lake. Meanwhile a Lord Eberwin sought clandestine help from one of the monks, Brother Martin, to free the young woman. Together they rescued the maiden from her captors under the cover of a thunderstorm. During their flight, lightning shattered the cells of the monastery, and an earthquake sank it into the lake.[48] The Scottish border ballads, "Kinmont Willie" (Child #186), "Jock O' the Side" (Child #187), and "Archie Cawfield" (Child #188), relate different kinds of capture and rescue tales that took place during a brief period of peace between England and Scotland in 1596. Although each story has a different twist, they resemble one another so thoroughly that they were probably different versions of the same or similar historical events.[49]

Unlike the successes and attempts of raiders in ballads, legends, and the movies, from the Revolution to Vietnam, except for the large Cabanatuan raid in World War II, Americans succeeded in rescuing relatively few prisoners from enemy hands. One reason for the failures is that contemporary raiding forces are in themselves inadequate. In general, the most bizarre forms of military assault become the calculated gambles of small, unconventional forces—Special Forces, Marine Force Reconnaissance, Navy SEALs, Air Force Commandos—that make high-risk assaults deep in enemy territory. With the few against the many, it is little wonder that success has been elusive.

Raids are also fundamentally humanitarian; raiders have a sincere passion for prisoners' welfare, as well as a personal sense of outrage at their treatment in captivity. General Stoneman cared about the Andersonville prisoners in 1864, and the Oflag 64 plan was drawn up because it appeared that the Allied POWs were about to be murdered in their camp. On the practical side, raids demand a great deal of preparation and coordination between intelligence communities and the special units. Coordinating intelligence-gathering and operational commands looks easy enough on paper, but in reality, it can be a nightmarish exercise in frustration. There has been little trust and less confidence between the two, and as raiders' recollections have shown, there is nothing more frustrating than to liberate an empty prison camp or one containing only dead prisoners. After Son Tay, for example, operators demanded to know why intelligence operatives had not told them that the prisoners had been removed from the camp. SEALs and other special warfare units believed that some of their BRIGHTLIGHT operations had been unknowingly compromised by a number of factors: enemy infiltration into friendly ranks, enemy intercepts of secret teletype messages, incompetence, negligence, or undetermined bad luck. Other instances in Vietnam reveal that central administrative intelligence and operational control may have delayed small unit commanders from initiating raids in time for successful rescues.[50]

From the time of Stephen Decatur, Jr., raids have consistently required tremendous personal daring against great odds, individual valor, high drama, overwhelming risk, and highly developed skills in unconventional warfare. The celebrated Marine rescue of Air Force Capt. Scott O'Grady on June 8, 1995, after his shootdown about twenty miles behind the lines in Bosnia, demonstrated these qualities yet again. After his aircraft was destroyed by a surface-to-air missile, he ejected and reached the ground safely. O'Grady evaded immediate capture by the Bosnian Serbs, who held many United Nations peacekeeping troops hostage at the time, and headed for the woods. Launched from two aircraft carriers, the USS *Kearsarge* and the USS *Theodore Roosevelt*, an assemblage of forty attack and cover aircraft, including two troop-carrying helicopters with forty-one Marines aboard, were deployed to rescue one pilot. After the force discovered the crash site, the pilots saw O'Grady's signal flares and landed. Nearly repeating James N. Rowe's 1968 rescue in Vietnam, O'Grady ran out of hiding and flung himself aboard the rescue helicopter. After the force returned to the *Kearsarge,* O'Grady told the press, "I'm no Rambo"; the "real heroes" were his rescuers.[51]

Although few raids have ever played significant roles in the overall military strategy of any war, they have acted as important tactical symbolic sideshows to the main events. The Kilpatrick-Dalhgren raid frightened the Confederates into moving Union POWs from Richmond. Stoneman's raid uplifted Union morale in Andersonville. Task Force Baum was symbolic of George Patton's concern for prisoners in the German stalags. The Cabanatuan and Son Tay raids significantly improved morale among the armies in the field and the folks at home. President Carter's Iran hostage raid responded to the public's call for military and humanitarian action to free civilian hostages, and the Bosnia rescue saved one pilot and provided the American media with an enormous amount of "heroic ink." This review of past events affords some optimism in that prison raids and SAR missions, whether successful or unsuccessful, raise hopes for repatriation and eventual liberation among helpless POWs or evaders on the run. With the exception of Decatur's raid against the Barbary pirates in 1804 and the Cabanatuan-Los Baños operations in the Philippines during World War II, very few have ever created the conditions for escape by other means on a large scale or changed the course of history.[52]

13

Escape and the Fortunes of War
Legacies and Reflections

Perhaps those little things are remembered because they are man's unconscious striving to achieve nobility.
—Steven Mellnik (1944)

Throughout America's military history, exactly how many prisoners escaped captivity remains only an estimate. Reasonably precise record-keeping on a large scale began during the Civil War, but all told, escapers were relatively few in comparison to the numbers of innocent people held as captives, indentures, slaves, POWs, or hostages for extended periods of time. Numbers aside, most of the individuals held in captivity had the overwhelming desire to go home, or, in the case of slaves, to break their bondage. A small minority felt driven to escape for its own sake; others felt compelled to join, or in some cases rejoin, active combat units still engaged in battle. The experiences of civilian captives and slave escapers show how the process of formulating an escape worked outside a purely military context. To be sure, individual escapes varied over time as circumstances of captivities changed, but some degrees of consistency have remained intact, not only in the patterns themselves but also in matters relating to risk, motivation, and rewards.

There has never been an accurate count of individuals taken captive during the Indian wars. Regardless of the actual numbers, fewer captives escaped than decided to remain with or assimilate into their captors' communities. Assimilation was relatively easy and far less dangerous than escape, where the stakes were considerably higher. For the very few committed natural escapers, the decision to flee captivity came easily. For others, those who were far more docile, pacifist, or trusting in values like justice, fairness, or traditional religious sanctions against murder, a distinctly evolutionary process of decision-making took place. At one end of the captivity spectrum, there were Indian captives like Mary Jemison who preferred to assimilate into their newly acquired tribal cultures. Others took varying amounts of time, depending on the circumstances of the individual captivities, to realize that living in captivity without end meant dying in captivity as well.[1] For those settlers firmly attached to their former cultures, like Barbara Leininger, a life sentence meant not only physical but emotional, psychological, and cultural death. Such losses must have been intolerable.

Committed escapers, especially the naturals, had to escape, or at least felt compelled to try again and again. No threats of reprisal against them personally or against the lives or the well-being of their prison communities lessened their spirit and determination. Beyond the motivational characteristics cited here, it has been shown that most escapers devised specific plans after one or more spontaneous attempts failed. Many escapers concocted simple plans that gambled on random opportunities, but others went well beyond mere chance when they banded together into small groups, pooled their resources, and made things happen. The best example of planned movement comes from the development of the slaves' maroon communities near the plantations, followed in the 1850s by the establishment of the Underground Railroad itself. This movement constituted the best organized escape line in the American experience until World War II.

What we have witnessed for more than three centuries, from the Bible and the ballads to the movies and the memoirs, have been the real dilemmas of those prisoners who arrived at their decisions slowly and deliberately. If captives attempted to escape and failed, a terrible fate awaited them at the hands of their captors. On the other hand, if military prisoners, regardless of their status as regulars or reserves, officers or enlisted, volunteers or conscripts, refused to attempt to escape, they failed to live up to the responsibilities imposed upon them by the tradition of arms. Military prisoners, civilian settlers, slaves, and hostages were caught in another web as well: if fear of reprisals against fellow prisoners grew too intense, escape became impossible, regardless of how committed individual escapers might have been. Yet one perceptive truth overrides all other factors: rightly or wrongly, overcoming the fear of death and conquering the uncertainty of prison life proved to be the most significant virtues of the committed escaper.

Although at times there remained some residual hostility on the part of prisoners left behind to face severe retributions caused by the activities of the escapers, the paradox is that the risk-takers themselves have received rich and lasting rewards. Of the 3,394 Medals of Honor awarded to date, thirty-five were presented to POWs, from the Civil War to Vietnam, who earned it for actions behind the wire, including successful escapers or those who made successive and determined attempts to escape. Confederate soldiers like Berry Benson never received any medals, but they earned respect and some adulation in the United Confederate Veterans' newsletter, *The Confederate Veteran,* during and after their lifetimes. In 1863, when the Medal of Honor took its place next to the Revolution's military medal, the Purple Heart (1782), the first soldiers to receive it were twenty Union escapers who were captured during failed raids deep in Confederate Georgia.

The 1,520 Civil War Medals of Honor included hundreds of awards for service as well as valor. Dr. Mary Walker, the only woman ever awarded the medal, received it for service. Dr. Walker was a volunteer civilian surgeon with the Union Army and a POW in Richmond for a short time. Following the Civil War, Congress took her medal away, along with hundreds of others.[2] Sgt. Daniel Ferrier earned his medal for valor. When he was a member of Company K, 2d Indiana Cavalry, Ferrier gave up his horse to his brigade commander during a retreat, an act that directly caused his capture. After confinement in several Confederate prison camps, Ferrier escaped and returned to Union lines.[3]

Following the Civil War, the military services reviewed the Medal of Honor's criteria and upgraded it to a valor-only award. Since that time, Congress has awarded the medal to only 1,898 servicemen. Many were hard-resisting POWs, and some were escapers. Michael McCarthy, a Canadian immigrant from St. Johns, Newfoundland, served with Troop H, 1st Cavalry and won his Medal of Honor in 1876 at White Bird Canyon, Idaho, during the Indian wars. After two different horses were shot from under him in battle, McCarthy was captured, but he escaped three days later. During World War I, Edouard Isaacs (Izac) won the medal for escaping from the German prison camp at Villingen. During World War II, Gen. Jonathan J. M. Wainwright, USA, Maj. Pierpont Hamilton, USAAF, T. Sgt. Vernon Garity, USA, and Maj. Gregory G. Boyington, USMC, each won the medal for gallantry in action and POW resistance. In Korea, Maj. Gen. William F. Dean, USA, Lt. John Koelsch, USN, Sgt. H. Miyamura, USA, Sp. R. E. Duke, USA, and Lt. J. L. Stone, USA, were all POWs and winners of the Medal of Honor, some posthumously for valor and POW resistance.

In Vietnam, Capt. D. G. Cook, USMC, won the medal posthumously for POW resistance. Col. George "Bud" Day, USAF, won the medal not only for resisting but for his escape and evasion. The Air Force awarded Capt. Lance Sijan the medal for valor after he died trying to escape, and Rear Adm. James B. Stockdale, USN, won his medal not only for extreme acts of resistance and acting as the senior ranking officer in Hanoi, but also for trying to facilitate escapes whenever feasible.[4] There were no Medals of Honor awarded after the Vietnam War until action in Somalia. During Operation Restore Hope, forty-four American soldiers were killed in action and eighty-four were wounded in Mogadishu alone. Among these casualties were Army M. Sgt. Gary Gordon and Sgt. 1c Randall Shughart. Both soldiers won the Medal of Honor posthumously for trying to rescue WO Michael Durant and save four other crewmen from capture. The men were lost; Durant became the sole survivor from his aircraft and the only prisoner. After his release, Durant commented, "I'm 100% convinced I would have been killed by gunfire if those guys had not been there."[5]

What about the enemy? Did captured soldiers, sailors, and internees sit quietly enjoying the benefits of benign quarantine captivity in relatively friendly hands? Did the Golden Rule apply to them? Were Americans all that friendly or even humane to their prisoners? Who escaped and why?

In most of America's international wars, enemy soldiers taken prisoner were relatively well treated, or at least fairly treated, in accordance with the rules held among nations and the American Army's internal rules at the time. There were exceptions. After the Pequot War in New England, the tribe's surviving remnant sued for peace and received harsh terms. The Treaty of Hartford, signed on September 21, 1638, stipulated that most of the Pequots became the property of the settlers' Indian allies: the Mohegans, the Narragansetts, and the Niantics. The name of the tribe was erased, and a few of its members were sent into slavery in the Caribbean.[6]

The Indian wars of the nineteenth century resulted in the capture and imprisonment of many tribal leaders. Chief Black Hawk of the Sauk and Fox tribes fought the American Army in Illinois and witnessed the massacre of his people along the Mississippi River on August 3, 1832. Having survived the action, he escaped north to Wisconsin, where he joined a group of Winnebagos. Black Hawk's captivity began when his hosts betrayed him to the Army for money. Nevertheless, he achieved considerable notoriety while in captivity for a year. Another leader, the Creek-Seminole warrior Oseola, famed for his defiance, was lured into captivity in Florida by Gen. Thomas Sidney Jesup. Oseola died of disease at Fort Moultrie, South Carolina, on January 30, 1838, still a POW. During the capture and removal of the Cherokee nation and four other tribes—the Choctaw, Chikasaw, Creek, and Seminole—from their homelands in Georgia and other states to Oklahoma in 1838–39, the eight-hundred mile forced march, known as "The Trail of Tears," killed more than four thousand innocent persons. After the Civil War, Indian prisoners in the Plains Wars suffered terrible mistreatment until the turn of the twentieth century. Many died in prison from abuse; some were executed or remained, like Geronimo, POWs confined to reservations for the rest of their lives.[7]

During the Revolution, the American Patriots despised the Loyalists. In 1776 and 1777, the new states required Test Acts, early kinds of loyalty oaths taken against King George III. In 1778, the stakes for Loyalists rose when several states passed exile laws, and the Continental Congress ordered their properties seized for sale or destroyed. States heavily populated by Loyalists, like Maryland and New York, earned millions of dollars from the sale of these properties, and five states disenfranchised Loyalists completely. Those Loyalists captured actively under arms were not exchanged; instead, they were returned in close confinement to their state of origin for disposition.[8] Even suspicions of Loyalism caused problems. The Continental Congress took some prominent pacifist Philadelphia Quakers as political prisoners and ordered them into temporary exile in Virginia for fear of their suspected loyalties to the crown.[9] By the end of the war, approximately one hundred thousand Loyalists left the United States for Britain or Canada, and as part of the peace process from 1783 until 1790, the British government established a claims commission that examined 4,118 claims and paid £3,292,452 in compensation. One cannot ignore the fact that the American Revolution was in part a vicious and unforgiving civil war.

Life was hard for captured enemy sailors in America too. The Americans held British sailors in two prison hulks, one in Boston, the other in New Haven, Connecticut, where the prisoners were treated as badly as the Americans were treated in the British hulks. Captured Hessian soldiers serving with the British Army fared a little better in American hands. Although many Hessians were tough professional soldiers, the Americans knew that many private soldiers were conscripted against their will at home, and with decent treatment, they could possibly be neutralized as a force. They were either exchanged, or, if they decided to remain with the Americans, paroled.[10] In general, the Continental Congress preferred to put those that were interned into loyal German-speaking villages and towns. Reading, Pennsylvania, was one example. Despite the efforts made by the Continental Congress to persuade Hessian conscripts to change sides during the war, the Hessian prisoners were never really welcome. Local Pennsylvania Germans were simply aghast at seeing the uniformed Hessians interned near their homes in America. After all, German institutional militarism was one of the principal reasons for their departure from Germany in the first place.[11] Although the Hessians were not held in close confinement like the British POWs, life often became very hard for them.

British soldiers captured in the Revolution and again in the War of 1812 were held in dungeons and makeshift jails and exchanged in much the same way Americans were.[12] Between 1812 and 1814, British officers were often free on parole and housed themselves with as much comfort as their means allowed.[13] In the Texas war and later in Mexico, the American Army paroled most captured enemy soldiers in the field; it had neither the desire nor the facilities to hold them as POWs. On the other hand, the American Army tried and executed most of the surviving members of the renegade San Patricio Battalion. This group of soldiers, mostly new immigrants, had been promised land and rank in Mexico if they fought for General Santa Anna. After the American victories at Vera Cruz and Cherabusco, fifty were hanged; others were flogged and imprisoned, and eleven were branded with a "D" on their faces near the eye.[14] Americans treated desertion and renegading very harshly in 1847 and 1848.

The Civil War at first continued the tradition of paroles in the field after the battle, but in time each side realized that the parole system was a failure, and captivity in general became a scandalous exercise in prisoner mistreatment on both sides. The Golden Rule was ignored more than flaunted because the Union POW camps held more than Confederate soldiers. Union camps also held political prisoners, who were jailed without habeas corpus for Confederate sympathies. Despite Chief Justice Roger Taney's judicial opposition in *Ex parte* Merryman (1861), from the beginning to the end of the war, Abraham Lincoln ordered his regional commanders to imprison anyone expressing even a hint of sedition against the government of the United States. Where insurrection existed or was suspected to exist, private citizens, the innocent as well as the guilty, went to jail, sometimes to Union POW camps, for extended periods of time.

Lincoln believed he held the legal high ground on the strength of Section 9, Article 1, of the Constitution, which gives the president extraordinary powers as commander in chief of the armed forces with the mandate to stop rebellion and invasion and to maintain public safety. Lincoln issued the first such proclamation on May 10, 1861, and directed the commander of Union forces in Florida, ". . . if he shall find it necessary, to suspend the writ of habeas corpus and to remove . . . all dangerous or suspected persons."[15] "Executive Order No. 1, Relating to Political Prisoners," was issued on February 14, 1862; however, as the war progressed beyond a police problem to a war of conquest, armed Confederates and Union troops became traditional prisoners of war.[16] By 1863, soldiers on both sides were protected by the *Rules of Land Warfare* in areas of military confrontation; civilians were not.

By the turn of the twentieth century, the United States had signed the 1899 Hague Convention and joined the international community in trying to ameliorate the horrors of war, especially for POWs and other innocents caught in the midst of the fighting. Western democracies, imperfect as they may be, subscribed to the provisions of the international conventions relative to POWs, and enemy escapes based on intolerable cruelty were rare indeed. At the end of World War I, the American Expeditionary Force held approximately 40,000 German POWs in Europe, and only 1,346 German servicemen in the United States. Aside from a few escapes into Mexico, there were no significant difficulties. In Europe, the American Expeditionary Force promptly repatriated its German POWs in 1919, shortly after hostilities ended according to the armistice agreement made in November 1918.

World War II was more complicated. Between 1942 and 1945, the enemy POW count rose significantly. The U.S. Army held more than 375,000 German, 50,000 Italian, and 5,000 Japanese war prisoners in some 511 POW camps placed in forty-four states, with thirty in Oklahoma alone and many around the sunbelt states with up to 4,000 men each.[17] In accordance with the provisions of the 1929 Geneva Convention, officers and senior sergeants were not required to work, but some did so simply to relieve their boredom. Treatment was proper, just, firm, humane, and generally consistent with the 1929 Geneva Convention requirements.[18]

For Axis prisoners there was no such thing as a typical POW experience in America. In *Nazi Prisoners of War in America* (1979), Arnold Krammer noted that the most significant problem for American camp authorities was distinguishing between the four kinds of Axis prisoners.[19] Political opportunists who used the POW experience for their own benefit were ever present. So too were German nationalists, who fought for the greater glory of the Reich. The nonpolitical soldiers, mostly draftees, formed the largest category. These men had worked in their respective professions before the war and wanted simply to be left alone in camp; their only wish was to go home unmolested by either the Americans or other prisoners. The smallest group included the dedicated Nazi Party members, sometimes members of the SS or Gestapo, who blended in with the other three groups, and who from time to time murdered their own men for political reasons while in American captivity.[20]

The CBS teleplay *The Incident* (1990) depicted just such an event. Walter Matthau played a small-town country lawyer called to defend a young German POW, who was wrongly accused of the murder of a Colorado doctor at a nearby POW camp and stood trial for his life. Although the lawyer lost his son in combat against his client's countrymen, he was prepared to defend the young German prisoner against injustice despite wartime prejudice and his own personal grief. During the pretrial investigation, the lawyer discovered that the real killer was a ranking sergeant and Nazi politico in the camp. Matthau showed that law in a civilized world can triumph over evil even in wartime, and that a country lawyer can defend the innocent successfully despite his feelings.[21] The obvious paradox was never lost on the audience.

Axis POWs may have shared experiences, but their cultural traditions varied greatly. For example, well-schooled German officers must have thought of imprisonment in terms of the university *Karzer,* prison cells for misbehaving students who were found drunk in public, or dueling illegally, or, perhaps, keeping dangerous dogs. For many, a stint in the *Karzer* became a badge of honor, and the experience was taken lightly. During his university days at Georg-August University in Göttingen, Otto von Bismarck spent eighteen nights in a *Karzer* for dueling, smoking in public, and other socially unacceptable offenses. In 1931, just before the Nazis radically changed Germany's political history forever, one student carved "Hotel zur Akademischen Freiheit" (Hotel of Academic Freedom) into the wooden door of his *Karzer.*[22] Humor was not lost among the German enlisted soldiers either. Often they joked that the "PW" painted on the back of their shirts stood for "Pensionierte Wehrmacht" or "Military Retiree," meaning that they considered themselves simply put out to pasture, in effect quarantined on a harmless working vacation with pay. Sometimes German prisoners harassed one another in ideological disputes, but most German POWs, both officers and enlisted men, spent their years uneventfully and, in some cases, enjoyably, so much so that many relocated to Canada and the United States as immigrants after repatriation.[23]

Noted military historians like Arnold Krammer in America, Erich Maschke, Günter Bischof, Hermann Jung, and Kurt Böhme in Germany, as well as former German POWs who became novelists, like Alfred Andersch, agreed that the German experience in American, British, and Canadian POW camps was relatively benign. German prisoners worked on farms; studied literature, history, and politics; played endless soccer matches and card games; developed their own theater; and attended church services often held by German-speaking American clergy. Keeping the provisions of the 1929 Geneva Convention to the end, even to the point of being accused of "coddling,"[24] the American government eventually paid all the former German POWs held in the United States their salaries concurrent with their ranks and the monies they earned for their work in the United States.

Each camp in the American system had a canteen, where prisoners bought personal sundries and had the opportunity to read in libraries full of books, including the important *Selections of the New World* (*Bucherreihe der Neue Welt*), a twenty-four volume collection published by Bermann-Fischer in Stockholm. Titles included Erich Maria Remarque's *All Quiet on the Western Front* (1929), Thomas Mann's *Zauberberg* (1924), Franz Werfel's *Song of Bernadette* (1941), and other literary classics that the Nazis had forbidden for more than a decade. In a short commentary in the intercamp journal, *Der Ruf,* German prisoner Curt Vinz wrote, "Had we only had the opportunity to read these books before, our introduction to life, to war, and the expanse of politics would have been different."[25] After the war, Fischer Verlag (Publisher) specialized in publishing inexpensive paperback volumes of classic literature and remains a popular publishing house in Germany today.

Produced in 1944–45 by the Prisoner of War Special Projects Division, Fort Phil Kearney, Rhode Island, *Der Ruf* followed in the tradition of the *Orgelsdorfer Eulenspiegel,* a camp literary and satiric newspaper published by German internees during World War I, and became the anti-Nazi newspaper that circulated throughout the entire POW camp system.[26] It achieved great popularity among the more literary German prisoners in the United States and continued as an important literary journal back home in Germany until 1947, when the American occupation authorities feared its left-leaning positions and banned it under the pretext that paper was scarce. After their beginnings in the American POW camps, postwar German literary efforts were not to be stopped, and if there was at least one long-range, positive effect of American captivity on modern German culture, *Der Ruf* served as the new beginning for German letters following the mass repatriations in 1946.[27]

Even better prison conditions existed in Canada, where German POWs enjoyed more than adequate treatment, so good that many ex-prisoners returned to settle in Canada after the war. Similar to Australia's policy, Canadian guards were not stern military police, as they were in the United States; the force consisted of many kindly old veterans of the Great War who patriotically volunteered for guard duty.[28] It is no small paradox that it was from law-abiding Canada that the most famous German committed natural escaper, twenty-six-year-old Luftwaffe Oberleutnant Franz von Werra, made his flight from captivity in 1941 before the United States entered the war.

In the salutary biographical thriller *One That Got Away* (1957), Kendal Burt and James Leasor celebrated the crafty von Werra's winter

Luftwaffe Hauptmann Franz von Werra's official photograph when it appeared in Germany announcing his death in 1941. By permission of the German Bundesarchiv Koblenz

escape from Canada across the frozen St. Lawrence River to the United States, where he received so much notoriety in the American popular media that the German embassy sent him secretly to Mexico. There they arranged a passport for him under an assumed name and secured his passage to Rio de Janeiro in mid-April 1941. From neutral Brazil, he flew to Rome and reached Germany on April 18, 1941.[29] At home after one of the most daring exploits of the war to that point, von Werra received a promotion and the Knight's Cross for valor. Many private parties were given in his honor, and he was featured in a full-page story in the widely circulated German Air Force propaganda magazine *Der Adler,* "Die Flucht des Oberleutnants v. Werra." Very little ever appeared in the German popular press about his escape, however, although articles and photos did find their way into the American press.[30]

His next immediate assignment with Luftwaffe Intelligence had some long-range effects on Allied airmen during the ensuing four years of hostilities in Europe. Beginning shortly after his shootdown over England in 1940 during the Battle of Britain, his first experiences with skilled British interrogators had been deceptively amicable. As a young man, he found these men cordial, elderly, and curious about seeming trivialities. In time, he discovered that skilled intelligence officers can piece together entire dossiers from the most trivial details thought to be next to nothing by POWs. He came to this realization when he began collecting the stories of other pilots in British hands and found that the easy-going, relatively cordial style that the British used was actually an effective tool for gathering military information from downed German pilots. Upon his escape, he shared this knowledge with German Intelligence, which expanded his after-action report into a booklet issued to all Luftwaffe pilots engaging the Western Allies.

In addition, von Werra participated in establishing interrogation procedures in the *Durchgangslager Luftwaffe,* the German Air Force's transient camp near Wetzlar, that existed to collect intelligence from captured Allied airmen.[31] He toured POW camps to forestall escapes based on intolerable cruelty and urged the German POW authorities to improve conditions in general. He wrote a book, *Mein Flucht aus England,* for popular consumption, but the German Propaganda Ministry banned its publication because it was too pro-British at the time.[32] On October 25, 1941, Franz von Werra died on a routine Luftwaffe patrol off the coast of Holland after his aircraft developed engine trouble and crashed into the sea. Long after his death and the conclusion of World War II, von Werra remained one of the war's most unusual characters. The von Werra story eventually found its way to the silver screen both in English as *The One That Got Away* (1957) and in German as *Einer Kam Durch.*

Some enemy POWs held by the United States, Britain, and Commonwealth countries became resisters and escapers for ideological reasons, most from a sense of duty. They also escaped for reasons of boredom or simple curiosity about what was on the other side of the metal barriers separating them from the outside world. All told, about two thousand German POWs escaped, most of whom were returned to camp by the military police, the Federal Bureau of Investigation, or the local police. Some were not escapers at all. Many German POWs on work details simply missed the buses that returned them to their camps and found themselves stranded in the American countryside. Some committed escapers, after realizing that there was no place to go, came back on their own. No one committed any acts of sabotage, which had been expected by the FBI and military intelligence, beyond occasional minor thefts of food, clothes, or cars.[33]

As the Allies pressed the war toward Germany and took many more prisoners, some of whom were submarine crews, escapers began to make their presence felt. Capt. Wolfgang Hermann Hellfritsch, for example, escaped from the POW camp at Crossville, Tennessee, on October 23, 1943. He spoke fluent English, found work as a farmhand, and was free for seven months before his recapture. Three German sailors escaped from Crossville into the Tennessee mountains, but when they stopped at a mountain cabin to get some water, an old woman shot at one of them and told the others to "git." When informed that she had shot at German POWs, the granny sobbed and replied, "I thought they wuz Yankees."[34]

Most German escapes were reactions to opportunities; the escape by the "Faustballers" imprisoned in Arizona was the exception. This group of twenty-five German submariners developed the only Axis great escape in the German POW experience in America, remembered as the "Faustball Tunnel." Led by Frigate Capt. Jürgen Wattenberg, a group of four hard-resisting naval officers, Hans Werner Kraus, Friedrich Guggenberger, August Maus, and Jürgen Quaet-Faslem, masterminded, built, and escaped through a 178-foot tunnel from Camp Papago Park near Phoenix on December 24, 1944.[35] The objective, as had been the case during World War I, was Mexico. The sixteen-foot-deep tunnel took nearly five months to dig, using tools requisitioned from the Americans. After the team strung the tunnel with electric lights, the men worked in ninety-minute shifts, beginning behind a bath house, then going under two fences and a road. After the breakout, one that was effectively covered by the other prisoners during a Christmas party in the camp, the German officers were free for only a short time. They had crude maps and no real plans except to head south to Mexico. As a result, all the Faustballers, including Wattenberg, were recaptured, although one prisoner, Walter Kozur, spent weeks in the Arizona mountains.[36]

The reasons for the escape varied from man to man. Wattenberg was one of the hardest resisters in an American POW camp and, much like his British counterpart, Douglas Bader, caused trouble and generated grudging respect wherever he went. German naval officers understood the 1929 Geneva Convention as well as the Americans, and on the occasions when the Americans used handcuffs for transporting those prisoners they considered to be dangerous, the Germans complained to the Red Cross authorities. Regardless of the charges and countercharges made to the International Committee of the Red Cross, the American POW authorities continued to use the handcuffs illegally.[37] In retrospect, something as minor as handcuffs may seem trivial at first, but to POWs living at the mercy of unpredictable jailers, the cuffs became symbols signifying the omnipotence of the captor. Remembering the popular story of the ill-fated Prussian Baron Frederick Trenck, who suffered a lengthy prison term at the hands of Frederick the Great and other powerful political adversaries in the eighteenth century, German prisoners were quick to ask what would come next from the whims of the Americans.[38] No one knew, and like such political prisoners as the Prussian Trenck and the Dutch Hugo Grotius, escape became an attractive option.

After Allied armies liberated Dachau, Buchenwald, Belsen, Flossenbürg, Auschwitz, and the other Nazi concentration camps in 1945, there were calls for retribution against German POWs in the United States. The Golden Rule crumbled. Cries of "coddling" appeared in the popular media, and rumors spread about something the German prisoners really feared—transfer to Dutch, French, or, worse, Russian prison camps in Europe, where formerly occupied countries were drafting German ex-soldiers for mine-clearing and massive reconstruction projects.

Even in the United States, conditions worsened rapidly for German POWs after May 8, 1945. Not only did the American authorities change their legal status from POW to Disarmed Enemy Personnel, but they also reduced food and tobacco rations and refused to restock empty canteen shelves. The prisoners had money, chits earned from working, but they had no place to spend it and little to spend it on. With a grim future in Europe and conditions becoming more difficult in the prison camps, some POWs looked to escape as an alternative. The last shipload of German POWs sailed for Europe and repatriation on July 23, 1946. Remaining behind in the United States were forty-three MIAs, among whom were twenty-eight German and fifteen Italian escapers known to be at large somewhere in the country.

In 1947, the FBI apprehended a handful of German escapers, then in 1953, the Bureau finally recaptured one of the most elusive, Sgt. Rheinhold Pabel, who had initially been captured in Sicily during the fighting in 1943. In 1944, he sat in Camp Ellis near Washington, Illinois, where he read the large selection of American newspapers and articles available to German POWs in the camp library. One article in particular interested him, J. Edgar Hoover's "Enemies at Large," published in the April 1944 edition of *American Magazine*. To the bored and escape-minded Pabel, FBI Director Hoover's warnings became his guidelines: do it alone and tell no one about the plans; have some ready cash; talk to no one unless it becomes absolutely necessary; and go as far as possible as quickly as possible.[39]

After the war's end in May 1945, Pabel began to suffer from the tensions caused by continuous hunger, the accelerated American reeducation program, and camp rumors about the proposed Morganthau Plan, which would limit Germany to a postwar future without industry or growth, and virtually no recovery at all. By August 1945, Pabel knew enough English to mingle freely with Americans and decided that the time was right to escape. He called his plan "Operation Vapor," the idea being that he would disappear into mainstream America and fend for himself.

Taking Hoover's advice, Pabel saved up fifteen dollars in contraband American cash and managed to acquire some road maps to Chicago, where he disappeared into the congestion of a large city full of European immigrants. He secured his first job washing dishes by identifying himself falsely as a Dutch refugee, Phil Brick. As Brick, Pabel married an American woman and opened a small bookstore, but in 1953, the FBI suddenly appeared in the store and arrested him as an escaped enemy POW and an illegal resident. After court proceedings, the government deported Phil Brick/Rheinhold Pabel to West Germany, but with visa in hand he returned to the United States and a television interview with Dave Garaway. After he published *Enemies Are Human* (1955), Pabel returned to Hamburg, where he continued his book business. The FBI also arrested two other German escapers: Harry Girth, a house painter in Atlantic City, in 1953, and Kurt Rossmeisl in 1959. Following their escapes, both men had established themselves in the United States but were promptly deported after recapture. The rest eluded the FBI and found permanent homes somewhere in the United States.[40] Georg Gaertner, a building contractor in Hawaii, was the last German escaper to surrender. He eluded his captors successfully, but he grew tired of living the life of a fugitive. He gave himself up to American authorities in 1985.[41]

In early postwar Europe, instances of escapes went unrecorded except in the memories of the escapers themselves, especially among the millions of war-weary, defeated German soldiers held in Europe after May 8, 1945. Knowing that the Allies were searching for them, many SS troops shed their uniforms and attempted to join the masses of German soldiers who filled the squalid Rhine Meadow camps, where they were held not as protected POWs but as unprotected Disarmed Enemy Personnel waiting for discharges. To prisoners starving and dying of illness in the huge, exposed camps along the Rhine River, escape looked good. If a way out arrived, they took it, legally or otherwise. A few, of course, were committed natural escapers; others were opportunists. For all those soldiers, the war was over, and they wanted to go home. By 1947, most had disposed of their uniforms, received discharges from the Allies, and started a new life.

Unbeknown to these former German soldiers, however, the politics of the Cold War had already begun to emerge. At noon on each October 24 from 1950 to 1954, the German police stopped traffic on streets and highways to remember the "Day of German Prisoners of War" and the men who remained captive in Russia. This action was intended to keep the issue in the public eye. As Konrad Adenauer, president of the new Federal Republic, reminded his nation, "Patience is the best weapon for the defeated"; in January 1954, Adenauer and the German Red Cross joined forces to facilitate the return of more than ten thousand German POWs from the Soviet Union. Many came home still wearing their tattered ten-year-old Wehrmacht uniforms.[42]

The end of World War II marked a new era in escapes. From 1945 to 1950, American intelligence officers in Austria established and used what they called the "Rat Line" to move Russian deserters to South America. This sophisticated American Army intelligence operation resembled the Underground Railway before the Civil War and *Comet* during World War II.[43] At the same time, Jewish organizations in Europe were transporting members of the Surviving Remnant—DPs or Displaced Persons who survived the Holocaust—to Palestine via their own Underground Railroad.[44]

As the 1950s gave way to the 1960s, Germans continued their own escape tradition in Cold War Central Europe. The open border in the divided city of Berlin was the only real window of opportunity until the Soviets closed the borders to the West and the East Germans built the Berlin Wall in 1961. For those people who rejected life in a socialist state, Berlin became more than simply a walled city; it was an enormous prison. Although most East Berliners accepted their fate with an angry resolve, some responded by finding ways to escape. On August 17, 1962, a young man named Peter Fechter attempted to climb the Wall, but he was shot down immediately. He cried, "Help me!" and although the West German border police tried to assist, he died in the hands of the East German border guards. In all, 187 people attempted to escape from East Berlin and the East German border to the Federal Republic and failed, in most cases, at the cost of their lives.

Several success stories balanced the books somewhat. A few escapers constructed ingenious hiding places in automobiles. Four people used cable drums that were simply rolled across the border. Others decided on deception and dressed themselves as Russian officers who crossed the closed border into West Berlin from time to time. East Berlin's great escape, however, took place on the nights of October 3 and 4, 1964, through a tunnel complex meticulously dug under the Berlin Wall. Beginning in an outhouse and ending in the cellar of a bakery, the tunnel was the product of an escape committee formed by thirty-six young people, mostly students, who dug for six months. In all, fifty-seven escapers freed themselves through the tunnel before it was discovered and destroyed by the East German police. One man built a mini-submarine that took him across the Baltic Sea to Denmark in 1968.[45] In 1979, two families, the Strelzyks and the Wetzels, joined forces and built a hot-air balloon that took them from East to West Germany. The Berlin Wall ceased to exist in 1989. For Germans who tried to escape during these sad years, the cost was high. Aside from the deaths, the East German communists arrested more than sixty thousand Germans, as well as eight hundred citizens of other countries. These people were tried, convicted, and imprisoned for attempting to flee or helping others to flee their political captivity in the East.[46] It is no wonder that by 1989, East Germans were bitter against the communist regime.

Throughout World War II in the Pacific, from 1941 to 1945, Allied forces took only 16,500 Japanese military personnel as POWs. Of this number, about 5,500 were Koreans and native Formosans drafted into

After six months' work, fifty-seven East Berliners escaped through the Berlin Tunnel on October 3–4, 1964. This photo shows a five-year-old boy being brought up to his new life in West Berlin. Courtesy of the Haus am Checkpoint Charlie Museum and Archive, Berlin

the Imperial Japanese Army, and neither group had succumbed to the Japanese death ethos inherent in militant Bushido. Unlike the militarized Samurai, neither the Koreans nor the Formosans were prepared to die in service to Japan and the emperor. That so few Japanese soldiers permitted themselves to be taken prisoner translated the death ethos into fact and remains, indeed, one of the most gruesome aspects of the Pacific war. Militant Bushido required absolute obedience and loyalty from all soldiers. Whereas duty to the Allied soldier required active expressions of hope in survival, duty in Japanese terms required a soldier to accept a sacrificial death willingly when all hope was lost. Captivity denied militant Bushido's highest honor to the soldier, and he became lost in shame and indignity.

If the Japanese soldier became a POW, then he was required to do something drastic to regain his honor. The two mass escape attempts from prison camps in Featherston, New Zealand, and Cowra, Australia, were examples of this fanaticism. Not really escape attempts at all, they were active responses to Bushido's requirement that Japanese soldiers express the ultimate outrage against the fundamental condition of captivity. The contradiction here is that the physical act of dying violently represented a form of spiritual rebirth and eternal life. At the Featherston prison camp, 48 Japanese prisoners died in a camp riot. In Cowra, New South Wales, 234 died when more than 1,000 Japanese prisoners rioted and attempted a major breakout. (Both these sites became sacred ground, much as Andersonville and Gettysburg did following the Civil War in the United States. Today, Japanese visitors come regularly to honor the memory of their sacred dead.) In the United States, 5,424 Japanese POWs were kept in five camps and Madrigan General Hospital in Washington, D.C. Spain acted as their protecting power. Of these POWs, twenty-four died in captivity, and—with the exception of three still buried in the Fort Sam Houston National Cemetery, Texas, three at Fort Riley, Kansas, and one at the Presidio in Monterey, California—all the bodies were returned to Japan by 1954. Two prisoners killed themselves, three were shot during an escape attempt at Denver's Fitzsimmons General Hospital, one died in an agricultural accident, and the remainder died from war wounds or natural causes. Only fourteen Japanese POWs attempted escapes, and all were promptly recaptured and returned to their camps.[47]

During the Korean War, the largest prison facilities for North Korean and Chinese POWs were on two islands south of the mainland: Koje and Cheju-do. In the years following World War II, Cold War realities changed American policy radically from requiring forced repatriations of the unwilling to accepting defectors as political refugees. In May and June 1952, communist POW resisters in the camps staged one of the most brutal camp uprisings in POW history. On May 8, 1952, after arming themselves with makeshift weapons, the prisoners seized the American camp commandant, Brig. Gen. Francis Dodd, and held him as ransom for political concessions. Brig. Gen. Charles Colson arrived quickly and negotiated Dodd's release with a wide range of promises to the communists. After Dodd's release on May 11, an outraged Gen. Mark Clark reneged on all the promises, and the prisoners rioted for nearly two months.

Action in Koje escalated dramatically, and Clark, frustrated that nothing worked, ordered several heavily armed combat units into the camp, including the 187th Airborne Regimental Combat Team, who stormed the camp and finally ended hostilities. All told, the Koje uprising cost the POWs seventy-seven lives and 140 wounded or injured. The Americans lost one soldier killed and fourteen wounded. What the Americans learned was that under the protection of the 1949 Geneva Convention, the North Korean and Chinese communist prisoners seized the opportunity not only to resist their captors individually, but also to reject quarantine and continue to develop new organizational structures to conduct mass operations. Were it not for the airborne soldiers' assault, Koje might well have evolved into the largest revolt and breakout in military history. Not far from Koje, in December 1952, civilian internees in Cheju-do rioted and attempted a mass breakout. That action cost eighty-five prisoners killed and more than one hundred wounded.[48] The answer to the resistance and insurrection problems in the South Korean camps came in part by separating communist and noncommunist prisoners upon arrival, and in part by some clever paper-shuffling by the American intelligence community. Beginning in 1952, many defecting communist POWs were killed on paper and reported dead so that armistice negotiations could proceed to their conclusion in Panmunjom.[49] In the end, the Korean war ended: only after a face-saving compromise did the communist side permit the POWs to go home. They allowed their own people who refused to return to stay in South Korea or Taiwan. There was no forced repatriation and no "final" POW stalemate.

During the Vietnam War, especially from 1965 to 1971 when American combat units took prisoners in the field, thousands of Vietcong and North Vietnamese soldiers fell into American hands. If prisoners were captured in uniform, the process was relatively simple and standard: they were sent to one of the island prison camps in South Vietnam to wait out the war in quarantine. North Vietnamese military prisoners were protected by the

1949 Geneva Convention and the 1964 agreement made by the United States and South Vietnam that North Vietnamese POWs were to be treated fairly and humanely, with oversight by the International Red Cross. Mobile surgical units and evacuation hospitals had POW wards, and the American Army made certain that wounded North Vietnamese and Vietcong soldiers received the same medical care as the American soldiers did.[50]

Vietnam, however, was as much a political as a military war, and there was another totally unsupervised prison system in place in the South. The Vietcong viewed itself as a force of national liberators and freedom fighters. Although the National Liberation Front was allied to the communist apparatus in the North, it saw itself as an independent force. The South Vietnamese government considered the Vietcong to be a collection of loosely organized indigenous guerrillas, more akin to the partisans in World War II than to soldiers defined in the 1949 Geneva Convention. As far as the Saigon authorities were concerned, "Charlie" was a criminal and deserved nothing more than treatment as one. Most American soldiers knew better and treated the captured Vietcong as soldiers. They were shocked that the South Vietnamese authorities felt differently. In 1970, for example, the Rules of Engagement in Vietnam required the Americans to turn Vietcong prisoners over to one of the South Vietnamese police forces within forty-eight hours after capture. Few American soldiers or sailors had any idea that their prisoners were heading for something other than POW camps.

What concerned the American intelligence community was neither forced repatriation nor finding refugees, as was the case after World War II and Korea. Hostilities in Vietnam included the not-so-covert mission of destroying the Communist Party. One ingredient in the formula became the *Chieu Hoi* program. The Americans and South Vietnamese invited any member of the party, that is, any level of political cadre, main force, local force, or guerrilla soldier, to change sides.[51] Captured soldiers, especially skilled sappers and other highly trained personnel, were especially welcome and became known as "Hoi Chanh," or ralliers. With no end to the war in sight, thousands of former prisoners, many of whom were willing or unwilling professional soldiers with no other training or skill, knew that a life sentence awaited them as POWs and decided to become refugees. They joined special units like the Kit Carson Scouts, who worked for the American Army directly, or the Province Reconnaissance Units (PRU), which worked for the CIA in the Phoenix program's combat arm. Both were political forces designed to aggressively destroy the South Vietnamese Communist Party.

The PRU, South Vietnamese National Police Field Force, and sometimes the Kit Carson Scouts, when they worked in units, arrested and jailed civilians whom they knew or suspected to be party members without habeas corpus. Under procedures styled after the British counterinsurgency activities in Malaya from 1948 to 1960, the political prisoners were first classified as detainees, then were often jailed in the Provincial Interrogation Centers.[52] If they were uncooperative or overtly resistant, they were frequently sent into squalid conditions such as those found on Con Son Island. This was the brutal and unforgiving side of the Vietnam War, with brutal and unforgiving tactics on both sides.

Political prisoners and communist cadre held by the South Vietnamese, often with the silent consent of the American intelligence personnel and advisors on the scene, received treatment similar to that given to their counterparts in North Vietnam. Neither state enjoyed POW status nor oversight by the International Red Cross, and this situation cast a shadow over American POW activities in South Vietnam. After the North Vietnamese Army's victory in 1975, the surviving detainees were freed from their terrible prisons, and any remaining North Vietnamese soldiers were repatriated. Tragedy enveloped the ralliers, or refugee-escapers, and they became victims of retributive wrath yet again. Often returned to their original combat units, they were executed as deserters. Abandoned by their American protectors in a lost war, they had no place to go and suffered the consequences.[53]

Following the Gulf War in 1991, captured Iraqi soldiers fell into two categories: those who participated in a failed rebellion against Saddam Hussein, and those who actively repressed their country's minorities. With the forced repatriations after World War II, the Korean prison revolts, and the South Vietnamese mistreatment of civilian detainees still in mind, American military authorities conducted rigorous screening of Iraqi POWs to determine which ones were likely to suffer political retribution and imprisonment following repatriation. Many of these prisoners were granted political asylum. Of the 4,600 Iraqi refugees permitted entry into the United States in 1993, 453 were former soldiers who deserted prior to the invasion of Kuwait.[54] Again, escapers were rewarded.

Although military personnel wear uniforms, they do not think uniformly. Reflecting on his captivity and escape from Davao Penal Colony in the Philippines during World War II, Steven Mellnik wrote, "Perhaps those little things are remembered because they are man's unconscious striving to achieve nobility."[55] Nobility may well be an answer for some escapers; survival is more consistent with history. Motivations vary with the actual circumstances, especially those entwined with experiences that generated great fears. In general, however, POWs, internees, and hostages found themselves having to choose from four alternatives: (1) survive the captivity experience by avoiding the captor's close scrutiny and pass the time in quarantine quietly; (2) survive it by actively resisting, even baiting and cajoling the captors to the breaking point; (3) survive by collaborating, even from time to time assimilating into the captor's culture; or (4) survive by escaping.

One thing most escapers agreed on is summed up by Winston Churchill's evaluation of life in captivity, "The whole atmosphere of prison . . . is odious. . . . You feel a constant humiliation in being fenced in by railings and wire, watched by armed men, and webbed about with a tangle of regulations and restrictions."[56] As Churchill pointed out, the captivity experience is fraught with fear, uncertainty, and boredom, each of which has contributed to someone's decision to escape. For other prisoners, guilt played a decisive role. War may have an insatiable appetite for heroics, but, to the prisoner, there is nothing heroic about one's unwilling capture or a surrender. With its emphasis on the negatives in life, guilt seemed to be a subtle, even subliminal, motivating factor, because most POWs suffer varying degrees of guilt for having fallen into the enemy's hands in the first place. If some prisoners determined that they were the cause, they may well have attempted to redeem themselves through escape.

On a more positive note, the military services have consistently created a work ethic based on success and achievement; even discussing captivity, although it is inevitable in war, tends to be humiliating. In 1988, the Australian Defense Force Academy conducted a seminar on POW behavior, an exercise that many student officers regarded as outrageous because it seemed defeatist. Yet the experiences of the past show there is something quite different about escapers, and the traits they exhibited may help to define individual stances to captivity in future wars. A prisoner of war needs self-discipline and determination simply to survive captivity. Brutal treatment may render either a committed escaper passive or a passive prisoner opportunistic. One need not be an obsessive escaper to begin to acquire, as soon as possible, some of the qualities needed for survival after an opportunistic escape—stealth, cunning, evasion, skill at hand-to-hand combat, and field survival. Keeping one's powder dry is not an obsolete notion; neither is the notion that gamblers win wars. A prisoner must be aware of the hazards as well as the positive aspects of small and large group escape attempts and, from the lessons of history, learn appropriate individual responses, from the "see no evil, hear no evil" stance of nonescapers to active individual, small group, or mass participation.[57]

What, then, might be remembered concerning escape after this historical journey? There is some lasting wisdom in Don Quixote's remark, "The fortunes of war are more fickle than any other."[58] Miguel de Saavedra Cervantes (1547–1616) knew what he was talking about. As he returned from the Battle of Lapanto in 1571, he was captured by Barbary pirates and made a slave for nine years. Following many escape attempts, he was ransomed in 1580. Committed escapers may fight windmills from time to time; more often, though, they fight for time, the right time. Airey Neave, a British Colditz escaper, noted in *Saturday at M.I.9* (1969), "My strongest motive was . . . to rid myself of the atmosphere of a POW camp."[59] After his own successful escape from Stalag Luft III in 1943, Eric Williams pointed out in *The Wooden Horse* (1949), "It was strange to be among people who had a purpose in life, who had somewhere to go, who were not just passing the time until the next roll-call or waiting for the soup to arrive."[60]

Although there is no way to predict who will or who will not make a successful escape, sometimes waiting for release or exchange is more prudent than risking escape at the wrong time. Just as important, throughout the history of the escape, many escapers found like-minded individuals in prison communities, even those that were often badly divided. Conversely, escape, both real and imaginary, formed a powerful reason to survive and united many POWs to continue the battle, not against each other but against their captors, especially if and when those captors acted contrary to the principles of common decency and the statutes of international law. For those who dared to flee, their oral, written, and popular media stories contain ten major components which function as distinct events that individuals recall with uncanny accuracy and detail: precapture circumstances, the capture itself, dangerous long marches or transfers, the prison landscape, and the decision to escape. After the commitment was made, they described their plans, the details of the escape itself, adventures along the way, contact with friendly forces, and reflections on or bearing witness to the experience.

In 1891, Ambrose Bierce, remembering his own experiences in the Union Army during the Civil War, observed, "An army in a line-of-battle awaiting attack, or prepared to deliver it, presents . . . precision, formality, fixity, and silence."[61] Sidney Lanier paralleled the experience from the Confederate side. "In a battle, as far as concerns the individual combatants, the laws and observances of civilization are abandoned, and primitive barbarism is king *pro tem*. . . . When the battle is over, to emerge from this temporary barbarism is difficult and requires a little time."[62]

So it has been in all of America's wars: from the colonial conflicts to the hostage crises in the Middle East, captivity remained the front line, where escapers continued the battle. Although the greatest escapes were precise, formal, and fixed acts of defiance in the face of clear and present dangers, there have never been any hard and fast rules, only individuals with confidence, luck, and a powerful motive, who escaped into history and affirmed their right to be free.

Appendix 1
Oral History Formats

Oral History Format for Escapers

DECISION: When and how did you decide to escape? Why? Was there an escape committee? Who ran it and how? Did you see any recaptured escapers killed, tortured, or both? Did you know the risks? Were you following what you understood as a "mandate to escape"? Were you aware of laws or codes for or against escape?

PLANNING: How did you prepare yourself to be on the run? If you planned the escape, how long did it take? How close were the friendly lines? Did you share escape plans with any other prisoner(s)? What were their reactions? Could you count on or receive any outside help after the escape? Were you part of a group? Did you go out by yourself, with someone else (whom?), a small group of three or more, or as part of a large group, eight or more? Were you a tunneler?

ESCAPE: Could you provide details of the actual escape? Who did what, when, where, why, and how? What were the escape route and destination? What kinds of events took place as you traveled in enemy territory?

CONTACT: When did you actually contact friendly forces? What happened? Were you repatriated immediately? Did you go back to your unit? Did you become a guerrilla fighter with indigenous friendly forces?

REFLECTIONS: Have you ever written about your escape? Looking back at the experience, was it worth it? Would you do it again?

Oral History Format for Raiders

BIOGRAPHY: Who you are: hometown; service; unit; year(s) in Vietnam, Korea, or World War II; war zone.

DATES: When did the rescue mission take place? Where?

MISSION: What was your specific job in the rescue mission? In what country did the mission take place? How was the mission planned? By whom? Civilians? Military? Both? How did you and your unit insert? By helicopter? By boat? How many days were you out on the mission? Did you have a guide to the camp? Were you wounded on the mission? How? Were you and/or your unit debriefed after you returned? Who or what organization debriefed you? Were you sworn to secrecy? Did you ever search for your files in the National

Archives or for your reports in military unit histories? Did you find anything?

CONTACT: Did you/your unit find any live American POWs? Dead American POWs? Allied POWs? Did you find any evidence of torture in the camp?

CAMP: What did the camp look like? Can you draw a map? Did you find any shackles or any torture devices? Did you find any evidence of recent departures?

REFLECTIONS: What went right on the mission? What went wrong on the mission? What were your feelings about the mission at the time? Now? In your view, might there be any other significant details?

Appendix 2
Eighteenth and Nineteenth Century Statistics

American Armed Vessels during the American Revolution (1776–1782)

	1776	1777	1778	1779	1780	1781	1782
Continental Ships	31	34	21	20	13	9	7
Number/Guns	586	412	680	462	266	164	198
Average Guns/Ship	19	12	32	23	20	18	28
Privateers	136	73	115	167	228	449	323
Number/Guns	1,360	730	1,150	2,505	3,420	6,735	4,845
Average Guns/Ship	10	10	10	15	15	15	15
Total Ships	167	107	136	187	241	458	330
Total Guns	1,946	1,142	1,830	2,967	3,686	6,899	5,043

Source: Edgar Stanton Maclay, *A History of American Privateers* (New York: Appleton, 1899), viii.

American Civil War Losses (1861–1865)

	Participants	Total Deaths	POWs	Paroled	Died in Captivity
Union	2,203,000	364,000	211,400	16,668	30,218
Confederate	1,000,000	133,821	220,000	Unknown	26,436

Source: William Best Hesseltine, *Civil War Prisons: A Study in Prison Psychology* (Columbus: Ohio State University Press, 1930), 256.

Appendix 3
World War II Allied Escapers and Evaders

By Theater of Operations

	Navy		Army		Air Force		Total	
	Escapers	Evaders	Esc.	Ev.	Esc.	Ev.	Esc.	Ev.
WESTERN EUROPE								
British Officers	10	6	106	36	46	401	162	443
British Troops	13	8	711	344	63	946	787	1,298
Dominion Officers	–	–	13	3	26	291	39	294
Dominion Troops	1	–	109	10	18	328	128	338
American Officers	–	–	37	3	105	1,380	142	1,383
American Troops	–	1	463	7	108	1,312	571	1,319
INDIA, SEAC, BAAG								
British Officers	4	13	14	16	3	34	21	63
British Troops	6	38	21	46	1	19	28	103
Dominion Officers	–	–	–	–	–	–	–	–
Dominion Troops	–	–	1	–	–	–	1	–
American Officers	–	–	1	–	5	10	6	10
American Troops	–	–	–	–	–	23	–	23
SWITZERLAND (Internment)								
British Officers	5	–	184	–	24	17	213	17
British Troops	7	–	2,276	–	17	35	2,300	35
Dominion Officers	–	–	40	–	20	1	60	1
Dominion Troops	–	–	1,392	–	15	11	1,407	11
American Officers	–	–	–	2	–	95	12	97
American Troops	–	–	–	12	12	106	12	106
MEDITERRANEAN WEST								
British Officers	12	–	393	–	36	15	441	15
British Troops	119	–	6,355	–	109	86	6,583	86
Dominion Officers	–	–	97	5	4	20	101	23

	Navy		Army		Air Force		Total	
	Escapers	Evaders	Esc.	Ev.	Esc.	Ev.	Esc.	Ev.
Dominion Troops	–	–	3,221	1	1	9	3,222	10
American Officers	–	–	31	–	103	1,039	134	1,039
American Troops	–	–	786	12	142	1,363	918	1,375
MEDITERRANEAN EAST								
British Officers	1	1	38	47	8	46	4	94
British Troops	3	17	163	121	23	130	189	268
Dominion Officers	–	–	16	36	2	16	18	52
Dominion Troops	–	–	351	982	8	12	359	994
American Officers	–	–	–	10	6	137	6	147
American Troops	–	–	–	–	11	187	11	187
Total American Officers							300	2,676
Total American Troops							1,512	3,010

Summary by Areas

	British	American
Western Europe (includes 70 Allied personnel, India, and SEAC)	3,631	3,415
	3,346	39
Switzerland	4,916	227
Mediterranean West	11,910	3,466
Mediterranean East (includes 2,089 Greeks rescued by IS 9 [M.E.] under special charter)	4,546	—
Totals	28,349	7,147

Summary by Services

	Officers	ORs	Total
Navy	53	212	265
Army	1,178	21,900	23,078
Air Force	1,016	1,831	2,847
Total			26,190

Summary by Nationalities

British	13,193
Dominion	7,058
Colonials	1,012

Summary by Nationalities *(continued)*

Indians	4,927
Allies*	2,159
Americans	7,147

*Greeks, Poles, French, Dutch, Czechs, Russians. Source: WO 208/3242, 65, quoted in M.R.D. Foot and J. M. Langley, "Return of Escapers and Evaders to 30 June 1945," in *MI 9: Escape and Evasion, 1939–1945* (Boston: Little, Brown, 1980), np.

Australian POWs in World War II

	RAN	AMF	RAAF	Total All Services
Europe/Germany	26	8,578	529	9,113
Japan	237	13,865	417	14,519
Totals	263	22,443	946	23,632

Source: *Australian Year Book 37, 1946–47*, and Gavin Long, ed., *Australia in the War of 1939–45* (Canberra, 1952), 77, cited in Jeffrey Grey, *A Military History of Australia* (Cambridge, UK: Cambridge University Press, 1990), 188.

Appendix 4
American Escapers in South Vietnam

According to American military records at the Pentagon, Marine Pvts. Joseph S. North, Jr., and Walker D. Hamilton were captured on October 18, 1965, and escaped in partnership eleven days later. Air Force St. Sgt. Jasper Page was captured on October 31, 1965, and escaped two days later. Army Pvt. Bruce A. Graening fell into enemy hands on March 9, 1967, and left after eighteen days. Army Sp. 4c Donald R. Braswell was captured on August 23, 1967, and escaped one day later. Army Pvt. Roger D. Anderson was taken on January 3, 1968, and escaped after nine days' captivity. During Tet's intense fighting, the Vietcong took Army Sgts. Edward C. Dierling and Robert W. Hayhurst prisoner on February 3, 1968. Their partnership resulted in an escape on February 23, 1968. Marine Cpl. William P. Taliaferro was captured on February 6 and escaped on February 13, 1968. Army Sp. 4c Thomas H. Van Putten was captured on February 10, 1968, and escaped on April 17, 1969, after a little more than a year in captivity. Army Sp. 5c Donald E. Martin was captured on March 2, 1968, and escaped on April 15, and Sp. 5c William B. Taylor's captivity lasted slightly more than a month, from March 20 until May 6, 1968. Marine Sgt. Albert S. Potter was captured with Frank C. Iodice on May 30, 1968; they escaped one day later. Marine Maj. Richard F. Risner lasted two days in captivity, from August 20–22, 1968. Army Sgt. Kenneth R. Gregory was captured on August 25, 1968, and spent nearly a year in captivity until he escaped on May 30, 1969. Army Sp. 4c Jerry L. Guffey, perhaps a committed natural escaper, was captured on March 4, 1969, and remained in enemy hands only one day.

Notes

Preface

1. Downey, "Eel-Eating Pilgrims," *Washington Post,* 22 November 1987; Ridpath, *History of the United States of America,* 775.

Introduction

1. Toffler and Toffler, "War, Wealth, and a New Era in History," 49.
2. Perplexed with questions about war and the laws of war when the Cold War reached one of its many zeniths, the noted jurist Quincy Wright suggested that events can hardly be described without a theory that determines what is important and what should be looked for. See Wright, "Outlawry of War," 368.
3. Foot and Langley, *MI-9: Escape and Evasion,* 329.
4. Hesseltine, *Civil War Prisons,* 259–82. See also Cole, *Civil War Eyewitnesses* and Byrne, "Prisons and Prisoners of War," in Nevins, Robertson, and Wiley, *Civil War Books: A Critical Bibliography,* 185–206. For more modern histories of Civil War escapes, see Shuster, *Great Civil War Escapes* and Denney, *Civil War Prisons and Escapes.*
5. This is by no means a comprehensive list from World War I or World War II. The postwar decades became very productive for former British/Commonwealth POWs in general and escapers in particular. From a long list of World War I titles, three examples: in England, *The Gold Stripe* published Merry's "My Escape from a German Prison" (1918); in Canada, McMullen and Evans published *Out of the Jaws of Hunland* (1918); and ten years later in Australia, White published *Guests of the Unspeakable.* For World War II examples, see Thomas, *Dare to Be Free* (1951); Rolfe, *Against the Wind* (1956); Pryce, *Heels in Line* (1958); and Deane-Drummond, *Return Ticket* (1953), to cite just a few of many. For a comprehensive history of the Canadian POW experience, see Vance, *Objects of Concern: Canadian Prisoners of War* (1994).
6. Personal correspondence from the Defense Intelligence Agency in response to FOIA requests and further correspondence with government research personnel on the subject.
7. H. C. Bates, "Escape," in Brickhill, *Escape or Die,* 15. See also Evans, *Escape and Liberation.* Evans served on the staff of MI-9, known as I. S. (Intelligence School) 9(d).

8. Neave, *They Have Their Exits,* 13.

9. Barker, *Behind Barbed Wire,* 147.

10. Garrett, *Jailbreakers,* 11.

11. Fellowes-Gordon, *The World's Greatest Escapes,* 10.

12. Peckham, *The Toll of Independence,* 132. See also Boudinot, *Journal of Historical Recollections,* 97, for a correlation between the thirteen colonies and the numbers of soldiers they contributed.

Chapter 1   The Dominance of Will:
Rejecting the Condition of Captivity

1. Lee, "Prisoners of War," 348.

2. Ibid., 349.

3. *Article of War* XIII of Richard II, 1385, cited in Prugh, "Prisoners at War," 123.

4. Lee, "Prisoners of War," 349.

5. Whewell, *Grotius on the Rights of War and Peace,* 354.

6. Ibid., 390.

7. Ibid., 354.

8. Clausewitz disdained moderation in war. He commented, "War is an act of force to compel our enemy to do our will. . . . To introduce the principle of moderation into the theory of war itself would always lead to logical absurdity," quoted in Howard, "Temporamenta Belli: Can War Be Controlled?" in *Restraints on War,* 1. See also Clausewitz, *On War.*

9. Flory, *Prisoners of War,* 147, 149.

10. Gray, *The Warriors,* 137.

11. Ackerley, *Escapers All,* 16.

12. Durand, *Stalag Luft III: The Secret Story,* 282. See also Vance, "The War Behind the Wire," 675–93.

13. Walzer, "Prisoners of War," 785.

14. Pape, *Boldness Be My Friend,* 91.

15. Gray, *The Warriors,* 27–8, characterizes *homo furens* as the fighting man who subordinates the peaceful aspects of his personality in combat and represses civilian habits of mind, especially when he closes with the enemy. Such madness as happens in combat cannot surface readily in the POW environment. It remains forcibly repressed in a prison camp but often drives the will to resist and escape.

16. Huizinga, *Homo Ludens,* 90.

17. Rudyard Kipling, "Half-Ballade of Waterval," in Rutherford, *Rudyard Kipling,* 194; Douglas Bader, quoted in Pape, *Boldness Be My Friend,* 91.

18. Romilly and Alexander, *The Privileged Nightmare,* 86–7.

19. Ibid., 87.

20. Aidan Crawley, quoted by Walzer, "Prisoners of War," 785. See also Crawley, *Escape from Germany* (1956).

21. H. E. Bates, Introduction in Brickhill, *Escape or Die,* 7.

22. Wilkinson, *American Tough,* 5.

23. See Slotkin, *Regeneration Through Violence;* Drinnon, *Facing West;*

and Doyle, *Voices from Captivity,* for different interpretations of the frontier dichotomy.

24. This analysis is an adaptation of anthropologist Robert Redfield's work with tribal communities. See Redfield, *The Little Community,* 4.

25. See Gray, *The Warriors,* 42. Other studies directly concerned with primary military units are Henderson, *Cohesion* (1985); Janowitz, *The Professional Soldier* (1960); and Mills, *American Military Thought* (1966).

26. Solzhenitsyn, *The Gulag Archipelago Three,* 126. For a critical essay about Solzhenitsyn and his relationship to American foreign policy, see Schlesinger, "The Solzhenitsyn Challenge," in *The Cycles of American History,* 111–17.

27. See Lord, "The Medal of Honor," 65, 67; McConnell, *The Story of Lance Sijan;* and Doyle, *Voices from Captivity,* 225. See also U.S. Senate Committee on Veterans Affairs, *Medal of Honor Recipients,* 922, for Sijan's full citation. Col. George E. Day, USAF, also received the Medal of Honor for escape attempts and resistance; his citation appears in the same source (826).

28. See Des Pres, *The Survivor,* 149–77.

29. Churchill, *My Early Life,* 259.

30. Garrett, *POW,* 90.

31. Barker, *Prisoners of War,* 79.

32. See Vischer, *Barbed Wire Disease* (1919). This short work is the first study dedicated to this prison camp phenomenon. Many more inquiries into it were published in medical and behavioral science journals.

33. Whewell, *Grotius on the Rights of War and Peace,* 390.

34. See Doyle, *Voices from Captivity,* 81–8, for an analysis of each stage of captivity.

35. de Tocqueville, *Democracy in America,* 14.

36. Personal interview with Henry Burman, Stalag Luft III, 1943–1945. See Vance, "The War behind the Wire," 690, and Vance, "The Politics of Camp Life," 109–26, for other POW commentary concerning fundamental motivations to escape quarantine captivity in Germany during World War II.

Chapter 2   Pioneers, Volunteers, and Privateers: Escape in the Wars of Musket and Sail

1. Van der Beets, *The Indian Captivity Narrative,* x.

2. For a chronology of the Indian Wars, see Billington, *The Westward Movement in the United States,* 16–78. See also Bischoff, "Der Western als amerikanischer Gründungsmythos," 3–29, for a critical overview of the captivity experience and its related narrative expression in western novels and stories as European immigrants and eastern settlers pioneered the West.

3. Baker, *True Stories of New England Captives,* 41, 44.

4. Keegan, "If You Won't, We Won't," 11.

5. Strong, "Captive Images," 51–6. See also Stockel, *Chiricahua Apaches in Captivity* for an account of the Apaches' illnesses and death in federal captivity beginning in 1886.

6. Coleman, *New England Captives,* 2, 276–7.

7. Cotton Mather, *Decennium Luctuosum* (1699), reprinted in Vaughan and Clark, *Puritans among the Indians*, 139. See also Derounian, "Puritan Orthodoxy and the 'Survivor's Syndrome,'" 82–93.

8. White, *Indian Battles*, 193.

9. Cotton Mather, "A Notable Exploit; wherein Dux Faemina Facti" reprinted in Lincoln, *Narratives of the Indian Wars 1675–1699*, 264. Cotton Mather published the Dustan story, "Narrative of a Notable Deliverance from Captivity," three times: As an Appendix to *Humiliations Followed with Deliverances* (1697); as "A Notable Exploit; wherein Dux Faemina Facti" in *Decennium Luctuosum* (1699); and again in *Magnalia Christi Americana* (1702). See Vaughn and Clark, *Puritans among the Indians*, 161–4. See also Caverly, *Heroism of Hannah Dustan*.

10. Baker, *True Stories*, 148.

11. White, *Indian Battles*, 191.

12. John Smith, *General History of Virginia* Book III (1624), quoted in Bischoff, "Der Western als amerikanischer Gründungsmythos," 4. For an example of a traditional British romance captivity-escape tradition, see Moreland, *Humors of History*, for the legend of Gilbert Beckett who was taken captive by the Saracens and while in prison won the affections of his jailer's daughter.

13. Washington, *The Journal of Major George Washington*, 8.

14. LeRoy and Leininger, "Narrative," 113, and subsequent quotes, 115–16.

15. See Smith, *Historical Account of Bouquet's Expedition;* Muhlenberg, "Regina, the German Captive," 82–92, and Winterburn, *History of the Great Trail*, 270–3. For a large collection of 311 Indian captivity narratives in 111 volumes, see Washburn, *The Garland Library of Narratives*.

16. See Billington, and Ridge, *Westward Expansion*, 147–9.

17. See Quaife, "A Journal of an Indian Captivity during Pontiac's Rebellion," 65–81.

18. Knight, "The Narrative of the Perils and Sufferings of Doctor Knight and John Slover," reprinted in Brackenridge, *Indian Atrocities*, 9. For a reprint of Slover's part of the escape, see Dorson, *American Rebels*, 298–300.

19. Knight, "Narrative," quoted in Brackenridge, *Indian Atrocities*, 13.

20. Ibid., 22–4.

21. Ibid., 25. See also Seaver, *A Narrative of the Life of Mrs. Mary Jemison*, 96–100, for Mary Jemison's version of the Crawford execution. Jemison noted in her narrative that she hated to witness these ritual tortures and rarely attended.

22. Ibid., 26–30. Dorson notes that Philip Freneau, the "Poet of the Revolution," first published "The Narrative of the Perils and Sufferings of Doctor Knight and John Slover" in the *Freeman's Journal* on April 30, May 7, May 14, and May 23, 1783, before it appeared as a pamphlet in the same year (p. 287). Another small edition was reprinted in Nashville in 1843 and again in 1867 for popular consumption in Brackenridge, *Indian Atrocities*, 9–30.

23. See also Seaver, *Mary Jemison*, 93–8; Sherrard, *A Narrative of the Wonderful Escape and Dreadful Sufferings of Colonel James Paul;* Brown, "'Crawford's Defeat,'" 311–27; and Butterfield, *An Account of the Expedition against Sandusky*, for further discussions concerning this expedition and Colonel Crawford's execution.

24. Pratt, *Preble's Boys*, 11; Maclay, *A History of American Privateers*, vii. See also Dorson, *America Rebels*, 167–70, and Andrews, *Concise Dictionary of American History*, 767–8, for a short description of naval and privateer operations during the Revolution. For John Paul Jones's concern about taking and exchanging prisoners, see Prelinger, "Benjamin Franklin and the American Prisoners of War," 272. Jones brought in two hundred British prisoners after defeating the *Drake* in 1778.

25. Cohen, "The Preachers and the Prisoners," 1.

26. Sherburne, *Memoirs of Andrew Sherburne*, 81.

27. Major published escape narrative memoirs of the Revolution include Greene, *Recollections of the Jersey Prison Ship*; Herbert, *A Relic of the Revolution: Voices from Captivity*, 42; Fooks, *Prisoners of War*, 272. For a strongly propagandistic version of life aboard the British prison ships in Wallabout Bay, see *Martyrs to the Revolution in British Prison-Ships* (1855).

28. Fooks, *Prisoners of War*, 272.

29. Garrett, *POW*, 35.

30. For a partial list of Continental Army officer prisoners exchanged through Elias Boudinot, Thomas Franklin, and John Adams, see Saffell, "British Prisons and American Prisoners," in *Records of the Revolutionary War*, 298–323. See also Bowman, *Captive Americans*, 42, for a description and full list of the British Navy's hulks in New York. For a tertiary study, see also Campbell, *The Intolerable Hulks*, for an examination of the social history of civilian British prison ships in England.

31. Garrett, *POW*, 42.

32. "Obituary: In Wolfborough, N. H. 18th of April last. Mr. Samuel Nowell, Aged 86," 1. The privateer officer Nathaniel Fanning also planned to take over the ship transporting him and other captured officers to England. His attempt failed. See an excerpt from Fanning's *Memoirs of the Life of Captain Nathaniel Fanning* (1808) in Dorson, *America Rebels*, 176.

33. Anderson, "American Escapes from British Naval Prisons," 239. Anderson quotes a communication from the Sick and Hurt Commissioners dated June 2, 1779, and concludes that Americans were relatively well treated in British prisons because they received monetary support from American representatives like John Thornton, as well as assistance in their escapes from dissenting Englishmen. Thornton's Memorandum to American Commissioners, January 5–7, 1778, is located in the *Arthur Lee Papers*, IV, II, Harvard University Library, Cambridge, Mass, cited by Prelinger, "Benjamin Franklin and the American Prisoners of War in England," 266–9. See also Anderson, "The Establishment of British Supremacy at Sea," 77–89, and "The Treatment of Prisoners of War in Britain," 63–83, and Cohen, "The Preachers and the Prisoners," 10.

34. Winslow, *Wealth and Honour*, 38. See also Colburn, "A List of the Americans Committed to Old Mill Prison," 74–5; 136–41; 209–13.

35. Abell, *Prisoners of War in Britain 1756 to 1815*, 224–7. See also Barney, *A Biographical Memoir of Commodore Joshua Barney* and Cranwell and Crane, "Joshua Barney Sails," in *Men of Marque*, 62–74.

36. Neeser, *Letters and Papers Relating to the Cruises of Gustavus Conyngham*, xix. See also Doyle, *Voices from Captivity*, 214–15. For the complicated

Franklin connection to American privateer POWs in England, see Prelinger, "Benjamin Franklin and the American Prisoners of War in England," 261–94.

37. See Cohen, "The Preachers and the Prisoners," 5–10.

38. Anderson, "American Escapes from British Naval Prisons," 238. See also Alexander, "Forton Prison during the Revolution," 369.

39. Alexander, "Forton Prison," 382–3. See also Alexander, "American Privateersmen in the Mill Prison, 1777–1782, 318–40.

40. Livesey, *Charles Herbert: A Relic of the Revolution,* 258, quoted in Anderson, "American Escapes," 238.

41. Anderson, "American Escapes," 239–40.

42. Moyne, "The Reverend William Hazlitt," 297.

43. Pratt, *Preble's Boys,* 200–1. According to Shepard, *Bound for Battle,* 18, from 1803 to 1812, the British Navy impressed about four thousand American sailors. See also Ferrell, *American Diplomacy,* 10–13, and Fredriksen, *Free Trade and Sailors' Rights.* Post-1814 naval activities engaged the American Navy against pirates in the Caribbean and the Mediterranean seas and supported American commercial activities worldwide.

44. *Historical Collections of the Michigan Pioneer and Historical Society,* vol. 15 (Lansing, 1880), 106–7, quoted in Ridge and Billington, *America's Frontier Story,* 268. See also Utley and Washburn, *Indian Wars,* 123.

45. Josephy, "Tecumseh," in Frazier, *Underside of American History,* 155.

46. Tecumseh died in battle at Thamesville; his body was never recovered. See Josephy, "Tecumseh," 157–9, for a description of the battle.

47. For a dated but interesting salutary treatment of the naval war, see Roosevelt, *The Naval War of 1812.* For a listing of American interventions, small wars from 1798 to 1945, see Rusk, "Instances of the Use of United States Armed Forces Abroad, 1798–1945," Hearing before the Committee of Foreign Relations and Armed Services, 87th Cong., 2d Sess., September 17, 1962, quoted in Jacobs and Landau, with Pell, *To Serve the Devil,* 338–55.

48. Dye, "American Maritime Prisoners of War, 1812–1813," in Runyan, *Ships, Seafaring and Society,* 293. See also Brannon, *Official Letters of the Military and Naval Officers of the United States* and Coggeshall, *History of American Privateers.*

49. Abell, *Prisoners of War in Britain,* 248–9.

50. Ibid., 237–9.

51. Ibid., 94.

52. Dye, *American Maritime Prisoners,* 319.

53. Hawthorne, *Yarn of a Yankee Privateer,* 242–52.

54. *The Negro Soldier,* 68–9. See Fabel's two articles concerning Crafus: "Self-Help in Dartmoor," 165–90 and "King Dick—Captive Black Leader," 58–61. See also "The Government of Dartmoor Prison," Portsmouth (N. H.) *Journal of Literature and Politics,* 2, for commentary concerning Crafus's leadership style.

55. Cobb, *Greenhorn's First Cruise,* 2, 224.

56. Ibid., 2, 225. See also Hawthorne, *Yarn of a Yankee Privateer,* 241–8, for other Dartmoor escape attempts.

57. Wildwood, *Thrilling Adventures,* 234–5.

58. Fletcher, *Preble's Boys,* 393–7. Fletcher makes the point that increasing military prowess maneuvered the Americans into a substantially stronger negotiating position at Ghent.

59. Shepard, *Bound for Battle,* 197. Porter captured ten armed British whalers and took 343 prisoners before being caught off Valparaíso, Chile, and destroyed by the British frigate *Phoebe* on March 28, 1814.

60. Abell, *Prisoners of War in Britain,* 255. See also Andrews, *The Prisoners' Memoirs, or, Dartmoor Prison;* Selman, "Extracts from the Journal of a Marblehead Privateersman," in Roads, *The Marblehead Manual,* 28–96; and Fowler, *Jack Tars and Commodores,* for other accounts of the American experience in Dartmoor.

Chapter 3   Soldiers of Manifest Destiny:
Escapes South of the Border

1. Haring, *The Spanish Empire in America,* 7. For an overview of the Texas issue and American responses, see Ridge and Billington, *America's Frontier Story,* 414–38.

2. *America's Historylands,* 386. See also Strack, "Texas History in Selected Works of Elmer Kelton," 23–4, and Williams, "A Critical Study of the Siege of the Alamo," 22–4.

3. R. M. Potter, "Hymn of the Alamo," in Colonial Dames of America, *American War Songs,* 58–9.

4. Fehrenbach, *Lone Star: A History of Texas,* 226; McCaffrey, *Army of Manifest Destiny,* 4; and Creel, *Sam Houston,* 145–56. See also Kelton, *Massacre at Goliad,* for a fictional treatment of the Goliad shootings.

5. J. M. Parmenter, "Texas Hymn" (1838), in Linenthal, *Sacred Ground: Americans and Their Battlefields,* 71. See also Nackman, *A Nation within a Nation,* 92.

6. Sam Houston in a letter to G. G. Burnet, president of the Republic of Texas, quoted in Ridge and Billington, *America's Frontier Story,* 436. See also Creel, *Sam Houston,* 172–84.

7. McCaffrey, *Army of Manifest Destiny,* 4.

8. Haynes, Preface, *Soldiers of Misfortune,* 4. Haynes cites Kendall, *Narrative of the Texan Santa Fe Expedition,* and Loomis, *The Texan-Santa Fe Pioneers.* See Andrews, *Concise Dictionary of American History,* 937; Bell, *A Narrative of the Capture and Subsequent Sufferings of the Mier Prisoners;* and Green, *Journal of the Texian Expedition against Mier.*

9. Haynes, *Soldiers of Misfortune,* 12.

10. Ibid., 19.

11. In the Preface to *Soldiers of Misfortune* (1990), Haynes suggests that the affair erupted as one of the most bitter incidents to occur during the short life of the Republic of Texas.

12. See Haynes, 106–8.

13. Ibid., 113.

14. McCutchan, *Mier Expedition Diary,* 192. See Day, *Black Beans and Goose Quill* and "Diary of James A. Glassock, Mier Man," 225–38. See also Zuber, "The Number of 'Decimated Mier Prisoners,'" 165–8. For a description of Peroté castle, see McGrath and Hawkins, "Peroté Fort—Where Texans Were Imprisoned," 340–5.

15. See Coulter and Barclay, *Volunteers: The Mexican War Journals,* 113. See also Walker, *Samuel Walker's Account of the Mier Expedition.*

16. McCutchan, *Mier Expedition Diary,* 119.

17. Ibid., 119.

18. See *The United States Magazine and Democratic Review,* 5–6, 9–10.

19. Andrews, *Concise Dictionary of American History,* 940–1.

20. *Encarnacion Prisoners Written by a Prisoner,* 37.

21. Smith and Judah, *Chronicles of the Gringos,* 270. See Oswandel, *Notes of the Mexican War* and *The Mexican War,* for contrasting treatments of events during the Mexican War.

22. Smith and Judah, *Chronicles of the Gringos,* 270.

23. Morris, *Encyclopedia of American History,* 208; Cunliffe, *Soldiers and Civilians,* 351. Military and naval costs exceeded $97,500,000.

24. Burr plotted an invasion of Mexico, but it was discovered. Subsequently, he surrendered himself to the acting governor of Louisiana on January 17, 1807. After he attempted an escape, Burr was sent to Richmond, Virginia, where he was tried for treason but was released for lack of evidence. See Thomas Jefferson, "Message on the Burr Conspiracy, January 22, 1807," quoted in Commager and Cantor, *Documents of American History,* 1, 195–7.

25. See Pratt, *Preble's Boys,* 377–80, for a discussion of Jean Lafitte and his brother Pierre, whose privateer activities in the Gulf of Mexico targeted Spanish rather than American ships from 1804 to 1814. The organization used the swampy area of Barrataria as a base and sold their plunder to the people of neighboring New Orleans, who always appreciated a bargain. Upon the recommendation of the Louisiana Legislature, President James Madison pardoned Jean Lafitte and his men of all crimes on February 6, 1815; however, Lafitte moved operations to Mexican Galveston and continued raiding until 1825, when he died in a brawl in Yucatan (p. 389). See Madison's pardon in Richardson, *A Compilation of the Messages and Papers of the Presidents, 1789–1897,* 1, 558–60.

26. Brown, *Agents of Manifest Destiny,* 67–88, quoted in McPherson, *Battle Cry of Freedom,* 106–7, 113–15. See also Schlesinger, *The Cycles of American History,* 152, for a description of the end of filibustering in Central and South America in the 1850s.

Chapter 4 Escape from *Durante Vita:* Breaking the Chains the Masters Made

1. Campbell, *The Intolerable Hulks,* 15, 62.

2. Bergman and Bergman, *Chronological History,* 2.

3. Ibid., 1.

4. See Tannenbaum, *Slave and Citizen,* 14–17. See also Parry, *The Establishment of the European Hegemony,* 149–61.

5. Tannenbaum, *Slave and Citizen,* 35.

6. Bergman and Bergman, *Chronological History,* 8.

7. Jacobs and Landau with Pell, *To Serve the Devil,* 89.

8. Tannenbaum, *Slave and Citizen,* 67.

9. "Virginia Slave Laws," in *Annals of America,* 1, 225.

10. See Francis Daniel Pastorius, "Resolution of the Germantown Mennonites, February 18, 1688," in Commager and Cantor, *Documents of American History,* 1, 37–8.

11. See Woodward, *The Negro in the Military Service.*

12. Davis, *The American Negro Reference Book,* 596. See also Carney, "Haiti: 'Treading on Loaded Barrels of Gunpowder,'" 34–6, for an abbreviated survey of Haiti's political difficulties with outside powers, including Spain, Britain, France, and the United States.

13. The bibliography on slavery as an institution in the American experience is vast. For an international perspective, see Miller, *Slavery and Slaving in World History,* for a solid literature review.

14. Bergman and Bergman, *Chronological History,* 16.

15. Blassingame, *The Underground Railroad,* 220.

16. Quote on a statue of W.E.B. Dubois (1868–1963) standing outside the Gallery of Fine Arts at Fisk University.

17. See McDougall, *Fugitive Slaves,* 54.

18. Blassingame, *Underground Railroad,* 395.

19. Ibid., 189.

20. Ibid., 303.

21. Douglass, *My Bondage and My Freedom,* 429–30.

22. Douglass, *Narrative of the Life of Frederick Douglass,* 112.

23. See Osofsky, *Puttin' On Massa,* 408–9, for a bibliographic essay that lists the most significant antebellum slave narratives that address escape as a major theme.

24. See Cade, "Out of the Mouths of Ex-Slaves," 322.

25. James W. C. Pennington, reprinted in Bayliss, *Black Slave Narratives,* 212.

26. Henry "Box" Brown, reprinted in Bayliss, *Black Slave Narratives,* 195–6.

27. Osofsky, *Puttin' On Massa,* 9. John Henry Falk recorded oral narratives of ex-slaves for the Works Projects Administration (WPA). See the Federal Writers' Project, *Slave Narratives: A Folk History of Slavery in the United States,* a collection of oral histories of slaves who lived in all slaveholding states. See also Cade, "Out of the Mouths of Ex-Slaves," 294–337. Black and white newspapers played a vital role in this regard as well. For comments concerning the important work of the *Liberator,* the New York *Anglo-American,* the *National Anti-Slavery Standard,* the *Christian Recorder,* the *Pacific Appeal,* *L'Union* and *Tribune* [*La Tribune de la Nouvelle Orléans*] in New Orleans, and the *Colored Citizen* published in Cincinnati, see McPherson, *The Negro's Civil War,* 345–7.

28. Douglass, *Narrative,* 111.

29. Blassingame, *Underground Railroad,* 395.

30. Ibid., 416.

31. Ibid., 426.

32. Chapman, *Steal Away,* 113.

33. Ibid., 84.

34. A local legend believed to be true in Bellefonte, Pennsylvania. Manchester, "POW Rally Proved Rich in Drama."

35. Douglass, quoted in Blockson, *Slave Testimony,* 110–11.

36. Butterfield, "Search for a Black Past," 101. See also Franklin, "Rebels, Runaways and Heroes," 92, 108, 110, 112–14, 116–20.

37. Butterfield, "Search for a Black Past," 101.

38. Douglass, quoted in Bergman, *Chronological History,* 225.

39. See "Report of General Butler to the Secretary of War, July 30, 1861," and "Frémont's Proclamation on Slaves, August 30, 1861," reprinted in Commager and Cantor, *Documents of American History,* 1, 396–8.

40. Davis, *The American Negro Reference Book,* 602.

41. McPherson, *The Negro's Civil War,* 213.

42. *Official Record,* ser. 3, vol. III, 1115, cited in ibid., 181.

43. Basler, *The Collected Works of Abraham Lincoln,* 6, 408–10, cited in ibid, 192.

44. Davis, *The American Negro Reference Book,* 607.

45. Ibid., 613. McPherson's numbers are higher in *The Negro's Civil War* (1965). From official records cited in Aptheker, "Negro Casualties in the Civil War," 12, 47–8, he commented that 178,985 enlisted men and 7,122 officers served in USCT regiments, nearly 10 percent of the Union Army. Losses totaled more than 37,300 (p. 237). Enlistment of USCT troops ended on June 1, 1865. See Davis, *The American Negro Reference Book,* for a review of African-American military activities from the colonial era to President Harry S Truman's order in 1951 to integrate the American military services fully during the Korean War. An early work on USCTs is Williams, *A History of the Negro Troops in the War of the Rebellion;* a modern study is Cornish, *The Sable Arm: Black Troops in the Union Army.* See also McPherson, *The Negro's Civil War,* 161–239. From 1987 to the present, considerable attention has been paid to the role of the postwar 8th and 9th Cavalry and the 24th and 25th Infantry Regiments, known generally as the "Buffalo Soldiers," and their roles in America's final wars against the Indian tribes in Texas and the Southwest. See Leckie, *The Buffalo Soldiers* and Carroll, *The Black Military Experience in the American West.*

46. See Cimprich and Mainfort, "Fort Pillow Revisited," 293–306, and Castel, "The Fort Pillow Massacre," 37–50.

47. *The Liberator* (22 October 1852), quoted in Osofsky, *Puttin' On Massa,* 29.

Chapter 5   Acts of Pure Cussedness: Escapes in the Civil War

1. During the Civil War 1.5 percent, or 3,171 Union POWs, escaped from Confederate prison facilities. Very few Confederate POWs, approximately 1,100, escaped from Union camps (see Appendix 2B: *American Civil War Statistics*). See U.S. House, *Report 45,* 40th Cong., 3d sess., 229, 737–70, cited in Flory, *Prisoners of War,* 147. For a sample of the postwar accusations coming from Confederate side, see Stephens's remarks in "The Treatment of Prisoners During the War Between the States," 123. Suffice it to say that both sides mistreated its prisoners.

2. Colonial Dames, *American War Songs*, 85–6.

3. Ibid., 134–5.

4. See Gragg, *The Illustrated Confederate Reader*, 211–15.

5. Duke, *History of Morgan's Cavalry*, 468. For an even more salutary account, see Hockersmith, *Morgan's Escape*.

6. See Ramage, "John Hunt Morgan's Escape," 22, and Hines, "Morgan and His Men Escape from Prison," quoted in Stern, *Secret Missions of the Civil War*, 165. Before capture, Hines served with Morgan as a trusted Confederate secret agent.

7. See Johnson, *The Partisan Rangers*, 365, 382, quoted in Rosenberg, "*For the Sake of My Country*," 14; Ramage, *Rebel Raider;* and *Confederate Veteran*, 413–14.

8. Ramage, "John Hunt Morgan's Escape," 28.

9. Benson, *Berry Benson's Civil War Book*, 86–7.

10. Ibid., 87. For Civil War spy stories set in fiction, see Bierce, "Parker Adderson, Philosopher" and "The Story of a Conscience," in his short-story collection, *In the Midst of Life: Tales of Soldiers and Civilians*, 77–82; 92–8.

11. According to the *Official Records of the War of the Rebellion*, ser. II, 8, 557 (see also 700, 705, 991–1002), from July 1863 until it closed in June 1865, Point Lookout held 52,264 Confederate prisoners, of whom only 50 (.09%) escaped. According to Beitzell, *Point Lookout Prison Camp*, 191, these figures are too low.

12. Older works on Elmira include Holmes, *The Elmira Prison Camp*, and King, *My Experience in the Confederate Army*. Materials on the camp are held by the Chemung County Historical Society, Elmira, New York. See Jaker's WSKG-TV documentary, *Hellmira*, for a balanced, less partisan discussion.

13. Garrett, *POW: The Uncivil Face of War*, 87; Doyle, *Voices from Captivity*, 217.

14. Berry Benson (b. February 9, 1843) died at the age of 80 in 1923. See Herman Hattaway, foreword, in Benson, *Berry Benson's Civil War Book*, x–xii.

15. Beitzell, *Point Lookout Prison Camp*, 195.

16. The manuscript version of the captivity of Sgt. James S. Wells, Company A, South Carolina Volunteers is part of the Confederate collections in the Archives Division of the South Caroliniana Library, University of South Carolina, Columbia, South Carolina. For a published version, see Wells, "Prison Experience," 324–9, 393–8, 487–91.

17. Luther B. Lake, quoted in ibid., 95–6.

18. Ibid., 96. See also *Confederate Veteran*, 6, and Reid, "Escaped from Fort Delaware," 271–9.

19. His captivity memoir, *The Adventures of a Prisoner of War and Life and Scenes in Federal Prisons: Johnson's Island, Fort Delaware, and Point Lookout by an Escaped Prisoner of Hood's Texas Brigade* (1865) was published in Houston, Texas, and is one of the few such accounts published on either side before the end of the conflict. See Shuffler, *Decimus et Ultimus Barziza*, ix.

20. Charles Leavelle, introduction to Dyess, *The Dyess Story*, 13–14. John Dyess's grandson, William E. Dyess, escaped from the Philippines during World War II and wrote the first narrative account of the Bataan March, a book that

enraged the American public in 1944. In this unusual case, escape ran in the family, albeit in two different wars in two succeeding centuries.

21. "Escape of Prisoners from Johnson's Island," 428–9.

22. Ibid., 430–1.

23. Alexander, "How We Escaped from Fort Warren," 208–13.

24. Witt, *Escape from the* Maple Leaf, 21, 22, 29. Witt cites John Uriah Green, *My Life in Prison and Escape;* "Thrilling Incident: Capture of the Federal Steamer *Maple Leaf,*" 165–71, and Browne, "Stranger Than Fiction: Capture of the United States Steamer *Maple Leaf,* Near Cape Henry, Half a Century Ago," 181–5.

25. Witt, *Escape from the* Maple Leaf, 36, quotes Special Order 159, Headquarters, Department of Virginia, VII Army Corps, Fort Monroe, Virginia, June 9, 1863.

26. Ibid., 31.

27. Ibid., 33, 37. Witt notes that Fuller had been released from a federal hospital some three weeks earlier with wounds to both arms. Although he accepted command of the ship, he did not join in the escape. Fuller died on July 25, 1863, as a POW at the officers' prison camp on Johnson's Island, Sandusky, Ohio.

28. Ibid., 76.

29. Ibid., 39.

30. Ibid., 76.

31. Ibid., 90–1.

32. Michael Corcoran's amusing book, *The Captivity of General Corcoran,* became one of the first Union captivity narratives published during the Civil War. Corcoran died in 1863 after he fell off his horse. See also Cunliffe, *Soldiers and Civilians,* 230.

33. Witt, *Escape from the* Maple Leaf, 44.

34. Ibid., 63.

35. Ibid., 68.

36. Johnson, "A Prisoner's Diary," in *Stories of Our Soldiers,* 244.

37. Cangemi and Kowalski, *Andersonville Prison,* 14.

38. English, "Life in Rebel Prison," 1: 2.

39. Hardy, "Andersonville Prison," courtesy of the Friends of Andersonville, Andersonville National Historic Site and National Cemetery, Andersonville, Georgia. All further quotes from Hardy come from this source.

40. William Wallace Hensley, "Autobiography," (unpublished manuscript, printed by the author, 1912), 45, for his family archives. Typescript was provided courtesy of William Crocken, Professor Emeritus of Theater Arts at Pennsylvania State University, University Park, Pennsylvania.

41. Hensley, "Autobiography," 46. See also Howe, *Adventures of an Escaped Union Prisoner,* for the story of another escaper who bore witness to slave help.

42. See also King, "Death Camp at Florence," 35–42. This article describes camp life and Confederate administration and contains fascinating camp drawings held by the Lackawanna Historical Society, Scranton, Pennsylvania, made by James E. Taylor, a Union prisoner in Andersonville.

43. Morton, *Sparks from the Campfire,* 205.

44. Ibid., 205.

45. Cavada, *Libby Life,* 167–76. For one of the earliest discussions of the Yankee Tunnel, see Johnston, *Four Months in Libby.*

46. See Wells, "Prisoners of War Tunnel to Freedom," 21–31, for a personal narrative of the Libby escape. Wells was one of the successful escapers who reached his own lines.

47. "Recollections of Libby Prison," 91–2.

48. Morton, *Sparks from the Campfire,* 381.

49. Barker, *Prisoners of War,* 13.

50. Foote remained in the Army until 1905. See Foote, "Narrative of an Escape from a Rebel Prison Camp," 50–60.

Chapter 6   *Homo Ludens:* Escape De Luxe in the Great War

1. *The Prisoner of War Problem,* 3.

2. General Order 100, *Rules of Land Warfare,* was first enacted by the United States government for the Union Army in 1863.

3. *Rules of Land Warfare* (1914), 25.

4. Ibid., 31. Article 78 is based on *Hague Rules: Annex to the Convention,* Chapter II, "Prisoners of War," Art. 8, para. 2. See also U.S. Department of the Army, *Treaties Governing Land Warfare,* 8–9.

5. Ibid., based on *Hague Rules,* Art. VIII and *General Order 100, 1863,* Art. 60.

6. Ibid., 30.

7. O'Brien, *Outwitting the Hun,* 38.

8. Ackerley, *Escapers All,* 18. Despite the great numbers of soldiers and mass killing, some acts of chivalry occurred, such as the Christmas Truce of 1914 between British and German front-line troops. See Weintraub, "The Christmas Truce," 76–85. Such activities were irregular and unusual. On the other hand, the chivalry between airmen was a regular practice and in part defined the bizarre nature of the air war.

9. Huizinga, *Homo Ludens,* 98.

10. According to Vance, *Objects of Concern: Canadian Prisoners of War,* 26–27, it was common practice early in the war for boards of inquiry to be called to determine the degree of guilt or innocence of British and Canadian soldiers taken prisoner in battle.

11. S. A. Kinner-Wilson, cited in Vischer, *Barbed Wire Disease,* 19.

12. Hall, "Escape De Luxe," 92.

13. Stevenson, *A Man Called Intrepid,* 9.

14. Everett Buckley's personal post-escape report to American Red Cross officials in Bern appears in Dennett, *Prisoners of the Great War,* 95–103. All subsequent quotes from Buckley come from this source. See also Microfilm M990, ser. M, vol. 9, which deals with captured American airmen during World War I, and Doyle, *Voices from Captivity,* 219.

15. Thomas Hitchcock cited in Dennett, *Prisoners of the Great War,* 104–5.

16. O'Brien, *Outwitting the Hun,* 12. All subsequent O'Brien quotes come from this source, 81, 82, 84, 243–4, 247, 277, 280.

17. Archibald, *Heaven High Hell Deep,* 232.

18. Ibid., 234.

19. Ibid., 239.

20. Puryear, "The Airman's Escape," 453–4.

21. Ibid., 457.

22. Messimer, *Escape,* 205.

23. Dennett, *Prisoners of the Great War,* 138–40.

24. Ibid., 142–4. Fresnes prison was used in World War II for the same purposes.

25. Gordon, *Lafayette Escadrille Pilot Biographies,* 174, cited in Messimer, *Escape,* 114.

26. Adde, "Prison Escapee Found Location of Enemy Subs," A4.

27. "Lieutenant Edward Victor Izac, USN Retired," Navy Office of Information, Internal Relations Division (OI-430), 26 September 1967, 1–5. See also Lt. Edouard Victor Isaacs, USN, letter of 13 November 1918 to the Secretary of the Navy, "Report on Imprisonment in Germany," 93–6.

28. Armstrong, *Escape,* 295–6; Dennett, *Prisoners of the Great War,* 291–315.

29. Ibid., 295–6.

30. Isaacs, *Prisoner of the U-90,* 180–2.

31. Harold Willis, quoted in Armstrong, *Escape,* 312–13.

32. See Isaacs, *Prisoner of the U-90,* 148–59, for details of his escape. See also Reeder, "Lieutenant Izac and His Escape," 1–13; Crews, "Medal of Honor," 16, 68; Gordon Hardy, ed., "Prisoner of the *U-90*: Edward Izac's Escape," in Editors, Boston Publishing Company, *Above and Beyond: History of the Medal of Honor,* 134–8. Dwight R. Messimer's *Escape* devotes most of the book to the Isaacs escape from the Villingen POW camp.

33. Armstrong, *Escape,* 289. Additional representative American POW narratives that discuss escape during World War I include Ellinwood, *Behind the German Lines* and Hoffman, *In the Prison Camps of Germany.*

34. See Messimer, *Escape,* 228–38, for a biography of Isaacs's life after his naval service.

35. See Paine, *The First Yale Unit,* 2, 329–49.

36. Hall, "Escape De Luxe," 92; 96–7; 103; and *My Island Home,* 211.

37. This contrasts with 260,000 Russians, mostly officers, who escaped from the Germans before Bolshevik Russia established the Treaty of Brest-Litovsk with the Germans in 1917. See Tolstoy, *Victims of Yalta,* 46. According to Tolstoy, German forces took 2,417,000 Russian POWs, approximately 70,000 of whom died in captivity, and about 2,000 Ukrainians joined the German Army. See also Brändström, *Among Prisoners of War in Russia and Siberia* and Davis, "Deutsche Kriegsgefangene in Ersten Weltkrieg in Russland," for commentary concerning German prisoners in Russia.

38. For data concerning the German experience in America, see National Archives, *World War I: Prisons and Prisoners—Prisoners of War and Allied Enemies in the United States,* Subject File NA RG 407/23.

39. Moore, *The Faustball Tunnel,* 69.

40. "Isaacs Report," quoted in Messimer, *Escape,* 141.

41. Ellinwood, *Behind the German Lines*, 47.

42. Ibid., 47.

43. Ackerley, *Escapers All*, 18.

44. Neave, *Saturday at M.I.9*, 19, 143. According to Neave, MI-9 paid particular attention to Henry Cartwright, who published *Within Four Walls* (1930), a book that chronicled five attempts and his final escape to neutral Holland in August 1918.

Chapter 7   Home Run Kriegies: Escape and Evasion in Europe

1. Shoemaker, *The Escape Factory*, 71–80. Shoemaker's work was highly regarded by ex-Kriegies in the Stalag Luft III Association, and his death in 1995 was noted in the obituary column of the *Kriegie Klarion* (Winter 1996), 8.

2. Pague, *United States Army in World War II*, 13.

3. Foot and Langley, *MI-9: Escape and Evasion 1939–1945*. MIS-X's figures exceed twelve thousand American escapers and evaders.

4. See Wyman, *DP: Europe's Displaced Persons*, for a discussion of postwar handling of civilians, and Bacque, *Other Losses*, for the catastrophic effects of the Allied status changes on German POWs after May 8, 1945. For an opposing view to Bacque, see Mackenzie, "Essay and Reflection," 717–31, and Günter Bischof's and Stephen Ambrose's attempt to refute Bacque in *Eisenhower and the German POWs*. The debate focuses on Bacque's research methods, his interpretation of the evidence concerning the numbers of dead German prisoners, and Dwight D. Eisenhower's intentions.

5. See Alfred Andersch, "Amerikaner—Erster Eindruck" (Trans. "Americans—A First Impression") in *Flucht in Etrurien*, 171–99, an essay written during his own captivity first published in the *Kölnische Zeitung* on April 25, 1944. See also Prugh, "Prisoners at War: The POW Battleground," 126–7; Mason, "German Prisoners of War in the United States," 198–215; and Tollefson, "Enemy Prisoners of War," 51–77.

6. See Pictet, "The New Geneva Convention for the Protection of War Victims," 462–75.

7. Hatch, *American Ex-Prisoners of War*, 18; Prittie and Edwards, *Escape to Freedom*, 7.

8. MIS-X Papers, Records Center, Suitland, Md., Record Group 332. Boxes 116–21 contain escapers' and evaders' reports. Captivity and escape materials can be found also in the Simpson Historical Research Center, USAAF, Maxwell AFB: 670-614-1 for Southeast Europe and 142-7621 for Northwest Europe from 1942 to 1945.

9. Spivey, *POW Odyssey*, 98–105.

10. See Williams, *The Wooden Horse* and *The Book of Famous Escapes*; Jerrome, "The Wooden Horse," *Tales of Escape*; and Doyle, *Voices from Captivity*, 221.

11. Interview with Henry Burman, POW 1943–1945, and member of the Stalag Luft III Association, State College, Pa., October 1990.

12. Spivey, *POW Odyssey*, 112.

13. Alan Johnson in a personal letter, March 31, 1990.

14. Baybutt, *Colditz: The Great Escapes,* 8.

15. Ibid., 9.

16. Reid, *The Colditz Story,* 9, 17, 23, 38, 220.

17. O'Donnell, *Shoe Leather Express,* 14–16.

18. Lamb, *War in Italy,* 162.

19. Brig. Gen. Rollo Price won his DSO decades later while serving with the United Nations' forces in the Congo. After enemy forces opened fire on an aircraft bringing in much needed reinforcements, Price walked straight toward the enemy positions and personally negotiated a cease-fire. Information concerning Rollo Price courtesy of Simon W. Duke.

20. Westheimer, Sitting It Out, 86–7. See also Westheimer's *Von Ryan's Express* and "Von Ryan's Express," *Houston Post,* reprinted in *Kriegie Klarion,* 5.

21. Lamb, *War in Italy,* 160. Lamb's research shows that the stay-in-place order was DDM P/W 87190, issued by one of the three deputy directors of MI-9, probably Brig. Gen. Richard Crockett, who was in charge of POW escape matters in London.

22. See Schunemann, with Meltesen, "Gustave E. Schunemann Finds a Safe Harbor," 35–9. See also Mann, *Over the Wire,* for a British account of an escape and subsequent experiences with Italian partisans.

23. In *Passages to Freedom: A Story of Capture and Escape* (1990), he severely criticized American behavior in general for being too individualistic and generally disorganized.

24. Robert W. Blakeney in a personal letter, October 10, 1990. Blakeney kindly responded in writing to an inquiry. See Appendix 1: *Oral History Format for Escapers.* All quotes come from this unpublished version of his narrative. For a British escape from Sulmona on December 7, 1941, see Deane-Drummond, *Return Ticket.*

25. Robert Blakeney's experience corresponds with remarks made in Smith, "None But My Foe," 9, a review of Absalom, *A Strange Alliance.*

26. This story, written from memory in his correspondence, was published in two parts in the 44th Bomb Group *Log Book* and later by the Air Force Escape and Evasion Society.

27. Warren Fencl in a personal letter, March 20, 1991. All quotes from Fencl are contained in this source.

28. Foot and Langley, *MI-9,* 244.

29. See de Zayas, *The Wehrmacht War Crimes Bureau,* for the German side of the partisan dilemma that surfaced during World War II.

30. Hatch, *American Ex-Prisoners of War,* 19.

31. Flammer, "Dulag Luft," 61. See also Cole, "Dulag Luft Recalled," 62–5.

32. See Vanderstock, *War Pilot of Orange.* After the war, Dr. Vanderstock emigrated from Holland to Virginia Beach, Virginia, where he practiced medicine until he died at age 77.

33. Jodl's diary, *Tagebuch Generaloberst Jodl.* Entries from January 6, 1943–May 21, 1945 (Freiburg, FRG: Bundesarchiv/Militararchiv), npn, stated on July 22, 1944: "Warnung in allen Kriegsgefangenenlagern: Wer ausbricht wird erschossen. Kein Sport, sondern Lebensgefahr." POW affairs came under the

High Command of the German Armed Forces, the OKW or *Oberkommando Wehrmacht* and the Army High Command, the *Oberkommando des Heeres.* The German military archive (BA-MA) at Freiburg holds very little relative to Allied POWs. In April of 1945, German authorities (*Wehrmachtauskunftstelle*) moved 377 cases of documents to the Drachenberg barracks in Meiningen, Thuringia, for safekeeping. After liberation, these cases fell first into American hands. Under the auspices of a joint commission of Allied officers, the documents were sorted and packed. After the Russians arrived, the Americans withdrew from Thuringia, and, by August 1945, the documents were lost. See also Durand, *Stalag Luft III: The Secret Story,* 123.

34. Interview with Henry Burman of State College, Pennsylvania, who, like Brickhill, served as a "stooge" or lookout for the "X" organization in Stalag Luft III's North Compound during the dig. Along with the other American officers, he was moved to South Compound before the breakout. After his removal and march east in January 1945, Hank Burman finally escaped from the huge concentration of American POWs held at Moosburg prior to the end of hostilities on May 8, 1945. Like many Kriegies, toward the end of hostilities, he feared SS execution squads and escaped in the confusion that reigned in the POW camps in the spring of 1945. See also *Behind the Wire,* an 84-minute documentary of airmen POWs in the ETO through interviews, photos, and archival film, produced by the 8th Air Force Association.

35. See James, *Moonless Night: One Man's Struggle for Freedom.* James participated in the escape from Stalag Luft III and was sent to the Sachsenhausen concentration camp after his recapture. Other great escapers in Sachsenhausen were Sydney Dowse and Jack Churchill.

36. Mitterand and Wiesel, *Memoir in Two Voices,* 119. See also Elie Wiesel, *Night;* Levi, *Survival in Auschwitz;* and Des Pres, *Survivor.*

37. Adler et al., "The Last Days of Auschwitz," 21. See also *Auschwitz: Nazi Extermination Camp,* 284, for a survey of political prisoners who escaped.

38. See Arad, *Belzec, Sibibor, Treblinka.* For a fascinating and frank first-person narrative account of early Jewish ghetto escapers who became partisans in an *atrad* or maroon community in eastern Poland, see Jack and Rochelle Sutin, *Jack and Rochelle: A Holocaust Story of Love and Resistance.* After the war, the Sutins emigrated from a devastated Europe to the United States.

39. Foot and Langley, *MI-9,* 259.

40. Seventeen American Jewish civilians died in Auschwitz, eleven at Dachau, and eight in Mauthausen. See Bard, "American Victims of the Holocaust," reprinted in Bird, *American POWs of World War II,* 129–37. See also Felsen, *The Anti-Warrior,* 178–245. Felsen was a member of the Lincoln Brigade in the Spanish Civil War and a declared communist. Wounded and captured as a member of the OSS with the cover rank of master sergeant, Felsen became a Kriegie in North Africa in 1943. Of special interest in this regard is Arnold Shapiro's documentary, *POW: Americans in Enemy Hands* (1988), part of which addresses Jewish-American POWs sent to the Berga work camp, and Leslie and Jeremy Milk, "Witness to the Holocaust," 29–31, 48–9. Sachsenhausen's prisoner population included mostly German political prisoners, but it had two barracks for Jewish

Häftling and two for POWs. The SS sent condemned British commandos to this camp and secretly executed most of them in their cells. The American military establishment never formally recognized this unusual form of POW incarceration.

41. Bailey, *Prisoners of War,* 79. See also Read and Fisher, *The Fall of Berlin,* 246–8, 289–90, for an account of Brig. Gen. Arthur W. Vanaman's negotiations with the SS regarding American POWs in 1945. Vanaman and Spivey finally escaped across the border into Switzerland.

42. Brickhill, *The Great Escape,* 151.

43. Letter to Geoffrey Forrest, quoted in Sullivan, *Thresholds of Peace,* 370. See also Durand, *Stalag Luft III,* 394–5, for reference to the Von Lindeiner Folder in the "Delmar T. Spivey Collection, 1943–1975," at the U.S. Air Force Academy Library and Von Lindeiner's unpublished personal memoir translated by Berthold Geiss.

44. See Weingartner, *Crossroads of Death,* for an excellent study of the Waffen SS, the Malmédy murders, and the subsequent war crimes trials. Many German prisoners, including Jochen "Blow Torch" Peiper, were held in solitary confinement for extended periods of time and severely interrogated at the former Dachau concentration camp prior to the trials.

45. Anonymous by request. Taped personal memoir prepared in 1989.

46. Foot and Langley, *MI-9,* 301; Mike Enfros of Toluca Lake, California, in a personal letter, June 9, 1993. See also Brown, "Our Unknown POWs," 106.

47. Lawson, "Escape to Russia," 19–20. See also Hays, *Home from Siberia.*

48. See Bethel, *The Last Secret;* Mather, *Aftermath of War;* Tolstoy, *Victims of Yalta;* and Wyman, *DP: Europe's Displaced Persons,* for the contesting sides of the forced repatriation issues that followed hostilities in 1945.

49. Foot and Langley, *MI-9,* 300.

50. Sanders, Sauter, and Kirkwood, *Soldiers of Misfortune,* 26.

51. Brown, "Our Unknown POWs," 74, 76, 106, and *Moscow Bound,* 266, 273. Brown's numbers, drawn from internal Allied communications, include Allied POWs taken late in the war in Germany, Austria, and the Mediterranean. According to Brown, 25,000 U.S. and 31,809 British and Commonwealth POWs were in Russian hands at the war's end. Brown also suggests that more than two million Japanese POWs taken in China and Korea were transported to the Soviet Union's remote slave labor camps. See also Volume IV of the German Maschke Commission's study, Raza, *Die deutschen Kriegsgefangenen in the Sowjetunion;* Karner, *Gefangen Rußland;* and "Prisoners of War in the Economy of the Former Soviet Union: 1941–1945," Eleventh International Economic History Conference at Milan *Conference Paper* (Prague: University of Economics, 1994), 175–99, for the German side of the story.

52. This theory includes Korea and Vietnam as well. National Public Radio reported on August 31, 1995, that the American embassy's POW/MIA hunters in Russia interviewed former Russian soldiers who witnessed American POWs in Russia in the 1950s. See Brown, *Moscow Bound* (1993); U.S. Senate *POW/MIA's: Report of the Select Committee on POW/MIA Affairs* (Kerry Hearings Report), 420; U.S. Senate, *An Examination of U.S. Policy toward POW/MIAs;* Brown and Ashworth, "A Secret That Shames Humanity," 1–12; and Sanders, Sauter, and

Kirkwood, *Soldiers of Misfortune.* See also Epstein, "The Next War," 20–7, 50–3, for a critical review of the Kerry Hearing conclusions.

53. See Karner, "Die Sowjetische Hauptverwaltung für Kriegsgefangene und Internierte," 447–71. Professor Karner heads the Ludwig Boltzmann Institute for the Study of War Consequences in Graz, Austria. With members of his staff, he went to the military archives in Moscow and found the records of the GUPVI, that is, the World War II POW records the Russians kept for POWs and internees. As prisoners in the Soviet GUPVI (POW) and GULAG (political) prison systems, the Russians forced former enemies to rebuild parts of the Soviet Union destroyed during the fighting in World War II.

54. Fleming, "Evasion in Enemy-Held Territory Was Dangerous," 26. For an extensive history of the evasion lines in northwest occupied Europe, see Neave's books, *They Have Their Exits, The Escape Room,* and *Saturday at M.I.9.*

55. Ballard, "Mail Call," 9–10.

56. Foot and Langley, *MI-9,* 317.

57. Watt, *Comet Connection,* 67. See also Neave, *Little Cyclone,* for the story of Andrée de Jongh, the Belgian woman whose courage and determination characterized the Belgian and French parts of *Comet.*

58. Sometimes men went to concentration camps too. Andre Rougeyron helped to rescue Allied airmen and put them into escape lines. He was caught by the Gestapo and sent to Buchenwald, where he remained until its liberation in 1945. See his *Agents for Escape,* which has been translated into English from the 1947 French edition.

59. Neave, *Saturday at M.I.9,* 20, 22.

60. Ibid., 226–38, for a description of the *Shelburne* escape line. See also Foot and Langley, *MI-9,* 63.

61. Maurice Quillien, quoted in Kaiser, *Veteran Recall,* 69.

62. Watt, *Comet Connection,* 90.

63. Derry, with MacDonald, "Vatican Pimpernel," in Verral, *True Stories of Great Escapes,* 344. See also Derry, *The Rome Escape Line* and the feature film *The Scarlet and the Black* (1983), directed by Bill McCutchan, with Gregory Peck, Christopher Plummer, and Sir John Gielgud.

64. Derry, quoted in Verral, 345. See also Lamb, *War in Italy, 1943–1945,* 169–70.

65. Kappler received a life sentence for war crimes, but he too escaped and died a fugitive in 1978. See Sancton, "Crazy Like a Fox," 25.

66. Derry, quoted in Verral, 346.

Chapter 8 Survival in the Pacific: Escape from Militant Bushido

1. Bosworth, *America's Concentration Camps,* 4–8. For contemporary issues concerning Japanese relocation and internment see Myer, *Uprooted Americans* and Brew, "Making Amends for History," 179–201. For congressional reviews, see U.S. Congress, House Commission on Wartime Relocation and Internment of Citizens, *Personal Justice Denied* by Miller, and the House Hearing before the Subcommittee on Federal Services, Post Office, and Civil Service of

the Committee on Governmental Affairs, *To Accept the Findings and to Implement the Recommendations of the Commission on Wartime Relocation and Internment of Civilians.* Internee literature is growing quickly. For example, see Weglyn, *Years of Infamy;* Higa et al., *The View from Within;* and Inada, *Legends from Camp* for three perspectives on internment.

2. For d'Aquino's sad history, see Kutler, "Forging a Legend: The Treason of 'Tokyo Rose,'" *Justice and Injustice in the Cold War,* 3–32. See also Fugita, *Foo,* for his complicated captivity story.

3. Foot and Langley, *MI-9,* 264–71. BAAG could easily be Ride's play on words. The British and Australians always called POW imprisonment being "in the bag."

4. Kerr, *Surrender and Survival,* 335.

5. Foreign Office Papers, Public Record Office, London, FO-46-596, MacDonald to the Foreign Office, 15 May 1905, cited in Towle, "Japanese Treatment of Prisoners in 1904–1905," 116.

6. FO-181-847 quoted in Towle, "Japanese Treatment of Prisoners in 1904–1905," 116.

7. See Burdick and Moessner, *The German Prisoners of War in Japan, 1914–1920,* for a study that shows how well the Japanese treated German prisoners.

8. See Carr-Gregg, "Japanese Personality and Value Orientation," in *Japanese Prisoners of War in Revolt,* 128–68. Carr-Gregg also discusses the complicated Japanese attitude toward death (p. 129).

9. Towle, "Japanese Treatment of Prisoners in 1904–1905," 117.

10. Vaughn, *Community under Stress,* 74.

11. Carr-Gregg, *Japanese Prisoners of War in Revolt,* 104–5. See also Keegan, *A History of Warfare,* 40–6, for a discussion of the samurai's role in Japanese military culture.

12. See Lory, *Japan's Military Masters,* 123, quoted in Carr-Gregg, *Japanese Prisoners of War in Revolt,* 106.

13. See Story, *History of Modern Japan,* 162, cited in ibid., 106.

14. Ibid., 115–16.

15. Van der Post, *The Night of the New Moon,* 36.

16. Ibid., 43–5.

17. See Roland, "Stripping Away the Veneer," 92.

18. Bailey, *Prisoners of War,* 37.

19. See McDaniel, White, and Thompson, "Malnutrition in Repatriated Prisoners of War," 793–810. See also Scott, *The Hague Conventions and Declarations of 1899 and 1907,* for relevant articles of the Hague Convention relative to POW escapes. The United States ratified the Hague Convention in 1909.

20. From the 1929 Geneva Convention. See U.S. Congress, House Committee on Foreign Affairs, *The Geneva Convention Relative to the Treatment of Prisoners of War,* for the 1949 version. See also Barker, *Behind Barbed Wire,* 218–19, for comparisons between the 1929 and 1949 treatments of escape.

21. Petak, *Never Plan Tomorrow,* 187.

22. Durnford, *Branch Line to Burma,* 1.

23. Ibid., 80. See also Giles, *Captive of the Rising Sun.* Rear Admiral Giles came to the same conclusion.

24. Lomax, *The Railway Man,* 80. See Glass, "The Big Stick," 7, for a review of Lomax's book.

25. Petak, *Never Plan Tomorrow,* xvi.

26. Whitcomb, *Escape from Corregidor,* 92. See also Wills, with Myers, *The Sea Was My Last Chance,* for another swimmer who jumped from a Japanese transport, escaped, and joined Filipino guerrillas in Mindanao.

27. Roskey, "Great Escapes," 68.

28. Whitcomb, *Escape from Corregidor,* 100–1.

29. Ibid., 107.

30. During World War II, Korea, and Vietnam, the American military services prohibited escaped prisoners from returning to their former theaters of war. Whitcomb's assignment, and later Wohlfeld's as well, became exceptions to this rule.

31. Meltesen, "From the Foxholes of Bataan," 26.

32. Meltesen, "Defenders of Corregidor," 33–4.

33. McCoy, Mellnik, and Kelley, *Ten Escaped from Togo,* 62–3.

34. Shoemaker, *The Escape Factory,* 205. Shoemaker points out that although MIS-X was very successful in Europe, it was ineffective in the Pacific theater (pp. 204–20).

35. Knox, *Death March,* xi–xiii.

36. Carl Nash in a personal interview, June 29, 1994.

37. Russell, *The Knights of Bushido,* 75.

38. See Perret, *There's a War to Be Won,* 497, for a slightly different version.

39. McCoy, et al., *Ten Escaped from Togo,* 64–6.

40. Leo A. Boelens was killed in action on January 22, 1944, fighting as a guerrilla against Japanese forces.

41. Dyess, *The Dyess Story,* 168.

42. Hawkins, *Never Say Die,* 59.

43. Grashio and Norling, *Return to Freedom,* 83.

44. Hawkins, *Never Say Die,* 109.

45. Ibid., 110.

46. Dyess, *The Dyess Story,* 177.

47. Ibid., 182. For expanded studies of Wendell M. Fertig's guerrilla activities in Mindanao see Fellowes-Gordon, " 'General' Fertig Carries On," in *The World's Greatest Escapes,* 232–9, and Keats, *They Fought Alone.*

48. See Lawton, *Some Survived* and Keats, *They Fought Alone,* 447–50, for a list of Americans, some escapers, some evaders, who fought with Colonel Fertig's guerrillas.

49. Grashio and Norling, *Return to Freedom,* 114.

50. See Knox, *Death March,* 292, and Lawton, *Some Survived,* 81–100.

51. Personal letter dated October 18, 1953, to Wohlfeld's friend and fellow prisoner, Carl Nash. See also Doyle, *Voices from Captivity,* 222.

52. Lawton, *Some Survived,* 92.

53. Ibid., 92.

54. Ibid., 96; Wohlfeld letter to Nash, 2. Two men were lost in the escape.

55. Wohlfeld to Nash, 3.

56. Fraser, *Quartered Safe Out Here,* 155.

57. Kerr, *Surrender and Survival,* 339–40.

58. Prisoner of War Exhibits, Australian War Memorial, Canberra, ACT, Australia, 1994.

59. Lt. Col. Garry J. Anloff, AUS, (Ret.), in a personal letter, November 24, 1990.

60. Copies of these prison camp reports are available from the American Ex-Prisoner of War Association, 3201 East Pioneer Parkway #40, Arlington, TX 76010.

61. Hawkins, *Never Say Die,* 58.

62. Some American POWs perished as a direct result of the Hiroshima bombing. According to David H. Rogers, director of the 494th History Project, 494th Bombardment Group (H) Association, the exact number is small, about eleven, most of whom were members of the 866th Bomb Squadron. See also Clarke, *Last Stop Nagasaki.*

63. For commentary about the POW trials, see Daws, *Prisoners of the Japanese,* 368–72.

64. Personal letter from Martin O'Hara to Walter S. Farquhar, Pottsville, Pennsylvania, dated December 5, 1945. "O'Hara Collection" in the Pattee Library, Pennsylvania State University, University Park, Pennsylvania. See also Ginn, *Sugamo Prison, Tokyo,* for another guard's story.

65. Personal letter, O'Hara to Farquhar dated March 10, 1946.

66. Ibid., np.

67. For discussions concerning more than 1,400 defendants, the 1,229 convictions, and more than 150 death sentences, see Brackman, *The Other Nuremberg;* Dower, *War without Mercy;* Minear, *Victors' Justice;* and Piccigallo, *The Japanese on Trial.*

68. See Daws, *Prisoners of the Japanese* (1994). Daws points out that Japanese POW camps were not homogenizing institutions but existed as tribal societies of Americans, British, Australians, Dutch—and Japanese. Inmates did what they had to do to survive and afterward lived with their guilt.

69. From a BBC World Service report broadcast in Germany in July 1995.

70. See Schermann, "Sins of the Fathers," 3, 34, for a discussion of this position taken by Ian Buruma, a Dutch journalist, concerned mainly about how a modern Germany deals with its newly uncovered war criminals.

Chapter 9   Tigers: The Will to Escape in Korea

1. According to the U.S. Department of Defense, *Selected Manpower Statistics* FY 1994, Table 2-23 (*Principal Wars*), 112, cited in *VFW Magazine* (February 1996), 8, combat losses amounted to 33,652 killed in action; noncombat losses reached 3,262, for a total of 36,914 American dead in Korea. *Dictionary of American History* (pp. 228, 239) noted that war costs also include money for veterans' benefits and interest on debts based on 1975/1976 dollars.

2. Stenger, 1986, in Williams, *Post Traumatic Stress Disorders,* 131. According to Stenger's report, 8, 177 remain unaccounted MIAs today.

3. "Escape from Butchery," 32. See Tomedi, *No Bugles, No Drums,* 51–9, 223–34, for different accounts of similar actions. See also the official Korean

War escaper debriefs in National Archives, Record Group 319, Entry 85, Item 950, 774.

4. See U.S. Senate Committee on Government Operations, *Korean War Atrocities,* for direct testimony from various survivors after repatriation.

5. Hubbell, "The Long Way Home," quoted in Verral, *True Stories of Great Escapes,* 111.

6. Ibid., 120.

7. Rubin Townsend, unpublished typescript, (1990), 104.

8. Ibid., 120.

9. For treatments of Chinese communist indoctrination procedures during the Korean War, see Pate, *Reactionary;* Thornton, *Believed to Be Alive;* Biderman, *March to Calumny;* U.S. Department of the Army, *Communist Interrogation and Exploitation of Prisoners of War;* and Department of Defense, *POW: The Fight Continues.* See also numerous articles on the subject of brainwashing in *Newsweek, Saturday Evening Post, Atlantic Monthly, Collier's,* and others published during and after the Korean War.

10. Townsend, unpublished typescript, 141.

11. Ibid., 141–2.

12. Ibid., 161.

13. Blair, *Beyond Courage,* 3–5. In his book, Blair described the Scheinz, Summersill, and Thomas evasions in great detail.

14. *Newsweek,* 30 October 1950, 32.

15. Melvin Shadduck, quoted in Blair, *Beyond Courage,* 171. Subsequent quotes come from this source: 187, 190, 195, 230, 240, 243, 245.

16. James Young's POW Debrief, National Archives Record Group 153, Entry 183, Box 6, quoted in Brown, *Moscow Bound,* 434.

17. Pate, *Reactionary,* 93–4.

18. See Hastings, "The Prisoners," in *The Korean War,* 328, 348.

19. Leonard Jones, quoted in Knox, *The Korean War,* 2, 335.

20. Farrar-Hockley, *The Edge of the Sword,* 72. Subsequent quotes from this source, 91–3, 105, 144, 178, 179–80, 232.

21. Laffin, *The Anatomy of Captivity,* 23.

22. See Hastings, "The Prisoners," in *The Korean War;* Vatcher, *Panmunjom;* and White, *The Captives of Korea.*

23. Biderman, *March to Calumny,* 180–1.

24. Alexis de Tocqueville, *Democracy in America,* quoted in Karsten, "American POWs in Korea and the Citizen Soldier," 375.

25. See Wubben, "American POWs in Korea," 3–19, for a discussion of collaboration cases in Korea. See also Doyle, *Voices from Captivity,* 195–212, for commentary and analysis of POW assimilation; Hunter, *Brainwashing,* for an analysis of interrogation techniques; and Pasley, *21 Stayed,* and her British edition, *22 Stayed,* for an extended discussion concerning the social backgrounds of the defectors. See also "Washed Brains of POWs: Can They Be Rewashed?" *Newsweek,* 4 May 1953, 37; "The Prisoners Who Broke," *U.S. News and World Report,* 21 August 1953, 30–1; and "Without Honor," *Newsweek,* 13 July 1953, 30, for a report on disloyal POWs or how progressives were picked for indoctrination. See

Sommers, *The Korea Story,* for a very strong pro-veteran approach. For descriptions of how United Nations forces treated North Korean and Chinese POWs, see Weintraub, *War in the Wards* and White, *The Captives of Korea.*

26. Biderman, *March to Calumny,* 156–7, 67. Popular American magazine treatments of the social decay thesis include "Korean Puzzle: Americans Who Stay," *U.S. News and World Report,* 24 December 1954, 104; "The Prisoners Who Broke," *U.S. News and World Report,* 21 August 1953, 30–1; "Washed Brains of POWs: Can They Be Rewashed?" *Newsweek,* 4 May 1953, 37; "Without Honor," *Newsweek,* 13 July 1953, 30; Berquist, "A Turncoat Comes Home," *Look,* 25 June 1957, 125–8; Bouscaren, "Korea, Test of American Education," *Catholic World* (April 1956), 24–7; Brean, "Prisoners of War the Reds Say Do Not Want to Come Home to America," *Life,* 19 October 1953, 44–5; Brinkley, "Almost All Released Prisoners Come Home Happily," *Life,* 7 September 1953, 126–7; and "Case History of Those 21: What Their Lives Show," *Newsweek,* 18 January 1954, 52–4.

27. Editors, "A Code of Conduct," in *Above and Beyond: A History of the Medal of Honor from the Civil War to Vietnam,* 272.

28. Hastings, 341; Bird, "Not Any Battlefield Heroics," 28–30, 32, 86–7.

29. Barker, *Prisoners of War,* 125.

30. U.S. Department of Defense, *POW: The Fight Continues,* vi–vii.

31. See Prugh, "The Code of Conduct for the Armed Services," 678–707.

32. Dwight D. Eisenhower, cited in Burgess, "Prisoners of War: Foreword," 676.

33. U.S. Department of Defense, *POW: The Fight Continues,* 20.

Chapter 10   Free from the Jungle Camps:
Escape in Laos and Vietnam

1. Personal letter from Douglas Cotton, 5 November 1995.

2. Cotton letter, 2.

3. Personal letter from Maurice G. Hughett to Maj. Gordon Close, April 23, 1986, courtesy of Douglas Cotton, London, England, one of the 1,100 British POWs taken from Singapore to Saigon in April 1942. Close served as the Saigon camp interpreter and kept other materials concerning Americans in a secret diary that he donated to the Imperial War Museum. Close sent one copy to Cotton for his personal use. Maurice Hughett, escaper and guerrilla, died on July 25, 1989, in Dallas, Texas.

4. Starin, "Combat SAR," 51. See also Sochurek, "Air Rescue Behind Enemy Lines," 346–69, and Tilford, *Search and Rescue in Southeast Asia 1961–1975.*

5. In the Afterword, Anderson told a streamlined version of the Hambleton story, saying that this fiction consisted of composite characters for lucidity only, and he did not alter the facts.

6. William Henderson, reprinted in Wyatt, *We Came Home.*

7. See Anderson, *Bat-21,* 218–22.

8. According to Bailey, *Solitary Survivors,* the United States recovered only

fifteen of the six hundred POWs lost in Laos. See also "Bibliography and Monographs," 10.

9. Marolda and Fitzgerald, *The United States Navy and the Vietnam Conflict*, 2, 381ff.

10. Starin, "Combat SAR," 54.

11. "Guards Said to Have Helped Pilot Escape in Laos," 2.

12. "Navy Flier, Captured by Laos Reds, Back in U.S.," 2. See also "The Mysterious Pentagon," 33.

13. See "U.S. Pilot's Escape from Reds in Laos Described by Navy," 4.

14. Dengler, *Escape from Laos,* 147–61. All the subsequent quotes come from this source unless specifically indicated.

15. See U.S. Senate, Armed Services Committee, *Imprisonment and Escape of Lieutenant Junior Grade Dieter Dengler;* Dengler, "I Escaped from a Red Prison," 27–33; "Snakes and the Angel," 32; and Dengler, *Escape from Laos.* See also Doyle, *Voices from Captivity,* 224.

16. Quoted in Editors of the *Army Times, American Heroes of Asian Wars,* 91.

17. Smith, *POW: Two Years with the Vietcong,* 298.

18. Ibid., 298.

19. Ibid., 300.

20. "A Tale of Two Prisoners," 27.

21. "Guests of the VC," 37.

22. Ibid., 37.

23. Rowe, *Five Years to Freedom,* 110. Unless otherwise indicated, statements made by Rowe come directly from this source: 122, 105, 200–1, 366–72. The narrative, based on Rowe's hidden diary, is one of the great classics of the Vietnam War, and is, perhaps, one of the most thorough personal reflections on military captivity ever written by an American military officer. See Doyle, *Voices from Captivity,* 225. For a summary of Vietnam POW narratives, see Dunn, "The POW Chronicles," 495–514, and "The Vietnam War POW/MIAs: An Annotated Bibliography," 152–8.

24. "Life with Charlie," 35.

25. "Obituary Note," 30; U.S. Department of State, Bureau of Diplomatic Security, *Significant Incidents of Political Violence against Americans,* 21.

26. Brown, "Escape in Indochina," 39–41.

27. Brown, *Moscow Bound,* 545, cites the number at thirty-one. For Col. Ben Purcell's two escapes and recaptures, see *Love & Duty,* 98–113, 163–74.

28. Personal conversation with Gen. William C. Westmoreland, USA (Ret.) in Baltimore, Maryland, on November 9, 1994. When asked about this situation specifically, General Westmoreland said, "That might have something to do with it."

29. Howes, *Voices of the Vietnam POWs,* 4.

30. Article 85 refers to the treatment of war criminals. It stipulates that POWs prosecuted under the laws of the detaining power for actions committed prior to capture retain the benefits of the convention. Article 108 empowers punishment and defines how detaining powers may carry out sentences. The Soviet Union and its satellite states rejected these concepts. See Barker, *Behind Barbed Wire,* 216–18, for a discussion of this problem in international law. See also Landon, "Geneva

Conventions—The Broken Rules," 34–9; Levie, "Maltreatment of Prisoners of War," 323–59; and "The Geneva Convention and the Treatment of Prisoners of War in Vietnam," 851, 856–8.

31. "Trial and Error," 35–6.

32. Gaither, *With God in a POW Camp,* 53.

33. Stockdale and Stockdale, *In Love and War,* 278.

34. Boot, *Great Photographers of World War II,* 8. See also North, "Hanoi Hannah Speaks Again," 18–24. Trinh Thi Ngo broadcast all sorts of war news from Radio Hanoi and stated in this interview article that she often used the American forces newspaper *Stars and Stripes* as well as popular magazines from the United States as her immediate sources. American prisoners in Hanoi were forced to listen to her regular broadcasts.

35. Summers, *On Strategy,* 65–7.

36. Schell, *The Real War,* 29.

37. Hilsman, *To Move a Nation,* 525. At the same time, the Americans lost 267 advisors killed in action. See also Kenny, *The American Role in Vietnam and East Asia,* 25. For an argument against American bloodlust, see Hatch, "One Despicable Part of the Vietnam War," 58, 60–2. Hatch points out that from 1965 to 1973, 201 Army personnel and 77 Marines were tried for crimes against Vietnamese civilians.

38. Howes, *Voices of the Vietnam POWs,* 184–7.

39. See Lord, "The Medal of Honor," 65, 67, and McConnell, *Into the Mouth of the Cat,* for more details concerning Lance Sijan's captivity, escape attempts, and death.

40. U.S. Senate Committee on Veterans' Affairs, *Medal of Honor Recipients,* 922.

41. Editors, *Above and Beyond: A History of the Medal of Honor,* 309.

42. Day, "Promises to Keep," 110, quoted from Day, *Return with Honor.*

43. U.S. Senate Committee on Veterans' Affairs, *Medal of Honor Recipients,* 825–6.

44. Stockdale and Stockdale, *In Love and War,* 467.

45. Coker, "P. W.," 45–6. See also Doyle, *Voices from Captivity,* 225.

46. Stockdale and Stockdale, *In Love and War,* 467–8.

47. Dramesi, *Code of Honor,* 18. Subsequent direct quotes also come from this source: 93, 111, 117–18.

48. Plumb, *I'm No Hero,* 219.

49. Stockdale and Stockdale, *In Love and War,* 466.

50. See Howes, *Voices of the Vietnam POWs,* 105.

51. Plumb, *I'm No Hero,* 224–5.

52. Towers, *Hope for Freedom,* 32–3.

53. Ibid., 74.

54. Ibid., 74.

55. The number was lowered to 2,234 in 1994.

56. See Grant, *Survivors,* and Schwinn and Diehl, *We Came to Help,* for one side of the Garwood story. See Groom and Spenser, *Conversations with the Enemy,* for Garwood's side. See also Nichols, "Article 105," 393–8, for a legal perspective on Vietnam POW behavior.

57. Groom and Spenser, *Conversations with the Enemy*, 344.

58. Ibid., 354.

59. Ibid., 365, for the myth of the renegade in the Vietnam War.

60. Personal interview with Tanh in Melbourne, Australia, May 1994.

61. Excerpt from a personal essay for admission to medical school in the United States that Bach kindly shared with the author in 1993.

62. See Yathay, "Escape from Cambodia," 1588–95.

63. See *Vietnam Investment Review,* quoted in *Indochina Chronology,* 4.

64. Howes, *Voices of the Vietnam POWs,* 22.

65. Richard Stratton made this comment in an interview for the documentary *POW: Americans in Enemy Hands.* See also "Controversial Prisoner Freed," 1; Blakey, *Prisoner at War;* and Stratton, "Turn on the Lights," 81ff, for his position on survival in captivity.

66. See McGrath, "Reading the Code of Conduct," 100–4.

67. Question posed by the author to Lt. Col. Garth Cartledge, Royal Australian Army, during a POW conference at the Australian Defense Force Academy, Canberra ACT, Australia, in May 1994. At the time, Lieutenant Colonel Cartledge was stationed with Land Headquarters at the Victoria Barracks in Sydney.

Chapter 11   The Pseudo-Wars: Civilian Hostages and Escapers

1. Dr. John Dalton, a Senior Lecturer in the Department of Politics, Monash University, provided the interview with Walter "Wally" Burgess, on May 12, 1994, in Melbourne, Australia. Burgess, an Australian, worked with UPI, ITN, and WTN during and after the Vietnam War. He left Cambodia in July 1974 and returned briefly in 1977. Tim Page is British.

2. See McFadden, *No Hiding Place,* 175–9. For a critical background essay concerning why Iranians were angry with both the Shah and the Americans, see Halberstam, *The Fifties,* 359–69.

3. Roberts, "The Year of the Hostage," 26–30.

4. See Santino, "Yellow Ribbons and Seasonal Flags," 19–33.

5. Raids are acts of war generated in wartime, not usually in peacetime unless a president or some other head of state is backed into a corner by hostage-takers. In 1978, H. Ross Perot formed a private rescue mission, the "Sunshine Boys," led by Arthur "Bull" Simons of the Son Tay raid, who freed two Perot representatives held hostage in Iran.

6. See Alnwick and Fabyanic, *Warfare in Lebanon,* for background on the Lebanese civil war, Low Intensity Conflict, and the role of the U.S. military in its execution.

7. Norland, "America's Forgotten Hostages," 41.

8. Pintak, *Beirut Outtakes,* 243.

9. Jacobsen, with Aston, *Hostage: My Nightmare in Beirut,* 38–9. See also Jacobsen, "How I Survived," 60; Anderson, *Den of Lions;* and Martin and Walcott, *Best Laid Plans.*

10. Aikman, "The World Is Fresh and Bright and Beautiful," 58.

11. Jacobsen, *Hostage,* 127–8; 186–7.

12. Aikman, "The World Is Fresh and Bright and Beautiful," 58.

13. Weir and Weir, with Benson, *Hostage Bound, Hostage Free,* 28–9.

14. Martz, "Even When It's Over, It Isn't Over," 37.

15. Jacobsen, *Hostage: My Nightmare in Beirut,* 195–6.

16. Thomas, *Journey Into Madness,* 80.

17. Levin, *Beirut Diary,* 175–6.

18. Ajemian, "Terror and Tedium," 50.

19. Ibid., 51–2.

20. Smith, "Escape from Beirut," 25.

21. "'Quiet Diplomacy' of Secretary-General Pays Off," 37.

22. See Summers, *On Strategy,* 35.

23. De Vattel, *The Law of Nations or the Principles of Natural Law,* reprinted in Falk, *The Vietnam War and International Law,* 23.

24. See Kaplan, "The Coming Anarchy," 44–76, subtitled as, "How scarcity, crime, overpopulation, barbarism and disease are rapidly destroying the social fabric of the planet." See also Colburn, *The Vogue of Revolution in Poor Countries,* who argued that socialist revolutions since 1945 have left hopeful revolutionaries morally, politically, and materially bankrupt. See also Toffler and Toffler, "War, Wealth, and a New Era in History," 46–52, for a comparative analysis of three stages of war and how shifting technologies reflect broad cultural changes.

25. Professor Duke's remarks were made on several occasions when this topic was discussed. See Best, *War and Law Since 1945,* who points out that troubles exist today accommodating international rules to the kinds of culture warfare going on in the Third World. For a competing view, see Alexander, *The Future of Warfare,* for case studies concerning future small wars that the author believes are based on past guerrilla/partisan forms of warfare fought in China and Vietnam.

26. See Santino, "Yellow Ribbons and Seasonal Flags," 19–33.

27. See Say and Knobler, *Forgotten: A Sister's Struggle to Save Terry Anderson;* Say, "The Dream That Died," 38; and "The Last Hostage," 28–33. See also Anderson, *Den of Lions.*

28. See Mann, *Holding On.* Sunnie Mann died in 1992, a year after her husband returned from captivity; Jackie Mann died on November 12, 1995.

29. Horowitz, Labi, Lofaro, and Rutherford, "An End to the Long Ordeal," 11.

30. Carlson, *One American Must Die.* See also "Transcript of World Airlines Hijacking Incident," 286.

31. See Levin, Bodman, and Levin, *Lebanon: Emblem of Captivity.*

32. "The Coldest Hostage Crisis," 27. In Yemen, seventeen French tourists were taken hostage during the Christmas holiday season in 1995. This group suffered no hardships; instead they dined with their captors who became their tour guides before their release. See Greenberg, with Thomas, "Travels with My Captor," 19.

33. See Gibson, *Warrior Dreams.* Gibson takes the concept of the pseudo-war into what he calls the myth of the "New War" conducted by paramilitaries inside the United States.

Chapter 12   Escape by Other Means: Prison Raids and Raiders

1. Janes's *Dictionary of Military Terms*, 135, cited in Kelly, "Raids and National Command," 20.

2. See McRaven, *Case Studies in Special Operations Warfare*, who developed the six principles for a raid: simplicity, security, repetition, surprise, speed, and purpose.

3. Gates had served as a regular British officer before emigrating to America. For a description of Gates's cordial relationship with Burgoyne, see Riedesel, *Letters and Journals Relating to the War of the American Revolution*, 113–35, quoted in Dorson, *America Rebels*, 228–31. See also Metzger, *The Prisoner in the American Revolution*, for a survey, and Sampson, *Escape in America*, for a British study of the Convention prisoners from an escape-and-evasion point of view.

4. *Clinton Papers* 1 Dec. 1781, quoted in Metzger, *The Prisoner in the American Revolution*, 39. According to Gen. Sir Henry Clinton, 6,259 rank and file soldiers, including 3,776 British, 1,600 Hessians, and 883 Provincials, mostly Loyalists and Canadians, surrendered at Yorktown to the Americans. In South Carolina at the same time, British forces surrendered 221 British, 48 Germans, and 257 Provincials. In 1782, Sir Guy Carleton replaced Clinton as commander in chief of British forces in America. At the end of the war in the American colonies, the British surrendered 8,516 uniformed personnel to the Americans. General Cornwallis was exchanged for Henry Laurens, who assisted Franklin with peace negotiations in Paris. The last fight of the Revolution took place at Comhabee River, South Carolina, on August 27, 1782.

5. Prelinger, "Benjamin Franklin and the American Prisoners of War," 272.

6. Dupuy and Baumer, *The Little Wars of the United States*, 26ff.

7. Pratt, *Preble's Boys*, 20. Preble was captured aboard the American privateer *Protector* in May 1781. In the prison ship *Jersey*, Lieutenant Preble nearly died of fever but survived through the efforts of a British Colonel Tyng, who served with his father in the colonial wars against the French. For the careers of Decatur and Bainbridge, see Pratt, *Preble's Boys*, 85–143.

8. Segal, "Combating Terrorism," 21–3; Lane-Poole, *The Story of the Barbary Corsairs*, 275–91; and Pratt, *Preble's Boys*, 94–5.

9. Sager, "A Boy in the Confederate Cavalry," 376.

10. Garrett, *The Raiders*, 63ff, 74. According to Stern, *Secret Missions of the Civil War*, 236, John Singleton Mosby enjoyed an interesting postwar career. He became a Republican and a friend of President Ulysses S. Grant and received assignments as the U.S. consul in Hong Kong, land agent in Colorado, and assistant attorney for the U.S. Department of Justice.

11. For a popular history of Quantrill's activities, see Hines, "Infamous Border Guerrilla William Clarke Quantrill Met His Fate," 16, 68–9.

12. One can find the "Ballad of Jesse James" in nearly every folk song collection available in the United States.

13. Thomas, "The Kilpatrick-Dahlgren Raid" (February 1978), 4–9, 46–8; (April 1978), 26–33. See also Basile, *The Civil War Diary of Amos E. Stearns*, 55.

14. Kinchen, *Confederate Operations in Canada,* 104, 108. See also Shepard, "The Johnson's Island Plot," 1–51.

15. See Bragg, "The Union General Lost in Georgia," 16–21.

16. See Sherriff, *Journey's End,* 10–136. See also Kosok, "Aspects of Presentation, Attitude and Reception in English and Irish Plays," in Stanzel and Löschnigg, *Intimate Enemies,* 343–64.

17. See Shoemaker, *The Escape Factory,* 114–26, for the aborted American plan to raid and evacuate Oflag 64.

18. See Baron, Baum, and Goldhurst, *Raid!: The Untold Story of Patton's Secret Mission.*

19. Ibid., 157.

20. Fruman, "Last Days at Stalag 7A," 6. See also Schemmer, *The Raid,* 59.

21. Baron, Baum, and Goldhurst, *Raid!: The Untold Story of Patton's Secret Mission,* 252–3.

22. Ibid., 271. For accounts of German raids to rescue their own prisoners from French partisans, see von Roon, *Zwischen Freiheit und Pflicht,* 179–80, and Kurowski, *Sturz in die Hölle,* 382–8. See Neave, *They Have Their Exits,* 158–65, for British raids in France and Holland to recover prisoners and evaders.

23. Johnson, *Hour of Redemption,* 21. See also "MacArthur's Back," 3–4.

24. Simpson, *Inside the Green Berets,* 128.

25. Johnson, *Hour of Redemption,* 19. See also Breuer, *The Great Raid on Cabanatuan* and Gleek, "The Rescue of the Los Baños Internees," 144–9. At the end of the war, 11,500 American POWs were liberated from Japan and only 1,500 from camps in the Philippines.

26. Crow, "Free at Last," 29.

27. Simpson, *Inside the Green Berets,* 129.

28. Schemmer, *The Raid,* 227.

29. Personal letter from Lee Roy Pipkin of Reno, Nevada, May 27, 1989. Pipkin served as a team leader of the 173d Airborne Brigade (LRRP) and also with "Dog" Company 4th BN, 503d ABN INF 173d Airborne Brigade in 1967–68.

30. Personal interview with David Beville (pseudo.) in September 1989.

31. For popular treatments, see Freemont, "Let's Go Get 'Em," 52–5, 79, and Caristo, "We Tried Hard," 57–9, 81.

32. Nearly every province in South Vietnam had a Provincial Reconnaissance Unit consisting of former Vietcong soldiers who had rallied to the Allied side. For remembrances written by Americans who worked with Vietnamese PRU personnel, see "Echoes of Honor," 43, 50.

33. Personal letter from Brian Rand, September 13, 1989. For a published narrative of a SEAL BRIGHTLIGHT mission, see Young, *The Element of Surprise,* 39–45.

34. 173d Airborne Brigade, "Brightlight After Action Report," dated 20 February 1971, quoted in Stanton, *Rangers at War,* 194.

35. Schemmer, *The Raid,* 171.

36. Andrade, "Bring Our POWs Back Alive," 22. See also Sidey, "How the Raid Was Planned," 36; Hemmingway, "Daring Raid at Son Tay," 20–3.

37. Schemmer, *The Raid,* 282.

38. Deering of Hendersonville, Tennessee, in "Mail Call," 6.

39. Schemmer, *The Raid,* 236, 267.

40. Ibid., 261.

41. Ibid., 286.

42. Kelly, "Raids and National Command," 22. See also Rowan, *Four Days of the Mayaguez.*

43. Courtesy of Guy H. Harris, Typescript, "Diary of the Fall of Saigon and the *Mayaguez* Incident," 1990. See also Rowan, *The Four Days of Mayaguez* and Guilmartin, *The Mayaguez and the Battle of Koh Tang.*

44. Lippman, "U.S. Team to Inspect Possible POW Prison in Laos," A34.

45. Patterson and Tipton, *The Heroes Who Fell from Grace,* 142.

46. Ibid., 153.

47. For even more criticism of Gritz and other POW/MIA issues, see Keating, *Prisoners of Hope* and Franklin, *MIA: Mythmaking in America.* Although Keating defends government actions and Franklin criticizes them severely, both come to the conclusion that no living prisoners are being held in Southeast Asia against their will.

48. Local legend collected in Münster, Germany, 1995.

49. See Child, *The English and Scottish Popular Ballads,* 3, 469–95.

50. As Naval Intelligence Officer, Ben Tre, RVN, 1970–1971, I observed several BRIGHTLIGHT operations firsthand and often discussed the problems with SEAL Team commanders in Kien Hoa Province. See Lt. Robert C. Doyle, USNR, "NILO Ben Tre," Typescript and "Oral History" Tape Recording, Naval Historical Center, Washington, D.C., 1978.

51. Vistica, "An American Hero," 28. This story headlined many American newspapers and news publications during that week. Sylvester Stallone's Rambo film character became an American stereotype of the Vietnam War veteran. In his novel *First Blood* (1972), the Canadian author David Morell created his complex fictional Rambo character as an escaper and sole survivor patterned after the French adventurer-poet Arthur Rimbaud. Much attention has been afforded to this image in the United States. See Gibson, *Warrior Dreams,* for an analysis of Rambo's effects as a mythic figure representative of what Gibson calls the "New Warrior" in the "New War." See also Rich, "The 'Rambo' Culture," A29.

52. Schemmer, *The Raid,* 295, 267. See also Doyle, *Voices from Captivity,* 226–7.

Chapter 13   Escape and the Fortunes of War: Legacies and Reflections

1. See Heard's study, *White into Red,* 2. Heard pointed out that for men, capture frequently ended in death by the most excruciating torments. For women, the fear was of lifelong bondage. As a result, frontier people kept on guard against Indian attack.

2. Congress restored Dr. Walker's Medal of Honor to her posthumously on May 4, 1977. See Walker, *Hit.* See also Editors, "The Only Woman," in *Above and Beyond: A History of the Medal of Honor,* 38–9; Edwards, "Dr. Mary Edwards Walker" (September 1958), 1160–2; (October 1958), 1296–8; Lockwood, "Pantsuited Pioneer of Women's Lib," 113–18; Poynter, "Dr. Mary Walker, M.D.,

Pioneer Woman Physician," 43–51; Snyder, *Dr. Mary Walker;* and Werlich, "Mary Walker: From Union Army Surgeon to Sideshow Freak," 46–9.

3. See *The Medal of Honor of the United States Army,* 153, for Sgt. Daniel T. Ferrier's citation.

4. See Cooke, *For Conspicuous Gallantry;* Jacobs, *Heroes of the Army;* Murphy, *Vietnam Medal of Honor Winners;* Reck, *Beyond the Call of Duty;* and *The Medal of Honor of the United States Army.*

5. "Somalia Service Provided Its Share of Heroes," 26–7.

6. Utley and Washburn, *Indian Wars,* 43. The Pequots have returned to Connecticut and now operate a successful gambling casino. See Johnson, "An Indian Tribe's Promised Land," 4–7.

7. See Barrett, "A Prisoner of War," in *Geronimo, His Own Story,* 156–60. See "Letter No. 57," in Catlin, *North American Indians,* 449–55, for a description of Oseola's death. See Utley and Washburn, *Indian Wars,* 137–8, for the Black Hawk capture, imprisonment, and national tour. See also Berkhofer, *The White Man's Indian,* for a critical analysis of American treatment of its aboriginal peoples.

8. Metzger, *The Prisoner in the American Revolution,* 26. See also Dorson, *America Rebels,* 133–66, for several revealing narratives written by American Loyalists. For Departmental and State Papers concerning British troops captured in America during the Revolution, see Andrews, *Guide to the Materials for American History.* See also Public Record Office, Information Bulletin 72, "Prisoners of War 1660–1919: Documents in the PRO," 1–7.

9. See Mekeel, "Suspicion of Quaker Treachery," 173–88, and "The Relation of the Quakers to the American Revolution," 3–18.

10. Of the 29,867 Hessians deployed to America from Germany, 5,000 defected. See Bowie, "German Prisoners in the American Revolution," 196.

11. The City of Reading, Pennsylvania, maintains a Revolutionary War site called Hessian Village. See Becker, "Prisoners of War in the American Revolution," 169–73.

12. "Treatment of American Prisoners!" 4.

13. For American complaints about British treatment of American prisoners, see U.S. Congress, House, *Report on the Spirit and Manner in Which the War Has Been Waged.* For a review of the incident that concerned the British treatment of Irish-American prisoners at sea and the American response, see Robinson, "Retaliation for the Treatment of Prisoners," 65–70.

14. For the sad story of the San Patricio Battalion in the Mexican War, 1846–1848, see *The American Star,* 23 September, 12 November 1847; Downey, "Tragic Story of San Patricio Battalion," 20–3; Hopkins, "The San Patricio Battalion in the Mexican War," 279–84; Mahoney, "50 Hanged and 11 Branded," 373–6; Wallace, "The Battalion of Saint Patrick in the Mexican War," 84–91, and "Deserters in the Mexican War," 374–83.

15. Richardson, *Messages and Papers of the Presidents,* 6, 17.

16. Ibid., 102–4.

17. Fincher, "By Convention, the Enemy Within Never Did Without," 133. Maschke noted in *Zur Geschichte der deutschen Kriegsgefangenen des 2. Welt-*

krieges, 3, that during and after World War II, over 10 million German soldiers were held as POWs in twenty countries.

18. Spindle, "Axis Prisoners of War in the United States," 63.

19. Krammer, *Nazi Prisoners of War in America,* vii.

20. Ibid., viii, and Spindle, "Axis Prisoners of War," 60–3. See also Whittingham, *Martial Justice,* for the story of the trial and execution of German soldiers who executed their own men.

21. *The Incident,* a teleplay directed by Joseph Sargent with Walter Matthau, was aired by CBS on March 6, 1990. The script was written by James and Michael Norell.

22. Mooney, "Slammer or Shrine?" A55. Mooney noted, however, that although they existed at Heidelberg and Göttingen, *Karzer*s for misbehaving students were not found at every German university.

23. See Fincher, "By Convention," 126–7.

24. The "coddling" issue arose and found its way into the popular press in 1944, after D-Day and the bitter fighting in France. It intensified in 1945, following the discovery of the Nazi death camps. For some examples, see Devore, "Our 'Pampered' War Prisoners," 144; Hirsh, "German Atrocities Raise Questions," 60–61; Shafer, "Here's How We Treat Nazi Captives," 9; "Do We Pamper Our POWs?" 78; "On Pampering Prisoners," 12.

25. Vinz, "Das freie Buch," in *Der Ruf,* privately reprinted by his wife on his eightieth birthday as a Festschrift. The issue of denazification and reeducation appeared regularly in the American popular press, especially in 1944 and 1945. Samples include "Re-Educating the Nazis," *America,* 26 August 1944, 515; Reynolds, "Experiment in Democracy," *Collier's,* 25 May 1946, 12–13; 41–42; Frost, "New Orleans Test Tube for German Democracy," *Times-Picayune Sunday Magazine,* 23 September 1945; "Re-Education Program for German Prisoners in Effect Here," *Publishers Weekly,* 24 June 1945, 24–39.

26. Copies of Volumes 1–26 of *Der Ruf* can be found in the Wisconsin State Library. See also Schwab-Felisch, *Der Ruf: Eine deutsche Nachkriegszeitschrift,* for a study of the postwar *Ruf.* Special thanks to Gerald H. Davis for a copy of "Biographical Essay on Re-Education of Prisoners of War in Two World Wars," an unpublished paper that he gave to the author at a conference at the Australian Defense Force Academy, Canberra, on May 12, 1994. See also Davis, " 'Orgelsdorf': A World War I Internment Camp in America," 249–65, and "Prisoners and Prisons," File O 68, Hoover Institution on War, Revolution and Peace at Stanford University.

27. The reeducation-denazification program in the United States initiated and run by the Prisoner of War Special Projects Division at Fort Phil Kearney, Rhode Island, is not an item for discussion here. For sources close to the time, see Brody, "Observation and Reëducation of German Prisoners of War," 12–19; Casady, "The Reorientation Program for POWs," 169–96; Ehrmann, "An Experiment in Political Education," 304–20; and McCracken, *The Prisoner of War Re-Education Program.* For further comment, see Robin, *The Barbed-Wire College.* Robin argues that the Special Projects Division failed to do anything more than to provide an American liberal arts college campus in the POW camps for Germans.

28. See Melady, *Escape from Canada.*

29. See Johann, *Schneesturn Heimweh und nächtlicher Bambus,* for an exciting fictional treatment of an around-the-world odyssey home made by German escapers.

30. "Die Flucht des Oberleutnants v. Werra," 42; Burt and Leasor, "The One That Got Away," in Verral, *True Stories of Great Escapes,* 416; and Melady, *Escape from Canada,* 98.

31. See Flammer, "Dulag Luft," 58–62, and Cole, "Dulag Luft Recalled and Revisited," 62–5. See also "Dulag Luft" Folder, "Camp Reports-Germany-Air Force Transit Camps" File, National Archives and Records Center, and "German Methods and Experiences of Prisoner Interrogation."

32. Von Werra escaped from Canada, not England. See Burt and Leasor, "The One That Got Away," in Verral, *True Stories,* 417. A search in the Military Bundesarchiv in Freiburg, Germany, failed to turn up a copy of *Mein Flucht aus England.*

33. Moore, *The Faustball Tunnel,* 70–1; Fincher, "By Convention," 127.

34. Moore, *The Faustball Tunnel,* 64–5.

35. See "Kriegsmarine Escape," 33–4; "Escape in Arizona," 16; and Fincher, "By Convention," 137–8. Friedrich Guggenberger later attained the rank of admiral in the West German Bundesmarine.

36. Thomas, "Jürgen Wattenberg, 94, POW Who Escaped," B9. After a long career in the beer business, Frigatten-Kapitän Wattenberg died in Hamburg at the age of 94 on November 27, 1995.

37. Moore, *Faustball Tunnel,* 44.

38. See Laffin, *The Anatomy of Captivity,* 104–13, for the Trenck story.

39. Pabel, *Enemies Are Human,* 165, and Moore, *Faustball Tunnel,* 243. See Hoover, "Enemies at Large," 29–30, and "Alien Enemy Control," 396–408. See also Jung, *Die deutschen Kriegsgefangenen in amerikanischer Hand—USA,* for a historical analysis of American captivity practices from a German point of view.

40. See Pabel, "It's Easy to Bluff Americans," 20–33.

41. See Gaertner, with Krammer, *Hitler's Last Soldier in America,* for Gaertner's escape and life as a fugitive in America.

42. Knopp, "Heimkehr, Flüchtlinge und Vertriebene," 8–11. For a personal narrative concerning German mass civilian escapes from the Red Army in East Prussia, see Fittkau, *Mein 33. Jahr: Erinnerungen eines ostpreußischen Pfarrers.*

43. These operations were super-secret at the time and were even kept from the State Department. See Milano, with Brogan, *Soldiers, Spies and the Rat Line.* See also Nelan, "Cold Light on the Cold War," 40–3, for a short survey of the Woodrow Wilson International Center for Scholars' new discoveries concerning the postwar clash between the United States and the USSR made available from the Russian archives.

44. See Milano, with Brogan, *Soldiers, Spies and the Rat Line,* 76–9. For a study of the surviving remnant's evacuation from Europe to America and the Middle East, see Wyman, *DP: Europe's Displaced Persons.* Wyman studied the complex period between the German surrender in May 1945 and the end of the Allied occupation; how DP camps worked; how Jews migrated west, many to British-controlled Palestine; who hated whom and why; the Baltic and Balkan

dilemmas; how attitudes changed toward Germans as the Cold War began; and how the politics of forced repatriation worked.

45. Hildebrandt, *It Happened at the Wall,* 52, 59.

46. Ibid., 77.

47. See Carr-Gregg, *Japanese Prisoners of War in Revolt* and Gordon, *Die Like a Carp,* for accounts of both breakout attempts. See also Ooka, *Taken Captive,* written by one of Japan's foremost literary critics. Regarding Japanese POWs in the U.S., see Krammer, "Japanese Prisoners of War in America," 85–90. See the Records of the Provost Marshal General's Office (Record Group 389) at the Modern Military Branch of the National Archives.

48. Summers, *Korean War Almanac,* 213, quoted in Brown, *Moscow Bound,* 442.

49. Based on several conversations with Stanley Weintraub, a former first lieutenant who participated in the program. See his *War in the Wards.* See also Tomedi, *No Bugles, No Drums,* who interviewed Professor Weintraub for his book.

50. Several oral histories given by American military nurses contain references to treating North Vietnamese and Vietcong POWs. See Walker, *A Piece of My Heart,* 99–100, 173–4.

51. This program operated similarly to what the Union Army did during the Civil War. See Brown, *Galvanized Yankees,* for a close study of Confederate prisoners who joined the Union Army to fight in the Indian wars but never against their former comrades. These highly effective volunteer units of former Confederate soldiers—the "galvanized Yankees"—were discharged in 1866.

52. See Sherry, *The Life of Graham Greene,* 2, 344, for the price list offered by the British in Malaya.

53. Most North Vietnamese POWs were repatriated in 1973 after the Paris Peace Accords were enacted. See Valentine, *The Phoenix Program,* for an extremely critical treatment of Phoenix. For a South Vietnamese evaluation of the suffering endured by members of special units after hostilities ended in April 1975, see Canh and Cooper, *Vietnam under Communism.*

54. Van Buskirk, "Enemy Ex-POWs in Our Midst?" 36.

55. McCoy, Mellnik, and Kelly, *Ten Escaped from Togo,* 71.

56. Churchill, *My Early Life,* 259.

57. On April 29, 1995, the Associated Press reported that the U.S. Air Force decided to drop resistance and escape training for Air Force Academy cadets.

58. Miguel de Saavedra Cervantes, *Don Quixote* (1605), quoted in Austin, *War,* 173.

59. Neave, *Saturday at M.I.9,* 53.

60. Williams, *The Wooden Horse,* 155.

61. Bierce, "One Officer, One Man," in *In the Midst of Life,* 108. See Fatout, *Ambrose Bierce,* 36–58, for his service as an infantry lieutenant in the 9th Regiment, Indiana Volunteers.

62. Greever and Abernathy, *Tiger-Lilies and Southern Prose,* 108.

Works Cited

Correspondence, Interviews, and Typescript Sources

Anloff, Lt. Col. Garry J., AUS (Ret.). Carmel, Calif. Personal letter, 24 November 1990.

Beville, David (pseudo). State College, Pa. Interview, 9 September 1989.

Blakeney, Robert W. Needham, Mass. Personal letter, 10 October 1990.

Burgess, Walter. Interview at Monash University, Melbourne, Australia, 18 May 1994.

Burman, Henry. State College, Pa. Interviews. 1991–94.

Close, Gordon. Unpublished diary. Courtesy of Douglas Cotton, October 1994.

Cotton, Douglas. South Norwood, London, England. Personal letter, 13 October 1994.

Doyle, Lt. Robert C., USNR. "NILO Ben Tre." Typescript. Naval Historical Center, Washington, D.C., 1978.

Enfros, Mike. Toluca Lake, Calif. Personal letter, 9 June 1993.

Fencl, Warren. Honolulu, Hawaii. Personal letter, 20 March 1991.

Harris, Guy H. Unpublished personal diary of the fall of Saigon and *Mayaguez* incident, 1990.

Hensley, William Wallace. "Autobiography." 1912. Typescript. Courtesy of William Crocken, Professor Emeritus of Theater Arts, Pennsylvania State University, University Park, Pa.

Hughett, Maurice. Dallas, Tex. Personal letter to Maj. Gordon Close, 23 April 1986. Courtesy of Douglas Cotton.

Johnson, Alan. Venice, Fla. Personal letter, 31 March 1990.

O'Hara, Michael. Personal letter to Walter S. Farquhar, Pottsville, Pa., 5 December 1945. *O'Hara Collection.* Pattee Library, Pennsylvania State University.

Pipkin, Lee Roy. Reno, Nev. Personal letter, 27 May 1989.

Nash, Carl. Harlem, Ga. Interviews in 1989 and letter, 29 June 1994.

Rand, Brian. Newark, Del. Personal letter, 13 September 1989.

Tanh (Full Name Withheld by Request). Interview, Melbourne, Australia, 18–20 May 1994.

Townsend, Rubin. Tempe, Ariz. Unpublished typescript, 1990; Personal letter, 3 March 1995.

Wohlfeld, Mark. Personal letter to Carl Nash, 18 October 1953. Courtesy of Carl Nash.

Published Works

Abell, Francis. *Prisoners of War in Britain 1756 to 1815: A Record of Their Lives, Their Romance and Their Sufferings.* London: Oxford University Press, 1914.

Absalom, Roger. *A Strange Alliance: Aspects of Escape and Survival in Italy 1943–45.* Florence: Leo Olschki, 1991.

Ackerley, J. R. *Escapers All: Being the Personal Narratives of Fifteen Escapers from War-time Prison Camps, 1914–1918.* London: John Lane The Bodley Head, 1932.

Adde, Nick. "Prison Escapee Found Location of Enemy Subs." *Fairfax Journal,* 12 April 1988, A4.

Adler, Jerry. "The Last Days of Auschwitz." *Newsweek International,* 16 January 1995, 14–26, 31.

Aikman, David. "The World Is Fresh and Bright and Beautiful." *Time,* 18 May 1992, 57–8.

Ajemian, Robert. "Terror and Tedium." *Time,* 27 August 1990, 50–2.

Alexander, Bevin. *The Future of Warfare.* New York: Norton, 1995.

Alexander, John K. "American Privateersmen in the Mill Prison, 1777–1782: An Evaluation." *Essex Institute Historical Collections* 102 (October 1966): 318–40.

———. "Forton Prison during the American Revolution: A Case Study of British Prisoner of War Policy and the American Prisoner Response to That Policy." *Essex Institute Historical Collections* 103 (1967): 365–89.

Alexander, J. W. "How We Escaped from Fort Warren." *New England Magazine* New Series 7, New Series 13 (September 1892–February 1893): 208–13.

Allen, Ethan. *The Narrative of Colonel Ethan Allen.* 1807. Ed. Brookes Hindle. Facsimile of the Walpole, N.H., 1807 Ed. New York: Corinth, 1961.

Alnwick, Kenneth J., and Thomas A. Fabyanic, eds. *Warfare in Lebanon.* Washington: National Defense University Press, 1988.

America's Historylands. Washington, D.C.: National Geographic, 1967.

The American Star. Mexico City, 23 September, 12 November 1847.

Andersch, Alfred. *Flucht in Etrurien. Zwei Erzählungen und ein Bericht.* Zürich: Diogenes, 1981.

Anderson, Olive. "American Escapes from British Naval Prisons during the War of Independence." *Mariner's Mirror* 41 (1955): 238–9.

———. "The Establishment of British Supremacy at Sea, and the Exchange of Naval Prisoners of War, 1689–1783." *English Historical Review* 75 (1960): 77–89.

———. "The Treatment of Prisoners of War in Britain during the American War of Independence." *Bulletin of the Institute of Historical Research* 28. 77 (May 1955): 63–83.

Anderson, Terry. *Den of Lions: Memoirs of Seven Years.* New York: Corgi, 1993.

Anderson, William C. *Bat-21.* 1980. Reprint, New York: Bantam, 1983.

Andrade, Dale. "Bring Our POWs Back Alive." *Vietnam Magazine,* February 1990, 22.

Andrews, Charles. *The Prisoners' Memoirs, or, Dartmoor Prison: Containing the*

Complete History of the Captivity of the Americans in England. New York: Privately printed, 1815.

Andrews, Charles M. *Guide to the Materials for American History, to 1783, in the Public Record Office of Great Britain.* 2 vols. Washington, D.C., 1912–1914.

Andrews, Wayne, ed. *Concise Dictionary of American History.* New York: Scribner's Sons, 1962.

Aptheker, Herbert. "Negro Casualties in the Civil War." *Journal of Negro History* 32 (January 1947): 10–80.

Arad, Yitzhak. *Belzec, Sibibor, Treblinka: The Operation Reinhard Death Camps.* Bloomington: Indiana University Press, 1987.

Archibald, Norman. *Heaven High Hell Deep, 1917–1918.* London & Toronto: Wm. Heinemann, 1935.

Armstrong, H. C. *Escape.* New York: Robert M. McBride, 1935.

Auschwitz: Nazi Extermination Camp. 2d enlarged ed. Warsaw: Interpress Publishers, 1985.

Austin, Alex, ed. *War.* New York: Signet, New American Library, 1957.

Australian War Memorial. *Prisoner of War Exhibits.* Canberra, ACT, Australia, 1994.

Bacque, James. *Other Losses: An Investigation into the Mass Deaths of German Prisoners at the Hands of the French and Americans after World War II.* Toronto: Stoddart, 1989.

Bailey, Lawrence, with Ron Martz. *Solitary Survivor: The First American POW in Southeast Asia.* New York: Brassey's, 1995.

Bailey, Ronald H. *Prisoners of War.* Alexandria, Va.: Time-Life Books, 1981.

Baker, C. Alice. *True Stories of New England Captives Carried to Canada during the Old French and Indian Wars.* 1897. Reprint, Bowie, Md.: Heritage, 1990.

Ballard, Leon. "Mail Call." *VFW Magazine,* August 1989, 9–10.

Bard, Mitchell. "American Victims of the Holocaust." *The Jewish Veteran* (Fall 1990), np.

Barker, A. J. *Behind Barbed Wire.* London: Purnell Book Services, 1974.

———. *Prisoners of War.* New York: Universe, 1975.

Barney, Joshua. *A Biographical Memoir of Commodore Joshua Barney.* Ed. Mary Barney. Boston: Gray and Bowen, 1832.

Baron, Richard, Maj. Abe Baum, and Richard Goldhurst. *Raid! The Untold Story of Patton's Secret Mission.* New York: Putnam, 1981.

Barrett, S. M., ed. *Geronimo: His Own Story.* New York: Ballantine, 1974.

Barziza, Decimus et Ultimus. *The Adventures of a Prisoner of War and Life and Scenes in Federal Prisons: Johnson's Island, Fort Delaware, and Point Lookout by an Escaped Prisoner of Hood's Texas Brigade.* Houston, Tex.: 1865.

Basile, Leon. *The Civil War Diary of Amos E. Stearns, a Prisoner at Andersonville.* Rutherford, N.J.: Fairleigh Dickinson University Press, 1981.

Basler, Roy P. *The Collected Works of Abraham Lincoln.* 9 vols. New Brunswick, N.J.: Rutgers University Press, 1955.

Baybutt, Ron. *Colditz: The Great Escapes.* Boston: Little, Brown, 1982.

Bayliss, John F., ed. *Black Slave Narratives.* London: Collier-Macmillan, 1970.

Becker, Laura L. "Prisoners of War in the American Revolution: A Community Perspective." *Military Affairs* 26: 4 (December 1982): 169–73.

Beitzell, Edwin W. *Point Lookout Prison Camp for Confederates*. Leonardtown, Md.: Published by the author for the St. Mary's County Historical Society, 1991.

Bell, Thomas W. *A Narrative of the Capture and Subsequent Sufferings of the Mier Prisoners in Mexico, Captured in the Cause of Texas, Dec. 26th, 1842, and Liberated Sept. 16, 1844. DeSoto County, Mississippi: Printed for the Author at the Press of R. Morris & Co. 1845*. Reprint, with editorial notes by James M. Day, Waco, Tex.: Texian Press, 1964.

Benson, Susan Williams, ed. *Berry Benson's Civil War Book: Memoirs of a Confederate Scout and Sharpshooter*. 1962. Athens: University of Georgia Press, 1992.

Bergman, Peter M., and Mort N. Bergman. *The Chronological History of the Negro in America*. New York: New American Library, 1969.

Berkhofer, Robert F., Jr. *The White Man's Indian: Images of the American Indian from Columbus to the Present*. New York: Vintage, 1979.

Berquist, Laura. "A Turncoat Comes Home." *Look*, 25 June 1957, 125–8.

Berry, William A., with James Edwin. *Prisoner of the Rising Sun*. Norman: University of Oklahoma Press, 1993.

Best, Geoffrey. *War and Law Since 1945*. Oxford: Clarendon Press, 1994.

Bevan, Donald, and Edmund Trzcinski. *Stalag 17: A Comedy Melodrama in Three Acts*. New York: Dramatist's Play Service, 1951.

"Bibliography and Monographs." *Indochina Chronology* 14. 4 (October–December 1995): 10.

Biderman, Albert D. *March to Calumny: The Story of American POWs in the Korean War*. New York: Macmillan, 1963.

Bierce, Ambrose. *In the Midst of Life: Tales of Soldiers and Civilians*. 1891. Reprint, intro. Clifton Fadiman. Secaucus: Citadel Press, 1946.

Billington, Ray Allen, and Martin Ridge. *Westward Expansion: A History of the American Frontier*. 5th ed. New York: Macmillan, 1982.

———. *The Westward Movement in the United States*. New York: D. Van Nostrand, 1959.

Bird, Roy. "Not Any Battlefield Heroics, But Sustained Bravery of Another Sort." *Military History* 10. 5 (December 1993): 28–30, 32, 86–7.

Bird, Tom. *American POWs of World War II: Forgotten Men Tell Their Stories*. Westport, Conn.: Praeger, 1992.

Bischof, Günter, and Stephen Ambrose. *Eisenhower and the German POWs: Facts Against Falsehood*. Baton Rouge: Louisiana State University Press, 1992.

Bischoff, Peter. "Der Western als amerikanischer Gründungsmythos: Die Tradition der Indian Captivity." *Studies in the Western* 11. 1/2 (1994): 3–29.

Blair, Clay. *Beyond Courage*. New York: David McKay, 1955.

Blakey, Scott. *Prisoner at War: The Survival of Commander Richard A. Stratton*. Garden City: Anchor Press/Doubleday, 1978.

Bland, Elizabeth, ed. *Escape Stories*. 1980. Reprint, London: Octopus Books, 1984.

Blassingame, Charles L. *The Underground Railroad*. New York: Prentice Hall, 1987.

Blockson, John W. *Slave Testimony.* Baton Rouge: Louisiana State University Press, 1977.

Boot, Chris. *Great Photographers of World War II.* London: Bison Books, 1993.

Bosworth, Allan R. *America's Concentration Camps.* 1967. Reprint, New York: Bantam, 1968.

Boudinot, Elias. *Journal of Historical Recollections of American Events during the Revolutionary War.* Philadelphia: Frederick Bourquin, 1894.

Boulle, Pierre. *Bridge over the River Kwai.* Trans. Xan Fielding. New York: Vantage, 1954.

Bouscaren, Anthony T. "Korea, Test of American Education." *Catholic World,* April 1956, 24–7.

Bowie, Lucy Leigh. "German Prisoners in the American Revolution." *Maryland Historical Magazine,* September 1945, 185–200.

Bowman, Larry G. *Captive Americans: Prisoners during the American Revolution.* Athens: Ohio University Press, 1976.

Brackenridge, Hugh Henry. *Indian Atrocities, The Narrative of the Perils and Sufferings of Doctor Knight and John Slover, among the Indians during the Revolutionary War.* 1843. Reprint, Cincinnati: U. P. James, 1867.

Brackman, Arnold C. *The Other Nuremberg: The Untold Story of the Tokyo War Crimes Trials.* New York: Morrow, 1987.

Bragg, William Harris. "The Union General Lost in Georgia." *Civil War Times Illustrated* 24. 4 (June 1985): 16–23.

Brändström, Elsa. *Among Prisoners of War in Russia and Siberia.* London: 1929.

Brannon, John. *Official Letters of the Military and Naval Officers of the United States in the War with Great Britain.* Washington City: Way and Gideon, 1823.

Brean, Herbert. "Prisoners of War the Reds Say Do Not Want to Come Home to America." *Life,* 19 October 1953, 44–5.

Breuer, William B. *The Great Raid on Cabanatuan: Rescuing the Doomed Ghosts of Bataan and Corregidor.* New York: Wiley, 1994.

Brew, Sarah L. "Making Amends for History: Legislative Reparations for Japanese Americans and Other Minority Groups." *Law and Inequality* 8 (1989): 179–201.

Brickhill, Paul. *Escape or Die: Authentic Stories of the RAF Escape Society.* New York: Norton, 1952.

———. *The Great Escape.* New York: Norton, 1950.

Brickhill, Paul, and Conrad Norton. *Escape to Danger.* London: Faber and Faber, 1946.

Brinkley, William. "Almost All Released Prisoners Come Home Happily." *Life,* 7 September 1953, 126–7.

Brody, Curt. "Observation and Reëducation of German Prisoners of War." *Harvard Educational Review* 14 (January 1944): 12–19.

Brooks, Janice Young. *Guest of the Emperor.* New York: Ballantine Books, 1990.

Brown, Alexander D. *Galvanized Yankees.* Urbana: University of Illinois Press, 1963.

Brown, Charles Brockden. *Edgar Huntly.* 1803. Reprint, intro. David Lee Clark. New York: Macmillan, 1928.

Brown, Charles H. *Agents of Manifest Destiny.* Chapel Hill: University of North Carolina Press, 1980.

Brown, F. C. "Escape in Indochina: Some U.S. POWs Found Freedom on Their Own." *Behind the Lines* (July/August 1994), 39–41.

Brown, Henry Box. *The Narrative of Henry Box Brown: Written by a Statement of Facts Made by Himself.* Boston: Brown & Stearns, 1849.

Brown, John M. G. "Our Unknown POWs." *The American Legion* (September 1995), 74, 76, 106.

———. *Moscow Bound: Policy, Politics and the POW/MIA Dilemma.* Eureka, Calif.: Veteran Press, 1993.

Brown, John M. G., and Thomas G. Ashworth. "A Secret That Shames Humanity." *U.S. Veteran News and Report* (29 May 1989): 1–12.

Brown, Parker B. " 'Crawford's Defeat': A Ballad." *Western Pennsylvania Historical Magazine* 64. 4 (October 1981): 311–27.

Brown, William Wells. *Narrative of William W. Brown, a Fugitive Slave.* 1847. Ed. William L. Andrews. *From Fugitive Slave to Free Man: The Autobiography of William Wells Brown.* New York: Mentor Book of the New American Library, 1993.

Browne, Junius Henri. *Four Years in Secessia.* Hartford, Conn.: O. D. Case and Company, 1865.

Browne, W. B. "Stranger Than Fiction: Capture of the United States Steamer *Maple Leaf,* Near Cape Henry, Half a Century Ago." *Southern Historical Society Papers* 39 (April 1914): 181–5.

Burdick, Charles, and Ursula Moessner. *The German Prisoners of War in Japan, 1914–1920.* Lanham, Md.: University Press of America, 1984.

Burgess, Alan. *The Longest Tunnel: The True Story of the Great Escape.* New York: Grove Weidenfeld, 1990.

Burgess, Carter. "Prisoners of War: Foreword." *Columbia Law Review* 56: 5 (May 1956): 676.

Burson, William. *A Race for Liberty: or My Capture, Imprisonment, and Escape.* Wellsville, Ohio: W. G. Foster, Printer, 1867.

Burt, Kendal, and James Leasor. *The One That Got Away.* New York: Ballantine, 1957.

———. "The One That Got Away." Charles S. Verral, Ed. *True Stories of Great Escapes.* Pleasantville, New York: Reader's Digest Association, 1977. 394–417.

Buruma, Ian. *The Wages of Guilt: Memories of War in Germany and Japan.* New York: Farrar, Strauss & Giroux, 1994.

Butterfield, C. W. *An Account of the Expedition against Sandusky under Colonel William Crawford in 1782.* Cincinnati: U. P. James, 1873.

Butterfield, Roger. "Search for a Black Past." *Life,* 22 November 1968, 90, 93–104B, 108ff.

Byrne, Frank. "Prisons and Prisoners of War." Eds. Allan Nevins, James I. Robertson, Jr., and Bell I. Wiley. *Civil War Books: A Critical Bibliography.* Baton Rouge: Louisiana State University Press, 1970. 185–206.

Cade, James B. "Out of the Mouths of Ex-Slaves." *Journal of Negro History* 22 (April 1935): 294–337.

Campbell, Charles. *The Intolerable Hulks: British Shipboard Confinement, 1776–1857.* Bowie, Md.: Heritage Press, 1994.

Cangemi, Joseph P., and Casimir J. Kowalski. *Andersonville Prison: Lessons in Organizational Failure.* Lanham, Md.: University Press of America, 1992.

Canh, Nguyen Van, and Earle Cooper. *Vietnam under Communism, 1975–1982.* Stanford, Calif.: Hoover Institution Press, 1983.

Caristo, Col. Fred, USA (Ret.). "We Tried Hard: POW Recovery Ops in Southeast Asia." *Soldier of Fortune,* February 1992, 57–9, 81.

Carlson, Kurt. *One American Must Die: A Hostage's Personal Account of the Hijacking of Flight 847.* New York: Congdon & Weed, 1986.

Carney, J. C. "Haiti: 'Treading on Loaded Barrels of Gunpowder.'" *VFW Magazine,* March 1995, 34–6, 10.

Carr-Gregg, Charlotte. *Japanese Prisoners of War in Revolt: The Outbreaks at Featherston and Cowra during World War II.* Brisbane, Australia: University of Queensland Press, 1978.

Carroll, John M. *The Black Military Experience in the American West.* New York: Liveright, 1971.

Cartwright, Henry. *Within Four Walls.* London: Edward Arnold, 1930.

Casady, Edwin. "The Reorientation Program for POWs at Fort Eustis, Va." *The American Oxonian* (July 1947): 169–96.

"Case History of Those 21: What Their Lives Show." *Newsweek,* 18 January 1954, 52–4.

Castel, Albert. "The Fort Pillow Massacre: A Fresh Examination of the Evidence." *Civil War History* 4 (1958): 37–50.

Catlin, George. *North American Indians.* 1844. Ed. Peter Matthiessen. New York: Penguin, 1996.

Cavada, Frederick Fernandez. *Libby Life: Experiences of a Prisoner of War in Richmond, Va., 1863–1864.* Philadelphia: King and Baird, 1865.

Caverly, Robert B. *Heroism of Hannah Dustan Together with the Indian Wars of New England.* Boston: Russell, 1874.

Chapman, Abraham. *Steal Away.* New York: Praeger, 1971.

Child, Francis James. *The English and Scottish Popular Ballads.* 5 vols. 1884–1888. Reprint, New York: Dover, 1965.

Chinese People's Committee for World Peace. *Shall Brothers Be.* Peking: Foreign Languages Press, 1952.

Chipman, Norton P. *The Horrors of the Andersonville Rebel Prison. Trial of Henry Wirz, the Andersonville Jailer: Jefferson Davis' Defense of Andersonville Prison Fully Refuted.* San Francisco, 1891.

———. *The Tragedy of Andersonville: The Trial of Captain Henry Wirz.* San Francisco, 1911.

Churchill, Winston S. *My Early Life: A Roving Commission.* 1930. Reprint, New York: Charles Scribner's Sons, 1958.

Cimprich, John, and Robert C. Mainfort, Jr. "Fort Pillow Revisited: New Evidence about an Old Controversy." *Civil War History* 28 (1982): 293–306.

Clarke, Hugh V. *Last Stop Nagasaki.* London: Allen and Unwin, 1984.

Clausewitz, Karl von. *On War.* 1832. Reprint, New York: Penguin, 1968.

Clavell, James. *King Rat.* New York: Dell, 1962.

Cobb, Josiah. *A Greenhorn's First Cruise Together with a Residence of Five Months in Dartmoor.* 2 vols. Baltimore: Cushing and Brothers, 1841.

Coggeshall, George. *History of American Privateers.* New York, 1876.

Cohen, Sheldon S. "The Preachers and the Prisoners." *Essex Institute Historical Collections* 126 (January 1990) 1: 1–26.

Coker, George T. "P. W." *United States Naval Institute Proceedings* 100. 9 (October 1974): 41–6.

Colburn, Forrest D. *The Vogue of Revolution in Poor Countries.* Princeton, N.J.: Princeton University Press, 1994.

Colburn, Jeremiah. "A List of the Americans Committed to Old Mill Prison Since the American War. When Taken, Vessels Taken in, When Committed, Place of Abode, Exchanged, Ran Away and Died in Prison. *New England Historical and Genealogical Register* 19 (January, April, July 1865): 74–5, 136–41, 209–13.

"The Coldest Hostage Crisis." *Newsweek International,* 22 January 1996, 27.

Cole, Garold L. *Civil War Eyewitnesses: An Annotated Bibliography of Books and Articles, 1955–1986.* Foreword by James I. Robertson. Columbia: University of South Carolina Press, 1988.

Cole, James L. "Dulag Luft Recalled and Revisited." *Aerospace Historian* 19. 2 (1972): 62–5.

Coleman, Emma Lewis. *New England Captives Carried to Canada.* 2 vols. Portland, Maine: Southgate, 1925.

Colonial Dames of America. *American War Songs.* Philadelphia: Privately printed, 1925.

Commager, Henry Steele, and Milton Cantor. *Documents of American History.* 2 vols. 10th ed. Englewood Cliffs, N.J.: Prentice Hall, 1988.

Condron, Andrew M., Richard Cordon, and Lawrence V. Sullivan, eds. *Thinking Soldiers.* Peking: New World, 1955.

Confederate Veteran 31: 413–14; 37: 6.

Connat, Jennet, with Zofia Smardz and Rod Norland. "And Then There Were Six." *Newsweek,* 30 September 1985, 32.

"Controversial Prisoner Freed." *New York Daily News,* 5 March 1973, 1.

Cooke, Donald E. *For Conspicuous Gallantry: Winners of the Medal of Honor.* Maplewood, N.J.: C. S. Hammond, 1966.

Cooper, Alonzo. *In and Out of Rebel Prisons.* Oswego, N.Y.: R. J. Oliphant, Printer, 1888.

Cooper, James Fenimore. *Last of the Mohicans.* New York: New American Library, 1980.

Corcoran, Michael. *The Captivity of General Corcoran.* Philadelphia: Barclay and Company, 1862.

Cornish, Dudley Taylor. *The Sable Arm: Black Troops in the Union Army, 1861–1865.* Lawrence: University Press of Kansas, 1987.

Coulter, Richard, and Thomas Barclay. *Volunteers: The Mexican War Journals of Private Richard Coulter and Sergeant Thomas Barclay, Company E, Second Pennsylvania Infantry.* Kent, Ohio: Kent State University Press, 1991.

Cranwell, John Philips, and William Bowers Crane. *Men of Marque: A History of Private Armed Vessels out of Baltimore during the War of 1812.* New York: Norton, 1940.

Crawley, Aidan. *Escape from Germany: A History of RAF Escapes during the War.* London: Collins, 1956.

Creel, George. *Sam Houston: Colossus in Buckskin.* New York: Cosmopolitan, 1928.

Crews, Ed. "Medal of Honor: The U.S. Navy Officer Had Vital Information to Deliver." *Military History* 7. 3 (December 1990): 16, 68.

Crow, Richard. "Free at Last." *AXPOW Bulletin* 40. 2 (February 1983): 29.

Cunliffe, Marcus. *Soldiers and Civilians: The Martial Spirit in America 1775–1865.* Boston: Little Brown, 1968.

Davenport, Basil. *Great Escapes.* New York: Sloane, 1952.

David, Clayton. *They Helped Me Escape: From Amsterdam to Gibraltar in 1944.* Manhattan, Kans.: Sunflower University Press, 1988.

Davis, Gerald H. "Biographical Essay on Re-Education of Prisoners of War in Two World Wars." Unpublished paper. POW Conference. Defense Studies Institute: Australian Defense Force Academy, Canberra, May 1994.

———. "Deutsche Kriegsgefangene in Ersten Weltkrieg in Russland." *Militärgeschichtliche Mitteilungen* 31 (January 1982).

———. "'Orgelsdorf': A World War I Internment Camp in America." *Yearbook of German-American Studies* 26 (1991): 249–65.

Davis, John P., ed. *The American Negro Reference Book.* Englewood Cliffs, N.J.: Prentice Hall, 1966.

Daws, Gavin. *Prisoners of the Japanese: POWs of World War II in the Pacific.* New York: William Morrow, 1994.

Day, George E. "Promises to Keep." *Reader's Digest* (December 1991), 107–11.

———. *Return with Honor.* Mesa, Ariz.: Champlin Fighter Museum Press, 1989.

Day, James M. *Black Beans and Goose Quills.* Waco: Texian Press, 1970.

———, ed. "Diary of James A. Glassock, Mier Man." *Texana* 1 (Spring 1963): 85–119; I (Summer 1963): 225–38.

Deane-Drummond, Anthony. *Return Ticket.* London: Collins, 1953.

Deering, John A. "Mail Call." *VFW Magazine,* January 1996, 6.

Dengler, Dieter. *Escape from Laos.* Novato, Calif.: Presidio, 1979.

———. "I Escaped from a Red Prison." *Saturday Evening Post,* 3 December 1966, 27–33.

Dennett, Carl P. *Prisoners of the Great War.* Boston: Houghton Mifflin Riverside Press, Cambridge, 1919.

Denney, Robert E. *Civil War Prisons and Escapes: A Day-by-Day Chronicle.* Foreword by Edwin C. Bearss. New York: Sterling Publishing Company, 1995.

Denton, Jeremiah A., Jr., with Ed Brandt. *When Hell Was in Session.* New York: Reader's Digest, 1976.

Der Adler 1941. Propaganda Magazine of the German Air Force. Hamburg: Jahr Verlag, 1977.

Der Ruf. Prison Camp Anti-Nazi Newspaper. 26 vols. Prisoner of War Special Projects Division. Fort Phil Kearney, Rhode Island, 1944–1945. Wisconsin State Library: Madison, Wisconsin.

Derry, Sam. *The Rome Escape Line: The Story of the British Organization in Rome for Assisting Escaped Prisoners of War, 1943–1944*. London: Harrap, 1960.

Derry, Sam, with David MacDonald. "Vatican Pimpernel." Ed. Charles S. Verral. *True Stories of Great Escapes*. Pleasantville, N.Y.: Reader's Digest Association, 1977. 341–6.

Derounian, Kathryn Zabelle. "Puritan Orthodoxy and the 'Survivor's Syndrome' in Mary Rowlandson's Indian Captivity Narrative." *Early American Literature* 22 (Spring 1987): 82–93.

Des Pres, Terrence. *The Survivor: An Anatomy of Life in the Death Camps*. New York: Oxford University Press, 1976.

Devore, Robert. "Our 'Pampered' War Prisoners." *Colliers*, 14 October 1944, 144.

Dick, Laurie Rothrock. "The Great Escape: Tunneling Out of Stalag Luft III Was a Test of Endurance, Ingenuity and Daring." *The Retired Officer Magazine* (September 1993): 66–70.

Dictionary of American History. Rev. ed. New York: Scribner's Sons, 1976.

"Die Flucht des Oberleutnants v. Werra." *Der Adler* 4 (1941): 42.

"Do We Pamper Our POWs?" *Colliers*, 2 June 1945, 78.

Dorson, Richard M. *America Rebels: Narratives of the Patriots*. 1953. Reprint, Greenwich, Conn.: Fawcett, 1966.

Douglass, Frederick. *My Bondage and My Freedom*. 1855. Reprint, New York: Arno Press, 1968.

———. *Narrative of the Life of Frederick Douglass, An American Slave, Written by Himself*. 1845. Reprint, New York: Signet, 1968.

Dower, John W. *War without Mercy: Race and Power in the Pacific War*. New York: Pantheon, 1986.

Downey, Charles. "Oh, Those Colorful Eel-Eating Pilgrims." *Washington Post*, 22 November 1987, 1L, 6L.

Downey, Fairfax. "Tragic Story of the San Patricio Battalion." *American Heritage* 6. 4 (June 1955): 20–3.

Doyle, Robert C. *Voices from Captivity: Interpreting the American POW Narrative*. Lawrence: University Press of Kansas, 1994.

Drake, James Madison. *Fast and Loose in Dixie*. New York: The Authors' Publishing Company, 1880.

———. *Narratives of the Capture, Imprisonment, and Escape of J. Madison Drake, Captain Ninth New Jersey Veteran Volunteers*. (N. P.) 1868.

Dramesi, John A. *Code of Honor*. New York: W. W. Norton, 1976.

Drinnon, Richard. *Facing West: The Metaphysics of Indian-Hating and Empire Building*. New York: New American Library, 1980.

Dufur, Simon Miltmore. *Over the Dead Line, or Tracked by Bloodhounds*. Burlington, Vt.: Printed by The Free Press Association, 1902.

Duke, Basil W. *History of Morgan's Cavalry*. Ed. Cecil Fletcher Holland. Bloomington: Indiana University Press, 1961.

"Dulag Luft" Folder. "Camp Reports—Germany-Air Force Transit Camps" File. Modern Military Branch, Record Group 389. Washington, D.C.: National Archives and Records Center.

Dunn, J. P. "The POW Chronicles: A Bibliographic Review." *Armed Forces and Society* 9. 3 (Spring 1983): 495–514.

———. "The Vietnam War POW/MIAs: An Annotated Bibliography." *Bulletin of Bibliography* 45. 2 (June 1988): 152–8.

Dupuy, Ernest, and William Baumer. *The Little Wars of the United States.* New York: Hawthorne, 1968.

Durand, Arthur A. *Stalag Luft III: The Secret Story.* New York: Simon and Schuster, 1988.

Durnford, John. *Branch Line to Burma.* 1958. Reprint, London: Four Square, 1968.

Dye, Ira. "American Maritime Prisoners of War, 1812–1813." Ed. Timothy J. Runyan. *Ships, Seafaring and Society: Essays in Maritime History.* Detroit: Wayne State University Press, 1987.

Dyess, William E. *The Dyess Story: The Eye-Witness Account of the Death March from Bataan and the Narrative Experiences in Japanese Prison Camps and Eventual Escape.* New York: G. P. Putnam's Sons, 1944.

"Echoes of Honor: Of Tragedy, Treachery and a Pointman's Valor." *Soldier of Fortune,* December 1989, 43, 50.

Editors of the *Army Times. American Heroes of Asian Wars.* New York: Dodd and Mead, 1968.

Editors of the Boston Publishing Company. *Above and Beyond: History of the Medal of Honor from the Civil War to Vietnam.* Boston, Mass: Boston Publishing Company, 1985.

———. "The Only Woman." *Above and Beyond: A History of the Medal of Honor from the Civil War to Vietnam.* Boston: Boston Publishing Company, 1985. 38–9.

Edwards, Linden F. "Dr. Mary Edwards Walker (1832–1919): Charlatan or Martyr?" *Ohio State Medical Journal* 54 (September 1958): 1160–2; 54 (October 1958): 1296–8.

Ehrmann, H. W. "An Experiment in Political Education: The POW Schools in the United States." *Sociology Review* 14 (1947): 304–20.

Ellinwood, Ralph. *Behind the German Lines: A Narrative of the Everyday Life of an American Prisoner of War.* New York: Knickerbocker Press, 1920.

Encarnacion Prisoners Written by a Prisoner. Louisville: Prentice and Weissinger, 1848.

English, James D. "Life in Rebel Prison: Narrative by an Ohio Boy Just Escaped from Andersonville, Georgia." *The Cincinnati Commercial,* 10 July 1864; *New York Daily Tribune,* 26 July 1864: 7: 1: 2.

Ennis, John W. *Adventures in Rebeldom; or Ten Months' Experience of Prison Life.* New York, *Business Mirror* Print, 1863.

Epstein, Miles Z. "The Next War: How Far Should Americans Go to Bring Them Home?" *American Legion Magazine,* March 1993, 20–7, 50–3.

"Escape in Arizona." *Time,* 8 January 1945, 16.

"Escape from Butchery." *Newsweek,* 30 October 1950, 32.

"Escape of Prisoners from Johnson's Island." *Southern Historical Society Papers* 18 (1890): 428–31.

Estabrooks, Henry L. *Adrift in Dixie; or, A Yankee Officer among the Rebels.* New York: Carleton, 1866.

Evans, A. J. *Escape and Liberation, 1940–1945.* London: Hodder & Stoughton, 1945.

Fabel, Robin F. A. "King Dick—Captive Black Leader." *New Hampshire Bulletin* 36 (1973): 58–61.

———. "Self-Help in Dartmoor: Black and White Prisoners in the War of 1812." *Journal of the Early Republic* 9 (Summer 1989): 165–90.

Falk, Richard A. *The Vietnam War and International Law.* Princeton, N.J.: Princeton University Press, 1968.

Famous Adventures and Prison Escapes of the Civil War. New York: Century, 1893.

Famous Plays of To-Day. London: Gollanz, 1929.

Farrar-Hockley, Anthony. *The Edge of the Sword.* London: Frederick Muller, 1954.

Fatout, Paul. *Ambrose Bierce: The Devil's Lexicographer.* Norman: University of Oklahoma Press, 1951.

Federal Writers' Project. *Slave Narratives: A Folk History of Slavery in the United States from Interviews with Former Slaves.* 17 vols. Washington, D.C.: U.S. Government Printing Office, 1941.

Fehrenbach, T. R. *Lone Star: A History of Texas and the Texans.* New York: Wings Books, 1991.

Fellowes-Gordon, Ian, ed. *The World's Greatest Escapes.* New York: Taplinger, 1967.

Felsen, Milt. *The Anti-Warrior: A Memoir.* Intro. Albert E. Stone. Iowa City: University of Iowa Press, 1989.

Ferguson, Joseph. *Life and Struggles in Rebel Prisons. A Record of the Sufferings, Escapes, Adventures, and Starvation of the Union Prisoners.* Philadelphia: J. M. Ferguson, 1865.

Ferrell, Robert H. *American Diplomacy: The Twentieth Century.* New York: Norton, 1988.

Fincher, Jack. "By Convention, the Enemy Within Never Did Without." *Smithsonian* 6 (1995): 125–43.

Fittkau, Gerhard. *Mein 33. Jahr: Erinnerungen eines ostpreußischen Pfarrers.* Köln: Verlag Wort und Werk St. Augustin, 1978.

Flammer, Philip. "Dulag Luft: The Third Reich's Prison Camp for Airmen." *Aerospace Historian* 19. 2 (1972): 58–62.

Fleming, Thomas. "Evasion in Enemy-Held Territory Was Dangerous to Both Downed Allied Airmen and Their Civilian Helpers." *Military History* (April 1994), 26–7, 84–6.

Flory, William E. S. *Prisoners of War: A Study in the Development of International Law.* Washington: American Council on Public Affairs, 1942.

Fooks, Herbert C. *Prisoners of War.* Federalsburg, Md.: J. W. Stowell, 1924.

Foot, Michael Richard D., and James M. Langley. *MI-9: Escape and Evasion 1939–1945.* Boston: Little, Brown, 1980.

Foote, Morris C. "Narrative of an Escape from a Rebel Prison Camp." *American*

Heritage 11. 4 (June 1960): 65–75; *Civil War Chronicles* (Summer 1993): 50–60.

Fowler, William M., Jr. *Jack Tars and Commodores: The American Navy, 1783–1815.* Boston: Houghton Mifflin, 1984.

Franklin, H. Bruce. *MIA: Mythmaking in America.* New York: Lawrence Hill, 1992.

Franklin, John Hope. "Rebels, Runaways and Heroes: The Bitter Years of Slavery." *Life,* 22 November 1968, 92, 108, 110, 112–14, 116–20.

Fraser, George MacDonald. *Quartered Safe Out Here: A Recollection of the War in Burma.* London: Haverhill/Harper Collins, 1992.

Fredriksen, John C., comp. *Free Trade and Sailors' Rights: A Bibliography of the War of 1812.* Westport, Conn.: Greenwood, 1985.

Freemont, Chuck. "Let's Go Get 'Em: *Soldier of Fortune* Interviews Colonel Fred Caristo—Top POW Hunter." *Soldier of Fortune,* February 1992, 52–5, 79.

Frelinghuysen, Joseph S. *Passages to Freedom: A Story of Capture and Escape.* Manhattan, Kans.: Sunflower University Press, 1990.

Frost, Meigs O. "New Orleans Test Tube for German Democracy." *Times-Picayune Sunday Magazine,* 23 September 1945.

Fruman, Norman. "Last Days at Stalag 7A." *Times Literary Supplement,* 5 May 1995, 6.

Fugita, Frank. *Foo: A Japanese-American Prisoner of the Rising Sun.* Denton: University of North Texas Press, 1993.

Gaertner, Georg, with Arnold Krammer. *Hitler's Last Soldier in America.* New York: Stein and Day, 1985.

Gaither, Ralph, with Steve Henry. *With God in a POW Camp.* Nashville, Tenn.: Broadman Press, 1973.

Garland, Brock. *War Movies.* New York: Facts on File Publications, 1987.

Garrett, Richard. *Jailbreakers.* London: Granada, 1983.

———. *POW: The Uncivil Face of War.* Devon (U.K.): David and Charles, 1981.

———. *The Raiders: The World's Most Elite Strike Forces That Altered the Course of War and History.* New York: Van Nostrand Reinhold, 1980.

"The Geneva Convention and the Treatment of Prisoners of War in Vietnam." *Harvard Law Review* 80 (1967): 851, 856–8.

"German Methods and Experiences of Prisoner Interrogation." A.D.I. (K) Report 388, Microfilm Roll A5405. Doc. F164. Troy H. Middleton Library. Baton Rouge: Louisiana State University.

Gibson, James William. *Warrior Dreams: Violence and Manhood in Post-Vietnam America.* New York: Hill and Wang, 1994.

Giles, Donald T., Jr. *Captive of the Rising Sun: The POW Memoirs of Rear Admiral Donald T. Giles.* Annapolis, Md.: Naval Institute Press, 1994.

Gillette, William. *Held by the Enemy: The Five Act War Drama.* 1898. Reprint, New York: Samuel French, 1925.

———. *Secret Service: A Drama of the Southern Confederacy in Four Acts.* 1898. Arthur Hobson Quinn, ed. *Representative American Plays: From 1767 to the Present Day.* 7th ed. New York: Appleton-Century-Crofts, 1953. 545–620.

Ginn, John L. *Sugamo Prison, Tokyo: An Account of the Trial and Sentencing of*

Japanese War Criminals in 1948, by a U.S. Participant. Jefferson, N.C.: McFarland, 1995.

Glass, Charles. "The Big Stick." *Times Literary Supplement,* 17 November 1995, 7.

———. *Tribes with Flags: A Dangerous Passage Through the Chaos of the Middle East.* New York: Atlantic Monthly Press, 1990.

Glazier, Willard W. *The Capture, the Prison Pen and the Escape.* New York: United States Publishing Company, 1868.

Gleek, Lewis E., Jr. "The Rescue of the Los Baños Internees." *Laguna in American Times: Coconuts and Revolucionarios Historical Conservation Society* 34 (1981): 144–9.

Gordon, Dennis. *Lafayette Escadrille Pilot Biographies.* Missoula, Mont.: The Doughboy Historical Society, 1991.

Gordon, Harry. *Die Like a Carp: The Story of the Greatest Prison Escape Ever.* Stanmore, Australia: Cassell Australia, 1978.

"The Government of Dartmoor Prison." Portsmouth, N.H.: *Journal of Literature and Politics* Saturday, 5 April 1834: 2: 2.

Gragg, Rod. *The Illustrated Confederate Reader.* New York: Harper and Row, 1989.

Grant, Zalin. *Survivors: American POW's in Vietnam.* 1975. Reprint, New York: Berkley, 1985.

Grashio, Samuel C., and Bernard Norling. *Return to Freedom: The War Memoirs of Col. Samuel C. Grashio USAF (Ret.).* Tulsa, Okla.: MCN Press, 1982.

Gray, J. Glenn. *The Warriors: Reflections on Men in Battle.* New York: Harcourt, Brace, 1959.

Green, John Uriah. *My Life in Prison and Escape: A Story of the Civil War.* Ed. J. G. Whitten. Navasota, Tex.: *Navasota Examiner* Review, 1952.

Green, Thomas Jefferson. *Journal of the Texian Expedition against Mier, Subsequent Imprisonment of the Author, His Sufferings and Final Escape from the Castle of Perote with Reflections upon the Present and Probable Future Relations of Texas, Mexico, and the United States.* New York: Harper and Brothers, 1845; Reprint, Austin: Steck, 1935.

Greenberg, Susan H., with Dana Thomas. "Travels with My Captor." *Newsweek International,* 12 February 1996, 19.

Greene, Albert. *Recollections of the Jersey Prison Ship from the Manuscript of Captain Thomas Dring.* New York: Corinth, 1961.

Greever, Garland, and Cecil Abernathy, eds. *Tiger-Lilies and Southern Prose.* Baltimore: Johns Hopkins University Press, 1945.

Grey, Jeffrey. *A Military History of Australia.* Cambridge, U.K.: Cambridge University Press, 1990.

Groom, Winston, and Duncan Spencer. *Conversations with the Enemy: The Story of PFC Robert Garwood.* New York: Putnam, 1983.

"Guards Said to Have Helped Pilot Escape in Laos." *New York Times,* 4 September 1964, 9: 2.

"Guests of the VC." *Newsweek,* 11 July 1966, 37.

Guilmartin, John. *The Mayaguez and the Battle of Koh Tang.* College Station: Texas A & M University Press, 1996.

Halberstam, David. *The Fifties.* New York: Fawcett Columbine, 1993.

Hall, James Norman. "Escape De Luxe." *Harper's Monthly Magazine,* 160 (December 1929–May 1930): 91–103.

———. *My Island Home: An Autobiography.* Boston: Little, Brown, 1952.

Hardy, Gordon, ed. "Prisoner of the *U-90:* Edward Izac's Escape." Editors of the Boston Publishing Company. *Above and Beyond: History of the Medal of Honor from the Civil War to Vietnam.* Boston, Mass.: Boston Publishing Company, 1985. 134–8.

Hardy, Hiram. "Andersonville Prison: A Short Contribution to History from an Authentic Source." *Big Rapids Pioneer,* 28 August 1879.

Haring, C. H. *The Spanish Empire in America.* New York: Harcourt, Brace, 1963.

Harrold, John. *Libby, Andersonville, Florence, the Capture, Imprisonment, Escape, and Rescue of John Harrold.* Philadelphia, Pa.: W. B. Selheimer, 1870.

Hasson, Benjamin F. *Escape from the Confederacy—Overpowering the Guards—Midnight Leap from a Moving Train—Through Swamps and Forest—Bloodhounds—Thrilling Events.* Byron, Ohio: Published by the author, 1890.

Hastings, Max. *The Korean War.* London: Guild Publishing, 1987.

Hatch, A. Francis. "One Despicable Part of the Vietnam War Is the False Portrayal of American Soldiers as Bloodthirsty Barbarians." *Vietnam Magazine,* August 1995, 58, 60–2.

Hatch, Gardner, ed. *American Ex-Prisoners of War.* Paducah, Ky.: Turner Publishing Company, 1988.

Hawkins, Jack. *Never Say Die.* Philadelphia: Dorrance, 1961.

Hawthorne, Nathaniel. *The Yarn of a Yankee Privateer.* 1846. Intro. Clifford Smyth. Reprint, New York: Funk and Wagnalls, 1926.

Haynes, Sam W. *Soldiers of Misfortune: The Sommervell and Mier Expeditions.* Austin: University of Texas Press, 1990.

Hays, Otis, Jr. *Home from Siberia: The Secret Odysseys of Interned American Airmen in World War II.* College Station: Texas A & M Press, 1990.

Heard, J. Norman. *White into Red: A Study of the Assimilation of White Persons Captured by Indians.* Metuchen, N.J.: The Scarecrow Press, 1973.

Hemmingway, Al. "Daring Raid at Son Tay." *VFW Magazine,* November 1995, 20–3.

Henderson, William Darryl. *Cohesion: The Human Element in Combat.* Washington, D.C.: National Defense University Press, 1985.

Herbert, Charles. *A Relic of the Revolution.* 1829. Boston: Charles H. Pierce, Reprint, 1847; Arthur, Reprint, 1855.

Hesseltine, William Best. *Civil War Prisons: A Study in Prison Psychology.* Columbus: Ohio State University Press, 1930.

Higa, Karen M., et al. *The View from Within: Japanese American Art from the Internment Camps 1942–1945.* Seattle: University of Washington Press, 1995.

Hildebrandt, Reiner. *It Happened at the Wall.* Berlin: Verlag Haus am Checkpoint Charlie, 1992.

Hilsman, Roger. *To Move a Nation.* New York: Doubleday, 1967.

Hines, James. "Infamous Border Guerrilla William Clarke Quantrill Met His

Fate in the Unlikely Eastern Setting of Kentucky." *Wild West* (October 1991): 16, 68–9.

Hines, Thomas H. "Morgan and His Men Escape from Prison." *Century Magazine* (January 1891) in Philip van Doren Stern. *Secret Missions of the Civil War.* Chicago: Rand McNally, 1959. 155–65.

Hirsh, Diana. "German Atrocities Raise Questions: Are Nazi POWs 'Coddled' Here?" *Newsweek,* 7 May 1945, 60–61.

Historical Collections of the Michigan Pioneer and Historical Society. vol. 15. Lansing, 1880.

Hockersmith, Lorenzo Dow. *Morgan's Escape. A Thrilling Story of War Times.* Madisonville, Ky.: Glenn's Graphic Print, 1903.

Hoffman, Andy. *Beehive.* Sag Harbor: Permanent Press, 1992.

Hoffman, Conrad. *In the Prison Camps of Germany: A Narrative of "Y" Service among Prisoners of War.* New York: Association Press, 1920.

Holmes, Clay. *The Elmira Prison Camp.* New York: Rickenbacker Press, 1912.

Hoover, J. Edgar. "Alien Enemy Control." *Iowa Law Review* 29 (March 1944): 396–408.

———. "Enemies at Large." *American Magazine* (April 1944), 29–30.

Hopkins, G. T. "The San Patricio Battalion in the Mexican War." *Journal of the U.S. Cavalry Association* 24 (September 1913): 279–84.

Horowitz, Janice M., Nadya Labi, Lina Lofaro, and Megan Rutherford. "An End to the Long Ordeal." *Time International,* 12 February 1996, 11.

Howard, Michael. *Restraints on War.* New York: Oxford University Press, 1979.

Howe, Thomas H. *Adventures of an Escaped Union Prisoner from Andersonville.* San Francisco, Calif.: H. S. Crocker, 1886.

Howes, Craig. *Voices of Vietnam POWs: Witnesses to Their Fight.* New York: Oxford University Press, 1993.

Hubbell, John. "The Long Way Home." Ed. Charles S. Verral. *True Stories of Great Escapes.* Pleasantville, New York: Reader's Digest Association, 1977. 111–20.

Huizinga, Johan. *Homo Ludens: A Study of the Play-Element in Culture.* 1944. Reprint, Boston: Beacon, 1964.

Hunter, Edward. *Brainwashing: The Story of the Men Who Defied It.* 1956. Reprint, New York: Pyramid, 1964.

Inada, Lawson Fusao. *Legends from Camp.* Minneapolis: Coffee House Press, 1993.

Isaacs, Edouard Victor. *Prisoner of the U-90.* Boston: Houghton Mifflin, 1919.

———. "Report on Imprisonment in Germany and Escape Therefrom." Letter of 13 November 1918 to the Secretary of the Navy. *Naval Historical Foundation Manuscript Collection 93–6.* Washington, D.C.: Library of Congress.

Jacobs, Bruce. *Heroes of the Army: The Medal of Honor and Its Winners.* New York: Norton, 1956.

Jacobs, Paul, and Saul Landau, with Eve Pell. *To Serve the Devil.* 2 vols. New York: Vintage, 1971.

Jacobsen, David. "How I Survived." *Accent on Living,* Winter 1992, 60.

———, with Gerald Aston. *Hostage: My Nightmare in Beirut.* New York: Donald J. Fine, 1991.

James, B. A. *Moonless Night: One Man's Struggle for Freedom, 1940–1945.* Tel Aviv, Israel: Sentinel Publishing, 1993.

Jane's Dictionary of Military Terms. Comp. P.H.C. Hayward. London: MacDonald, 1975.

Janowitz, Morris. *The Professional Soldier.* New York: Free Press, 1960.

Jerrome, Edward. *Tales of Escape.* Belmont, Calif.: Fearon-Pitman, 1959, Reprint 1970.

Jodl, Alfred. *Tagebuch Generaloberst Jodl, Chef der Wehrmacht Führengsstabes des Oberkommandos der Wehrmacht.* BA-MA 2/33. Entries from January 6, 1943–May 21, 1945. Freiburg, FRG: Bundesarchiv/Militärarchiv.

Johann, A. E. *Schneesturm Heimweh und nächtlicher Bambus: Roman einer Fucht nach Hause.* Gütersloh: C. Bertelsmann Verlag, 1951.

Johnson, Adam R. *The Partisan Rangers of the Confederate States Army.* Ed. William J. Davis. Louisville, 1904.

Johnson, Forrest Bryant. *Hour of Redemption: The Ranger Raid on Cabanatuan.* New York: Manor Books, 1978.

Johnson, Hannibal A. "A Prisoner's Diary." *Stories of Our Soldiers: War Reminiscences, by "Carleton" and by Soldiers of New England.* Boston: The Journal Newspaper Company, 1893. 235–44.

Johnson, Keith. "An Indian Tribe's Promised Land." *New York Times* Reprint. *Vocable* 1 February 1995: 4–7.

Johnston, Isaac N. *Four Months in Libby.* Cincinnati: Methodist Book Concern, 1864.

Josephy, Alvin M., Jr. "Tecumseh, the Greatest Indian." Ed. Thomas R. Frazier. *Underside of American History: Other Readings.* 2 vols. New York: Harcourt Brace Jovanovich, 1971. 131–60.

Jung, Hermann. *Die deutschen Kriegsgefangenen in amerikanischer Hand—USA.* München: Gieseking, 1972.

Kaiser, Hilary. *Veteran Recall: Americans in France Remember the War.* Paris: Published by the author, 1995.

Kantor, Mackinlay. *Andersonville.* New York: World Publishing, 1955.

Kaplan, Robert. "The Coming Anarchy." *Atlantic Monthly,* February 1994, 44–76.

Karner, Stefan. "Die Sowjetische Hauptverwaltung für Kriegsgefangene und Internierte." *Vierteljahrshefte für Zeitgeschichte* 42: 3 (July 1994): 447–71.

———. *Gefangen Rußland: Die Beiträge des Symposions auf der Schallaburg 1995.* Conference Proceedings. Graz, Austria: Ludwig Boltzmann-Institut für Kriegsfolgen-Forschung, 1995.

———. "Prisoners of War in the Economy of the Former Soviet Union: 1941–1945." Eleventh International Economic History Conference at Milan. Conference Paper. Prague: University of Economics, 1994. 175–99.

Karsten, Peter. "American POWs in Korea and the Citizen Soldier." Ed. Peter Karsten. *The Military in America: From the Colonial Era to the Present.* New York: Free Press, 1980. 370–8.

Keating, Susan Katz. *Prisoners of Hope: Exploiting the POW/MIA Myth in America.* New York: Random, 1994.

Keats, John. *They Fought Alone.* New York: J. B. Lippincott, 1965.

Keegan, John. "If You Won't, We Won't: Honor and the Decencies of Battle." *Time Literary Supplement,* 24 November 1995, 11–12.

———. *A History of Warfare.* New York: Vintage, 1993.

Keenan, Brian. *An Evil Cradling.* London: Vintage, 1992.

Keith, Agnes Newton. *Three Came Home.* Boston: Little Brown, 1947.

Kelly, Peter A. "Raids and National Command: Mutually Exclusive." *Military Review* 60 (April 1980): 20–2.

Kelton, Elmer. *Massacre at Goliad.* New York: Ballantine, 1965.

Kendall, George Wilkins. *Narrative of the Texan Santa Fe Expedition.* 2 vols. New York: Harper, 1850.

Kenny, Henry J. *The American Role in Vietnam and East Asia: Between Two Revolutions.* New York: Praeger, 1984.

Kerr, E. Bartlett. *Surrender and Survival: The Experience of American POWs in the Pacific 1941–1945.* New York: William Morrow, 1985.

Kinchen, Oscar A. *Confederate Operations in Canada and the North.* North Quincy, Mass.: Christopher, 1970.

King, John R. *My Experience in the Confederate Army and in Northern Prisons.* Clarksburg, W.Va.: Stonewall Jackson Chapter 1333, United Daughters of the Confederacy, 1917.

King, Wayne. "Death Camp at Florence." *Civil War Times Illustrated* (January 1974): 35–42.

Kinkead, Eugene. *In Every War But One.* New York: Norton, 1959.

Kirkwood, James. *Some Kind of Hero.* New York: Thomas Y. Crowell, 1975.

Knight, John. "The Narrative of the Perils and Sufferings of Doctor Knight and John Slover." 1782. Ed. Hugh Henry Brackenridge. *Indian Atrocities.* "Narrative of the Perils and Sufferings of Doctor Knight and John Slover, among the Indians during the Revolutionary War." Nashville, Tenn. 1843; Reprint, Cincinnati, Ohio: U. P. James, 1867. 9–30.

Knopp, Guido. "Heimkehr, Flüchtlinge und Vertriebene." *Damals* (December 1994): 8–11.

Knox, Donald. *Death March: The Survivors of Bataan.* New York: Harcourt Brace Jovanovich, 1981.

———. *The Korean War: Uncertain Victory.* 2 vols. New York: Harcourt Brace, 1988.

"Korean Puzzle: Americans Who Stay." *U.S. News and World Report,* 24 December 1954, 104.

"Korean War Losses." *VFW Magazine,* February 1996, 8.

Kosok, Heinz. "Aspects of Presentation, Attitude and Reception in English and Irish Plays about the First World War." Eds. Franz Karl Stanzel and Martin Löschnigg. *Intimate Enemies: English and German Literary Reactions to the Great War 1914–1918.* Heidelberg: Universitätsverlag, 1993. 343–64.

Krammer, Arnold. "Japanese Prisoners of War in America." *Pacific Historical Review* 52.1 (February 1983); 67–91.

———. *Nazi Prisoners of War in America.* New York: Stein and Day, 1979.

"Kriegsmarine Escape." *Newsweek,* 8 January 1945, 33–4.

Kurowski, Franz. *Sturz in die Hölle: Die deutschen Fallschirmjäger 1939–1945.* Munich: Wilhelm Heyne Verlag, 1986.

Kutler, Stanley I. *Justice and Injustice in the Cold War.* New York: Hill and Wang, 1982.

Laffin, John. *The Anatomy of Captivity.* London: Abelard-Schuman, 1968.

LaForte, Robert S., and Ronald E. Marcello, eds. *The Ordeal of American POWs in Burma, 1942–1945: Building the Death Railway.* Wilmington, Del.: Scholarly, 1993.

Lamb, Richard. *War in Italy, 1943–1945: A Brutal Story.* New York: St. Martin's Press, 1994.

Landon, Walter J. "Geneva Conventions—The Broken Rules." *Naval Institute Proceedings* 99. 2 (February 1973): 34–9.

Lane-Poole, Stanley. *The Story of the Barbary Corsairs.* New York: G. P. Putnam's Sons, 1896.

Langworthy, Daniel Avery. *Reminiscences of a Prisoner of War and His Escape.* Minneapolis, Minn.: Byron Publishing Company, 1915.

"The Last Hostage: Her Little Brother Terry Anderson Was Free at Last. Now They Had to Learn to Live with That." *Life,* February 1992, 28–33.

Lawson, Thomas E. "Escape to Russia." *AXPOW Bulletin* 50. 2 (February 1993): 17–20.

Lawton, Marion R. *Some Survived: An Epic Account of Japanese Captivity during World War II.* Chapel Hill, N.C.: Algonquian, 1984.

Leckie, William H. *The Buffalo Soldiers.* Norman: University of Oklahoma Press, 1967.

Lee, J. Fitzgerald. "Prisoners of War." *Army Quarterly* 3 (1921–1922): 348–56.

LeRoy, Marie, and Barbara Leininger. "The Narrative of Marie LeRoy and Barbara Leininger." *Pennsylvania German Society Proceedings* 15 (1906): 111–22.

Levi, Primo. *Survival in Auschwitz.* New York: Macmillan, 1959.

Levie, Howard S. "Maltreatment of Prisoners of War in Vietnam." *Boston University Law Review* 48. 3 (Summer 1968): 323–59.

Levin, Jerry, Herbert Bodman, and Sis Levin. *Lebanon: Emblem of Captivity; Forgotten Hostages.* Radio Show. Research Triangle Park: National Humanities Center, 1986.

Levin, Sis. *Beirut Diary: A Husband Held Hostage and a Wife Determined to Set Him Free.* Downers Grove: InterVarsity Press, 1989.

"Life with Charlie." *Time,* 10 January 1969, 35.

Lincoln, Charles H., ed. *Narratives of the Indian Wars 1675–1699.* 1913. Reprint, New York: Barnes and Noble, 1966.

Linenthal, Edward Tabor. *Sacred Ground: Americans and Their Battlefields.* Urbana and Chicago: University of Illinois Press, 1991.

Lippman, Thomas W. "U.S. Team to Inspect Possible POW Prison in Laos: Mysterious Walled Site Was Target of Clandestine Raid Sponsored by CIA in 1981." *Washington Post,* 16 January 1994, A34.

Livesey, R. *Charles Herbert: A Relic of the Revolution.* Boston, Mass.: Charles H. Pierce, 1847.

Lockwood, Allison. "Pantsuited Pioneer of Women's Lib, Dr. Mary Walker." *Smithsonian,* March 1977, 113–18.

Lomax, Eric. *The Railway Man: A POW's Searing Account of War, Brutality and Forgiveness*. New York: Norton, 1995.

Loomis, Noel M. *The Texan-Santa Fè Pioneers*. Norman: University of Oklahoma Press, 1958.

Lord, Lewis. "The Medal of Honor." *U.S. News and World Report,* 10 June 1991, 65, 67.

Lory, Hillis. *Japan's Military Masters*. New York: Viking, 1943.

"MacArthur's Back." *Time Pacific Poney Edition* (19 February 1945): 3–4.

Mackenzie, S. P. "Essay and Reflection: On the Other Losses Debate." *International History Review* 14. 4 (November 1992): 717–31.

Maclay, Edgar Stanton. *A History of American Privateers*. New York: Appleton, 1899.

Mahoney, Tom. "50 Hanged and 11 Branded: The Story of the San Patricio Battalion." *Southwest Review* 32: 4 (Autumn 1947): 373–6.

Manchester, Hugh. "POW Rally Proved Rich in Drama." *Centre Daily Times,* 7 August 1993.

Mann, George. *Over the Wire*. Freemantle, Australia: Freemantle Arts Centre Press, 1988.

Mann, Sunnie. *Holding On*. London: Bloomsbury, 1990.

Marolda, Edward J., and Oscar P. Fitzgerald. *The United States Navy and the Vietnam Conflict*. Washington, D.C.: Naval Historical Center, 1986.

Martin, David C., and John Walcott. *Best Laid Plans: The Inside Story of America's War against Terrorism*. New York: Harper and Row, 1988.

Martyrs to the Revolution in British Prison-Ships in the Wallabout Bay. New York: W. H. Arthur, 1855.

Martz, Larry. "Even When It's Over, It Isn't Over." *Newsweek,* 16 December 1991, 37.

Maschke, Erich. *Zur Geschichte der deutschen Kriegsgefangen des 2. Weltkriegs: Eine Zuzammenfassung*. Munich: Gieseking, 1974.

Mason, John Brown. "German Prisoners of War in the United States." *American Journal of International Law* 39 (1945): 198–215.

Mather, Sir Carol. *Aftermath of War: Everyone Must Go Home*. London: Brassey's, 1993.

McBrayer, James D. *Escape! Memoir of a World War II Marine Who Broke Out of a Japanese POW Camp and Linked Up with Chinese Communist Guerrillas*. Jefferson, N.C.: McFarland, 1995.

McCaffrey, James M. *Army of Manifest Destiny: The American Soldier in the Mexican War, 1846–1848*. New York: New York University Press, 1992.

McCarthy, John, and Jill Morrell. *Some Other Rainbow*. London: Corgi, 1995.

McConnell, Malcolm. *Into the Mouth of the Cat: The Story of Lance Sijan, Hero of Vietnam*. New York: Norton, 1985.

McCoy, Melvyn H., Steven M. Mellnik, and Welbourn Kelley. *Ten Escaped from Togo*. New York: Farrar and Rinehart, 1944.

McCracken, George E. *The Prisoner of War Re-Education Program in the Years 1943–1946*. Washington, D.C.: Special Studies Division, Office of the Chief of Military History, Department of the Army, 1953.

McCutchan, Joseph D. *Mier Expedition Diary: A Texan Prisoner's Account*. Ed.

Joseph Milton Nance. Austin: University of Texas Press, 1978.

McDaniel, Frederick L., Benjamin V. White, Jr., and Charles M. Thompson. "Malnutrition in Repatriated Prisoners of War." *United States Naval Medical Bulletin* 46 (June 1946): 793–810.

McDougall, Marion Gleason. *Fugitive Slaves 1619–1865.* 1891. Reprint, New York: Bergman, 1967.

McFadden, Robert. *No Hiding Place.* New York: Times Books, 1981.

McGrath, James H. "Reading the Code of Conduct." *Naval Institute Proceedings* 112/6/1000 (June 1986): 100–4.

McGrath, J. J., and Wallace Hawkins. "Peroté Fort—Where Texans Were Imprisoned." *Southwestern Historical Quarterly* 48 (1944–1945): 340–5.

McMullen, Fred, and Jack Evans. *Out of the Jaws of Hunland.* Toronto: William Briggs, 1918.

McNab, Andy. *Bravo Two Zero.* New York: Bantam, Doubleday, Dell Publishing Group, 1993.

McPherson, James M. *Battle Cry of Freedom: The Civil War Era.* New York: Oxford University Press, 1988; Ballantine, 1989.

———. *The Negro's Civil War: How American Negroes Felt and Acted during the War for the Union.* New York: Vintage, 1965.

McRaven, William H. *Case Studies in Special Operations Warfare: Theory and Practice.* Novato, Calif.: Presidio, 1995.

The Medal of Honor of the United States Army. Washington, D.C.: U.S. Government Printing Office, 1948.

Mekeel, Arthur J. "The Relation of the Quakers to the American Revolution." *Quaker History* 65 (1976): 3–18.

———. "Suspicion of Quaker Treachery and the Virginia Exiles." *The Relation of the Quakers to the American Revolution.* Lanham, Md.: University Press of America, 1979. 173–88.

Melady, John. *Escape from Canada: The Untold Story of German Prisoners of War in Canada, 1939–1945.* Toronto: Macmillan, 1981.

Mellnick, Steven M. *Philippine Diary.* New York: Van Nostrand, Reinhold, 1969.

Meltesen, Clarence R. "Defenders of Corregidor." *AXPOW Bulletin* 51. 5 (May 1994): 33–7.

———. "From the Foxholes of Bataan." *AXPOW Bulletin* 51. 4 (April 1994): 23–7.

Merry, D. Bilson. "My Escape from a German Prison: A Thrilling Experience." *The Gold Stripe* 1 (1918): 85–7.

Messimer, Dwight R. *Escape.* Annapolis, Md.: Naval Institute Press, 1994.

Metzger, Charles H. S. J. *The Prisoner in the American Revolution.* Chicago: Loyola University Press, 1971.

The Mexican War. Alexandria, Va.: Time-Life Books, 1978.

Milano, Col. James V., USA (Ret.), and Patrick Brogan. *Soldiers, Spies and the Rat Line: America's Undeclared War against the Soviets.* Washington, D.C.: Brassey's, 1995.

Milk, Leslie, and Jeremy Milk. "Witness to the Holocaust." *American Legion Magazine* (August 1994); 29–31, 48–9.

Miller, Joseph C. *Slavery and Slaving in World History: A Bibliography, 1900–1991.* Millwood, N.J.: Kraus International, 1993.

Mills, Walter. *American Military Thought.* New York: Bobbs-Merrill, 1966.

Minear, Richard H. *Victors' Justice: The Tokyo War Crimes Trial.* Princeton, N.J.: Princeton University Press, 1971.

Mitterand, François, and Elie Wiesel: *Memoir in Two Voices.* Trans. Richard Seaver and Timothy Bent. New York: Arcade, 1996.

Mooney, Carolyn J. "Slammer or Shrine? How German Students Left Their Mark on the Wall of a Campus Prison." *Chronicle of Higher Education* (1 March 1996): A55.

Moore, John Hammond. *The Faustball Tunnel: German POWs in America and Their Great Escape.* New York: Random House, 1978.

Moreland, Arthur. *Humors of History.* London: Daily News Ltd., 1921.

Morrell, David. *First Blood.* New York: Fawcett Crest, 1972.

Morris, Richard B., ed. *Encyclopedia of American History.* Revised and enlarged edition. New York: Harper, 1961.

Morton, Joseph. *Sparks from the Campfire.* Philadelphia: Keystone, 1892.

Moyne, Ernest J. "The Reverend William Hazlitt: A Friend of Liberty in Ireland during the American Revolution." 3d Series. *William and Mary Quarterly* 21. 2 (April 1964): 288–97.

Muhlenberg, H. M. "Regina, the German Captive." *German-American Society Proceedings* 15 (1906): 82–92.

Murphy, Edward F. *Vietnam Medal of Honor Winners.* New York: Ballantine, 1987.

Myer, Dillon S. *Uprooted Americans: The Japanese Americans and the War Relocation Authority during World War II.* Tucson: University of Arizona Press, 1971.

"The Mysterious Pentagon." *Newsweek,* 14 September 1964, 33.

Nackman, Mark E. *A Nation within a Nation: The Rise of Texas Nationalism.* Port Washington, N.Y.: Kennikat Press, 1975.

National Archives. *World War I: Prisons and Prisoners—Prisoners of War and Allied Enemies in the United States.* Subject File NA RG 407/23.

"Navy Flier, Captured by Laos Reds, Back in U.S." *New York Times,* 3 September 1964, 2.

Neave, Airey. *The Escape Room.* New York: Doubleday, 1970.

———. *Little Cyclone.* London: Hodder & Stoughton, 1954.

———. *Saturday at M.I.9: A History of Underground Escape Lines in North-West Europe in 1940–1945 by a Leading Organizer at M.I.9.* London: Hodder & Stoughton, 1969.

———. *They Have Their Exits.* London: Hodder & Stoughton, 1953; New York: Beagle Books, 1971.

Neeser, Robert Wilden. *Letters and Papers Relating to the Cruises of Gustavus Conyngham: A Captain of the Continental Navy 1777–1779.* New York: DeVinne, 1915.

The Negro Soldier: A Select Compilation. 1861. Reprint, New York: Negro Universities Press, 1970.

Nelan, Bruce W. "Cold Light on the Cold War." *Time,* 18 March 1996, 40–3.

Nichols, Charles L. "Article 105: Misconduct as a Prisoner." *Air Force JAG Law Review* 11 (Fall 1969): 393–8.

Norland, Rod. "America's Forgotten Hostages." *Newsweek,* 20 October 1986, 38–42.

North, Don. "Hanoi Hannah Speaks Again." *Vietnam Magazine,* April 1996, 18–24.

"Obituary: In Wolfborough, N. H. 18th of April last. Mr. Samuel Nowell, Aged 86." *Portsmouth Journal of Literature and Politics* (Saturday, 16 November 1833): 3: 1.

"Obituary Note—James N. Rowe." *Military Affairs* 4. 5 (October 1989): 30.

O'Brien, Pat. *Outwitting the Hun: My Escape from a German Prison Camp.* New York: Harper and Brothers, 1918.

O'Donnell, Joseph P. *Shoe Leather Express—Book II.* Hamilton, N.Y.: Published by the author, 1986.

"On Pampering Prisoners." *Collier's,* 12 August 1944, 12.

Ooka, Shohei. *Taken Captive: A Japanese POW's Story.* Trans. and ed. Wayne P. Lammers. New York: Wiley, 1996.

Orgelsdorfer Eulenspiegel. Hoover Institution on War, Revolution and Peace. European War: Prisoners and Prisons. File O 68. Stanford, Calif.: Stanford University.

Ortiz, Juan. *True Relations of the Gentleman of Elvas.* Eurora, 1557.

Osofsky, Gilbert, ed. *Puttin' On Massa.* New York: Harper and Row, 1969.

Oswandel, J. Jacob. *Notes of the Mexican War, 1846–47–48.* Rev. ed. Philadelphia, 1885.

Pabel, Rheinhold. *Enemies Are Human.* Philadelphia: John C. Winston, 1955.

———. "It's Easy to Bluff Americans." *Collier's* 16 May 1953, 20–33.

Pague, Forrest C. *United States Army in World War II, European Theater of Operations: The Supreme Command.* Washington, D.C.: Department of the Army, Office of the Chief of Military History, 1954.

Paine, Ralph D. *The First Yale Unit: A Story of Naval Aviation 1916–1919.* Cambridge, Mass.: Riverside, 1925.

Pape, Richard. *Boldness Be My Friend.* London: Pan Books, 1955.

Parmenter, J. M. "Texas Hymn" (1838), in Edward Tabor Linenthal *Sacred Ground: Americans and Their Battlefields.* Urbana and Chicago: University of Illinois Press, 1991. 71.

Parry, J. H. *The Establishment of the European Hegemony: 1415–1715: Trade and Exploration in the Age of the Renaissance.* 3d ed. rev. New York: Harper and Row, 1966.

Pasley, Virginia. *21 Stayed: The Story of American GIs Who Chose Communist China—Who They Were and Why They Stayed.* New York: Farrer, Strauss and Cudahay, 1955.

———. *22 Stayed.* London: W. H. Allen, 1955.

Pastorius, Francis Daniel. "Resolution of the Germantown Mennonites, February 18, 1688." In Henry Steele Commager and Milton Cantor, eds., *Documents of American History.* 2 vols. Englewood Cliffs, N.J.: Prentice Hall, 1988. 1, 37–8.

Pate, Lloyd. *Reactionary*. New York: Harper, 1956.

Patterson, Charles J., and G. Lee Tipton. *The Heroes Who Fell from Grace*. Canton, Ohio: Daring, 1985.

Peckham, Howard H., ed. *The Toll of Independence: Engagements and Battle Casualties of the American Revolution*. Chicago: Clements Library Bicentennial Studies, 1974.

Perret, Geoffrey. *There's a War to Be Won: The United States Army in World War II*. New York: Random House, 1991.

Petak, Joseph A. *Never Plan Tomorrow: The Saga of the Bataan Death March and Battle of Corregidor Survivors 1942–1945*. Valencia, Calif.: Aquataur, 1991.

Philpot, Oliver S. *Stolen Journey*. London: Hodder & Stoughton, 1950.

Piccigallo, Philip R. *The Japanese on Trial: Allied War Crimes Operations in the East, 1945–1951*. Austin: University of Texas Press, 1979.

Pictet, Jean S. "The New Geneva Convention for the Protection of War Victims." *American Journal of International Law* 45 (1951): 462–75.

Pintak, Larry. *Beirut Outtakes: A TV Correspondent's Portrait of America's Encounter with Terror*. Lexington, Ky.: Lexington Books, 1988.

Plumb, Charles. *I'm No Hero*. Independence, Missouri: Independence, 1973.

Poynter, Lida. "Dr. Mary Walker, M.D. Pioneer Woman Physician." *Pan American Medical Women's Journal* 53. 10 (October 1946): 43–51.

Pratt, Fletcher. *Preble's Boys: Commodore Preble and the Birth of American Sea Power*. New York: William Sloane, 1950.

Prelinger, Catherine M. "Benjamin Franklin and the American Prisoners of War in England during the American Revolution." *William and Mary Quarterly* 3d ser. 32 (1975): 261–94.

The Prisoner of War Problem. Washington, D.C.: American Enterprise Institute for Public Policy Research, 1970.

"Prisoners and Prisons," File O 68, Hoover Institution on War, Revolution and Peace, Stanford University.

"The Prisoners Who Broke." *U.S. News and World Report*, 21 August 1953, 30–1.

Prittie, T.C.F., and W. Earle Edwards. *Escape to Freedom*. London: Hutchinson, 1953.

Prugh, George S. "The Code of Conduct for the Armed Services." *Columbia Law Review* 56: 5 (May 1956): 678–707.

———. "Prisoners at War: The POW Battleground." *Dickinson Law Review* 16. 2 (January 1956): 123–38.

Pryce, J. E. *Heels in Line*. London: Arthur Barker, 1958.

Public Record Office. Information Bulletin 72. "Prisoners of War 1660–1919: Documents in the PRO." (London: 1987), 1–7.

Purcell, Ben and Anne. *Love & Duty*. New York: St. Martin's Press, 1992.

Puryear, George W. "The Airman's Escape." *Atlantic Monthly* 123 (January–June 1919): 452–62, 615–27.

Quaife, Milo M. "A Journal of an Indian Captivity during Pontiac's Rebellion in the Year 1763, by Mr. John Rutherford, Afterward Captain, 42 Highland Regiment." *American Heritage* 9. 3 (April 1958): 65–81.

"'Quiet Diplomacy' of Secretary-General Pays Off with Release of Hostages, Prisoners." *UN Chronicle* (December 1991), 37.

Ramage, James A. "John Hunt Morgan's Escape from the Ohio State Penitentiary." *Civil War Quarterly* 10 (September 1987): 22–8.

———. *Rebel Raider: The Life of General John Hunt Morgan.* Lexington: University Press of Kentucky, 1987.

Ransom, John L. *Andersonville Diary, Escape, and List of Dead.* Auburn, N.Y.: Published by the author, 1881.

Raza, Werner. *Die deutschen Kriegsgefangenen in der Sowjetunion—Der Factor Arbeit.* München: Gieseking, 1973.

Read, Anthony, and David Fisher. *The Fall of Berlin.* New York: W. W. Norton, 1993.

Reck, Franklin M. *Beyond the Call of Duty.* New York: Crowell, 1944.

"Recollections of Libby Prison." *Southern Historical Society Papers* 11 (January to December 1883): 91–2.

Redfield, Robert. *The Little Community.* Chicago: University of Chicago Press, 1955.

Reeder, Col. Russell P., Jr., USA. "Lieutenant Izac and His Escape." *Medal of Honor Heroes.* New York: Random House, 1965. 1–13.

"Re-Educating the Nazis." *America,* 26 August 1944, 515.

"Re-Education Program for German Prisoners in Effect Here." *Publishers Weekly* (24 June 1945): 24–39.

Reid, Patrick S. *The Colditz Story.* 1952. Reprint, London: Coronet, 1972.

———. *The Latter Days of Colditz.* London: Coronet, 1954.

———. *Men of Colditz.* New York: Lippincott, 1954.

Reid, Patrick S., and Maurice Michael. *Prisoner of War.* London: Hamlyn, 1984.

Reid, Warren D. "Escaped from Fort Delaware." *Southern Historical Society Papers* 36 (1908): 271–9.

Reynolds, Quentin. "Experiment in Democracy." *Collier's,* 25 May 1946, 12–13; 41–2.

———. *He Came Back: The Story of Commander C. D. Smith.* 1945. New York: Pyramid, 1962, Reprint 1971.

Rich, Frank. "The 'Rambo' Culture." *New York Times,* 11 May 1995, A29.

Richardson, Anthony. *Wingless Victory: The Story of Sir Basil Embry's Escape from Occupied France in the Summer of 1940.* London: Odhams Press, 1950.

Richardson, James D. *A Compilation of the Messages and Papers of the Presidents. 1789–1897.* 53d Cong., 2d sess. House of Representatives. 8 vols. Washington, D.C.: U.S. Government Printing Office, 1897.

Ridge, Morton, and Ray Allen Billington. *America's Frontier Story: A Documentary History of Westward Expansion.* New York: Holt, Rinehart & Winston, 1969.

Ridpath, John Clark. *History of the United States of America.* 2 vols. Cincinnati, Ohio: Jones Brothers, 1912.

Riedesel, Baroness Frederike Charlotte Luise von Massow. *Letters and Journals Relating to the War of the American Revolution and the Capture of the German Troops at Saratoga.* Trans. William L. Stone. Albany, N.Y.: Joel Munsell, 1867.

Roberts, Steven. "The Year of the Hostage." *New York Times Magazine,* 2 November 1980, 26–30.

Robin, Ron. *The Barbed-Wire College: Reeducating German POWs in the United States during World War II.* Princeton, N.J.: Princeton University Press, 1995.

Robinson, Ralph. "Retaliation for the Treatment of Prisoners in the War of 1812." *American Historical Review* 49. 1 (October 1943): 65–70.

Roland, C. G. "Stripping Away the Veneer: POW Survival in the Far East as an Index of Cultural Atavism." *Journal of Military History* 53 (January 1989): 79–94.

Rolfe, Cyril. *Against the Wind.* London: Hodder & Stoughton, 1956.

Romilly, Giles, and Michael Alexander. *The Privileged Nightmare.* London: Weidenfeld and Nicolson, 1954.

Roon, Arnold von. *Zwischen Freiheit und Pflicht: Geschichten aus der Fallschirmtruppe.* Friedburg: Podzun-Pallas Verlag, 1989.

Roosevelt, Theodore. *The Naval War of 1812.* 2 vols. New York: G. P. Putnam's Sons, 1900.

Rosenburg, R. B., ed. *"For the Sake of My Country": The Diary of Col. W. W. Ward, 9th Tennessee Cavalry, Morgan's Brigade, CSA.* Murfreesboro, Tenn.: Southern Heritage Press, 1992.

Roskey, Bill. "Great Escapes: POWs Break Through the Wire." *Soldier of Fortune,* May 1991, 68.

Rougeyron, Andre. *Agents for Escape: Inside the French Resistance, 1939–1945.* 1947. Trans. Marie-Antoinette McConnell. Baton Rouge: Louisiana State University Press, 1996.

Rowan, Roy. *Four Days of the Mayaguez.* New York: Norton, 1975.

Rowe, James N. *Five Years to Freedom.* New York: Ballantine, 1971.

Runyan, Timothy J. *Ships, Seafaring, and Society: Essays in Maritime History.* Detroit: Wayne State University Press, 1987.

Rusk, Dean. "Instances of the Use of United States Armed Forces Abroad, 1798–1945." U.S. Congress. House. Hearing before the Committee of Foreign Relations and Armed Services. 87th Cong., 2d sess., September 17, 1962.

Russell, Lord Edward. *The Knights of Bushido.* London: Transworld, 1958.

Rutherford, Andrew, ed. *Rudyard Kipling: War Stories and Poems.* London: Oxford University Press, 1992.

Sabre, Gilbert E. *Nineteen Months a Prisoner of War. Narrative of Lieutenant G. E. Sabre, of His Experience in the War Prisons and Stockades of Morton, Mobile, Atlanta, Libby, Belle Isle, Andersonville, Macon, Charleston, and Columbia, and His Escape to the Union Lines, to Which Is Appended a List of Officers Confined at Columbia during the Winter of 1864 and 1865.* New York: The American News Company, 1866.

Saffell, W.T.R. *Records of the Revolutionary War.* 3d ed. Baltimore: Charles C. Saffell, 1894.

Sage, Jerry. *Sage.* Wayne, Pa.: Miles Standish, 1985.

Sager, Carl F. "A Boy in the Confederate Cavalry." *Confederate Veteran* 36. 10 (October 1928): 376.

Salinger, Pierre. *America Held Hostage.* New York: Doubleday, 1981.

Sampson, Richard. *Escape in America: British Convention Prisoners, 1777–1783.* Chippenham, Wiltshire (U.K.): Picton Publishing, 1995.

Sancton, Thomas. "Crazy Like a Fox." *Time,* 24 June 1996, 25.

Sanders, Jim D., Mark A. Sauter, and R. Cort Kirkwood. *Soldiers of Misfortune: Washington's Secret Betrayal of American POWs in the Soviet Union.* Washington, D.C.: National Press Books, 1992.

Santino, Jack. "Yellow Ribbons and Seasonal Flags: The Folk Assemblage of War." *Journal of American Folklore* 105 (Winter 1992): 19–33.

Say, Peggy, and Peter Knobler. *Forgotten: A Sister's Struggle to Save Terry Anderson, America's Longest-Held Hostage.* New York: Simon and Schuster, 1991.

Say, Peggy. "The Dream That Died." *Redbook,* December 1992, 38.

Say, Peggy, as told to Edward Barnes. "The Last Hostage." *Life,* February 1992, 28–33.

Schell, Jonathan. *The Real War: The Classic Reporting of the Vietnam War.* New York: Pantheon Books, 1987.

Schemmer, Benjamin F. *The Raid.* New York: Harper and Row, 1976.

Schermann, Serge. "Sins of the Fathers." Review. *New York Times Book Review,* 26 June 1994, 3, 34.

Schlesinger, Arthur M., Jr. *The Cycles of American History.* Boston: Houghton Mifflin, 1986.

Schunemann, Gustave E., with Clarence R. Meltesen. "Gustave E. Schunemann Finds a Safe Harbor." *AXPOW Bulletin* 51. 8 (August 1994): 35–9.

Schwab-Felisch. *Der Ruf: Eine deutsche Nachkriegszeitschrift.* Munich: 1962.

Schwinn, Monika, and Bernhard Diehl. *We Came to Help.* New York: Harcourt Brace Jovanovich, 1976.

Scott, Charles. *Pieces of the Game.* Atlanta: Peachtree, 1984.

Scott, James Brown, ed. *The Hague Conventions and Declarations of 1899 and 1907.* New York: Oxford University Press, 1918.

Seaver, James E. *A Narrative of the Life of Mrs. Mary Jemison.* 1824. Foreword by George H. J. Abrams. Reprint, Syracuse, N.Y.: Syracuse University Press, 1990.

Segal, David. "Combating Terrorism: Can We Learn from the Past?" *VFW Magazine,* April 1991, 21–3.

Selman, Francis G. "Extracts from the Journal of a Marblehead Privateersman Confined on Board British Prison Ships, 1813, 1814, 1815." Reprinted in Samuel Roads Jr., *The Marblehead Manual.* Marblehead, Mass.: Statesman Publishing Company, 1883. 28–96.

Shafer, Jack. "Here's How We Treat Nazi Captives." *PM,* 1 May 1945, 9.

Shepard, Betty, ed. *Bound for Battle: The Cruise of the United States Frigate Essex in the War of 1812 as Told by Captain David Porter.* New York: Harcourt, Brace & World, 1967.

Shepard, Frederick J. "The Johnson's Island Plot, An Historical Narrative of the Conspiracy of the Confederates, in 1864, To Capture the U.S. Steamship *Michigan* on Lake Erie, and Release the Prisoners of War in Sandusky Bay." *Publication of the Buffalo Historical Society* 9 (1906): 1–51.

Sherburne, Andrew. *Memoirs of Andrew Sherburne: A Pensioner of the Navy of the Revolution Written by Himself.* Providence, R.I.: H. H. Brown, 1831.

Sherrard, Robert A. *A Narrative of the Wonderful Escape and Dreadful Sufferings of Colonel James Paul.* Cincinnati: J. Drake, 1869.

Sherriff, R. C. "Journey's End: A Play in Three Acts," 1928, in *Famous Plays of To-Day.* London: Gollanz, 1929. 10–136.

Sherry, Norman. *The Life of Graham Greene.* 2 vols. London: Jonathan Cape, 1994.

Shoemaker, Lloyd R. *The Escape Factory: The Story of MIS-X.* New York: St. Martin's, 1990.

Shuffler, Henderson. *Decimus et Ultimus Barziza: The Adventures of a Prisoner of War.* Austin: University of Texas Press, 1964.

Shuster, A. I. *Great Civil War Escapes.* New York: G. P. Putnam's Sons, 1967.

Sickmann, Rocky. *Iranian Hostage: A Personal Diary.* Topeka, Kans.: Crawford, 1982.

Sidey, H. "How the Raid Was Planned: Attempt to Rescue POWs." *Life,* 4 December 1970, 36.

Simpson, Charles M. *Inside the Green Berets: The First 30 Years.* Novato, Calif.: Presidio, 1983.

Slotkin, Richard. *Regeneration Through Violence: The Mythology of the American Frontier, 1600–1860.* Middletown, Conn.: Wesleyan University Press, 1973.

Smith, Dennis Mack. "None But My Foe." Review. *Times Review of Books,* 31 January 1992, 9.

Smith, George E. *POW: Two Years with the Vietcong.* Berkeley, Calif.: Ramparts, 1971.

Smith, George Winston, and Charles Judah, eds. *Chronicles of the Gringos: The U.S. Army in the Mexican War, 1846–1848. Accounts of Eyewitnesses and Combatants.* Albuquerque: University of New Mexico Press, 1968.

Smith, William. *Historical Account of Bouquet's Expedition against the Ohio Indians in 1764.* Cincinnati: Robert Clarke, 1907.

Smith, William E. "Escape from Beirut: Where Iran and Syria Duel, An American Hostage Goes Free." *Time,* 31 August 1987, 24–5.

"Snakes and the Angel." *Time,* 23 September 1966, 32.

Snyder, Charles McCool. *Dr. Mary Walker: The Little Lady in Pants.* New York: Vantage, 1962.

Sochurek, Howard. "Air Rescue Behind Enemy Lines." *National Geographic* 134. 3 (September 1968): 346–69.

Solzhenitsyn, Aleksandr I. *The Gulag Archipelago Three 1918–1956.* New York: Harper and Row, 1976.

"Somalia Service Provided Its Share of Heroes." *VFW Magazine,* August 1994, 26–7.

Sommers, Stan, ed. *The European Story.* Marshfield, Wisc.: American Ex-Prisoners of War Association, 1980.

———. *The Japanese Story.* Marshfield, Wisc.: American Ex-Prisoners of War Association, 1980.

———. *The Korean Story.* Marshfield, Wisc.: American Ex-Prisoners of War Association, 1981.

Spindle, Jake W., Jr. "Axis Prisoners of War in the United States 1942–1946: A Bibliographical Essay." *Military Affairs* (June 1950): 60–3.

Spivey, Delmar T. *POW Odyssey: Reflections of Center Compound, Stalag Luft III and the Secret German Peace Mission in World War II.* Attleboro, Mass.: Published by the author, 1984.

Staden, Hans. *True History of His Captivity among the Tupi Indians of Brazil.* Marburg, 1557. Ed. and Trans. Malcolm Letts. Reprint, London: Routledge, 1928.

Stanton, Shelby L. *Rangers at War: LRRPs in Vietnam.* New York: Ivy Books, 1992.

Stanzel, Franz Karl, and Martin Löschnigg, eds. *Intimate Enemies: English and German Literary Reactions to the Great War 1914–1918.* Heidelberg: Universitätsverlag, 1993.

Starin, Mark A. "Combat SAR: Search and Rescue Operations in Southeast Asia from 1964 to 1975." *Chronicle of War* 1. 4 (Winter 1989): 50–2, 54, 57, 60–1, 88–9.

Stenger, Charles. "Report." 1986. In Tom Williams, *Post Traumatic Stress Disorders: A Handbook for Clinicians.* Cincinnati: Disabled American Veterans, 1987.

Stephens, Alexander Hamilton. *Recollections of Alexander H. Stephens.* New York: Doubleday, Page & Company, 1910.

———. "The Treatment of Prisoners during the War between the States." *Southern Historical Society Papers* 1. 3 (March 1876): 113–221; 1. 4 (April 1876): 225–327.

Stern, Philip van Doren. *Secret Missions of the Civil War.* Chicago: Rand McNally, 1959.

Stevenson, William. *A Man Called Intrepid: The Secret War.* New York: Harcourt Brace Jovanovich, 1976.

Stockdale, James B., and Sybil Stockdale. *In Love and War: The Story of a Family's Ordeal and Sacrifice during the Vietnam Years.* New York: Harper and Row, 1984; Bantam Books, 1985.

Stockel, H. Henrietta. *Chiricahua Apaches in Captivity.* Reno: University of Nevada Press, 1993.

Story, Richard. *History of Modern Japan.* Hammondsworth, U.K.: Penguin, 1960.

Strack, Manfred. "Texas History in Selected Works of Elmer Kelton." *Studies in the Western* 1. 1 (1992–93): 17–25.

Stratton, Richard. "Turn on the Lights." *Naval Institute Proceedings* 11 (September 1985): 81ff.

Strong, Pauline Turner. "Captive Images." *Natural History* 94. 12 (December 1985): 51f.

Sullivan, Matthew Barry. *Thresholds of Peace: Four Hundred Thousand German Prisoners and the People of Britain 1944–1948.* London: Hamish Hamilton, 1979.

Summers, Harry G., Jr. *Korean War Almanac.* New York: Facts on File, 1990.

———. *On Strategy: A Critical Analysis of the Vietnam War.* New York: Dell, 1984.

Sutin, Jack, and Rochelle Sutin. *Jack and Rochelle: A Holocaust Story of Love and Resistance*. Ed. Lawrence Sutin. Minneapolis, Minn.: Greywolf Press, 1995.

"A Tale of Two Prisoners." *Time*, 8 July 1966, 27.

Tannenbaum, Frank. *Slave and Citizen*. 1946. Reprint, Boston: Beacon Press, 1992.

"Taps." *Kriegie Klarion* (Winter 1996), 8.

Thomas, Emory M. "The Kilpatrick-Dahlgren Raid." *Civil War Times Illustrated* (February 1978): 4–9, 46–8; (April 1978): 26–33.

Thomas, Gordon. *Journey into Madness*. London: Bantam, 1988.

Thomas, Robert McG., Jr. "Jürgen Wattenberg, 94, POW Who Escaped." *New York Times*, Obituaries, 4 December 1995, B9.

Thomas, W. B. *Dare to Be Free*. London: Allan Wingate, 1951.

Thornton, John W. *Believed to Be Alive*. Middlebury, Vt.: Eriksson, 1981.

"Thrilling Incident: Capture of the Federal Steamer *Maple Leaf*." *Southern Historical Society Papers* 24 (January–December 1896): 165–71.

Tilford, Earl H. *Search and Rescue in Southeast Asia 1961–1975*. Washington, D.C.: Office of Air Force History, 1980.

Tocqueville, Alexis de. *Democracy in America*. 1848. Ed. J. P. Mayer and Trans. George Lawrence. Reprint, New York: Harper and Row, 1988.

Toffler, Alvin, and Heidi Toffler. "War, Wealth, and a New Era in History." *World Monitor*, May 1991, 46–52.

Tollefson, Dean. "Enemy Prisoners of War." *Iowa Law Review* 32 (1946): 51–77.

Tolstoy, Nikolai. *Victims of Yalta*. 1977. Reprint, London: Corgi, 1979.

Tomedi, Rudi. *No Bugles, No Drums: An Oral History of the Korean War*. New York: John Wiley and Sons, 1993.

Towers, Edwin L. *Hope for Freedom: Operation Thunderhead*. LaJolla, Calif.: LaLane and Associates, 1981.

Towle, Philip A. "Japanese Treatment of Prisoners in 1904–1905—Foreign Officers' Reports." *Military Affairs* 39. 3 (October 1975): 115–17.

"Transcript of World Airlines Hijacking Incident." *Weekly Compilation of Presidential Documents* 21: 27 (2 July 1985): 286.

"Treatment of American Prisoners!" *New-Hampshire Gazette* (Portsmouth) 4 April 1815: 1: 4.

"The Treatment of Prisoners during the War Between the States." *Southern Historical Society Papers* 1. 3 (March 1876): 113–221; 1. 4 (April 1876): 225–327.

"Trial and Error." *Newsweek*, 1 August 1966, 35–6.

U.S. Congress. House. *Report on the Spirit and Manner in Which the War Has Been Waged by the Enemy*. 1813. Reprint, New York: Garland, 1978.

———. House. Commission on Wartime Relocation and Internment of Citizens. *Personal Justice Denied* by George Miller. 102d Cong. 2d sess. Committee Print no. 6. Washington, D.C.: U.S. Government Printing Office, 1992.

———. House. Committee on Foreign Affairs. *The Geneva Convention Relative to the Treatment of Prisoners of War*. Washington: U.S. Government Printing Office, 1970.

———. House. Hearing before the Subcommittee on Federal Services, Post Office, and Civil Service of the Committee on Governmental Affairs. *To Accept the*

Findings and to Implement the Recommendations of the Commission on Wartime Relocation and Internment of Civilians. 100th Cong. 1st sess. Washington, D.C.: U.S. Government Printing Office, 1987.

U.S. Department of the Army. *Communist Interrogation and Exploitation of Prisoners of War.* Washington, D.C.: U.S. Government Printing Office, 1956.

———. *Rules of Land Warfare.* Washington, D.C.: U.S. Government Printing Office, 1914.

———. *Treaties Governing Land Warfare.* Washington, D.C.: U.S. Government Printing Office, 1956.

U.S. Department of Defense. *POW: The Fight Continues after the Battle: The Report of the Secretary of Defense's Advisory Committee on Prisoners of War.* Washington, D.C.: U.S. Government Printing Office, 1955.

———. *Selected Manpower Statistics* FY 1994, Table 2-23 (*Principal Wars*), 112, in *VFW Magazine,* February 1996, 8.

U.S. Department of State. Bureau of Diplomatic Security. *Significant Incidents of Political Violence against Americans.* Washington, D.C.: U.S. Government Printing Office, 1989.

U.S. Federal Writers' Project. *Slave Narratives: A Folk History of Slavery in the United States from Interviews with Former Slaves.* 17 vols. Washington, D.C.: U.S. Government Printing Office, 1941.

U.S. National Archives. *Korean War Escape Debriefs.* Record Group 319, Entry 85 Item 950, 774.

———. *World War I: Prisons and Prisoners—Prisoners of War and Allied Enemies in the United States.* Subject File NA RG 407/23.

U.S. Navy Office of Information. "Lieutenant Edward Victor Izac, USN Retired." Annapolis, Md.: Internal Relations Division (OI-430), 26 September 1967: 1–5.

U.S. Senate. Armed Services Committee. *Imprisonment and Escape of Lieutenant Junior Grade Dieter Dengler,* USNR. Washington, D.C.: U.S. Government Printing Office, 1966.

———. Committee on Government Operations. *Korean War Atrocities.* Washington, D.C.: U.S. Government Printing Office, 1954.

———. Committee on Veterans Affairs. *Medal of Honor Recipients 1863–1978.* Washington, D.C.: U.S. Government Printing Office, 1981.

———. *An Examination of U.S. Policy Toward POW/MIAs (The Helms Report).* Minority (Republican) Staff of the Committee on Foreign Relations. Washington, D.C.: U.S. Government Printing Office, 1991.

———. *POW/MIAs: Report of the Select Committee on POW/MIA Affairs.* 103d Cong., 1st sess. Washington, D.C.: U.S. Government Printing Office, 1993.

———. War Department. *War of the Rebellion: A Compilation of the Official Records of the Union and Confederate Armies.* Washington, D.C.: U.S. Government Printing Office, 1880–1901.

The United States Magazine and Democratic Review 17 (July–August 1945): 5–6, 9–10.

"U.S. Pilot's Escape from Reds in Laos Described by Navy." *New York Times,* 21 November 1964, 4: 4.

Utley, Robert M., and Wilcomb E. Washburn. *Indian Wars.* New York: The American Heritage Library; Boston: Houghton Mifflin, 1977.

Valentine, Douglas. *The Phoenix Program.* New York: William Morrow, 1990.

van Buskirk, Steve. "Enemy Ex-POWs in Our Midst?" *VFW Magazine,* January 1994, 36.

Vance, Jonathan F. *Objects of Concern: Canadian Prisoners of War through the Twentieth Century.* Vancouver: University of British Columbia Press, 1994.

———. "The Politics of Camp Life: The Bargaining Process in Two German Prison Camps." *War and Society* 10. 1 (May 1992): 109–26.

———. "The War behind the Wire: The Battle to Escape from a German Prison Camp." *Journal of Contemporary History* 28 (1993): 675–93.

Van der Beets, Richard. *The Indian Captivity Narrative: An American Genre.* New York: University Press of America, 1984.

Van der Post, Laurens. *The Night of the New Moon.* London: Chatto and Winden, 1985.

Vanderstock, Bram. *War Pilot Orange.* Missoula, Mont.: Pictorial Histories, 1987.

Vatcher, William H. *Panmunjom: The Story of the Korean Military Armistice Negotiations.* New York: Frederick A. Praeger, 1958.

Vattel, Emmerich de. *The Law of Nations or the Principles of Natural Law* (1758) in Richard A. Falk. *The Vietnam War and International Law.* Princeton, N.J.: Princeton University Press, 1968. 17–23.

Vaughan, Alden T., and Edward W. Clark. *Puritans among the Indians: Accounts of Captivity and Redemption 1676–1724.* Cambridge, Mass.: Belknap, 1981.

Vaughn, Elizabeth Head. *Community under Stress: An Internment Camp Culture.* Princeton, N.J.: Princeton University Press, 1949.

Verral, Charles S., ed. *True Stories of Great Escapes.* Pleasantville, N.Y.: Reader's Digest Association, 1977.

Vietnam Investment Review 28 April–3 May 1994, in *Indochina Chronology* 13. 2 (April–June 1994): 4.

Vinz, Curt. "Das freie Buch." *Der Ruf* 26 (1 April 1946).

"Virginia Slave Laws." *Annals of America.* vol. 1. Chicago: Encyclopedia Britannica, 1968.

Vischer, A. L. *Barbed Wire Disease: A Psychological Study of the Prisoner of War.* London: John Bale, Sons & Danielsson, 1919.

Vistica, Gregory. "An American Hero." *Newsweek,* 19 June 1995, 24–33.

Vonnegut, Kurt, Jr. *Slaughterhouse-Five or The Children's Crusade.* New York: Delacourt, 1969.

Walker, Keith. *A Piece of My Heart: The Stories of Twenty-six American Women Who Served in Vietnam.* New York: Ballantine, 1985.

Walker, Mary Edwards. *Hit.* New York: American News, 1871.

Walker, Samuel. *Samuel Walker's Account of the Mier Expedition.* Ed. Marilyn McAdams Sibley. Austin: Texas State Historical Association, 1978.

Walker, William. *The War in Nicaragua.* New York, 1860.

Wallace, Edward S. "The Battalion of Saint Patrick in the Mexican War." *Military Affairs* 14. 2 (July 1950): 84–91.

———. "Deserters in the Mexican War." *The Hispanic American Historical Review* 15. 2 (August 1935): 374–83.

Walzer, Michael. "Prisoners of War: Does the Fight Continue after the Battle?" *American Political Science Review* 63 (1969): 777–86.

Washburn, William. *The Garland Library of Narratives of North American Indian Captivities.* New York: Garland, 1978.

"Washed Brains of POWs: Can They Be Rewashed?" *Newsweek,* 4 May 1953, 37.

Washington, George. *The Journal of Major George Washington Sent by the Hon. Robert Dinwiddie to the Commandant of the French Forces in Ohio.* 1754. Reprint, Williamsburg, Va.: Colonial Williamsburg, 1959.

Watt, George. *The Comet Connection: Escape from Hitler's Europe.* Lexington: University Press of Kentucky, 1990.

Weglyn, Michi Nishiura. *Years of Infamy: The Untold Story of America's Concentration Camps.* Seattle: University of Washington Press, 1995.

Weingartner, James J. *Crossroads of Death: The Story of the Malmedy Massacre and Trial.* Berkeley: University of California Press, 1979.

Weintraub, Stanley. "The Christmas Truce." *MHQ: The Quarterly Journal of Military History* 5. 2 (1992): 76–85.

———. *War in the Wards: Korea's Unknown Battle in a Prisoner-of-War Hospital Camp.* New York: Doubleday, 1964; 2d ed. San Rafael, Calif.: Presidio, 1976.

Weir, Benjamin, and Carol Weir, with Dennis Benson. *Hostage Bound. Hostage Free.* Philadelphia: Westminster, 1987.

Wells, James M. "Prisoners of War Tunnel to Freedom." *McClure's Magazine,* 1904; reprinted in *Susquehanna Monthly Magazine* 16. 1 (January 1991): 21–31.

Wells, James T. "Prison Experience." *Southern Historical Society Papers* 7 (1879): 324–9, 393–8, 487–91.

Werlich, Robert. "Mary Walker: From Union Army Surgeon to Sideshow Freak." *Civil War Times Illustrated* 6. 3 (June 1967): 46–9.

Westheimer, David. *Sitting It Out: A World War II POW Memoir.* Houston: Rice University Press, 1992.

———. *Von Ryan's Express.* New York: Doubleday, 1964.

———. "Von Ryan's Express: At Maxwell Preflight He Was the Ironass Captain." *Houston Post,* 5 November 1986; *Kriegie Klarion.* Stalag Luft III Former Prisoners of War (Fall 1991), 5.

Whewell, William, ed. *Grotius on the Rights of War and Peace: An Abridged Translation.* Cambridge: Cambridge University Press, 1853.

Whitcomb, Edgar D. *Escape from Corregidor.* Chicago: Henry Regnery, 1958.

White, Henry. *Indian Battles: With Incidents in the Early History of New England.* New York: D. W. Evans, 1859.

White, T. W. *Guests of the Unspeakable: An Australian Airman's Escape from Turkey in the First World War.* 1928. Reprint, Crow's Nest, NSW (Australia): Little Hills Press, 1990.

White, William Lindsay. *The Captives of Korea.* New York: Scribner, 1957.

Whittingham, Richard. *Martial Justice: The Last Mass Execution in the United States.* Chicago: Henry Regnery, 1971.

Wiesel, Elie. *Night.* 1958. Trans. Stella Rodway. New York: Avon, 1960.

Wildwood, Warren [pseudo]. *Thrilling Adventures among the Early Settlers.* Philadelphia: John E. Potter, 1861.

Wilkinson, Rupert. *American Tough: The Tough-Guy Tradition and American Character*. New York: Harper and Row, 1986.

Wills, Donald H., with Rayburn W. Myers. *The Sea Was My Last Chance: Memoir of an American Captured on Bataan in 1942 Who Escaped in 1944 and Led the Liberation of Western Mindanao*. Jefferson, N.C.: McFarland, 1995.

Williams, Amelia. "A Critical Study of the Siege of the Alamo and of the Personnel of Its Defenders." *Southwestern Historical Quarterly* 37 (July 1933), 22–4.

Williams, Eric. *The Book of Famous Escapes*. New York: Norton, 1954.

———. *The Wooden Horse*. 1949. Reprint, New York: Harper, 1958.

Williams, George W. *A History of the Negro Troops in the War of the Rebellion 1861–1865*. New York: Harper, 1888.

Williams, Tom. *Post Traumatic Stress Disorders: A Handbook for Clinicians*. Cincinnati: Disabled American Veterans, 1987.

Winslow, Richard E., III. *Wealth and Honour: Portsmouth during the Golden Age of Privateering, 1775–1815*. Portsmouth, N.H.: Portsmouth Marine Society, 1988.

Winterburn, Gary. *History of the Great Trail: From the Forks of the Ohio to the Tuscarawas Valley*. Published by the author, 1993.

"Without Honor." *Newsweek*, 13 July 1953, 30.

Witt, Jerry V. *Escape from the Maple Leaf*. Bowie, Md.: Heritage Press, 1993.

Woodward, Elon A. *The Negro in the Military Service of the United States*. 8 vols. Washington, D.C.: U.S. Government Printing Office, 1888.

Wright, Quincy. "The Outlawry of War and the Law of War." *American Journal of International Law* 47 (1953): 365–76.

Writers Guild of America News (May 1976), 22.

Wubben, H. "American POWs in Korea." *American Quarterly* (1972): 3–19.

Wyatt, Frederic A. *We Came Home*. Toluca Lake, Calif.: P.O.W. Publications, 1977.

Wyman, Mark. *DP: Europe's Displaced Persons, 1945–1951*. Philadelphia: Balch Institute Press, 1989.

Yathay, Pin. "Escape from Cambodia." *National Review*, 22 December 1978, 1588–95.

Young, Darryl. *The Element of Surprise: Navy SEALs in Vietnam*. New York: Ivy, 1990.

Zayas, Alfred M. de. *The Wehrmacht War Crimes Bureau, 1939–1945*. 1979. Reprint, Lincoln: University of Nebraska Press, 1989.

Zuber, W. P. "The Number of 'Decimated Mier Prisoners.'" *Texas State Historical Association Quarterly* 5 (July 1901–April 1902): 165–8.

Films and Documentaries

Behind the Wire. Documentary. Prod. 8th Air Force Association.

The Bridge on the River Kwai. Dir. David Lean. With William Holden, Sessue Hayakawa, and Alec Guinness. Great Britain, 1957.

The Colditz Story. Dir. Guy Hamilton. With John Mills and Eric Portman. Great Britain, 1957.

Glory. Dir. Edward Zwick. With Matthew Broderick, Denzel Washington, Morgan Freeman, and Cary Elwes. Tri-Star Pictures, 1990.

Grand Illusion. Dir. Jean Renoir. With Jean Garbin and Erich von Stroheim. France, 1937.

The Great Escape. Dir. John Sturges. With James Garner and Steve McQueen. United Artists, 1963.

The Hanoi Hilton. Dir. Lionel Chetwynd. With Michael Moriarty and Jeffrey Jones. Cannon, 1977.

Hellmira. Dir. Bill Jaker. Documentary. WSKG-TV, Elmira, N.Y. Public Telecommunications Council, 1993.

Hostage. Dir. David Wheatley. HBO, 1992.

Hostage: An Endless Terror. ABC News Documentary. With Peter Jennings. CRM Films, 1978.

The Incident. Dir. Joseph Sargent. With Walter Matthau. CBS-TV, 1990.

The One That Got Away. Dir. Roy Baker. With Hardy Krüger, Alec McCowen, Michael Goodleffe, and Colin Gordon. U.K. Rank, 1957. [German Version: *Einer Kam Durch,* 1957]

POW: Americans in Enemy Hands. Dir. Arnold Shapiro. Documentary. Narrated by Robert Wagner. USAA, 1988.

The Scarlet and the Black. Dir. Bill McCutchan. With Gregory Peck, Christopher Plummer, and Sir John Guilgud. ITC-Raj, Italy, 1983.

The Story of Andersonville. Documentary. Friends of Andersonville Historic Site. Wells Communications, 1991.

Index

Dean, William F., 260
Decatur, Stephen, Jr., 238, 239, 256
Deering, John A., 252
Dengler, Dieter, xxv, 9, 191–95, 202
Denton, Jeremiah, 206, 216
Derry, Sam, 146
displaced persons (DPs), 272, 322 n. 44
Dix, John A., 87
Dobervich, Michael, 160
Dodd, Francis, 276
Dodge, David, 220–21, 228
Dodson, James S., 196–97, 202
Donaldson, John Owen, 112
Dorsey, William E., 85–87
Douglass, Frederick, 57, 65, 70–71
Douglass, Levi, 64
Dowse, Sydney, 305 n. 35
Dramesi, John, 206–7, 209–12
Duke, Basil W., 75
Duke, R. E., 260
Dumais, Lucien, 145
Durant, Michael, 261
Durnford, John, 155
Dustan, Hannah, 17–18, 174
Dyess, John George, 81
Dyess, William E., 160–63, 165, 167, 299 n. 20

Early, Jubal, 78
Eaton, William, 238
Eckes, Walter W., 196–97, 202
Eisenhower, Dwight D., 186
Ellinwood, Ralph E., 119–20
Ellison, Wallace, 102
Enfros, Mike, 141
escape: American attitudes to, x–xi, xxiv, 6–8; and boredom, 11; British attitudes to, x, xxiv, 3–6; from East Berlin, 273–74; and frontier mythology, 6–7; legal definition of, 3; narratives, xvii–xxiv, 15; psychology of, ix–x, xv–xvii, 258–59, 278–79. See also escapers, types of; committed natural escapers
escape lines, 124, 146–47; Comet, xxv, 108, 144–46, 272; Rat Line, 272; Shelburne, 145; Underground Railroad, xi, 56, 69–71, 92, 145, 259, 272; in War of 1812, 33–34
escapers, types of, 4–6, 8–10. See also committed natural escapers
executions, 1; and black soldiers, 73; and Civil War, 77, 80, 82, 86, 239, 240; and

Filibusters, 56; and Iran, 219; and Kashmir, 235; and Korean War, 171, 174, 176, 182, 248; and Lebanon, 227, 235; and Native Indians, 262; and Texan War, 44–46, 49–50, 53, 263; and Vietnam War, 195–96, 199, 203, 214; and World War II (Europe), 101, 135, 137–38, 139, 140, 143, 306 n. 40; and World War II (Pacific), 150, 155, 158, 160, 161, 188
Executive Order 10631. See Code of Conduct

Fadlallah, Sheik Mohammed Hussein, 222
Fannin, James, 44–45, 54
Fanning, Nathaniel, 25, 293 n. 32
Farrar-Hockley, Anthony, xxiv, 180–82, 183, 187
Faustball Tunnel, 269–70
Fechter, Peter, 273
Felsen, Milt, 305 n. 40
Fencl, Warren, 133–34
Ferrier, Daniel, 260
Fertig, Wendell W., 163, 165
Finney, Molly, 18
Fisher, Don, 201
Fisher, William, 48
Flynn, Sean, 218
Foote, Morris C., 98
Ford, Gerald R., 148, 207, 253
Forrest, Nathan Bedford, 52, 73, 239, 240
Fralik, R. S., 188
Franklin, Benjamin, 25, 33, 55, 237
Frelinghuysen, Joseph S., 130
Frémont, John C., 71
French and Indian Wars, 14–15, 19–21; and assimilation, 258; Pontiac's Rebellion, 22; at sea, 34; the "Trail of Tears," 262. See also Native Americans
Fruman, Norman, 245
Fugita, Frank, 149
Fuller, Emelius W., 85–86, 300 n. 27

Gaertner, Georg, 272
Gage, Thomas, 22
Gaither, Ralph, 203
Galinski, Edward, 138
Garity, Vernon, 260
Garnet, Rev. Henry Highland, 70
Garrison, William Lloyd, 65, 70
Garwood, Robert, 213–14
Gates, Artemus L., 117
Gates, Horatio, 236

About the Author

Dr. Robert C. Doyle is a native of Philadelphia, Pennsylvania. He earned his B.A. and M.A. in comparative literature at Penn State University, and his Ph.D. in American culture studies at Bowling Green State University. A Navy veteran of the Vietnam War, Dr. Doyle served in the USS *Steinaker* (DD-863) from 1968 to 1969, and later in South Vietnam as a naval intelligence liaison officer (NILO Ben Tre) with numerous Army, Navy, and Coast Guard units operating in the Mekong Delta in 1970 and 1971. This book is partially an outgrowth of that experience.

While teaching American studies, popular culture, and folklore at Penn State, Dr. Doyle wrote many trade and scholarly articles on various topics, including captivity. In 1994, Dr. Doyle published the first interdisciplinary study of the American military captivity experience, *Voices from Captivity: Interpreting the American POW Narrative,* and became a Fulbright Lecturer of American Studies at the Westfälische Wilhelms-Universität-Münster (Germany). He has lectured and participated in international conferences on POW issues in the United States, France, Germany, Austria, and Australia, and taught American civilization at the Université des Sciences Humaines de Strasbourg II in France.

Dr. Doyle and his wife, Beate, reside in Steubenville, Ohio.

The **Naval Institute Press** is the book-publishing arm of the U.S. Naval Institute, a private, non-profit, membership society for sea service professionals and others who share an interest in naval and maritime affairs. Established in 1873 at the U.S. Naval Academy in Annapolis, Maryland, where its offices remain today, the Naval Institute has members from around the world.

Members of the Naval Institute support the education programs of the society and receive the influential monthly magazine *Proceedings* and discounts on fine nautical prints and on ship and aircraft photos. They also have access to the transcripts of the Institute's Oral History Program and get discounted admission to any of the Institute-sponsored seminars offered around the country.

The Naval Institute also publishes *Naval History* magazine. This colorful bimonthly is filled with entertaining and thought-provoking articles, first-person reminiscences, and dramatic art and photography. Members receive a discount on *Naval History* subscriptions.

The Naval Institute's book-publishing program, begun in 1898 with basic guides to naval practices, has broadened its scope in recent years to include books of more general interest. Now the Naval Institute Press publishes about 100 titles each year, ranging from how-to books on boating and navigation to battle histories, biographies, ship and aircraft guides, and novels. Institute members receive discounts of 20 to 50 percent on the Press's nearly 600 books in print.

Full-time students are eligible for special half-price membership rates. Life memberships are also available.

For a free catalog describing Naval Institute Press books currently available, and for further information about subscribing to *Naval History* magazine or about joining the U.S. Naval Institute, please write to:

Membership Department
U.S. Naval Institute
118 Maryland Avenue
Annapolis, MD 21402-5035
Telephone: (800) 233-8764
Fax: (410) 269-7940
Web address: www.usni.org